POST-WAR WOMEN'S WRITING
IN GERMAN

POST-WAR WOMEN'S WRITING IN GERMAN

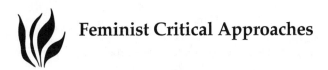 Feminist Critical Approaches

Edited by

Chris Weedon

Berghahn Books
Providence • Oxford

Published in 1997 by

Berghahn Books

Editorial offices:

165 Taber Avenue, Providence, RI 02906, USA

Bush House, Merewood Avenue, Oxford, OX3 8EF, UK

Library of Congress Cataloging-in-Publication Data

Postwar women's writing in German : feminist critical
   approaches : [a study of women's writing in the Federal Republic,
   the German Democratic Republic, Austria and Switzerland,
   1945–1990] / edited by Chris Weedon.
        p.   cm.
   Includes bibliographical references and index.
        ISBN 1-57181-902-9 (alk. paper). — ISBN 1-57181-048-X (pbk. :
   (alk. paper)
        1. German literature—20th century—History and criticism.
   2. German literature—Women authors—History and criticism.
   3. Feminism and literature—Europe, German-speaking.   I. Weedon,
   Chris.
   PT405.P625   1996
   830.9'9287'09045—dc20   95-50634
                                                               CIP

British Library Cataloguing in Publication Data

A CIP catalogue record for this book is available from
the British Library.

Printed in the United States on acid-free paper

Front Cover Illustration

Hannah Hoech, *Heller Kopf 1940*

 # CONTENTS

 PREFACE

This book offers the first broad-ranging study of contemporary women's writing in German in the context of wider literary developments. It combines a number of overview chapters with more detailed readings of individual authors. It outlines the development of women's writing in the four major German-speaking countries in the post-war period. Writers are located in relation to the social position of women and developments in gender politics. In the more detailed studies of individual authors, the book presents readings of selected texts informed by current debates in critical theory. These debates themselves are presented to the reader in chapter 2.

Certain key themes are addressed throughout the book. We ask what *Frauenliteratur* (women's writing) as a concept signifies in the different countries and how this relates to issues raised by recent feminist criticism. Central here is the question of whether it is possible to identify a specifically 'female' or 'feminine' aesthetic and what this might mean. Thus we look at the degree to which we can talk of common issues, themes, literary forms and use of language in the work of women writers.

This book was conceived during my time as Alexander-von-Humboldt fellow at the Freie Universität Berlin. I am very grateful to the Alexander von Humboldt-Stiftung in Bonn for its support. I should also like to thank contributors and translators and particularly Franziska Meyer and Helmut Peitsch for their generous help with the final stages of the book.

Chapter One

 INTRODUCTION
Chris Weedon

In German-speaking Europe, as in other parts of the Western world, the last three decades have seen increasing interest in writing by women. Both feminist presses, such as the Verlag Frauenoffensive, Orlanda, Ulrike Helmer Verlag (Edition Klassikerinnen), Antje Kunstmann Verlag and Kore in Germany, Wiener Frauenverlag in Austria and eF eF and ala in Switzerland, and mainstream publishers have published a range of new and old work by women writers. The Fischer Verlag, for example, has a long standing series *Die Frau in der Gesellschaft* (Women in Society), Ullstein has *Die Frau in der Literatur* (Women in Literature) and Rowohlt *Neue Frau* (New Woman). In addition to new work, many texts by women, both fiction and non-fiction, which have been out of print for decades or even centuries, have been republished.

This increase in the availability of German women's writing has gone hand-in-hand with an interest on the part of feminist literary critics and historians in writing by women. Scholars have begun to recover the forgotten history of women's writing, producing among other things, the essential bibliographical information which helps further research.[1] They are producing new annotated editions of texts long since out of print and developing new ways of reading.[2] This work is part of a more general feminist tendency in the humanities and social sciences which is particularly strong in cultural history and criticism. It draws its inspiration from feminist cultural politics.

New forms of feminist culture developed quickly after 1968 with the growth of new women's movements throughout the Western world. Feminists began to question the male bias of established cultural traditions and modes of literary and cultural analysis, linking

---

Notes for this section can be found on page 8.

them to the reproduction of patriarchal relations in society. Patriarchy is one of the founding concepts of contemporary feminism. It refers to structural social relations that privilege male interests over those of women. Feminist concepts of patriarchy were initially developed in the context of the radical social movements of the late 1960s. Among other things, the 1960s saw the advent of ideas of individual liberation which focused on the free expression of repressed sexuality. Writers such as Herbert Marcuse gained popularity with their theories of the unhealthy repression of sexuality in Western capitalist societies.[3] The answer for many 1960s radicals seemed to be 'free love' and the free expression of sexual needs and desires. For women, 'free love' was made possible by more than just ideas of sexual liberation. The introduction of the contraceptive pill had revolutionary implications. Whatever its long-term side effects, it gave women control over their own fertility, independently of any action on the part of their male partners. Promiscuity and 'free love', however, did not change male attitudes towards women. The expectation that a liberated woman should be sexually available to men was often experienced as yet another way of men controlling women. This negative experience of sexual liberation, together with experience of sexism in the male-dominated radical movements of the 1960s – the civil rights movement, the student movements and the anti-war movements – led to the founding of new women's liberation movements in most Western countries.

The women's movements in the Federal Republic, Austria and Switzerland, as elsewhere in the West, developed via networks of self-help, campaigning and consciousness-raising groups into strong forces for social change. Both the extent and degree of radicality of feminism in the three countries varied significantly. The Federal Republic was at the forefront of developments. In Austria and Switzerland things developed more slowly. Feminists set themselves political and social agendas designed to improve the situation of women in society. These included demands for equal access to education and public life, equal pay, full-time nursery facilities, free contraception and abortion, lesbian rights and an end to domestic and sexual violence.

The new feminism also affected education, culture and the arts. In looking to traditional sources of knowledge for an understanding of their social position, women found themselves invisible. History, sociology, literature, art history, philosophy all took men as their focus. Women's lives were absent from social history, women's writing from literary history, women's art from art history. Where women were represented, as, for example, in psychological theories of sexual difference, they were defined by male standards against male norms which were assumed to be universal.

The assumption that 'man' is coterminous with 'human' has been a feature of modern Western thought since the Renaissance. For centuries the 'Rights of Man' had indeed been the rights of (middle- and upper-class, white) men. Women's difference from men, which was always related back to their capacity for motherhood, had long been interpreted as proof of their inferiority to men.[4] Traditionally, women were seen as more emotional and intuitive and less rational than men. This difference was said to justify restrictions placed on women's access to education, the professions and public life. The response of liberal feminists from the 1700s onwards was to argue that rationality was the defining feature of human beings and that, given the same opportunities, women could be equally rational and capable in public life as men. Physical bodies – male or female – should not determine how one is seen and treated as a human being. For Mary Wollstonecraft in Britain in the 1790s and for Hedwig Dohm in Germany in the 1870s, the social and cultural construction of ideas of women's nature was a central focus of political struggle. It remains so for contemporary feminist movements. Many contemporary feminists, however, would move beyond a liberal framework, drawing on radical feminist, Marxist and poststructuralist theories.

The history of German-speaking feminism in the late nineteenth and twentieth centuries is a history of struggle under social and political conditions inhospitable to feminist aspirations. Key figures such as Luise Otto in Germany in the 1840s and Hedwig Dohm in the 1870s, or Rosa Mayreder in turn of the century Austria, were confronted with deep-seated beliefs in women's natural difference from men. These were supported by a broad-ranging body of contemporary medical, psychological, philosophical and religious writings.[5] Motherhood was regarded as the basis of women's essential nature. Her exclusive role was to be wife and mother. So strong was this belief, that it shaped the form of much German feminism even during its highpoint from 1880 to 1914. Unlike Hedwig Dohm (who remained a strong feminist polemicist until her death in 1919) and other radicals, moderate feminists stressed a philosophy of difference. Rather than suffrage, equal education and access to the professions, many bourgeois feminists argued for women's special social role as mothers. This included bringing uniquely female mothering qualities into public life. While the emancipation of women in the Weimar Republic made considerable advances, by 1933 German women would once again find themselves ideologically reduced to their biological and social roles as mothers. These ideas would be officially extended to Austria after annexation in 1938.

Gender relations in the post-war German-speaking world were marked by the legacy of Nazi ideas about women, which had deep roots in German cultural history. The splitting of Germany into two states along radically different ideological lines meant that women's writing would develop differently in East and West. While the German Democratic Republic pursued policies ostensibly based on women's emancipation through involvement in paid work and political and cultural life, many aspects of patriarchal thinking remained intact, particularly in the domestic sphere. As chapter ten demonstrates, women's writing would come to play an important critical role in contesting patriarchal gender relations. Yet it was not only different social and economic systems that led to the separate development of women's writing in East and West. East German (GDR) cultural policy played an important role in shaping literature by both women and men.

In the immediate post-war decades, social life in West Germany and Austria was marked by traditional ideas about the nature and primary domestic role of women. The Nazi legacy, together with long-established traditional thinking about women, was compounded by moves, found throughout the Western world, to encourage women to abandon their new-found roles and highly skilled jobs in the wartime production industries. With the return of men from the front, women were expected return to the home. In Switzerland gender roles were equally traditional. In looking at women's writing in the Federal Republic, Austria and Switzerland in the post-war period, it is clear that the widely held assumption that a writer will succeed, if only she or he is good enough, fails to take account of the gender power relations both within and between the various literary institutions. While literature has always been subject to historical changes in taste, a naive believe in quality cannot explain, for example, why so many works of male authors have been canonised while the works of women authors have not. Nor can it explain the negative connotations of triviality still ascribed by many writers and critics to the very term *Frauenliteratur*. To understand this we need to look at the gender politics of the literary institutions. This is one focus of the following chapters.

The current place of *Frauenliteratur* within the powerful institution of the university might help to clarify institutional aspects of the problems it faces. Under the present day conditions of academic life, the study of women's writing, whether in teaching or research, is confronted by a serious dilemma. The interest of women scholars in texts by women authors is often part of a much more broad reaching ghettoisation in research. In teaching, this finds its expression in the fact that courses on women's writing are for the most part taught by women and attended by women students. Once these courses are established the few set texts by women authors which have long belonged to the canon often disappear from the syllabi of male colleagues. The result of this is that the teaching of women's writing is left to a small number of women lecturers. If one of these women moves on or takes maternity or study leave, the newly discovered female classics disappear altogether because male colleagues do not wish to teach them, or do not consider themselves qualified to do so. On the other hand – and here lies the dilemma – the gender-specific division of labour within universities makes feminist research and teaching all the more urgent.

Gender has long been a fundamental but often unacknowledged category in the understanding of literary texts in their historical context, whether these are written by women or men. This is clear from the methodological blind spots of those courses which – usually drawing on unquestioned academic common sense – identify history, politics and literature automatically with the history of men. The changes in approach to the study of German literature which have come about since the 1970s and which have given rise internationally to a large number of feminist works, remain strikingly marginal to the publications of the majority of male academics. They continue to work with implicit gender norms which refuse to take women's marginalisation and questions of gender power seriously. In order to counteract this methodological blindness, a change in the self-understanding of women's researchers is necessary. Friendly and polite invitations to male colleagues to fill in the gaps in their knowledge via 'gender studies' can easily overlook the fact that – as Christa Wolf remarked – privileges in history have never been relinquished willingly. Feminist approaches insist on a thorough-going critique of patriarchal assumptions and power relations and on changes in the practice of both women and men which would make feminist critique redundant.

Gender is also a fundamental category in writing itself, not for essentialist reasons, but because patriarchal societies place women differently in all spheres of life. What gives post-war texts by women writers a unity beyond their historical differences, whether we look at the late 1940s, the 1980s or the 1990s, is the fact that women are working under conditions and within structures that are patriarchal. As we shall see in the decades under consideration here, gender-specific ways of writing were always formulated quite clearly. The category 'gender' is in no way a late discovery of feminists. The sex of the author is almost always a decisive factor in the way in which male literary criticism evaluates writing. It is used to define the boundaries of women's writing as a category of exclusion.

This book is a reply, necessarily partial and selective, to the exclusion and marginalisation of women's writing in the post-war period. It divided into five parts. While the introduction outlines the range and objectives of the volume, chapter 2 discusses recent theoretical approaches to reading women's writing. Here I outline the issues at stake in reading women's writing and introduce different ways of reading developed by modern critical theory. Particular emphasis is given to feminist critical theories. These include both deconstructive and woman-centred theories of women's writing and 'female' or 'feminine' aesthetics.

Part Two focuses on the Federal Republic of Germany. In chapter 3 Franziska Meyer looks in detail at the position and work of women writers in West Germany during the immediate post-war years. Having set a context, she then offers a more detailed study of the short prose work of Elisabeth Langgässer. In chapter 4, Meyer examines developments in West German women's writing in the 1950s, paying particular attention to the work of Gisela Elsner. Chapter 5 offers a detailed study of the work of Ruth Rehmann. In chapter 6, Cettina Rapisarda charts the transition to explicitly feminist women's writing, concentrating on the politicised works of the 1970s. She looks, in particular, at the ideas about the nature of women, prevalent in the 1970s, many of which stressed female difference and authenticity. In chapter 7, Margaret Littler looks at shifts in women's writing in the 1980s and 1990s, paying particular attention to those texts which can be read as addressing the concerns of the 'postmodern' world. In chapter 8, Johanna Bossinade offers a detailed reading of a short story by

Anne Duden drawing on Freud and Derrida. In chapter 9, Isolde Neubert looks at writing by Turkish women in Germany focusing on the work of Emine Sevgi Özdamar. This chapter raises questions of racism, ethnicity and identity which are marginalised in mainstream German women's writing.

Part Three looks at women's writing in the German Democratic Republic. Eva Kaufmann (chapter 10) outlines the very different cultural and sexual political contexts of women's writing in the GDR and looks at its development over the forty years of the state's existence. In chapter 11, she examines the responses of women writers to the events of 1989 and the subsequent changes in East German society. She considers the position of women writers from the former GDR in the new united Germany and looks at the contributions that they are currently making to German literature. In chapter 12 I take three important novels by the key GDR writer Christa Wolf, and read these texts in the context of GDR cultural politics, arguing for the importance of historical understanding in the reading of Wolf's work. I go on to consider Wolf's role as a specifically *woman* writer and discuss the relevance of theories of a female aesthetic to Wolf's work.

Part Four focuses on Austria. Allyson Fiddler (chapter 13) looks at the development of women's writing in Austria in the post-war period. She locates writers in relation to social and sexual-political developments and places them within the broader context of post-war Austrian writing. In chapter 14, Elizabeth Boa offers a detailed reading of the work of Austria's most famous woman writer Ingeborg Bachmann. In chapter 15, Fiddler offers a detailed study of selected works by the controversial writer Elfriede Jelinek. She considers the relevance of recent feminist theory to reading Jelinek and asks whether Jelinek's work throws light on the question of 'female' aesthetics.

Part Five looks at Switzerland. Chapter 16 outlines the development of Swiss women's writing in relation to the social position of women in Switzerland and in the context of developments in cultural and gender politics. It relates Swiss women's writing to the broader literary context and offers more detailed readings of the work of Eveline Hasler and Gertrud Leutenegger.

The brief afterword draws some conclusions about the usefulness of concepts of 'women's writing' and 'female' or 'feminine' aesthetics and the development and reception of women's writing in the post-war period. We hope that the volume will serve as a useful and interesting resource for teachers, researchers and students and encourage others to continue the task of reclaiming women's writing and fighting for the serious consideration of gender in literary studies.

Notes

1. Gisela Brinker-Gabler, Karola Ludwig and Angela Wöffen (1986) have compiled an extremely helpful reference book on women's writing in German 1800–1945. For the post-war period see Gnüg 1985, Brinker-Gabler 1988a and 1988b. Bibliographies of texts translated into English include Resnick and de Courtivron 1984 and Frederiksen 1989.
2. The literature on feminist ways of reading is immense. Useful introductory anthologies include Showalter 1985, Greene and Kahn 1985, Belsey and Moore 1989, and Eagleton 1991.
3. See in particular Marcuse 1969.
4. See Jaggar 1983.
5. Turn of the century sexist writings include, for example, Möbius 1900 and Weininger 1980 (orig. 1903).

Chapter Two

READING WOMEN'S WRITING
Feminist Critical Approaches

Chris Weedon

In German-speaking Europe, as elsewhere in the Western world, the 1970s and 1980s saw the development of a wide-ranging feminist culture. This included new writing, art, film-making and theatre. Yet these years also saw the development of new approaches to the study of literature and culture more generally. Gender became an explicit component of this work. Established disciplines were challenged for their perpetuation of patriarchal images of women and their practice of excluding or marginalising women's cultural production. A concerted effort was made to redress the absence of women's lives, experience, and creative work from history, literature, sociology, psychology and the arts. In the process new feminist forms of analysis and new ways of reading culture were developed.

The founding texts of this new feminist criticism and literary history were explicitly committed, political interventions aimed at exposing and transforming the structures, beliefs and imagery that underpin patriarchy. In addition to Simone de Beauvoir's *The Second Sex*, which first appeared in German as early as 1951, key early texts written in English were widely read in the German-speaking world. These included books by Kate Millett, Germaine Greer, Betty Friedan and Shulamith Firestone.[1] Their objectives were to redress the silencing of women in patriarchal culture and to understand and transform patriarchy itself.

Where literature was concerned, critics set out to analyse how literary texts naturalise conservative ideas about gender difference, privileging male views of women as different and usually inferior. Perhaps the classic text of this genre is Kate Millett's *Sexual Politics* first published in English in 1970 and in German in 1971. In this book Millett analyses the work of a range of male authors and theorists, exposing the sexist assumptions that underpin their representations of women.

As will become clear from the detailed discussions of both literary institutions and texts in this book, patriarchal societies position women and men in different ways. Such societies function according to what is called the 'sexual division of labour'. While men are seen to have primary responsibility for the public spheres of work, culture and politics, women's primary responsibility is seen to lie in the so-called 'private' sphere of the family. This social division is founded on assumptions about what is naturally appropriate for men and women and it has had profound effects on women as producers of cultural texts. As the first chapter by Meyer (below) suggests, the broad-based sexual division of labour, together with conservative assumptions about women's nature and gender roles, had particularly profound effects on women's access to the literary institutions and market in West Germany in the 1950s. While similar forces were in play in Austria and Switzerland (chapters 13 and 16), Eva Kaufmann (below) shows clearly how the situation was different for women in the German Democratic Republic.

Among the founding assumptions of feminist criticism was the belief that cultural practices, including literature, art, theatre and film, play an important role in forming both our ideas about what is natural and appropriate and our subjectivity, that is, our conscious and unconscious senses of self. The key projects of feminist criticism have included making these processes visible by looking at representations of women in male-authored texts. Soon, however, many feminist literary critics changed focus to look at if and how *women* writers contest patriarchal gender definitions in their work. This new perspective raised fundamental questions in feminist criticism about whether women write differently and if there is such a thing as a 'female' or 'feminine' aesthetic.

In the German-speaking world, Silvia Bovenschen's essay 'Über die Frage: Gibt es eine weibliche Ästhetik?' (1976, 'Is There a Feminine Aesthetic', 1977) and her substantial study *Die imaginierte Weiblichkeit. Exemplarische Untersuchungen zu kulturgeschichtlichen und literarischen Präsentationsformen des Weiblichen* (1979) helped set the terms of the debate. In the 1980s, much pioneering work was conducted at the Hamburg Centre for Women and Literary Studies, *Frauen in der Literaturwissenschaft*. Sigrid Weigel summarised the perspective behind this project in her influential essay 'Double Focus' (1985, German original 1983):

> Feminist literary criticism investigates the consequences of the patriarchal order for the aesthetic representation of women in literature written by men (that is, *images of women*) as well as for the possible existence and actual examples of literature written by women (that is, *women's literature*). This division into images of women and women's literature is merely a conceptual aid; it should not lead to a schematic confrontation between 'masculine' and 'feminine' culture. Instead, it should allow a detailed investigation into the relations between the two and prompt the questions: How far do the images of women in male discourse and male poetics take women's social and individual reality into account? And, does women's literature reproduce these images of women or does it liberate itself from them and if so, how? (1985: 59)

Since the early 1980s, feminist critics from the Hamburg centre, together with the Argument Verlag, have published a series of influential volumes of feminist literary theory and criticism, hosted path-breaking conferences and produced an important newsletter.[2] This *Rundbrief*, which reached its forty-third edition in December 1994, continues to play a crucial role in co-ordinating feminist literary studies in the German-speaking world.

Feminist Critical Approaches

Feminist criticism has developed over the last three decades into a wide-ranging body of work which varies radically in objectives and approaches. The early concern with patriarchal imagery and language and the move into the study of women's writing, were linked to ideas of sisterhood predominant in the late 1960s and early 1970s. Since the mid-1970s, with the diversification of an initially mainly white, middle-class women's movement, differences between women have come to the fore. This shift in feminist politics has affected both women's writing and literary studies. Most feminists now explicitly recognise that Western patriarchal societies are governed by power relations of class, race and sexual orientation as well as gender. Moreover, Western women enjoy privileges not shared by women from the 'Third World'. Whereas sisterhood might still be a desirable goal, women do not all share the same oppression but are differentially placed in society by these other forms of power relation.

Yet feminist literary studies have not only been affected by changes in the politics of the women's movement. As the various chapters in the book demonstrate, feminist criticism draws on a wide range of very different theories. These include, for example, perspectives that stress female difference, those that draw on psychoanalysis and those that use poststructuralist theories of meaning and subjectivity. Contemporary forms of feminist critical analysis can be loosely grouped together according to their founding assumptions about the nature of women, language, meaning and subjectivity. In the following, I outline key approaches under two main headings: 'woman-centred' criticism and 'poststructuralist' approaches. The aim of this is to give the reader a framework within which to locate the readings of texts which follow in individual chapters. Those chapters dealing with individual authors or texts draw more directly and explicitly on influential forms of critical theory than the more historical overview chapters (for example, chapter 8 draws heavily on Freud and Derrida, chapters 14 and 15 on a range of poststructuralist and psychoanalytic ideas). Yet all the chapters implicitly address those questions that have been most central to feminist criticism namely:

- How do texts construct the meaning of gender and women's subjectivity?
- Do women in patriarchal societies write differently from men?
- Is there an identifiable female or feminine aesthetic?
- How does women's writing subvert dominant patriarchal meanings?

Woman-Centred Criticism

Woman-centred criticism developed partly in response to early feminist work on 'images of women' which analysed the representation of women in texts by men. Woman-centred criticism seeks to redress the absence of women's writing and women's perspectives in the traditional study of literature. It argues that women's writing is different from writing by men precisely because women themselves and their experience of life are different. It seeks to recover and interpret this difference. Woman-centred approaches ask how women's writing is different and how it relates to the patriarchal societies in which it has been written.

Four questions stand out in woman-centred criticism: Do women use language differently from men? Does there exist an identifiable female aesthetics? How might we account for such differences as do exist? How can women use existing language to express their differences and to resist patriarchal forms of subjectivity? Woman-centred criticism can be categorised according to the ways in which it understands difference. It works with three main approaches to the question of women's difference from men. These can be described as theories that are: (1) biological, (2) psychoanalytic and (3) social and historical. The theoretical assumptions that ground different woman-centred approaches to reading have profound implications for how we read literary texts.

In biologically based theories, men and women are seen as different because their bodies are different. This is the assumption behind much radical feminist critique. It breaks with the tendency in liberal feminism to dismiss the importance of the body.[3] Radical feminist theories posit an essential, natural womanhood which has been deformed by patriarchal social relations. They look to women's bodies: their cycles, their sexuality and their capacity for motherhood and celebrate these as sources of positive strength and female identity which defy male definition and control. Women's cultural production, including writing, should reflect aspects of women's true nature and experience.

The most influential texts in radical feminist thinking were published in the United States in the 1970s and 1980s. A powerful example of such work is Mary Daly's *Gyn/Ecology*, originally published in English in 1978 and German in 1981. This text demonstrates several key feature of radical feminist theory and politics. It understands patriarchy as a world system of oppression which affects women everywhere. Daly takes examples of repressive social practices from different continents and historical periods – European witch burning, clitoridectomy, Chinese footbinding, Indian *suttee*, Nazi and U.S. gynaecology – and shows how they have functioned to control women. She also shows how, in writing about these practices, male scholars have played down or masked their violent and repressive aspects. In opposition to this, Daly envisages a new and creative female culture, separate from men, in which patriarchal definitions of women's nature are rejected, language is reclaimed by women and given new meaning, and women's bodies and minds are set free from patriarchal control.

Radical feminist ideas about women and their cultural production tend to be founded on an absolute difference between women and men. They reverse the patriarchal norms according to which the male is valued above the female and celebrate a womanhood which is often defined as closer to nature, as nurturing, emotional, maternal, sometimes homoerotic and often mystical.[4] Rationality loses its privileged status to a view of subjectivity which values the physical and emotional. From this perspective, which revalues qualities seen as of lesser importance by patriarchal societies, woman's special, different nature is the source of her unique cultural productivity.

A central problem with biologically based approaches to female difference is that they reinstate many of those aspects traditionally seen as feminine, revaluing them but leaving the patriarchal mainstream intact. To be defined by our bodies has mostly meant to be denied access to those spheres of life not obviously connected with women's domestic, caring roles. In the context of radical feminism as a political movement, however, this is not an issue, since the only way forward for women is separatism.

The second major type of woman-centred criticism looks to rewritings of psychoanalytic theory for its understandings of difference. Psychoanalysis has long been a controversial subject for feminist writers and critics. While early texts like Kate Millett's *Sexual Politics* were highly critical of Freud for his sometimes openly misogynist and sexist theories, subsequent feminist critics, influenced by Lacan, have reinterpreted and rewritten aspects of psychoanalytic theory for feminist ends. In the English-speaking world, Juliet Mitchell's *Psychoanalysis and Feminism* (1975), which brought together Althusserian Marxism and Lacanian psychoanalysis and appeared in German in 1976, helped begin this process.[5]

Criticism of Freud has focused on texts such as *Some Psychic Consequences of the Anatomical Differences Between the Sexes* (1974), in which Freud outlined his theory of penis envy. Yet an influential group of feminist critics has found other much more useful ideas in Freudian theory and in its further development in the work of the French psychoanalyst Jacques Lacan. Feminists turned to Freud for a theory of gender difference which does not tie it to biology. In Freud, masculinity and femininity are acquired in the process of psychosexual development. We are not born already masculine or feminine. Indeed Freud posits the existence in the infant of what he calls 'polymorphous perversity'. Sexual desire can, at this stage, go in any direction. The processes of psychosexual development in Freudian theory, through which the infant becomes a normal, gendered adult, involve the repression of those aspects of sexual desire that are incompatible with either adult male or female sexual identity and behaviour. The process of repression involves the formation of the unconscious which becomes a site of resistance which continually threatens the precarious stability of adult sexual identity.

The idea that both masculinity and femininity are social constructs founded on repression has been central to the development of feminist psychoanalytic criticism. The normatively patriarchal aspects of Freudian theory which so worried Kate Millett, for example the role and status of the penis in psychosexual development, have tended to be seen as reflections of the patriarchal society that produced Freudian theory rather than as a fundamental flaw in psychoanalysis.

Feminist rewritings of Freud, which have helped shape woman-centred psychoanalytical criticism, fall into two main groups, one North American and one French. In the United States, feminist psychoanalysts such as Nancy Chodorow and Dorothy Dinnerstein produced new versions of psychosexual development which stress the importance of the infant's differential relationship with its mother for the formation of gender identity.[6] The mother's body has a privileged role in psychoanalytic theory because it is the child's first love object. In traditional Freudian theory, however, it is the intervention of the father which disrupts the pre-Oedipal symbiotic relationship between mother and infant. In the process, the penis comes to signify control of the satisfaction of desire, and having or not having a penis and the possibility of losing it become crucial elements in the different psychosexual development of girls and boys. Feminist rewritings of this theory emphasise the primary importance of the pre-Oedipal phase of development.

Much more influential in literary analysis, however, has been the other main school of feminist psychoanalytic criticism which initially developed in France, drawing on the work of Jacques Lacan. Its key figures are Julia Kristeva, Luce Irigaray and Hélène Cixous.[7] The Lacanian theory of the split subject, the unconscious, the symbolic order and the Other have become widely used in both psychoanalytic and some poststructuralist feminist criticism.

Lacan produced a general theory of the acquisition of gendered subjectivity within what he terms the *symbolic order*, that is, the realm of the law, language and social organisation. Like Freud before him, Lacan posits ungendered desire (or libido) in the pre-Oedipal infant. The acquisition of gendered subjectivity requires entry into language – the realm of the symbolic order – and at the same time the repression of aspects of desire incompatible with the laws governing the symbolic order. This involves the formation of the unconscious which, in feminist appropriations of Lacan, becomes the site of the repressed feminine.

In Lacanian theory the process of psychosexual development which results in entry into a patriarchal symbolic order and the acquisition of gendered subjectivity involves an additional phase, the mirror stage. This marks the end of the pre-Oedipal symbiotic relationship of the infant with its mother and the beginning of the acquisition of subjectivity. According to Lacan, in the pre-Oedipal phase, the infant is unable to distinguish between things associated with its own body and the external world. It has neither a sense of physical separateness from the rest of the world nor of its own physical unity as an organism. Its main sensation is fragmentation. The initial conscious recognition by the infant of its body as something separate from the world around it comes with its first identification with a mirror image of itself or another complete, unified body. Through this identification the child gains an imaginary experience of what it must be like to be in control of one's body and one's needs.[8] This identification is based on what Lacan calls *misrecognition*. The child is unable to distinguish between the form that it identifies with and itself. The structure of misrecognition of the self-as-other remains the basis for all future identifications even after the child has acquired language and entered the symbolic order. This idea of a disunified, split subject has become crucial in much feminist theory and was further developed by Kristeva into her influential theory of the 'subject in process'.[9]

Language in Freudian and Lacanian psychoanalysis is motivated by the wish to control desire. To symbolise control over the presence and absence of objects, above all for the infant, the mother's breast, is symbolically to control the source of the satisfaction of desire. The actual position of control – the source of meaning and the laws that govern society – is what Lacan calls the position of the Other. No one can actually occupy this position but individuals identify in an imaginary relationship with the Other when they speak.

In feminist appropriations of Lacanian theory, the questions of women's difference and their relation to a patriarchal symbolic order have been theorised in a number of ways. The emphasis on language as the site for the acquisition of gendered subjectivity led Julia Kristeva to develop a theory of the feminine and masculine aspects of language. In her book, *Revolution in Poetic Language* (1984, original 1974), she looks at writing as a site of resistance to the patriarchal symbolic order. She sees the language of the symbolic order as masculine, reflecting its patriarchal structure. This order represses the feminine aspects of language which have their roots in the pre-Oedipal and which reside in what Kristeva calls the *semiotic chora*, a dimension of the unconscious. The feminine constantly threatens to disrupt the masculine language of the symbolic order, reasserting itself most visibly in poetic language. This shift of focus away from men and women to language suggests that masculine and feminine aspects need not be tied to biological maleness and femaleness.

The appropriations of Lacan to be found in the work of both Hélène Cixous and Luce Irigaray are rather different. For Cixous, gender is cultural and is constructed according to a set of binary oppositions which underpin patriarchal society and require transformation. In this context the repressed feminine aspects of language can be expressed through a return to the female body, the body of the mother, which was central in the pre-Oedipal phase of psychosexual development. Cixoux develops a theory of *écriture féminine* (feminine writing) which involves 'writing the body'.[10]

Luce Irigaray goes much further than either Kristeva or Cixous in transforming Lacanian psychoanalysis. She develops the idea of a separate and different female libido which, repressed by patriarchy, is the site of female power. Women's culture, including writing, should in this model give expression to woman's essential difference.[11]

The third group of woman-centred approaches to reading are those which look to social, historical and cultural explanations of women's difference. Focusing on the work of women authors, such works seek to identify what makes women's writing different and to construct female traditions which can serve as the basis for ideas of a female aesthetic. A classic example of feminist criticism written in this tradition is *The Mad Woman in the Attic* (1979) by Sandra Gilbert and Susan Gubar. In their analysis of nineteenth-century women's writing, they identify depictions of madness as a form of resistance to patriarchy through which an authentic female voice can assert itself.

This kind of woman-centred criticism places great emphasis on women's experience. It tends to avoid any thorough consideration of how language constructs rather than reflects the meaning that we give to our experience. To address this issue, feminist criticism found it necessary to move away from models of language as expression of female experience or a female libido, to poststructuralist approaches in which language constructs both gender and the meaning of experience.

Poststructuralist Feminist Criticism

Difference, in poststructuralist theory, is an effect of language. Indeed subjectivity depends on *access to language*. Language, in the form of competing discourses which propose different versions of what is natural or true, is a key site of political struggle, including sexual political struggle. Part of the social role of literature and literary criticism, for example, can be seen as the reaffirmation of subject positions and forms of subjectivity for women and men, which foreclose any questioning of the social power relations which they sustain. The effect of this is to render patriarchal relations not only seemingly natural but even desirable.

Poststructuralist theory, particularly that influenced by Foucault, suggests that a whole range of social institutions and practices are concerned with constituting the meaning of sexual difference – for example, science, medicine, literature, psychology, social science, religion, education, the media and the law. These forms of discursive practice not only constitute the meaning of sexual difference in language, they involve material practices that shape our conscious, unconscious and physical identities and our desire. Different types of discourse play different roles in the constitution of gendered subjectivity, for example, academic disciplines offer theories of gender which often claim scientific truth, religion sees the guarantees of the nature of gender difference in divine will, and literature addresses the emotional as well as rational dimensions of subject formation.

Poststructuralism offers a way of deconstructing representations and the ways in which signifying practices construct subjectivity. In poststructuralist theory, signifying practices not only tell us what we are and should be and how we should look, but they constitute the nature of our desires in gender specific ways. As Rosalind Coward argues in *Female Desire*:

> Representations of female pleasure and desire from fashion to food to family life and sex produce and sustain feminine subject positions. These positions are neither distant roles imposed on us from outside which it would be easy to kick off, nor are they the essential attributes of femininity. Feminine positions [and also masculine

subject positions] are produced as responses to the pleasures offered to us; our subjectivity and identity are formed in the definitions of desire which encircle us. These are the experiences which make change such a difficult and daunting task, for female desire is constantly lured by discourses which sustain male privilege. (1984: 16)

Structuralist theories, for example those important in the development of poststructuralism, namely Saussure's linguistics, Levi-Strauss' anthropology and the Marxism of Althusser's *Reading Capital*, look for deep structures which determine the forms taken by everyday social life. Levi-Strauss, for instance, sought to identify universal principles of kinship regulation governing modern societies. Saussure attempted to outline a general, universally valid theory of language which could serve as the basis for semiology, the name he gave to a naissant 'science of signs'.[12] It was on the basis of a critique of this theory of language and corresponding critiques of the model of subjectivity implicit in Saussure's theory and in most of the Western philosophical tradition that poststructuralist theory developed.

Saussurean theory of language was radical in its break with ways of seeing language as expressive or reflective of a world outside of itself. Saussure insisted that language does not label meaning, which is already constituted in the world, but constructs meaning by dividing up experience of the world into meaningful segments which are distinguished by their difference from one another. The language system is composed of chains of signs, consisting of signifiers (sound or written images) and signifieds (meanings) which are related to each other in an arbitrary way, that is, there is no natural connection between the two. The meaning of signs is given by their relation of difference from all other signs in the language system. For example, there is nothing natural and intrinsic to the signifier 'woman' that gives it its meaning. Meaning is given by the difference of the signifier 'woman' from other signifiers such as 'man', 'child' or 'girl'. As such, meaning is social and historical rather than natural.

Poststructuralism takes up Saussure's theory that meaning is constructed in language and is the product of the difference between terms, but contests the possibility of fixing meaning in the positive terms which Saussure called signs. Instead of speaking of signs as fixed terms, poststructuralist discourse speaks of *signifiers* whose meaning is always plural, constantly deferred, and can never be fixed once and for all. The poststructuralist critique of

Saussurean structural theory of language involves challenging both the fixity of meaning in the sign and the intentional speaking subject as author and guarantee of meaning. These ideas promised feminists a way of theorising and transforming both patriarchal language and subjectivity.

Both these aspects of poststructuralist theory are clearly articulated in the writings of Jacques Derrida which have influenced much poststructuralist feminist textual analysis.[13] Derrida rejects what he calls Saussure's *logocentrism*, according to which signs have a meaning prior to their articulation in speech or writing, a meaning which is recognised and used transparently by the rational speaking subject. Derrida locates meaning in an infinite process of textuality. He replaces Saussure's concept of language as a system of chains of signs, each of which has a fixed meaning, with a concept of *différance*, in which meaning is produced via the dual strategies of difference and deferral. From a poststructuralist perspective there can be no fixed signifiers (meanings); signifiers are subject to an endless process of deferral. The effect of fixing meaning, that is the effect of representation, is always a temporary, retrospective fixing, dependent on its discursive context, but always open to a plurality of meanings.

The very practice of cultural criticism is an illustration of the process whereby critical readings attempt to define and fix the meanings of cultural texts or practices. Yet rereadings are always not only possible but inevitable. The meanings of the signifiers 'woman' or 'man', for example, as they are articulated in discourse, vary according to discursive context and are open to constant challenge and redefinition. This is the case whether we are concerned with rereading nineteenth-century fiction, contemporary television, religious discourse, or the categories of critical analysis itself. Language is thus not only plural but political.

Feminist writers of both fiction and non-fiction have attempted to deconstruct discourses of femininity, masculinity and heterosexism, showing them to be neither natural nor inevitable but rather socially specific and historical. Deconstruction, as developed by Derrida, theorises the basis of discourses as sets of primary oppositions in which one term is privileged over the other. This discursive process of privileging and marginalising forms the basis of access to social power. As Hélène Cixous points out in her influential text *The Newly Born Woman* (1987), key oppositions structure patriarchal discourse: man/woman, active/passive, culture/nature, rational/emotional. They also structure racist discourse: white/black, developed/underdeveloped, civilised/ primitive, First World/Third World and all other discourses concerned with the reproduction of power relations. Yet, post-structuralism suggests, both these oppositions and the attempts to fix meaning and social relations as natural and inevitable are undermined by the very structure of signification itself which eludes such fixing.

It is in the inevitably temporary fixing of meaning, necessary for communication, that subjectivity is constituted. Even simple reversals of dominant hierarchies, which seek to determine what is natural or true, can have far-reaching effects on our sense of ourselves as subjects. A good example of this is the essay by Adrienne Rich 'On Compulsory Heterosexuality and Lesbian Experience' (1981), in which she argues that feminism and feminist analysis would be 'more accurate, more powerful, more truly a force for change' if it did not take the hierarchical opposition heterosexual/homosexual for granted. To question the nature of this opposition would be 'to deal with lesbian existence as a reality, and as a source of knowledge and power available to women or with the institution of heterosexuality itself as a beachhead of male dominance'. Rich argues that most feminist analysis does not raise the fundamental question of whether, 'in a different context, or other things being equal', women would choose heterosexual coupling and marriage. Heterosexuality is presumed to be the 'sexual preference' of 'most women', either implicitly or explicitly. It is not explained as an institution imposed on women by patriarchy that powerfully affects 'mothering, sex roles, relationships and societal prescriptions'. Ideas of 'preference' or 'innate orientation' are not questioned. To raise these questions, reversing the heterosexual/ lesbian opposition, is to produce a difference of view which has far-reaching consequences for how we understand contemporary gender relations.

If Derrida offers a powerful critique of the fixing of meaning and intentional subjectivity which has influenced much feminist deconstructive work, this theory has arguably less to offer when it comes to the analysis of the social construction of subjectivity and meaning in historically specific discourses, both inside and outside hegemonic social institutions and practices. It is here that feminists anxious to use poststructuralist principles in ways directly concerned with making visible and challenging power relations have placed Derridean principles of how language works and of deconstruction in a context which takes detailed account of existing social and institutional relations. Poststructuralist feminists have drawn here on Michel Foucault's historical accounts of the penal system and of sexuality which attend to how particular discourses, legitimating specific forms of social practice, constitute individuals as subjects inserted into specific forms of power relation.[14]

In *The History of Sexuality. Volume One* (1981), for example, Foucault attempts an analysis of the discourses which constitute sexuality and their implications for the production and government of sexual subjects. *The History of Sexuality* is concerned with locating:

> The forms of power, the channels it takes and the discourses it permeates in order to reach the most tenuous and individual modes of behaviour, the paths that give it access to the rare or scarcely perceivable forms of desire, how it penetrates and controls everyday pleasure – all this entailing effects that may be those of refusal blockage and invalidation, but also of incitement and intensification. In short, the 'polymorphous techniques of power'. (1981: 11)

This analysis is concerned with the ways in which social power relations are produced and sustained in the discursive production of historically specific sexuality, the subjects which it constitutes and governs, and the emergence of resistance to this power. Sexuality is seen as a primary locus of power in contemporary society, constituting subjects and governing them by exercising control through their bodies. The ways in which discourses of sexuality constitute the body, mind, emotions and desires of individuals are always historically and socially specific and a site of constant struggle. Sexuality and sexual difference have no essential nature or meaning.

In poststructuralist feminist analysis, language is not an abstract system but rather a set of historically and socially specific discourses, produced within social institutions and defining social life and subjectivity. A wide range of discourses and allied social practices – including literature – are concerned to constitute, define and fix gender difference. The same signifiers may occur in different discourses and signal radically different meanings, legitimating different modes of producing and governing individuals as sexual subjects. This is particularly clear, for example, in the ways in which radical feminists ascribe new meanings to traditionally feminine qualities, be these positive or negative in patriarchal discourse. In doing so they attempt to organise social relations in ways different from the patriarchal mainstream, a difference focused by the concepts of being woman-centred and woman-identified. For example, emotionality and intuition are posed as superior female qualities, not available to men, and conventionally negative signifiers such as 'hag', 'crone' and 'spinster' are invested with positive, creative meanings (Daly 1979).

However, mainstream discourses also use signifiers of sexual difference, femininity and masculinity in conflicting and contradictory ways. For example, signifiers of femininity ranging from sexual woman to housewife and mother are invested with different meanings and different values by different discursive practices, and from one historical moment to another. Literature is a key site for studying these differences and contradictions.

Poststructuralist theory breaks radically with the dominant humanist model of subjectivity. Instead of positing a unique essence with which each individual is born and which she or he develops, poststructuralism sees the individual as the site for the construction of modes of subjectivity which may well be contradictory, and which will demand the repression or marginalisation of other possibilities. Literature plays an important role in this process of constructing individuals as gendered subjects.

Different discourses, often reflected in literary texts, offer different sets of oppositions which attempt to lay out principles of difference and meaning. They also offer different gendered modes of subjectivity structured by, or in opposition to, patriarchal power relations. Thus this way of looking at language and subjectivity does not amount to a pluralist model of language and society, since different discourses have varying roles in defining social practices both inside and outside formal social institutions like education, the family, the media and the law. The subject positions which discourses offer involve differential access to social power.

Literary criticism based on this type of poststructuralist theory needs to look at literary constructions of gender in the context of other discourses of gender in circulation. Such analysis can point to weak points, contradictions, and resistances in patriarchally defined orders of meaning. It is only by analysing the mechanism of power at this level that it is possible to identify the potential for resistance and transformation.

The two major groups of feminist theory outlined here disagree radically about the nature of subjectivity, language and meaning. Whereas woman-centred criticism tends to see women's writing as an expression of a female perspective, be this based on experience or the feminine dimensions repressed by a patriarchal order, poststructuralist criticism stresses fictional texts as a site for the

construction of the meaning of gender and subjectivity. Both, however, share the assumption that the patriarchal order in which
women live places them differently from men. This different positioning involves relations of power and is likely to produce different forms of negotiation and resistance in women's writing.

The chapters which follow do not subscribe to ideas of woman's essential difference as the source of women's creativity. In
their different ways, they are interested in how writers negotiate
and offer resistance to patriarchal definitions of women. It is
women's different positioning in patriarchal societies and the
contradictory nature of competing definitions of femininity under
patriarchy, which make it likely that many women will write differently from their male counterparts. The rest of this volume
investigates this possibility, seeking to analyse the particular contribution of women writers to postwar writing in German.

Notes

1. Betty Friedan's *The Feminine Mystique* was published in German in 1966 by
   Rowohlt; Kate Millett's *Sexual Politics* (1970) was published by Kurt Desch
   Verlag in 1971 and reprinted in 1974 by dtv; Germaine Greer's *The Female
   Eunuch* (1971) by Suhrkamp in 1971; and Shulamith Firestone's *The Dialectic of
   Sex* by Fischer in 1975.
2. These publications include, for example, *Die verborgene Frau, Feministische Literaturwissenschaft* and *Frauen. Weiblichkeit. Schrift.*
3. For a substantial overview of feminist approaches to women's 'nature', including women's bodies, see Jaggar 1983.
4. For a sense of the concerns and power of radical feminist writing see Daly 1979
   and Griffin 1982 and 1984.
5. For an introduction to psychoanalytic criticism see Wright 1984. For a useful
   guide to concepts in feminist psychoanalytic criticism see Wright 1992.
6. See Chodorow 1978 and Dinnerstein 1987.
7. For an introduction to Lacan see Gallop 1985. For a brief introduction to Kristeva, Irigaray and Cixous see Moi 1985.
8. See Lacan 1977.
9. For a selection of Kristeva's important writings see Moi 1986.
10. See Cixous and Clément 1987 and Sellers 1994.
11. See Irigaray 1985.
12. See Levi-Strauss 1969, Saussure 1974 and Althusser 1970.
13. Texts of key importance in the early development of feminist forms of decon-
    struction are Derrida 1973 and 1976.
14. See, in particular, Foucault 1979 and 1981.

Chapter Three

Women's Writing in Occupied Germany, 1945–1949

Franziska Meyer

When studying the work of both female and male authors, regardless of the period in which it was written, it is important to bear in mind the following questions. Which texts do we read and when do we read them? What conditions were necessary for these texts not only to be produced, but to be published and to find their way to a broad reading public? In other words, who decides which works are important and of aesthetic value and what criteria do they use in deciding this issue? Why, for example, do we find in a 1979 edition of the weekly newspaper *Die Zeit* an article entitled '100 Books of World Literature' which only includes one female author – Anna Seghers (Wiggershaus 1989: 416)?

All these questions are central to an analysis of patriarchal power structures within literary institutions. An historical survey of women's writing in West Germany from the year 1945 to 1968 enables us to recognise the mechanisms of exclusion and devaluation of women writers more easily than is often the case in our immediate present. In this period the publishing industry, the organisation of writers in groups, and last but not least, media literary criticism played a decisive role in determining whether texts were published and widely distributed.

Literary studies, as taught in schools and universities, and research into literature also play an extremely important part in the canonisation of texts. Here decisions are made about what is important and, in this case, what is representative of West German literature of the post-war period. In looking at writing by women in the first two decades of the Federal Republic, it is imperative to

Notes for this section begin on page 42.

investigate the conditions of literary production for women writers inside the literary institutions.

Hanser's *Sozialgeschichte der deutschen Literatur vom 16. Jahrhundert bis zur Gegenwart* (Fischer 1986a) is a standard reference book which deals with the Federal Republic up until 1967. If we look here for accounts of women's writing in the years 1945 to 1968, the result is striking. Index entries for the terms 'female' and 'femininity' point to a small number of articles on children's literature and popular romances. Writers such as Ingeborg Drewitz, Ruth Rehmann and Barbara König – not to mention Marieluise Fleisser – whose work had been known for some considerable time are not only missing from the index of names but also from the almost nine-hundred page long book itself. Gisela Elsner, who was extremely successful in the 1960s, suffers a similar fate and is only mentioned once as a marginal imitator of Günter Grass. These absences are proof of a significant methodological failure: the well-known editor and the contributors still believed in 1986, that they could disregard more than fifteen years of feminist research. But it is more than this. What we see here is an institutionalised forgetting of women writers.

The failure of one of the most well-regarded literary histories to address the question of gender is all the more significant since the series sees itself explicitly as a *social* history. It claims to deal with 'the literary culture of a period' in the context of 'political, economic and social relations [and] social mentalities' (Fischer 1986a: 9). The editor, Ludwig Fischer, writes in his preface 'public institutions – the literary market, educational institutions and the media – play a particular important role here. They are not separate from literature, they decisively effect its quality, its range and the way in which it is received in a particular period'. Given this approach, the blindness to gender is all the more serious. The index contains the concepts 'racism', 'class struggle' and '*Sexualfeindlichkeit*' (hostility to sexuality). Once and once only is the term *Frauenliteratur* mentioned and it is dismissed as a term connected with protest literature of the 1970s.

Periodisation in literary histories does not usually rely on the self-definitions of the writers involved. This sort of periodisation ties *Frauenliteratur* to a narrowly defined historical phase and explicitly negates texts which were written before 1968. These are given a quasi pre-literary status.[1] In the following many examples will be given of how a covert stigmatisation of women writers, particularly in the literary climate of the 1950s, not only decisively affected the reception of texts written by women but also hindered their production.

The persistent way in which women writers have been excluded from the canon is evident in the naive, well-meant but patronising title of a volume published with a large print run in 1979: *Frauen schreiben. Ein neues Kapitel deutschsprachiger Literatur* (Serke 1979). In stressing the apparent newness of this writing, Jürgen Serke's emphatic subtitle ignores the works of women writers of earlier decades.

Even feminist literary studies are often not completely innocent of this type of periodisation which can easily lead to exclusions. All too often we find women's writing identified with texts influenced by the new women's movement of the 1970s. The often undifferentiated use of the terms 'feminist' and 'pre-feminist' literature is also methodologically questionable. The search for so-called 'precursors' of the feminist texts of the 1970s in early periods easily falls into a teleological way of thinking. This runs the risk of disregarding the different historical and social contexts of writing by women and of projecting present-day feminist expectations back onto earlier decades. This can lead to a reading of women writers of the 1950s in terms of the aesthetic and often moralising concept of 'conventionality' (Weigel 1989: 29) and to an unhistorical use of the more radical standards of the 1970s. It is like accusing naturalism of not being expressionist enough.

This type of simplified periodisation suppresses the disparities, the complexities and the contradictions of literary discourse in the 1950s and 1960s. If actual texts of this period are lost from view, then a critic like Sigrid Weigel can construct general and false oppositions such as the following: 'While women writers of the 1950s and 1960s were still totally preoccupied with love, the absence of love in women's writing of the 1970s is striking' (1989: 215).

In this chapter, I would like to encourage a rereading of a period which is often over-simplified even in feminist accounts. The history of women's writing in the first two decades of the Federal Republic demands a revision of the canon of West German literature of the post-war years. Up until now this period has been identified with the (male) literature of *Gruppe 47* (Group 47) – Andersch, Böll, Lenz, Grass, Johnson, Walser, supplemented by Arno Schmidt and Koeppen. This rereading does not seek to discover a female 'Other', nor does it concentrate exclusively on literary texts without asking about the conditions of their production.

As late as 1983, Sigrid Weigel – in my view correctly – criticised an exclusively metaphorical way of talking about women's writing and regretted the absence of 'the interpretation of actual texts in theoretical discussions' (1983b: 150). How we read is also important. Numerous recent readings of texts by women writers use French poststructuralist and psychoanalytic theory (Irigaray, Cixous, Derrida, Lacan). In the process they often reduce literary texts to illustrations of pre-existing theoretical models. For example, the question of *écriture feminine* (feminine writing) is arguably unproductive if the answer is known in advance. Despite their high theoretical aspirations and often thought-provoking results, these types of interpretation – which are usually applied repeatedly to a relatively limited selection of writers – tend to reduce completely different texts to sameness.

In contrast to this, women's writing will be discussed in the following three chapters in its broader social and historical context. Where ways of writing and genre are concerned, it is imperative to look at the appropriate literary traditions. Every woman writer is at the same time a reader. For example, Marie Luise Kaschnitz and Elisabeth Langgässer's change to short-story writing after 1945 was part of a more general tendency in Germany to model literature on the American short story. The early prose work of Ingeborg Bachmann and Ruth Rehmann can only be fully understood if we take account of the reception of French existentialism in the late 1940s in West Germany. Gisela Elsner's satirical texts clearly belong – in spite of many contradictory elements – to the new realism of the 1960s. Strong traces of the French *nouveau roman* (for example, Nathalie Sarraute) – which was widely read in the 1960s – can be found in the early prose of Renate Rasp, Gabriele Wohmann and Hannelies Taschau.

As early as the first decades of the twentieth century, European modernist literature by both female and male authors was marked by strong doubts about language and ideas of language as a prison. After 1945 writers also searched for the 'right' language – with very varied results.[2] This search is a feature of the immediate post-war period, the avant-garde literature of the 1950s, and the 'new realism' of the 1960s. As will be seen in chapter 6, the innovative interventions made by feminist literature in the 1970s included the thematisation of the patriarchal and sexist nature of existing language.

Numerous woman writers of the period 1945 to 1968 take up themes which have become identified with feminist literature of the 1970s. In women's writing from the 1950s onwards, we find lesbian love, abortion, women's search for identity in the prison of existing norms of youth and beauty, as well as illusionless depictions of marriage and authoritarian patriarchal family structures. Examples include the prose of Johanna Moosdorf, Gabriele Wohmann, Gisela Elsner, Marie Luise Kaschnitz, Ruth Rehmann, Ingeborg Bachmann and, last but not least, Hannelies Taschau's first novel which was published in 1967.[3] Yet, before 1968, these themes were not and could not be depicted via a wide-ranging discourse of emancipation.

When interpreting actual texts I consider the following points. In looking at the level of fictional representation I ask what access women's writing can give us to the everyday reality of women and men in post-war Germany. On the ideological level I am interested in constructions of femininity and masculinity 'which must not necessarily differ from those of male authors' (Weigel 1983b: 149). The utopian dimension of texts by woman writers lies in their existence as 'the second sex' (Simone de Beauvoir). Do traces of this 'different way of being in the world' (Christa Wolf) occur in the texts? Are there contradictions and breaks in the way in which life is perceived and narrated which could point towards a possible 'freeing of writing' from 'male perspectives'? (Weigel 1983b: 150)

Rarely have traditional relationships between the sexes been so radically disturbed as they were in the immediate post-war years. Like women in other European countries involved in the Second World War, German women had to work hard on the so-called 'homefront'. They were not only responsible for the survival of their families; in addition to this they also performed (as in the First World War) all sorts of heavy physical work in industrial production, for example, in the munitions industry. The writer Elisabeth Langgässer, who lived in Berlin, was conscripted to a cable factory in 1944. Later she would describe her experiences in the short story 'An der Nähmaschine' (1980a).

The strong position of women in social and economic life persisted into the immediate post-war period. It was mostly women who, left to their own devices, fought for survival on an everyday basis in a world governed by ruins and starvation. In a city such as Berlin, at the end of the war, women made up 64.2 percent of the population (Rapisarda 1987a: 88). Even today the striking number of elderly single women testifies to the effects of the war.

In May 1945 the majority of the German population was overcome by worry and uncertainty about the safety of their next-of-kin.

More than ten million people were on the move as refugees. The majority of men had either been killed in the war or were still in prisoner-of-war camps. Of those who returned many were disabled and suffering from their traumatic war experiences. In addition to this, the majority of the population regarded the allied victory over Hitler's Germany not as liberation from fascism but as total defeat. The collapse of a fascist master-race identity was experienced by those who had identified with it as a complete humiliation.

At home these men often found themselves confronted by completely changed circumstances. Their wives were managing perfectly well on their own, had become alienated from their husbands, or in the course of the long years of separation had found other partners. School-aged children met complete strangers – their fathers – for the first time. Experiences at the front and as refugees, hunger, destroyed marriages, and last but not least, the much repeated theme of the homecomer, provided the material for numerous short stories by young male authors such as Böll, Borchert, and Andersch.[4] A large number of these men were neither physically nor psychologically in a position to resume their pre-war role as head of the family. In no other phase of post-war German history would male identity be so badly shaken.

Thousands of *Trümmerfrauen* (rubble women) of all ages and social backgrounds began the work of clearing up and rebuilding the bombed cities. Christa Reinig's story 'Eine Ruine', first published in 1949, is the only example known to me of a literary representation of this typical everyday experience of women (Reinig 1989). Referring to these unusual circumstances, an article written in 1946 on women's writing, which is otherwise explicitly conservative, rejects any distinction between male and female writing as an unwarranted labelling:

> Many novels written by women are in no way recognisable as such … The differences in ways of life have largely disappeared in the last few decades. Women have almost as many opportunities as men and are just as burdened. They have emerged from their centuries-long position of being looked after. This is a result both of their own efforts, of war and the post-war period. The stamp of a different way of life must, therefore, become ever less pronounced in women's writing and eventually more or less disappear. (Seyffarth 1946: 193)

For a brief period of time it seemed as if women and men might have equal access to writing and publishing. In the immediate post-war period, before the onset of the Cold War in 1947, women writers played a comparatively prominent role in the literary and cultural life of all zones of occupation. Despite the extremely hard conditions of everyday life, the political and cultural life which came into being shortly after the end of the war was marked by an enormous sense of renewal. Women were well represented in a literary arena where anti-fascism ruled the day. Luise Rinser, who was a literary correspondent for the famous Munich *Neue Zeitung* from 1945 to 1953, recalls opportunities of which women in West Germany ten years later could only dream:

> At that time we women had chances as never before to involve ourselves in politics, even in leading positions. What wasn't I offered back then. Control of women's affairs for Bavarian broadcasting, the job of chief editor of the literary supplement of a newly founded newspaper ... a leading job in the new SPD [Social Democratic Party], a position in the special ministry for de-nazification. I refused them all ... I wanted to write other things. (1981: 399)

Women writers who had to deal with domestic arrangements and the material welfare of their families, like for example Rinser, wrote under extremely difficult circumstances:

> I earned a good living but I couldn't buy anything with the money. The black market was a closed book to me ... we were starving ... during the day I looked after domestic concerns, at night I wrote by the dull light of a small petroleum lamp beside the kitchen stove which grew colder and colder. (1981: 402)

Berlin writer Ingeborg Drewitz, who in 1951 would produce the first West German post-war drama to include scenes from a concentration camp, describes her experiences in 1945:

> I ... had tenants, my father-in-law lived with me, you had to queue for everything. You got your rations ... every ten days, you queued from seven in the morning until the afternoon in order to buy your rations ... I could only steal a bit of time to write. (Rapisarda 1987b: 10)

One of the most prominent women writers in West Germany, the Catholic writer Elisabeth Langgässer, was obsessed by her literary work – an activity which the author herself called 'the gentle madness of artistic compulsion' (1979, II: 235). Her writing was the only source of income for the family. She was also burdened by worries about her eldest daughter Cordelia who had been persecuted as Jewish. Not until 1946 would she learn that Cordelia had survived Auschwitz.[5] In a letter written in January 1947 we read about the infamous winter of hunger and cold:

> Hunger, no shoes for the children or myself, a wearisome struggle from one day to the next ... the temperature in the room where we lived ten degrees centigrade. In spite of this I started a new piece of work. (Hetmann 1990: 81)

In the summer of the same year Langgässer used her own work as an exchange object on the black market: 'I gave a Catholic priest in the country, who begged me for a copy of a novel, a book on condition that he give me its weight in flour' (Hetmann 1990: 82).

Both Elisabeth Langgässer (b. 1899) and Luise Rinser (b. 1911) belonged to a generation of women writers who had already published before the end of the war. Rinser, who was arrested in 1944 for 'high treason' and 'defamation of the army',[6] saw her large body of prose translated into more than thirty languages. In 1984 she achieved a degree of popularity as the Green candidate for the Federal Presidency which extended far beyond the literary arena. In contrast to Rinser, Langgässer's work was forgotten in the course of the 1950s. Yet 'at least between 1945 and 1955 Elisabeth Langgässer was undoubtedly considered one of the most important writers in Germany' (Krüger in Langgässer 1980a: 346).[7] Her premature death in 1950 was deplored by the newspaper *Frankfurter Allgemeine Zeitung* as 'the most important loss to our literature since the death of Ricarda Huch' (Hetmann 1990: 95).

Elisabeth Langgässer's literary career had already begun in the 1920s when she worked for the literary magazine *Die Kolonne* with, among others, Peter Huchel and Günter Eich. In 1932 she received the *Deutsche Staatsbürgerinnenpreis* (German Citizen's Prize) for her novellas which were often compared to Droste-Hülshoff's prose. Also employed as a teacher, domestic demands were even at that time too much for the writer and mother. I know of no comparable exasperated expression of desperation by a male author:

> Yesterday I simply burst into tears. I couldn't stand the noise any more ... One thing is certain, if you have a child then your day is completely full. Or a profession – then you have to have somebody else care for the child. Both our fathers ('women belong in the home') and Soviet-Russia did the absolutely right thing. (Hetmann 1990: 46)

In 1936 Langgässer was forbidden to write because of her 'half-Jewish' origin. Her powerful novel *Das unauslöschliche Siegel* was written in secret and in constant danger of discovery over the next nine years. When it was published in 1946, this text caused a furore and earned the writer the Büchner prize posthumously in 1951. Today this is still the most important German literary award.

After 1945 the range of non-fascist literature by writers who had remained in Germany, choosing so-called 'inner emigration', proved to be extremely narrow. The expected drawerfuls of literature, written in secret as a form of resistance, did not materialise. The drawers were empty and Langgässer's novel is constantly cited as one of the few valuable examples of such writing. Langgässer's extremely modern, unconventional and provocative Christian novel was blacklisted by the Catholic church because of its representation of lesbian love and other 'erotic liberties'.[8]

In 1947 Langgässer gave one of the main addresses at the first Congress of German Writers. There she sharply condemned those writers who had opted for 'inner emigration' in Nazi Germany and who claimed to have written in a language of veiled resistance. The 'enormous self-deception' of these harmless nature poets was 'an anacreontic dancing around with flowers on the dreadful gaping chasm of the mass graves covered by these flowers'. Language, she argued, was the thing that should link authors of all types and which needed to be radically scrutinised:

> Many people still think that they can take over a language and a mode of expression which was previously used by terrible criminals and horrifying idiots in the destruction and demise of our continent … People don't think that they can put new wine into old bottles neither those of 1933 nor those of 1923. (Langgässer 1947: 41)

At this Berlin Congress writers from all four zones of occupation were able to meet for the first and last time. Just one year later the outbreak of an open Cold War would divide intellectuals too. Prior to this, women writers still played an exceptionally important and representative role. Eighty-three year old Ricarda Huch, the grand old lady of German literature, was made honorary president of the Berlin Congress. In 1930 Huch had been the first woman to gain admittance to the Prussian Academy of Arts which she left in 1933 in protest against the persecution of Jewish members – unlike her colleagues Gottfried Benn and Ernst Jünger. Three very different women writers at this congress, Huch, Langgässer and the Communist writer Anna Seghers who had just returned from exile in Mexico, formed the 'triumvirate of great contemporary women novelists' (Rapisarda 1987a: 96).

In the immediate post-war years, publishers faced difficult circumstances: on the one hand the reading public had a great hunger for books, on the other, there was an immense shortage of paper complemented by the Allies' policy of re-education and licensing. While book production in the partially destroyed publishing houses only got under way again slowly and with difficulty, it was the right time for newspapers and magazines. The numerous newly founded literary and cultural journals became the most important outlets for literature and offered authors the chance to publish and to make a living. This boom would come to an end with the currency reform in 1948.

The very titles of these magazines – *Die Wandlung* (Change), *Der Aufbau* (Reconstruction), *Ost und West* (East and West), *Ende und Anfang* (End and Beginning) and last but not least *Der Ruf* (The Call) – bear witness to the immense impetus for renewal during these years, irrespective of political differences. Writers took the educational potential of literature extremely seriously and radically overestimated it. Langgässer and Geno Hartlaub both worked as editors for *Aufbau* and *Die Wandlung* in addition to their writing. Even novels were distributed *en masse* in a newspaper format. In 1946 the publisher Harry Rowohlt brought out the famous *Rowohlt-Rotations-Romane* (Rowohlt-Rotation-Novels).[9] 'In times of austerity it is no longer a question of how something is produced only of what is produced. The hunger for good books cannot be satisfied in traditional ways' (Reith 1987: 124). Anna Segher's world-famous exile novel *Das siebte Kreuz* (1946, *The Seventh Cross*, 1942) first published in New York reached a German audience in an edition of a 100,000 copies each priced at fifty pfennig.

Distribution via newspapers and magazines was both democratic and cheap and also helped establish the short story, the 'pride of post-war German literature' (Reich-Ranicki). The short story became the genre of so-called *Trümmerliteratur* ('rubble literature', Böll 1961). It was not only authors like Heinrich Böll who made their successful literary debut with this genre. Both Luise Rinser and Elisabeth Langgässer created significant contributions to this important chapter of German post-war literature.[10] Later, Gabriele Wohmann, who was born in 1932, followed in their footsteps. In the 1950s and 1960s she became one of the best known German short-story writers: 'In the area of short story writing there are only very few writers who can surpass or even equal this writer in the whole of the German-speaking world' (Reich-Ranicki 1967: 281).

The same can be said for the short prose works by Elisabeth Langgässer. It does not seem to me to be an overstatement to include Langgässer's short stories among the most penetrating texts of the immediate post-war years. To begin with, the author published in the East Berlin magazine *Eulenspiegel*. In 1948 a collection of these stories appeared under the characteristic title *Der Torso*. However, with a few exceptions, most of these stories were never reprinted in the decades that followed. It was only in the 1970s that publishers began to show a widespread renewed interest in texts by women writers. More than thirty years after their initial publication a new edition of Langgässer's complete works was finally published in 1979.

It is not easy to label Langgässer's stories as *Trümmerliteratur*. Most of the stories do not have the male protagonists and lonely spartan heroes which are so often found in other post-war stories by male authors. Langgässer tends to narrate her stories from a female perspective or often from the perspective of a child. In this way she guides the reader from the present of the post-war period back into normal everyday life under the Nazis. Her stories take up the questions of the guilt and the responsibilities of individuals. Her characters lack all heroism. It is not the large-scale crimes, but rather small thoughtless and opportunistic deeds – and acts of omission – committed by supposedly innocent people which are questioned in a deeply thoughtful way. Langgässer's themes include the persecution of the Jews – for example in 'Untergetaucht' ('In Hiding', 1984) and 'Saisonbeginn'; the experiences of civilians in air raids – 'Der Erstkommunionstag' and 'Jetzt geht die Welt unter'; forced labour – 'An der Nähmaschine'; and the last days of the war as seen from the perspective of a Russian woman who is conscripted to work in Germany – 'Lydia'. The shocking ending of the story 'Saisonbeginn' perhaps points most cleverly to the irresponsible behaviour of the inhabitants of an idyllic holiday resort. They act like Nazi fellow travellers.

These texts question the widespread resistance to the question of guilt in the German population ('we did not know anything about it'). They also question the feeling of being merely the victim of a political catastrophe. An angry report by the exiled writer Erika Mann, the eldest daughter of Thomas Mann, who travelled to post-war Germany as a newspaper correspondent in American uniform, gives an impression of this attitude:

That they don't want to be occupied ... is the nicest thing. Much less attractive is the way in which they are dripping with a self-pity which never considers the suffering of others because such suffering would have to be someone's fault, because this someone in the final analysis is called Germany and because Germany *should not* be allowed to have such an *unbounded* self-pity if it is guilty of other peoples' similar misery. (Quoted in von der Lühe 1994: 212)

Langgässer's great artistic achievement lies in her ability to involve her readers in the plots of her stories. First person narratives and personal ways of telling stories, such as the frequent use of dialogue, create a strong identification effect. Here we can see quite clearly the influence of the American short story (such as those by Hemingway). The very first sentence engages the reader, drawing her or him into the plot: '"I was after all only human", the imposing woman repeated over and over' ('Untergetaucht', 1980a: 206); 'When the people came out of the bunker the unknown dog ... was still lying in the corner of the bedroom and refused to move' ('Jetzt geht die Welt unter', 1980a: 222).[11]

Going beyond these classical features of the short-story genre we often find a dialogical structure which attempts to engage the reader. Stories frequently use the following kind of introduction: 'Whether or not he is still alive today, I really can't say. My husband has heard nothing from this branch of the family for a long time, and in any case I am not keen on long family histories' ('Die Sippe auf dem Berg und im Tal', 1980a: 193). Alternatively a 'harmless listener', taking the place of the reader, listens to someone else's stories: 'There began a story which I really had to listen to; and I have always liked stories like these: nothing special and the sillier the better. They make you feel less alone' ('Untergetaucht', 1980a: 206). The strength of such a narrative style lies in the way it emphasises an individual perspective on what is being represented. There is no omniscient narrator telling 'general truths'. Rather, we are confronted by a variety of subjective interpretations of events and of history. The stories explicitly thematise the role of narrative as a particular way of interpreting the past. In this way history is presented to us by the various characters as already linguistically structured – that is textualised. These meanings and interpretations do not require the reader's endorsement. Where characters attempt to create coherence the text itself makes the contradictions and incoherences obvious. The attitudes of the characters who narrate the stories are also represented as historically changeable. The frequently used perspective of a first person narrator who turns to the reader in order to explain things can have a didactic effect: 'I now know why my best friend's kitchen ... was increasingly filled with strangers towards the end of the war ... but at that time I simply found this story unpleasant' ('Lydia', 1980a: 211).

This dialogical structure of the stories appeals to the reader to become actively engaged with the narrative. Here we find an extremely clever aspect of Langgässer's art that is aimed at reaching both the heart and mind of her readers. The author herself once formulated her intentions as follows: 'There must be something in every short story – like a silent drum beat – if you like, but one which marks the point after which nothing can ever be the same again' (quoted in Kaschnitz 1979: 18).

The story 'Glück haben' is a very well crafted example of this effect. Together with the story 'Saisonbeginn' it has become part of the canon in so far as both texts are repeatedly included in anthologies and school textbooks. 'Glück haben' is an impressive example of Langgässer's extremely well thought out use of artistic means, which was so admired by Marie Luise Kaschnitz.[12] In this story, too, the 'process of story telling' and the 'process of listening to stories' are explicitly thematised. Once again they have a quite particular importance. Alongside the plot which is being narrated, the way in which characters tell the story is particularly accentuated. The scene of the plot is a mental hospital after the war, 'a real paradise ... which lies just beyond the cemetery' (1980a: 231). The story is told from the perspective of a first person narrator who is visiting a bomb victim and finds herself confronted by chance with the life story of a mad woman: 'I heard this conversation that the woman was having with herself and which ended so strangely while I was sitting on a bench in the garden' (230). This opening sentence of the framing narrative points, in a way that is untypical of short stories, towards an unexpected ending. Through the ears of the hard-nosed visitor, who is disturbed by her own misfortune and who listens unwillingly, we hear a personal account of more than forty years of German history which ends in madness. The woman tells the story of her 'good luck' in a totally indifferent tone of voice. For the readers, however, who become more and more disturbed, it proves to be a chain of increasingly gruesome examples of individual misery. The hard-boiled attitude of the mad narrator, who continues to seek happiness in unhappiness by constantly repeating 'but we were lucky' could not contrast more sharply with the content of the story.

The girl grows up spoiled and without a care in life in a wealthy home during the Wilhelmenian era. 'I was a child of Fortune' (1980a: 233). Inconsequentially and incidentally we learn about the death of her father and how 'the World War went by without harming us'. The young woman is 'always lucky'. She has 'plenty of proposals of marriage even though many young men were killed in the war' (233). Her eventual husband, a highly gifted lawyer who worked for the state and is 'a kind good fellow', soon makes a lot of money. With two children the family moves further East. 'This was the sign of the times' and they buy 'a "little" country estate'. However, the woman's luck slowly begins to change. 'I no longer know exactly when our bad luck begun. Perhaps we should not have moved so far from the West, but who could have known?' (234).

The use of extended narrative time is extremely clever – insignificant events are described in detail – as is the use of summary. Terrible things are passed over with increasing speed in order once again to reach the conclusion, 'but we were lucky'. The woman's attempt to conform to Nazi policies on the birthrate – 'it was fashionable to have lots of children' (234) – ends in several miscarriages. In 1939, the year in which the war begins, her husband dies unexpectedly but she is comforted by the career success of her two children. Her daughter, 'tall and blond', is put in charge of forced workers and a (concentration) camp in occupied Poland. Her son who is 'technically gifted' is not at first sent to the front. The increasing blows to their private happiness which follow correspond exactly with the decreasing success of fascist war policies. Her ambitious son pays for his promotion in the German army with his death at Monte Cassino. Admittedly, her daughter has a son at this very moment by an 'SS comrade', but unfortunately her fiancé, a high-ranking pilot, is killed during the Allied landings in Normandy. Nonetheless 'she was lucky and was married to him before this by proxy'.

The defeat of Germany, which is gaining speed, is experienced by the protagonist as Hitler's increasing bad luck: we 'noticed that the Führer had lost his good luck'. The victory of the Soviet Army over the German army, which would play a decisive role in the liberation of Germany from fascism, is reported as a misfortune: 'Everything went wrong. The Russians [*der Russe*] were coming closer and closer' (235). The remainder of the family has to flee. The mother is forced to watch the gruesome death of her daughter and grandson on a crowded refugee train. But, in spite of this she soon arrives 'happily' uninjured in a Berlin camp for refugees. 'We were conquered, I was lucky, the suburb was handed over to the Russians almost without a shot'. The turning point which follows – creating the catharsis – is occasioned by something comparatively harmless. Searching desperately for potatoes the woman puts her hands in excrement: 'Both my hands were full of shit, full of brown stinking slimy shit ... I have reached the height of my misfortune' (236). It is this brown filth (*Dreck*) – and here Langgässer's choice of word is extremely ambiguous – which opens the eyes of the pro- tagonist in order finally, as she sees clearly for the first time, to rob her of her sanity. Her 'luck' is shown actually to be madness and the lie of her life (Durzak 1980b: 395). 'This shitty life! I cried ... Shitty life ...shitty ...'. And even the disturbed woman listening joins in the screaming: 'Shitty life, she screamed, and I screamed too' and ends up staying in the institution for four weeks.

'Glück haben' is not only the story of continuous attempts at repression and lying about life, it is also the story of a wealthy middle-class family under fascism whose 'harmlessly apolitical' roots stretch back to the imperialism of the Wilhelmenian era.

The luck of the mad woman appears to the readers who are lis- tening in as incomprehensible misfortune. The story leaves open the pressing question of the individual responsibility of this woman who was destroyed by the war. The narrative perspective has the effect, in the first instance, of encouraging the reader to identify spontaneously and empathically with the misfortune of the vic- tim. However, a closer reading does not allow a response of mere sympathy since the text repeatedly and incidentally points to the extent to which this 'victim' identified her personal happiness and the career success of her family with Hitler's 'good luck'. Through the figure of the mad woman, we get to know one of millions of fel- low travellers who internalised the fascist war aims even to the point of using Nazi propaganda terms such as *'der Russe'*. Lang- gässer points in a historically concrete way to the battle fields which were decisive for the course of the Second World War. If everything had not gone wrong on the Eastern front – in the central battle for Stalingrad – and if the woman's son and son-in-law had been more successful in Monte Cassino and in Normandy, this family history would undoubtedly have had a 'happier' ending. Linked as it was to world history, the price of this family's happi- ness would have been no less than the victory of Hitler's Germany.

The recognition of this forces readers to change from the ex- clusive perspective of the victim and become involved. The text profoundly questions a way of thinking which treats politics and history in a dangerously personalised manner. The self-satisfied unwillingness to probe how one's own individual happiness creates misfortune for others, including one's own family, is depicted as both a lack of political responsibility and ultimately self-destructive. The reader is called upon to disengage the apparently unconnected experiences of the luck and 'bad luck' of the mad woman, which appear to happen by chance, from a private individual fate. (Langgässer analyses a similar case of individualistic thinking in her story 'Untergetaucht'. In this case the man had 'just been accepted by the Nazi party ... this thoroughly good-hearted man', 207). Langgässer also stresses the lack of linguistic responsibility through the constant weaving in of everyday clichés. The second woman, who is listening, is a master of trivia. She cannot be relieved of responsibility any more than the mad woman. This is made clear by her close friendship with the nurse who she soon finds 'particularly nice': 'She used to be engaged to a gasman. Oh well. But that's a different story' (237). Both the outward appearance of this nurse – 'a fat blue and white striped locomotive' (232) and her former fiancé's job could only connote Auschwitz in the mind of the reader of 1948. The inability to make connections, the indifference and the unwillingness to think shown by this woman are, in the final analysis, all too similar to the mad woman's attitude of 'let's put a brave face on it'. This point is made, among others, by the concluding sentence 'But that's a different story'. The repetition of this phrase reiterates the central idea of the story as a whole. Neither the bomb victim, the gasman, the death of the family nor the madness of the woman are simply 'different stories' which have nothing to do with each other. They are part of the same German history as the ambitious wife of a 'highly gifted lawyer' who, as a sign of the times, moved to the East, and the proud mothers of women running concentrations camps and the bright SS brides who wanted to earn a fashionable medal for motherhood (*Mutterkreuz*).

In her narrative, Langgässer gives explicit expression to linguistic defence mechanisms using the example of the listening woman. Ways of speaking are exposed which to a large extent characterised the everyday consciousness of the population of post-war Germany: 'There was so much unhappiness at this time that more or less unhappiness no longer mattered – people have forgotten about it. (Today I say, thank God. Where would that get us?)' (232). This involuntary defensive rhetorical question ('Where would that get us?'), which is repeated several times in the course of the story, and the no less frequent 'That's the way things are', force the reader to examine these phrases closely and to reflect upon their implications. Both clichés express nothing less than the refusal to think. Langgässer makes drastically clear, through the terrible misfortune of the mad woman, that the refusal to think which marks a spontaneous bid for private advantage can have deeply self-destructive implications. A moralistic condemnation by the narrator is not needed here. Both fellow travellers, one of whose life is already over, reveal themselves. Langgässer refuses to relieve the individual of her political responsibility, not in spite of but precisely because of the suffering she has experienced. The considerable power of this impressive anti-fascist text results not least from the fact that the personal suffering of the guilty victims is taken extremely seriously. Langgässer's work is aimed at reflective readers who by the end of the story have gone far beyond the characters. Appealing to a limited sympathy with the severely punished 'child of fortune', the text attempts to make suggestions about how people can come to terms with suffering in a way which will prevent future misfortune. The appeal to take responsibility for recent German history does not need large-scale pathos. Instead of this, Langgässer insists on the responsibility of the individual. Regarding history as an individualistic list of chance, luck or bad luck leads to a perspective which helplessly sees it as merely fate or catastrophe. The implications of 'Where does that get us?' as a way of thinking are graphically depicted in 'Glück haben'. Complacency, and the unwillingness to think beyond personal interest robs the individual of her mind, leaving her in the garden of the mental asylum.

Translated by Chris Weedon

Notes

I would like to thank my late friend Marion Farouk-Sluglett (Salt Lake City) for her immense help in providing the published literary translations for this and the following chapter. Thanks also to Cettina Rapisarda for most helpful discussions of chapters 3, 4 and 5. Except for translations from published English editions referenced and listed in the bibliography, all translations from German texts cited in this chapter and chapters 4 and 5 are by Chris Weedon.

1. The volume on 1968–1990 also follows the same logic, since we now find a lot of space given to women's writing. See Briegleb and Weigel 1992.
2. See, for example, the early prose of Ingeborg Bachmann, the collection of stories *Das dreißigste Jahr* (1961/1986 The Thirtieth Year 1987). In her 'Frankfurt Lectures' given in 1959–1960, Bachmann had repeatedly emphasised this tradition.
3. Moosdorf and Kaschnitz are covered in more detail in Stephan et al. 1986a.
4. Many writers saw themselves as a 'lost generation' and began to write as prisoners of war. Experiences at the front influenced their way of writing even to the extent of their using *Landser* (private) language. A comparative reading of short stories by male and female authors would be well worthwhile. Authors like Böll and Andersch, schooled in the hard hitting realism of American writers, who took as their models Hemingway and Steinbeck depicted the prototype of the saintly motherly beautiful German woman in their stories. These images of women contrasted starkly with the actual lived reality of women. The female figures in these texts merely serve as caring motherly projections for defenceless insecure male anti-heroes who are often psychologically destroyed. See, for example, Böll 1947/1987, trans. 1977, Weyrauch 1989 and Durzak 1980a.
5. Langgässer's attitude towards her daughter is open to debate. At the age of fifteen, the daughter was deported via Theresienstadt to Auschwitz. The 'anger of the survivor' (Edvardson 1991a: 114) towards the 'blind, stupid … loved and hated mother' (Edvardson 1991b: 21,135) permeates the later autobiographical prose of the daughter. In Langgässer's letters from the crucial period, she articulates, admittedly at considerable intervals, desperate concern for Cordelia. Yet, despite this, the daughter's absence from most of the letters is somewhat mystifying. After her liberation, Cordelia, who had survived because of her role as secretary to the infamous concentration camp doctor Mengele, lived first in Sweden and later emigrated to Israel.
6. See Rinser 1977, *Gefängnistagebuch* (trans. 1987) first published in 1946.
7. It is all the more perturbing that the two 'standard works' on post-war women's writing (Stephan et al. 1986a and Weigel 1989) do not mention this writer, who received many awards, by name. The same is true of Serke 1979/1982.
8. See Krechel in Langgässer 1979, II. The author herself reflected on how her work was radically different from conservative tendencies in Christian literature: 'I was dismissed as a "Christian writer" – which, of course, I am, but I would prefer "Christian writer" without the connotations of literary triviality. And because I am dismissed in this way, I have attracted the aversion of liberals for who I am an emetic' (Krechel in Langgässer 1979, II: 235).

9. This term referred to the way these texts were printed on a rotary press. Even today the brand name of Rowohlt's paperback series 'rororo' (*Rowohlts-Rota-tions-Ro*mane) is a reminder of the conditions of post-war book production.

10. See, for example, Rinser's impressive story 'Die rote Katze' in Durzak 1980a. This story has deservedly become part of the canon of German short stories. On the occasion of Rinser's first and only reading to *Gruppe 47*, it was dismissed as mere kitsch.

11. The substantial difference between this and the classical way of beginning a novella becomes clear if we compare the first sentence of Langgässer's story 'Mars' written in 1932: 'In O. a small town on the Rhine in 1920 during French occupation the following event happened:' (1980a: 7).

12. Marie Luise Kaschnitz also changed to writing short stories after 1945. Full of admiration she tells of her first encounter with Langgässer at a writer's meeting in 1948 in Royaumont in France. Rooms are being allocated:

> Well, three bedrooms and as it turned out giant rooms with two beds next to each other and one in the corner. The young woman from the Herder publishers had already chosen that one when we got there. So. Elisabeth Langgässer and I side by side and I was scared of Frau Langgässer's cool penetrating look, and I go and get the screen and pull it between our beds, impolitely enough. Yet during the very first night we talk and all of the nights that follow without the screen. Conversations about techniques of short story writing are a preferred form for both of us now. I am amazed at Elisabeth Langgässer's self-conscious work, her superior application of artistic means, her clear analytical mind. (Kaschnitz 1979: 18)

Chapter Four

WOMEN'S WRITING IN THE 1950S AND 1960S

Franziska Meyer

By the beginning of the 1950s women writers were disappearing from the public arena. In the areas of social and more especially family policy, there was a general restoration of traditional gender relations. Adenauer's social order – marked by reconstruction and the economic miracle – favoured an image of women which identified female self-realisation with the 'three K's': *Kinder, Küche, Kirche* (children, kitchen and Church).

In comparison with the immediate post-war years, the opportunities open to women writers within the male-dominated literary institutions diminished. Differences between the super powers, particularly since the onset of the Cold War in 1947, had a significant curtailing influence on cultural life. The currency reform of 1948 led to the widespread demise of the literary magazines which had recently been founded with so much enthusiasm. This meant the loss of literary outlets which would have offered publishing possibilities to younger authors. This is not the only reason why the concept of 'pre-currency reform literature' is useful in periodising post-war literature (Lettau 1967: 94). In the cultural sphere, 1949 marked a much less significant break than is often assumed. Whereas the writer's congress of 1947 was still influenced to a considerable extent by women writers, by 1950 only six women were included among the 150 intellectuals from numerous countries who took part in the Congress of Cultural Freedom – *the* Western organisation of the cultural Cold War (Meyer 1987: 34).

Gruppe 47, founded by Hans Werner Richter in 1947, had a huge influence on the development of literature in the post-war Federal

Republic. The group as such came together once or twice a year for a few days. Richter invited mostly younger, unknown authors to read from as yet unpublished works which were then criticised by those present. In this way writers such as Heinrich Böll, Günter Grass and Peter Weiss were helped to establish themselves. Only two women – both Austrian – Ilse Aichinger and Ingeborg Bachmann became famous through *Gruppe 47* in the 1950s.

Aichinger's prize-winning 'Spiegelgeschichte' (1978b, orig., 'Story in Reverse' 1972) marked the end of so-called *Trümmerliteratur* (Böll 1961: 339). Rejecting the direct realism (*Realismus des Unmittelbaren*) of the post-war years, authors now turned to the aesthetics of modernism. In the early 1950s prose writing and more particularly experimental poetry and radio plays were influenced by Kafka and French existentialism (particularly Sartre and Camus). Bachmann's poetry was highly regarded for years. The first prose work by this poet, the story 'Alles' (1961, 'Everything', 1964) was much acclaimed at the 1959 meeting of the group. During the twenty years of the group's existence, the two Austrians remained the only woman writers to win the Group's much sought after prize. Later accounts, written by men, of their special place in *Gruppe 47*, attributed it to 'male gallantry' (Rapisarda 1991: 194, 200). Apart from these two (women) authors, particularly Bachmann, women writers faced hard times.

In the early 1950s there was still a critical awareness among men of the striking absence of women writers from the literary scene. Commenting on a meeting of *Gruppe 47*, the *Neue Zeitung* wrote: 'Among the twenty people reading from their works there were only two women. This is very strange when compared with Anglo-Saxon countries. In Germany, however, it is the usual picture' (Lettau 1967: 53). Yet people quickly became used to all-male meetings in public and literary life and soon this was no longer commented on. The models of 'normal' relations between the sexes quickly shifted to the disadvantage of women.

In 1987 the author Ingrid Bachér summed up the situation as follows: 'The Gruppe 47 Almanac of 1962, edited by Hans Werner Richter, lists all the authors who took part in meetings during the first fifteen years, eighty-six men and ten women. This is not many women, but it is a normal quota when measured against other areas of public life' (Bachér 1988: 91).[1] A similar quota can be found in most well-known anthologies of prose from the 1950s and 1960s. Compared with an anthology from 1947, which included almost 40 percent women, female writers are barely

visible. The same is true of the two most important literary magazines of the 1950s, in particular Alfred Andersch's *Texte und Zeichen*
(1955–1957).

However, in the late 1950s and 1960s, the second of the two
journals, *Akzente*, edited by Walter Höllerer and Hans Bender,
became an outlet for first publications by among others Ruth
Rehmann, Gabriele Wohmann, Gisela Elsner, Helga Novak and
Renate Rasp. In addition to this, *Akzente* printed texts by women
writers who had no access to *Gruppe 47*. Of particular significance
here were the impressive prose writings of Geno Hartlaub and the
Büchner prize winner, Marie Luise Kaschnitz.[2] Meanwhile, behind
the scenes, women were playing an important role translating, for
example, works by Alain Robbe-Grillet, Natalie Sarraute, Samuel
Beckett and Ernest Hemingway.

On the whole, the 1950s are marked by a process of institutionalised forgetting of women writers. Klaus Nonnenmann's portraits *Schriftsteller der Gegenwart*, published in 1963, contained
alongside forty-nine portraits of male writers and the two Austrians Bachmann and Aichinger, only two further women authors.
These were Christa Reinig and Gabriele Wohmann, who had made
a successful debut in the *Gruppe 47* in the late 1950s. Even the traces
of those women who were repeatedly or regularly invited to meetings of *Gruppe 47* in the 1960s, for example, Bachér, Rehmann, Barbara König and Wohmann, disappeared from numerous later
accounts and memoirs of *Gruppe 47*. This exclusion – begun by
Nonnenmann and Richter – became a consistent feature of male
literary history writing in the following decades. Thus a recent
book, published to accompany a six-part literary documentary
for television, reduces women's writing in West Germany between 1945 and 1970 to the single Austrian name of Bachmann
(Bohn 1993).

In order to understand the renewed exclusion of female authors
from the canon, which Sigrid Weigel has called a 'systematic forgetting' (1989: 12), it is necessary to consider the conditions of
women's access to the literary sphere. Women required more
courage, stamina and perseverance than their male colleagues to
gain access to the literary life of *Gruppe 47*. When they appeared at
readings in front of an almost exclusively male public, they were
treated not only as exotic but were confronted with an increasing
degree of sexism from critics which meant a considerably higher
danger of public humiliation. Both men and women experienced
reading aloud, while sitting on Hans Werner Richter's 'electric

chair', as an *angst* inducing torture. Barbara König's report is typical of many others:

> These readings, what a ritual! At the front of the hall there are two chairs with a small table between them. On the left-hand side sit the authors deadly pale. On the right hand-side sits Richter [the German word for judge] – how the name suits him! – cold and unmoved. He says: 'Begin', claps his hands and casts his animal trainer like eye over the rows of people. This silences even the most persistent talkers. (König 1988: 73)

In the founding years of the group, it was predominantly men who had the word at the end of readings. In the mid-1950s, with the increased representation of publishers and professional literary critics at these meetings, sexism increased even further. This marked a historical change in the perception of women authors. A shameful lack of respect towards women writers, which would not have been allowed in the late 1940s, became fashionable. Whereas for instance Ricarda Huch, Elisabeth Langgässer and Anna Seghers had been seen as respected representatives of a broad-based public anti-fascism, women writers now had to engage with a literary climate that resembled a private men's club.

The appearance of the writer and her style of reading became the subject of smug, sexually inflected comments which literary histories would repeat continually over the following decades. Ilse Aichinger is said to be '… quite different from a plump girl rather more a beautiful woman – a bit masculine' (Richter 1986: 69). Ingeborg Bachmann is described as 'a bad actress from the provinces who is trying to imitate a shy poetess' (Reich-Ranicki 1967: 38).[3] In the case of Barbara König, the comments read '… good God, a mixture of snake and cat. What does she want here?' (Richter 1986: 193).

We see here that 'gender' was an implicit category in literary criticism and was in no way a later discovery of feminists. Criteria of so-called 'femininity' served both the erotic enhancement of the author and the literary degradation of the text. As late as 1987, Joachim Kaiser could still unquestioningly invoke this long established form of sexism without having to fear any question from his (male) interviewer: 'Usually, of the five readings, three ranged from mediocre to weak, one was quite nice, women's writing or light fiction' (Schutte 1988: 11–12). It is hardly by chance that Reich-Ranicki turns to military language in order to express fantasies of conquest: 'It was [General] Schlieffen who said that nothing is harder to calculate in advance than the outcome of a battle or the resistance of a girl. This is also true of literature' (Lettau 1967: 141). Indeed, Dieter Wellershoff is quite right when, looking back critically in 1988 at the way that the people involved saw themselves, he talks of 'the illusion of an alienation-free social space' (1988: 128). The disregard for gender politics inside Richter's group is a part of this illusion which has doggedly survived into the present.

Before *Gruppe 47* could make any decision about the literary quality of a text, it had to be presented to the influential ears of the group. 'To get an invitation to a group meeting, a new author had to be recommended by a member whose judgement was trusted by Hans Werner Richter and his council of elders' (Wellershoff 1988: 126). Anyone who was able to rely on an old boy network, for example, acquaintance with critics, publishers or other literary agents, had a considerably easier start. Milo Dor, who completed his successful 'relay race' for entry into *Gruppe 47* with an 'erotic appetite', 'many pernods' and 'hangovers', has described this in detail (1988: 55–59).

The conditions under which Ruth Rehmann gave her first reading in 1958 were quite different. She could not rely on Dor's notorious network, nor could she travel around and make contacts of various types due to her family commitments. For these reasons, Rehmann found herself up against a closed circle of insiders who talked:

> … mostly about people who you don't know and who all know each other and call each other by their Christian names. They don't discuss literature. It seems as if they have come to this remote place in order to have a drink together and to tell each other the latest jokes. (Rehmann 1988b: 48)

The reason why Rehmann 'always felt a bit of an outsider' became clear when she realised that: 'Most women came because of a man. They were wives or girlfriends or companions. A very few of them were writers … For the most part women did not say anything at readings … Almost only men talked' (1988a: 115). Rehmann experienced her own first reading as a 'witch trial' (1988b: 50).

The competition between the critics promoted vanity and a loud desire to project an impressive image at the expense of others. Kaiser remembers in an almost self-critical manner how 'these five critics, Mayer, Reich-Ranicki, Jens, Höllerer and little me, formed this ominous quintet which probably talked too much and in this way, perhaps, also stopped other people from speaking'

(Schutte 1988: 16). Following the advice of Ilse Aichinger and others, Richter plucked up the courage in 1961 to exclude one of the most aggressive critics, Reich-Ranicki, from the meeting. His attempt failed on account of his timidity. He ventured to exclude another type of clientele in the same year with less fear of conflict and more courage. This time it was a case of writers' wives whose participation was thought likely to be disruptive given the expected turbulent debate about the building of the Berlin wall (Schutte 1988: 81, 89–90, 257).

In the early 1960s, Gisela Elsner, a discovery of 1962, was much debated by *Gruppe 47*. Her reading of a chapter from *Die Riesenzwerge* (1964/1985, *Giant Dwarfs*, 1965) was felt by many to be very good. In spite of this it caused considerable disquiet in the male dominated auditorium. With its destructive and almost surreal perspective on the Federal Republic of the economic miracle, it challenged preconceptions about women's writing, but was not able to dislodge rigid traditional expectations on the part of male critics. The writer had not only dared to use satire – a way of writing generally thought to be male – but had shaken one of the pillars of patriarchal consensus, sexuality. The international success of *Die Riesenzwerge*, which was soon translated into fourteen languages, was impressive.

On publication this three-hundred-page long text consciously dispensed with genre and bore the simple subtitle *Ein Beitrag*. As a sober 'ethnographer' of West German society (Gerhardt 1980: 91), Elsner – often using grotesque distortions – pointed a finger at the hastily recovered self-confidence of her philistine 'dwarves', puffed up into 'giants'. In the 1950s fat stomachs were often seen as the proud insignia of economic recovery and prosperity in the young Republic. The wave of gluttony that had been conjured up was now to wash away the evil spirits of the German past and give large parts of the West German population a false new sense of self value. In the microcosm of the petty bourgeois family, Elsner depicts an oppressive horror scenario of unrestrained gluttony and egocentric greed whose all-devouring patriarchal force rises to the level of cannibalism.

The story is told from the perspective of five-year-old Lothar, the son of a timid mother and an all-powerful father who is a high school teacher by profession. He is a paragon of German virtue, 'He doesn't smoke ... he doesn't drink ... he eats whatever is put on the table' (1965: 27). Even his surname, Leinlein, a doubled diminutive suffix, indicates the dwarf-like proportions of the hero.

This 'father' is the murderer of Lothar's biological father. The latter became the victim of a cannibalistic orgy during a family visit to a restaurant – an orgy into which his boss, a senior teacher, had goaded the mob of hungry guests. In order to compensate for this event, the murderer marries the mother: '"I don't know," my mother says, "whether I was right or not, but I'm not pretty and I don't know how to dress. And he was so attentive towards me"' (26). Both fathers are every bit as hideous as each other and are indistinguishable to the boy.

The very first sentence of the novel, 'My father is a good eater' leads us straight to the heart of the matter. This apparently harmless beginning is soon followed by a meticulous description of a bestial act of eating, which is all the more revealing when seen from the laconic perspective of a child. 'He raises his arse a little from the chair. He leans across the table … so that he can see what is in the dishes … Then he pitches in. He serves himself … one forkful after another, one spoonful after another until he has a great heap on the plate' (1). Potatoes, meat and gravy. The boy's 'heap' is considerably smaller. Smaller still is the mother's heap. The father's meal becomes a threatening, randy, copulation-like sublimation:

> His belly touches the edge of the table. There is a gap between his thighs wide enough for a head to fit between them. His legs are wrapped around the chair legs. He carries big forkfuls to his mouth and chews them with great care, his eyes fixed on the centre parting of my mother's hair. (1–2)

The displaced object of desire, the mother, 'holds her head so low … that her hair hangs down into the food' (2). 'Hastily [she] lifts a tiny mouthful into her mouth, washes it down unchewed … the mouthfuls that get smaller and smaller … I see how differently my parents eat' (2, 3). Only the father's brusque commands interrupt the silent eating: 'At meals … we don't talk' (2). The son, too, should learn to appreciate the price of his gross size, this oral lust for which he has worked so hard: 'He should finally learn what it means to earn his daily bread'(130). The mother's behaviour is timid and obsequious:

> 'Will there be enough?' she asks with twitching lips … Only when my father starts belching at his third heap which is made up of what is left in the serving dishes, my plate and my mother's half-heap, does she suddenly wince … 'That was good', he says … 'I can serve up again', she says. 'I'm no glutton', says my father and gets up. (4–5)

Under the dry x-ray eyes of the child the adults respectively become mere functions of an authoritarian or obsequious order. Elsner's satiric typification rejects all forms of individualisation and psychologisation of the characters. Their indistinguishability is made clear not only by the 'two fathers' but also, drastically, when the boy sits down by mistake with the wrong parents at a big feast. The figures' literal 'lack of character' has a repulsive, alienating effect, which makes the power structures in family and gender relations all the more visible. The figure of the devoted mother functions as negative complement to the monstrous father. Everyday she handles 'lumps of raw red meat' (27) in order to satisfy her husband's greed. Her only thought is not to upset father. With a bowed head and bent back, and with clothes and a bearing indistinguishable from the mass of her sex, the giggling, obsequiousness of this female figure is hardly less provocative than the self-important tyranny of her husband.

On leaving the familial dining room, the text takes us into the outside world of a small town governed by aggressive dog owners. The institutions of the school – where the senior teacher's régime reminds us of fascism – and the Catholic Church perpetuate unbroken patriarchal power in the public sphere. The priest and the doctor represent the classical pillars of an authoritarian, philistine, petty bourgeois world. In the smooth, faceless town – a not atypical image of the newly reconstructed towns of the 1950s – between tower blocks, department stores, churches and cinemas, we also find the familiar sight of disabled ex-servicemen. In shocking style, the figure of the stick-in-the-mud cripple, Herr Kecker (*keckern* also means 'to shit') with his dangling stump, represents the broken, castrated masculinity of the defeated warrior. Addicted to war films, Herr Kecker – with his aggressive victim mentality – turns his self-hatred, full of anger against an intimidated world: 'So you think the sight of me is contagious like leprosy!... as though a stump were as disgusting as a worm!' (92–93).

Yet this nasty picture of social and moral relations in the 1950s would be incomplete if we did not accompany the young protagonist on the forced ritual of their Sunday family outing. Elsner's picture of the collective, individual 'love of nature' felt by people from the town now becomes grotesque. 'Get up, get up ... Today we're off on a hike!' (126) is the battle cry of the father on departure through the allotments into the German forest. The mother, 'wailing', 'stumbled along, constantly turning her ankle or getting her heels stuck in the cracks between the cobbles, behind my father by the width of two men' (128). They meet crowds of other day trippers, large families, mostly quiet, the children with bowed heads. '"Isn't it beautiful here," said my father. "All right, all right," murmured my mother' (144). Even the boy, with blistered feet in shoes too small for him, has difficulty following the head of the family marching smartly in front like a soldier. '"He's got no spunk, the weakling!"' (150). Yet the father's attempts to develop the virility of his son in a military fashion misses the mark. Elsner's mixture of familiar army sayings still resonate in the ears of many people who grew up in West Germany in the 1960s: '"Stand up straight! Breathe deeply!", said my father to me, "don't hobble around like an old woman!"' (144). The boy eventually finds a welcome relief from his constant torture in the unexpected discovery of a couple having sex behind the bushes:

> They lay stomach to stomach, the man on top, the woman underneath ... The woman stretched out her naked arms and legs as far away from herself as she could. Motionless and without even making an effort to shake him off ... She held up the weight of the man. Her head laid on the side, her face turned away she was looking between the trees into the distance without the slightest trace of anger or irritation ... but as though the whole thing were none of her concern. (145–146)

The open, sober, naive realism of the style in which the child observes the event makes clear to the reader the woman's lack of pleasure and the way in which she is used. This perspective on the hierarchy in sexual intercourse is also emphasised in the chapter 'Das Achte' which Elsner presented to *Gruppe 47*. Here Elsner plays a blasphemous game with the creation myth. After seven years of celibacy, two helpless parents are forced to have sex by their seven children – minors – who are completely out of control. After the children have discovered from watching their naked parents – chained to the bed – that their sexual intercourse is no different from that of dogs, they are laid on one another and forced to produce another child by the pressure of the children's hands.

Some male critics were not happy with this kind of rewriting of a myth, also familiar in literary history. Wolfdietrich Schnurre's accusation of 'anti-family pornography' (Lettau 1967: 172) totally misrecognised the decidedly anti-pornographic effect of the scene. Some contemporary criticism pointed to similarities with the work of Günter Grass. Grass's depictions of sexual intercourse, which were not prudish but rather erotic, had admittedly upset some of the bourgeois literary supplements. It would have been more appropriate to call them pornographic. Elsner's intertextual reply to the *Die Blechtrommel* (1959/1962, *The Tin Drum*, 1961) demonstrates a decisive difference precisely where the representation of sexual relations are concerned. The voyeurism of the young Oskar Matzerath, which invites identification, is explicitly counteracted by Lothar Leinlein. Whereas from Oskar's perspective 'the distasteful soon becomes tasteful again', Elsner's young male hero refuses even secretly to consent to what he is watching (Gerhardt 1980: 90). Whereas a pornographic perspective seeks out the consensual gaze of the usually male observer – objectifying the subject represented[4] – Elsner's sober, reserved and distanced narrative emphasises the objective alienation of the female character. Both representations of sexual intercourse found in her text break with and disappoint patriarchal expectations of pornography.[5] *Die Riesenzwerge* not only concentrates on the aggressive omnipotence of the fathers but also the inhibited rigid sexual morality and the sexual exploitation of women. Structurally, these elements are concentrated in the motif of gluttony which runs through most of the loosely connected chapters. The maxim 'The way you eat, that's the way you are!' (4) governs the whole text. Under this motto the 'giant dwarfs' elevate oral consumption to a symbol of their social identity. Here Elsner's social criticism dissolves into psychological generalisations, which see the patriarchal nuclear family as representative of a predatory society compulsively fixated on 'having things'. This perspective on the West German economic miracle has striking resemblances to the otherwise so different texts of Ruth Rehmann and Gabriele Wohmann. All three authors choose the butcher's shop as the social space in which to mirror, bloodily distorted, a society fixated on gluttony. Rehmann's work is discussed in detail in chapter 5.

Elsner invites us to experience the twenty-fifth anniversary of the butcher's shop. Here, at last, the characters are offered something for nothing: free meat for the numerous greedy customers, 'dripping hot sausages … you can eat as much as you want to' (164). Even the butcher helps himself voluptuously from his own pots. The scene of this butcher eating can be read as the finale of the whole text. The 'bald moist top of his skull' (164) reminds one of George Grosz's obese 1920s caricatures of the 'pillars of society'.[6] The images that we find here have become familiar. The description of the wolf-like butcher, 'his mouth, with its prominent

Punishment follows immediately. Grass has the woman die from fish poisoning, her 'face devastated by pain and nausea', to the relief of the male members of her family. The fearful Grass mummifies the threatening, beautiful woman in order to idealise her once again in death: 'Once she had been washed and lay there in her shroud, she had her familiar, round, shrewdly naive face again' (156). In contrast, Elsner counters this literary portrayal of a female sacrifice with the self-castration of the male killer-hero.[8]

In 1964, male critics reacted violently to the publication of this text. The often patronising and aggressive reviews show how accurately Elsner had touched a sensitive nerve in many of her male contemporaries. The *'femme fatale'*, 'Cleopatra' and 'cold-blooded sphinx' (quoted in Flitner 1995: 56) had struck a terrible blow. With their backs against the wall, the critics tried to defuse the provocative nature of the text by referring to the sex of the writer. They quickly drew a contrast between the youth and beauty of the author and the 'ice-cold' and 'disgusting' nature of her text. Four years later in reviews of Elsner's no less provocative novel *Der Nachwuchs*, this contrast was taken up again: 'Many people were shocked ... to see this remarkably good-looking woman messing around with such filth with such obvious pleasure' (Flitner 1995: 56). Critics also asked 'why such a pretty woman wrote such gruesome male prose' (Flitner 1995: 56).

Despite the documented sexism of literary critics in the 1950s and 1960s, more and more women writers were appearing on the literary scene and gradually the conditions for women's writing began to change. During the course of the 1960s, there was a process of fundamental change in the social and political consensus in the Federal Republic. In the most disparate areas, the rigid conservativism of the Adenauer era began slowly to dissolve. 'Engagement' became the slogan of numerous writers who increasingly came to see the function of literature as social criticism. The influence of *Gruppe 47*, which was so strong at the end of the 1950s and the beginning of the 1960s, and which met for the last time in 1967, began to pale. Literary institutions diversified.

In 1961, a new writers' organisation, which called itself *Gruppe 61*, formed in Dortmund in opposition to *Gruppe 47*. In 1970, it became the influential *Werkkreis Literatur der Arbeitswelt* (Worker Writers' Circle for Literature from the World of Work). Writers belonging to *Gruppe 61* demanded literary engagement with the world of industrial work and turned to the task of representing working-class life in literature. At the end of the 1960s, Erika

Runge would become one of the most important representatives of this group.

In 1965, a group of mostly young authors gathered around Dieter Wellershoff to form the so-called *Kölner Schule* (Cologne School). Following in the footsteps of the French *nouveau roman* – particularly Natalie Sarraute whose work had a considerable influence on Wohmann's writing – this new way of writing tried to break with established conceptions of realism. In a way similar to Elsner's *Riesenzwerge*, psychoanalysis was rethought along critical social lines and became a central reflective component within writing. It was women writers of the Cologne School, like Renate Rasp, who developed this complex understanding of realism into *Schwarzer Realismus* ('black realism', Esselborn 1986: 468). The rigorous criticism of the family found in Rasp's prize-winning novel *Ein ungeratener Sohn* (1967, *A Family Failure*, 1970) followed in the satirical footsteps of Elsner's prose. Rasp represents upbringing as a process of 'amputation' and 'rape' (Serke 1979: 276–277) using the example of a boy who is trimmed and pruned literally to be planted later as a tree in the garden.

Women writers of the younger generation, such as Wohmann, Elsner and Novak, whose successful literary debuts were closely linked to *Gruppe 47*, would later follow very different paths. Novak, who had moved to West Germany from the GDR and whose poetry had initially caused a sensation, would concentrate intensively on female experience. Later feminist critics would distance themselves from Wohmann, whose writing was highly praised by mainstream critics and appeared in large print runs. This distancing was mutual. The author herself stressed, 'I can manage perfectly well on my own' (Siblewski 1982: 46). On the other hand, Elsner, who like several other authors took the part of German Communist Party (DKP) in the 1970s and was, as a result, exposed to sharp anti-Communist criticism, would place the representation of class conflict in the forefront of her later prose.[9]

Looking back on women's writing of the first two decades of the post-war period, we can establish the following. Apart from the immediate post-war years, when women writers played an important representational role, women's writing in the Adenauer era was far more threatened and isolated than in later decades. It faced the sexist conditions of a patriarchal literary industry. These conditions could only later be challenged with the support of a broad-based feminist movement (see chapter 6).

The validity of historical accounts of West German post-war literature must be measured against a recognition of these conditions. Just as it is wrong to ascribe unity to the non-conformist literature of the Adenauer period, so it is wrong to judge it according to the feminist criteria of later years. The historically inexact and teleological perspective, which sees such writers as so-called precursors of feminist literature, is just as inaccurate as the suggestion that there was a *Stunde Null* (zero hour) in women's writing. An answer to the question of a female perspective in post-war literature calls for a precise reading of individual texts in their particular historical context. Every literary text confronts us with an historically specific way of perceiving and constructing the world. Literary constructions can simultaneously confirm, question or even undermine the expectations of the reader. Readers' expectations are just as historically conditioned as the author's perceptual framework.

The significant role played by gender in numerous texts by women writers emerges from their attention to realism and exact observation. The texts function as a sensitive seismograph of the experiences and conditions of women's lives in post-war Germany. The illusionless depiction of patriarchal marriage, the nuclear family and love relationships between the sexes is shared by many texts from the 1950s onwards. The identity of the female characters is riven by conflict. They find themselves exposed to the conservative gender norms underpinning the utilitarianism of the economic miracle. The existential realism of Ruth Rehmann's early prose (see chapter 5), the grotesque surreal distortions of Elsner's writing and the disillusioned ironic sarcasm of Wohmann's short stories disturbed the literary consensus and broke implicit patriarchal rules. These disruptions – although not explicitly articulated in terms of gender politics – were perceived as shocking departures from the female norm.

Whatever the differences in their themes and modes of writing, these women writers refused to consent to dominant gender relations and patriarchal constructions of femininity. The negative utopian potential of their texts, which should not be underestimated, lies in this refusal. Using 'unfeminine' weapons such as malice, the women authors expose social wounds whose obvious need for healing requires a thorough-going change in social relations. Looking back in 1973, Gabriele Wohmann remarked: 'The wasteland which I describe in my books should be an impetus for change' (Knapp 1981: 28). Extensive utopian perspectives would only be formulated by the women's movement in the decades that followed. These would not only revolutionise the conditions under which women were writing and public discourse on sexual politics, but would also release new liberating literary forces.

In January 1968, *Akzente* printed five poems by Renate Rasp. Here the female poetic voice articulates in a sharp and demanding fashion an impatient hunger for change:

> To eat/ what one has never tasted/ never to be full whatever is available/... to be able to do everything at once and oneself/ continuously/ never too much/ like breathing ... / That no one has thought of it yet'. (Rasp 1968: 54, 58)

Translated by Chris Weedon

Notes

1. See also von der Lühe 1988.
2. These authors are covered in more detail in Stephan et al. (eds) 1986a.
3. For an analysis of male reaction to Bachmann see von der Lühe 1982a.
4. For a deeper understanding of pornography as an effect of representation see Kappeler 1986.
5. The sex scene in the forest refers clearly to the one on the sofa in *Tin Drum*: 'under Matzerath she lay, and on top of her lay Matzerath ... Through Matzerath's parted fingers Maria stared at the carpet and seemed to follow the pattern under the table' (Grass 1989: 279–280).
6. Grosz's huge oil painting of 1926 whose title alludes to Henrik Ibsen's play represents a judge, a journalist, a member of parliament, a priest and an army officer as the 'Stützen der Gesellschaft', all in the same butcher-like way as fat, self-satisfied and blood-thirsty. (Berlin, Neue Nationalgalerie.)
7. See Grass's fantastic fantasies about the phallic connotations of this fish: 'one of the doctors ... told me about a married woman who tried to take her pleasure with a live eel. But the eel bit into her and wouldn't let go; she had to be taken to the hospital and after that they say she couldn't have any more babies' (1989: 146).
   And Grass's little boy has learned his lesson: '... with both fists I landed an uppercut in the exact same spot where she had admitted Matzerath. She caught my fists ... whereupon I sank my teeth into the same accursed spot and, still clinging fast, fell with Maria to the sofa' (1989: 284).
8. For an outline of the history of sacrificed women in literature see Weigel 1983a.
9. Elsner could never again match her initial great success. In the 1980s she fell more and more into oblivion. Her publisher Rowohlt stopped reprinting her texts and the author lived in poverty. In 1992 she committed suicide.

Chapter Five

THE EARLY NOVELS OF RUTH REHMANN

Franziska Meyer

In 1958 Ruth Rehmann (b. 1922) caused a literary sensation when she read a chapter from her first novel *Illusionen* (1959/1989, *Saturday to Monday*, 1961) in front of *Gruppe 47*. (The conditions under which Rehmann read her work to *Gruppe 47* are described in the previous chapter.) Together with Ingrid Bachér's highly praised reading and Günter Grass's *Blechtrommel* (1959/1962, *The Tin Drum*, 1961) literary critics praised Rehmann's text as one of the high points of this meeting. Later it would go down in history as a 'mere women's meeting' (Richter 1986: 277). With its quiet yet insistent social criticism, Rehmann's novel – together with a very few others – went against mainstream writing of the 1950s, which consisted mainly of consoling family and war novels (Peitsch 1991).

Rehmann's *Illusionen* paints a picture of human coldness and the poverty of relationships in the midst of an affluent society, governed by the laws of functional utilitarianism. The plot is set in an average, medium-sized, West German town in the 1950s. The story is told from the changing perspectives of four office workers employed in administration.[1] 'Correctly and unobtrusively dressed ladies, who are so difficult to tell apart and are actually inter-changeable – only their functions are irreplaceable' (Rehmann 1961: 7) work here in the 'crystal transparency' of their glass 'cells'. They are like a swarm of bees working for economic progress, 'a discreet, smoothly running well-muffled motor, driven by the sensitive nail-polished finger tips of typists' (1961: 6). However, we soon see that Rehmann's characters – 'industrious, useful, decent colleagues, their minds concentrated on orderliness and security'

(41) – are caught in a net of internalised norms which govern their whole existence.

It is the external view of the narrator, with the eyes of a window cleaner, who disturbs the cold majesty of this clearly hierarchically ordered system: 'He, on the other hand, knows the office personnel better than their files know them, better than they know each other, for he is the only one who can look into the peep shows of the office building from the outside and see things no one else can see' (5).

Through his eyes, as if through the focal lens of a camera, things that at first appeared undifferentiated gain distinct contours. As the focus sharpens, however, individual figures become visible as sites of different, conflicting attitudes, wishes and motives. Multi-dimensional individuals emerge from the one-dimensional figures who are there only to carry out a particular function. These individuals are neither unified in themselves nor among themselves. The following quotation brings out the narrative project of the text as a whole:

> That is how the window cleaner sees them … each in his place, fig-ures in a toy that has stopped running … But as soon as he stops and watches more closely they seem to move away without leaving their places, they blur and dissolve into innumerable fleeting pic-tures that scurry past him softly, shadows and reflexes, four people, each one seen by three others and by himself, mirrored, fragmen-tary, falsified … taken apart and put together again with the addi-tion of foreign elements. (8)

Each of the four figures – three single women of different gener-ations and a man – is the focus of numerous unfulfilled individual conceptions of happiness. There is the sixty-three year-old Frau Schramm – personal assistant, head secretary and office manager – 'with the dry hands, warped from typing … who has sacrificed her private life on the altar of the firm' (13). Her forty years of maternal care for her boss and for the firm are badly invested emotions. They offer no protection against unexpected premature dismissal.

At Frau Schramm's suspicious side works her possible succes-sor Carmen Viol: hungry for love, 'at present melancholy … her beauty fading. No possibility of finding out her age (8) … Hurling her masks, her disguises, curls, faces, against powerfully advanc-ing time' (11). For both women the office is their 'true vocation' (12). They find the 'youthfulness … display[ed] so casually' of the apathetic, uninterested nineteen-year-old Therese, a 'pretty super-fluous doll' (10) who is persecuted by Viol's 'poisonous envy', all the more threatening. For her the office is no more than 'a macabre show' (70). And finally there is the only married person among them, 'dry, downtrodden', thirty-year-old Paul Westermann, who has been to university and who, his academic hopes betrayed, translates French business correspondence (14).

The relations between these colleagues are marked by the pressure of competition, condescending pity, and false superiority. They serve as objects for the projection of each other's contempt and fears for the future. Their inability to communicate, the hopeless 'dialogue of voices which seek and miss their mark' (208) render impossible their perceiving any form of shared experience in their private sufferings which they hide from one another. As readers, we accompany these figures on one of their many typical weekends where their feelings of isolation extend into their free time.

Illusionen draws the reader into a maelstrom from which is it difficult to escape. Internal monologues and streams of consciousness give us disturbing insights into the individual depths of a desperate illusionary search for identity. The changing perspectives of the characters reveal helpless heroes with unattractive weaknesses. None of the characters invites a positive identification. As at work so too are their friendships and sexual relationships distorted and instrumental. Theodor W. Adorno's statement, 'wrong life cannot be lived rightly' (1969/1987: 39) could serve as the motto governing the private lives of Rehmann's characters. Older Frau Schramm's only personal contact, a pensioner Fräulein Krumbach, whom she 'has acquired ... as a friend through an advertisement in the paper' serves, at the weekend, as a rubbish basket 'for her painfully dammed-up need to communicate' (13). The lonely secretary is only able to develop an anonymous sense of belonging at the market where she takes on the levelling role of consumer: 'The consciousness of being solitary, isolated, separate, was gone ... she enjoyed a precious sense of belonging, a nameless submersion beyond all destiny, in a sea of people, all of whom were alike' (41). Using the example of this older character, Rehmann emphatically investigates the historical continuities and consequences of an attitude to life unconsciously governed by abstract and inhuman notions of duty and order. The narrative successfully merges the horizons of the contemporary economic miracle and the past everyday world of war under the Nazis. The repressed past overcomes the secretary – 'distinguished for courage and active participation in the big push of 1944' (127) – as she imagines that she smells ruins among the new buildings (142).

Associations of repulsion, lust and fear revive the image of a man who was helplessly dependent on her, a deserter with wounds stinking of decay, who hid illegally in her loft. This memory forcefully penetrates the ordered everyday life of the former air raid warden. Where previously her ego had refused human sympathy, fleeing behind the instrumental management of crises, where this ego in order 'to stand by her nation in its hour of need' (47) preached to the helpless refugee unthinking phrases about the national task – 'our lives don't belong to us alone' (49). Now the extremely hygienic environment of a butcher's shop offers refuge from dirty stinking feelings of guilt. The dangers lurking in the sausages, meat and blood, the forbidden pleasures of the anal drives, are here hygienically tamed between 'hanging baskets of luxurious leaf plants ... of flowery innocence ... under glass' (46). Work which denies the effort put into it and the medical hygiene of this wealthy world of flesh cover the traces of its bloody origins.[2] Frau Schramm's belief in authority, which is focused on her male boss, and her rigid feelings of duty only offer an incomplete armour behind whose carefully hidden gaps lurk the depths of a repressed past. The obsessional fixation of this character with cleanliness, like her condescending pity which can suddenly change into unexpected aggression towards her weekend friend, is identifiable – following Freud – as a classical symptom of an obsessional neurotic.

Rehmann's youngest character, the unhappy narcissistic Therese, does not belong anywhere. Following a failed school leaving exam and a monotonous marriage entered into at the wish of her father, she randomly searches for happiness without direction in love affairs. The student Christoph whom she at least finds attractive knows 'more about [her spiritual life] than she did ... [and] had taken it upon himself to educate her, which was decent of him' (71). His patronising efforts to educate her do not, however, meet her needs for consumerism to which – 'blindly, greedily, like a fish on the hook' (72) – she constantly has to give in. The pressure to conform and the modes of identity, which change with fashion, offered by her trendy clique of young friends provoke strong feelings of loss and conflict: 'If only she could have split in two ... like an earthworm, but ... there was nothing left for her to do but be one, or at any rate pretend to be one, which was ... why she never could cope with her funny life, which tended to split up into many compartments, and she would have liked nothing better than to experience all of them at the same time' (73).

Herr Westermann also flees in vain from the everyday 'tread-mill' into the 'hopeless mediocrity' of the nuclear family and the private life of his unhappy marriage. With its stylistic references to Wolfgang Borchert's striking anti-war manifesto (1949), Paul Westermann's drunken self-accusation rises in a crescendo of desperate appeals to missed moments of happiness:

> If anybody ever tells you he'd have done this or that if this or that hadn't kept him from doing it, don't believe him ... If anybody ever tells you he'd have finished college if circumstances or some nitwit of a women hadn't prevented it – stuff and nonsense, just plain rot. Are you listening? He didn't have to marry her, did he? He could have married somebody else, the great love of his life ... And if anybody ever tells you he would have written poetry or painted a picture or composed music if only the struggle for existence had left him time for it, then laugh at him and tell him: What doesn't come out isn't inside, and what isn't inside doesn't come out ... If a man stays in this city, then he belongs in this city, if he stays behind glass, he belongs behind glass, and if he marries Gerda, he's got what he had coming to him. (157–158)

The man, who is himself only thirty, projects his goals in life onto his small son 'who wasn't quite finished yet, who was new, indefinite, who had possibilities' (158). Ingeborg Bachmann developed this theme of a failed father's omnipotent fantasy of creating the unspoiled 'design' of an completely new person with far fewer compromises in her story 'Alles' (1961, 'Everything', 1964) which was written at the same time.

As a full-time housewife and mother, Westermann's wife has no choice but to identify herself with the career of her husband. Forced into a monotonous normative lifestyle, she plays no less a functional and conformist role than the furniture:

> Kidney-shaped table and Acrylon rug, at the love seat, the philo-dendron, the picture of their wedding, Nolde besides Dürer's little hare, the whole apartment haphazard, anonymous, unnecessary, stereotypical and in the middle of it Gerda, the charming hostess ... running back and forth eagerly on her spiked heels, her shoes uncomfortable, with salt sticks and cheese crackers, with little plates and ashtrays ... babbling about Italian food and Bert Brecht, about Existentialism, Freud and Christianity, about Communism and modern child care. (104)

From a critical perspective, unusual in this period, Rehmann examines 1950s' lifestyles. The anti-authoritarian criticisms of the next generation would do the same in a much harsher fashion, denouncing their parental homes as the epitome of bourgeois narrow-mindedness.

However, it is the tragic character of Carmen Viol who embodies a general lack of authenticity most clearly.[3] Surrounded by normative images of young female beauty, this restless narcissistic woman is unable to achieve any unified sense of self. Constantly conforming to her environment and changing her role like she changes her clothes, her face too, is 'a planned controlled system' (84). As in the fairy tale *Snow White*, a mirror is the most important thing in this woman's life. Yet the more frequently and intensely Carmen Viol attempts to fix her dispersed identity through projections onto others, the more hopeless the result. The image remains empty, like a house of mirrors at a fair which reflects images to the point where they disappear beyond an infinite vanishing point:

> When she recognises the face in the mirror … as her own, and when she takes the dried mask off … only to find another mask underneath it, and another, and still another, and she lays them bare one after the other, and asks each one, 'Who are you?' and never gets an answer, never hears a clear and distinct 'I', … In the mirror nothing moves – a smooth, white oval, impersonal, unlined, empty … the heroine … expects suggestions from outside which do not come. (243)

Carmen Viol's mistaken question, 'Mirror, mirror on the wall who is the fairest of them all?', is ironically undermined by the narrative commentary on the 'heroine'. Snow White – a figure in a patriarchal myth and a projection of unobtainable picture-book femininity – is dead and uninteresting as a counterpart. New images of imaginary ideal femininity are repeatedly rejected by the narrator who stands at the side of her character offering critical support. This narrative unmasking of Carmen Viol's prison, at the same time cautiously points towards a utopian moment of liberation.

As in contemporary stories by Gabriele Wohmann, most of which are written from a female perspective, Rehmann brings to her female and male figures equally divided feelings. The character who is best educated and yet a loser, Herr Westermann, realistically represents the contemporary educational gap between the sexes. With an observant eye, the text questions the price of traditional forms of desirable femininity in the 1950s. This sensitivity of Rehmann's work cannot be overestimated in the face of the extremely conservative and misogynist climate of the late 1950s.[4]

Readers are presented with the self-sacrificing motherliness of both Frau Schramm and Herr Westermann's wife, as well as the self-destructiveness of Carmen Viol and Therese's fixation on men. It is remarkable – and here *Illusionen* differs radically from literature of the same period in the GDR – that having a profession 'does not create identity for any of the four characters' (Stephan 1986: 236). Even Frau Schramm's 'hard won self-image' is, in the end, condemned to fail: 'None of the women is emancipated. Having a job is merely a temporary solution' (Stephan 1986: 236). Whereas feminist texts of the 1970s challenge patriarchal images of women using emancipated heroines and perspectives which emphasise collective solidarity and liberation, Rehmann appeals cautiously to the strength of the individual. Fifteen years later, workers and employees like Frau Schramm or Herr Westermann would find a politicised literary voice in the *Werkkreis Literatur der Arbeitswelt* (see chapter 6). Rehmann's text, dating from the late 1950s, moves between the individual existentialist desire for change and realistic insights into irresolvable social contradictions. The fact that this tension can be seen so clearly adds to the emancipatory power of the novel, a power which overcomes the lack of emancipated female characters identified – somewhat ahistorically – by Stephan. It is precisely the non-affirmative narrative perspective which points a particularly sensitive finger at the inadequacies of the female characters, making them visible for what they are.

The committed, human quality of *Illusionen* resides in its empathetic perspective on the misery of the characters. The narrative voice, with its cautious comments, makes the reader aware of the social nature of the isolated views of individual characters. The private unhappiness of the characters puts into question all the more forcefully the inhuman structures of the affluent society. The 'atmosphere of the economic miracle and the general mood of renewal has no liberating power ... because it is based on old social structures and ideological patterns ... Surrounded by images, men and women become trapped in these old structures which make them functional for the apparatus' (Stephan 1986: 238). On the empirical level, we learn much about the social and political nature of gender relations. We are led to understand that the social conditions do not exist which could do away with the isolation felt by young Therese Pfeiffer and Carmen Viol. Just as Paul Westermann has to get drunk in order to believe in the individual, anarchic, liberatory effects of action ('Every man is what he does and does what he is and that's all there is to it', 158), so the figure of Carmen Viol is left to her own devices when it comes to countering her prison of alienation. The narrative voice refuses the characters both approval and victim status.

The text makes implicit suggestions about liberation through individual autonomy. This shows traces of the existentialist philosophy of Jean-Paul Sartre which was widely read in the 1950s. However, it is also clear that Rehmann's socially weak anti-heroes are overtaxed by existentialist 'grand designs' of free-floating intellectuals. In its choice of subject matter, Rehmann's novel is very different from many other socially critical texts of its time (Fischer 1986a: 64). The concentration on the little world of the employees – especially of secretaries – decisively favours a gendered perspective from below.[5] In the face of the historical lack of a broad-based political and social movement which could resolve and integrate their disparate illusions, Rehmann's unhappy, divided female characters are in no way bearers of hopes for successful emancipation.

Ten years later Rehmann wrote a counterpart to her city novel *Illusionen*, her novel of rural life *Die Leute im Tal* (1968). As early as 1961 and 1963 she had read preliminary sketches for this text to *Gruppe 47*, where she had received some devastating criticisms. The author's change to a rural setting was taken amiss. The politically provocative nature of her text can be seen from the fact that critics were not deterred from finding an alleged connection between *Die Leute im Tal* and *Blubo* (*Blut und Boden Literatur*), a tradition of writing popular under fascism (Lettau 1967: 161, 163). The publication of these preliminary sketches in the quality Munich-based paper, *Süddeutsche Zeitung*, brought the conservative 'Bavarian soul to the boil' and Rehmann 'numerous death threats' (Lettau 1967: 183).

Set in the Bavarian village surroundings which Rehmann had adopted as her home, *Die Leute im Tal* was awarded the prize *Der Bauer in der Industriegesellschaft* (The Farmer in Industrial Society) even before it was published. When it appeared in 1968, however, it was ignored by prominent critics. In the literary context of the 1960s, Rehmann's novel, which examined what the dust jacket called 'reactionary intolerance' and the conservative clerical atmosphere of small town rural milieus, seemed totally alien. A considerable part of the increasingly socially critical literature of the late 1960s and early 1970s was already under way. This thematised the working environment of the industrial proletariat and the living conditions of people employed in the large-scale factories, for example, Günter Wallraff's *Industriereportagen* (1966) and Erika Runge's *Bottroper Protokolle* (1968). These texts were closely connected to a broader political movement which was directing its critique of capitalism at the power of monopolies and the domination of large-scale capital. It was only in the later 1970s and more particularly in the 1980s that regionalism in literature made a comeback with the growth of interest in ecological concerns. Examples of this are the dialect village novels of Maria Beig and Franz Xaver Kroetz's texts, which were strongly influenced by Marieluise Fleisser.

In the 1960s, Rehmann's novel could not be subsumed within any contemporary literary tendency. It took up the themes and modes of characterisation found in a long tradition of critical rural novels. As late as 1961 the author had to put up with such dismissive names 'Tante Ganghofer' and 'Tante Homer' (Lettau 1967: 161, 164).[6] Yet twenty years later, Martin Walser in his euphoric afterword to Maria Beig's much praised novel *Rabenkrächzen. Eine Chronik aus Oberschwaben* (1982) praised in particular the way in which the text was written 'in the style of Homer' (Beig 1983a: 126). From this example we can see very clearly the changes in criteria of value. The blurb which accompanied Beig's novel recommended it expressly 'as a book for alternative and Green people'.

A rereading of *Die Leute im Tal* makes the left intellectual taboo, shared by *Gruppe 47*, where rural material was concerned seem decisively disconcerting. Rehmann's characters are simultaneously modern and obsessed by tradition, oriented towards the future and reactionary. The unstoppable process of modernisation and urbanisation in the 1960s provide material for persistent conflicts in the village community. Rehmann's text shows clearly how the contradictions between economic necessity on the one hand, and traditional, religious and social ties on the other, not only divide individuals and their families but whole communities. Unlike in *Illusionen*, we find here narrative perspectives which come predominantly from male characters. Rehmann looks at a rural social space where the public sphere is almost exclusively male. Its authoritarian, patriarchal and even brutal laws, which even allow murder and rape, are portrayed with relentless realism.

The text is framed by the burial of old Bruckner, a key figure in the valley, and a man who rules powerfully over the richest and oldest estate. The wake becomes the occasion for numerous memories and stories. Here, once again, Rehmann shows herself to be a mistress of narrative technique. Without falling into Bavarian dialect, the narrator comes close to colloquial language on a syntactical level. In long passages the narrator listens to what people really say and comes so close to them that s/he merges with them in a first person plural. It is precisely the feigned naivety of this narrative which gives the text its critical edge.[7] Monstrosities are related in an apparently harmless manner and are exposed by the casual comments of the narrator. The constantly changing perspectives of the characters create a distancing effect. The interweaving stories form patterns with the very different characters and attitudes.

Bruckner and his eldest son Rass are always at the centre of these memories. The two of them are estranged from one another because the father refuses to hand over the estate to the modernising ideas of his son. Still more unforgivable for the father, however, is Rass's forbidden love for a woman who is not from the area. She is called 'die Rote' (the red head) and as a child had been evacuated to the valley during the war. The son is disinherited for his disobedience, a move only reversed on the father's deathbed. Rass solves the conflict by doing the unimaginable: he looks for work in a urban nitrogen factory and moves in with his girlfriend on a housing estate called 'Neue Heimat', which is a focal point for people who have left the valley.

The case of the obese second son, Bürschi, who is eleven years younger, is no less hopeless in the eyes of his father. With two left hands and complete lack of practical skills, he is given a classical grammar-school education at the wish of his mother which is supposed to lead to the priesthood. It is wasted on him. Bürschi, whose damaged masculinity is imbued from his earliest years with the religious mania of his mother, strives to become a soldier. Fascistic in his way of thinking, he punishes his own family by treating them with condescending contempt.

Die Leute im Tal is an anti-family novel *par excellence* in the ways in which it makes clear the violent structures of family life. The patriarchal rural family is presented as an economic unit which chains people together for better or for worse. Fathers make their sons 'work extremely hard ... for clothing, food and pocket money' (1968: 35–36) creating forms of personal dependency not dissimilar to serfdom. The emotional relationships which spring from such structures are brutal, marked by a helpless poverty of verbal and physical communication. Rehmann uncompromisingly refuses any transformation into a rural family idyll: 'Whereas for summer visitors it would appear to be a peaceful scene in which the farmer's family sit there together after work in the half light … at a scrubbed table by the nest-like warmth of the tiled stove' (70) the malicious nosy neighbours know 'that the Bruckners do not talk to one another at all. Either they are silent or they shout' (5).

Love and marriage are determined by economic necessities and future marriages are arranged by families. An archaic patrilinear tradition of inheritance makes it the sons' duty to take over their fathers' farms. The opposite is true for women, who have to marry into another farm and family. Financial consideration and a dowry are still important factors in the choice of a bride. Sexuality can only develop within the prison of rigidity and double standards provided by village Catholicism. This is something which the enlightened 'red head' discovers in her love for Rass. In vain she tries to free her lover from 'a few centuries of Christianity soured by the stale air of rural life' (155). Rass, too, 'was not someone one finds in rural folk theatre, climbing through his sweetheart's window, sleeping together cheerfully in the hay loft and in the cornfields. He has been brought up in the dark, in an atmosphere of shame and dirty jokes at the beer table' (153).

If religion, as the most powerful force in the valley, condemns Bürschi and Rass to an emotional and sexual prison, for their mother it is a source of partial liberation. With stubbornness and obstinacy, using the priest as an ally, she is able to revenge herself on her husband through Bürschi's religious education. Her husband has 'taken everything from her: innocence, beauty, youth, money, children. But he won't get his hands on this son' (91). Her active subjection to the power of a higher Lord deprives the domestic patriarch of his power and even provides a suitable means 'to smoke him out of the house': 'This constant smell of incense, Bruckner said in the pub, the whole house stinks of incense … he can't bear the smell. He has to get out and be among men with his beer … but at home he can't say anything … he has to keep his mouth shut in his own house like a castrato' (100–101). Compared to the other women in the valley the 'red head' is an emancipated woman. As an employee in a pharmaceutical factory she has 'more brains than a good girl should have' (45). She chooses Rass herself at a dance. Her economic independence is provocative, since it questions the traditional role of women in the valley.

The strength of the text lies in the way in which it makes visible the 'non-contemporaneities'[8] in the heterogenous everyday consciousness of the people who live in the valley. Rehmann refuses to caricature her characters. They are depicted as individuals.

Furthermore we are shown the co-existence of varied feelings and attitudes which are often in conflict with one another. Both the young and the old Bruckner are inwardly divided. The latter is both victim and perpetrator. Just as Rehmann refuses to depict the father merely as a caricatured representative of a putatively vegetating farming community, so, too, his no less obdurate and rebellious son does not represent a clear break with his father. And even Rass' emancipated urban girlfriend dreams of a future existence as a farmer's wife, which would free her from waged labour.

Given the authoritarian family structure which hands down paternal power in a violent form across generations, the continually repeated conflicts are pre-programmed. The shrewdness of old Bruck fails in the final analysis because of the incompatibility of an old-fashioned patriarchal ideology with modern economic demands. Bruck's dogged insistence on the way things were visits the sins of his own father on his son.

However, this ancient father-son conflict gains new dimensions with the possibility, for the first time, of economic independence, social mobility and the chance of escape. The break between Bruckner and his son is a sign of irreversible changes in agricultural production, in family relationships, and last, but not least, in the relationship between the sexes. In highlighting of these aspects, Rehmann's text resembles a social novel which encompasses much more than the narrow realm of the valley. Whereas Rass' father could only free himself from dependence on his own authoritarian father through violence, the economic changes in the increasingly industrialised Federal Republic offer his son's generation the possibility of emancipation. The movement of farm workers and their children to factories in the cities frees them from forms of personal dependency. Yet it also means the proletarianisation of people who might otherwise have become independent landowners. From the perspective of the 'red head', who is dependent on waged labour, the possibility of self-determined work in the valley seems attractive.

Those farmers who stay in the valley experience the sight of 'workers who had gone away and on their return call for whisky … as if they were important people' (67) as a provocation. Here, in the pub, Rehmann reveals to her readers the basis of reactionary thinking in the 1960s. In the cosy, beery atmosphere in which the men meet, reactionary ways of thinking can unite them temporarily. Fear of the future can be turned into hostility towards other people. A rosy picture of the Nazi era, an unbroken anti-Semitism, racism and xenophobia directed at the new *Gastarbeiter* (guest workers) form ideological bonds between the industrial workers, farmers, agricultural workers and the sons of the middle class. Among those who become victims of this collective witch hunt are Rass' brother-in-law, the 'red teacher', who, as an advocate of comprehensive schooling, is suspected of being a Communist and Rass' friend, the garage owner Flinz, who is also scared out of the valley. He, too, is not from the valley and keeps company with 'longhaired unwashed lay-abouts from Neue Heimat ... precisely those people who no decent person would touch with the barge pole.... Communists should be hung up by their pricks ... away with whores and pimps!' (135)

In picking up these fascist slogans, Rehmann captures very precisely elements of right-wing thinking of the late 1960s. A little later, slogans of this sort would dominate the broad-based public campaign against the student movement, which was largely initiated by the influential Springer press. In addition, because Rehmann's valley is not only a traditional rural enclave, we also come across representatives of this protest generation in the form of school students from the north, whose anti-nationalist football commentaries provoke an aggressive response in the pub: 'They all were in agreement on this point: these milk sops should get themselves proper jobs before they start opening their mouths in order to foul their own nests' (67–68).

From the middle of the 1960s onwards, the lack of credibility and integrity shown by parts of their parents' generation, a repressive upbringing at home and at school, and the disturbing questions about Germany's past under fascism became the driving forces behind the politicisation of the younger generation. In the cities this revolt expressed itself increasingly publicly and politically. Eventually it led to the comprehensive social criticism of the so-called 'student's movement' which came to a head in West Germany in 1967 and 1968. In the following encounter between Rass and one of the school students, Rehmann brings together two angry young men whose mutual understanding is destroyed by a still greater gulf between town and country. While the farmer's son and the grammar-school student are unable to communicate, the narrator suggests to the reader that they share anti-authoritarian ideas:

Are you one too? ... the boy had asked. Do you want to kill everything that's different? ... Rass did not answer ... nothing passed

from one to the other, no word, no look, no breath of understanding
even though both of them were filled with an anger whose cause
was not so different as it seemed to them. Only communication was
not possible. (68)

The narrator's sympathies are divided. Already sufficiently familiar with the unhappy character of Rass, readers are forced to interpret the enlightened, arrogant reaction of the 'towny', who thinks
he knows better, as politically naive narrow-mindedness: 'You see
the farmers never learn anything … Just let a new Hitler come
along … and they'll all vote NPD [the Neo-Nazi Party, the *Natio-
naldemokratische Partei Deutschlands*]' (69). One of the main strengths
of Rehmann's narrative technique is sharply observed and dili-
gent differentiation which refuses to reconcile things which under
these conditions are irreconcilable.

If we look closely, we find numerous breaches in the unity of
the villagers beyond the pub. These contradictions are not independent of the economic situation which has decidedly divisive
effects upon them. It creates competition and envy between the
small landowners. They keep an eye on their own interests, spying on their neighbours and conducting intrigues in the farmers'
and refugees' organisations. Their methods are no different from
people who live in the town. The farmer, Gehrke, who, twenty
years after the end of the war, still attracts hostile abuse because of
his former refugee status, will never be accepted as belonging to
the village and will always be put down: 'Fine Mr Gehrke … he
has cheap loans thrown at him, you have to be a refugee … He can
fetch his workers from Pommerania or wherever he comes from'
(109–111). More friendly attitudes to outsiders only occur when
there is something to be gained. Pinkus, who became a millionaire
with the compensation that he received in return for building
land, serves as an object for the projection of a shared pride among
the farmers. They can compensate for their own misery narcissis-
tically in the mirror of this *nouveau riche*:

> Someone just like them … that was the wonderful thing about it ….
> Each one of them in the pub could so easily have been a Herr
> Pinkus if the Lord God had not laid them by chance in the cradle in
> this valley rather than in the home of Herr Pinkus…. It could have
> happened to us, anyone of us, we too could be decent, magnani-
> mous and noble, if only we had millions. (171, 173)

In spite of what appears at first glance to be a narrow subject,
Rehmann captures far more of the world in her rural valley than

in her city novel *Illusionen*. The novel of rural life (*Bauernroman*) becomes both a *Zeitroman* and a *Gesellschaftsroman* (a novel dealing with a period of contemporary history and with a society). The rural valley enlarges into a melting pot, a differentiated social system of representatives of different backgrounds and varied social and political attitudes. This expanded narrative horizon shows, more clearly than in the first novel, that individual scope for action is not independent of the social structures and constraints into which one is born and which one has to confront. Historical, political and economic developments in post-war Germany and their inevitable influence on the life of people are evoked just as vividly as the social and political dynamite of an unbroken mystification of the German past. Through the examples of the young extreme right-winger Bürschi and the older liberal doctor, Rehmann avoids undifferentiated simplification which would understand the social rebellion of the late 1960s simply as a generational conflict.

As in *Illusionen*, the text shows a clear desire to do justice to unsympathetic individual characters.[9] Yet unlike in the city novel, the psychologisation of the characters does not produce a reconciling effect. On the contrary, the different internal perspectives serve as a narrative means of depicting the irreconcilable contradictions even more drastically and hopelessly. The artistic accomplishment of this insistent realism lies precisely in the incorruptibility of the narrator. S/he observes very slowly and exactly and remains unaffected by the fatherly misery of old Bruck. Rehmann's famous colleague the Bavarian *Volksdichterin* (folk poet) Marieluise Fleisser interpreted this realism in her enthusiastic review as 'tragedy':

> No deception is possible, there is no pretence ... opposition is useless ... people are discarded even if they try to fight. The way they fight gets to you, the way they cannot give up and in the process become guilty and ugly. There is no glossing things over, everything is almost too real. (Fleisser 1968)

Both the figure of Gehrke's completely isolated wife going mad in the country, wanting to be an opera diva, and Rass' hard-working mother show the personal costs of the lives of two women who have to fit in with the plans of their husbands on the farm. In her support for Rass' and the red head's escape, the narrator not only takes the part of young people but uncompromisingly refuses consent to traditional gender roles. Rehmann's clear sensitivity towards the oppressive gender relations which constantly directs attention towards the brutality of this archaic rural male society gives the novel an almost singular status within the genre of *Bauernroman*.[10]

Translated by Chris Weedon

Notes

1. See also Stephan 1986.
2. See also Gabriele Wohmann's depiction of a butcher shop in her story 'Die Schwestern', 1966 ('The Sisters', 1974), which was written in 1957 and first published in 1963. For further information on Wohmann see Knapp 1981.
3. In front of *Gruppe 47* (Group 47) Rehmann read one of the Carmen Viol chapters ('Das erste Kleid'). This chapter and another chapter of *Illusionen* were published again in 1978 as stories under the title 'Bei Tageslicht' and 'Ein Kleid für den Winter'. See Rehmann *Paare* (1983).
4. As late as 1967, for instance, the *Handbuch der Sekretärin* (Guidelines for Secretaries) praised 'good feminine qualities, like, for example, tact, gentleness, motherliness' (Niehaus 1967: 16); women are warned however against vanity in the workplace: 'don't immediately use ... a break in the workprocess like Snow White's stepmother to admire yourself in the mirror. Use this time ... to keep your workplace in order' (1967: 23).
5. Here Rehmann's text conforms with the tradition of the *Angestelltenroman* ('employees novel') of the 1930s, see for instance Irmgard Keun's *Gilgi – eine von uns* (1931/1990). Munich: dtv. (I am grateful to Cettina Rapisarda for this point.)
6. This refers to the rural novels of the Bavarian writer Ludwig Ganghofer (1855–1920) in which we often find a religious transfiguration of nature.
7. This unmasking is comparable to Irmgard Keun's subtle narrative style.
8. For this term compare Ernst Bloch's *Heritage of Our Times* (1991: 100 ff), a book which was of major influence in West Germany in the 1960s.
9. This psychologisation in *Die Leute im Tal* is quite different from Elfriede Jelinek's rural satire *Die Liebhaberinnen* 1975. See chapter 15.
10. Rehmann's later prose of the 1970s, 1980s and 1990s is marked by a very wide range of themes and styles of writing. See, for instance, the novels *Der Mann auf der Kanzel. Fragen an einen Vater* (1979, *The Man on the Pulpit* 1995b); *Abschied von der Meisterklasse* (1985); *Die Schwaigerin* (1987) and her autobiographical text on German unification *Unterwegs in fremden Träumen. Begegnungen mit dem anderen Deutschland* (1993, *Travelling in Alien Dreams* [Excerpts],1994).

Chapter Six

 WOMEN'S WRITING, 1968–1980

Cettina Rapisarda

The year 1968 is a landmark which commemorates not only the student movement named after it but also the beginnings of the new women's movement in the Federal Republic of Germany. If we look at literary developments in their socio-historical context, it is apparent that the women's movement, which expanded rapidly and diversified in the 1970s, was a crucial influence on many women writers.[1] Starting from the women's movement, to which writers reacted in very different ways, some very critically, it is possible to identify various dominant trends in women's writing. The following chapter examines the central themes and styles of individual prose works, particularly those which were well received on publication,[2] revealing various phases in women's writing in the context of the changing political situation and the changing literary public. The purpose is not to reduce the diversity of literature produced in this period to a common denominator under the label of 'feminist writing', although feminist literature as a new phenomenon, specific to the period, will certainly form a focal point. The term 'women's writing' applies here to writing which was written not only *by* but *for* women and was explicitly related to the new, informal feminist debate which developed in this period with the aim of encouraging discussion between women from various walks of life and areas of work, not the least between women writers and their public. This was the background – a period of critical reappraisal of academic disciplines – which gave rise to the beginnings of feminist literary studies.

The influence of the post-1968 women's movement in the cultural sphere can be attributed primarily to its broad conception of politics. In the Federal Republic of Germany, as in other Western

European countries, feminism arose in the context of a confrontation with the New Left. The women's movement seized upon the New Left's political ideas and developed them further applying them to the relationship between the sexes. This confrontational climate was already apparent in 1968 when, at a conference of the SDS, (*Sozialistischer Deutscher Studentenbund*, German Socialist Students' League) the 'Aktionsrat zur Befreiung der Frau' (Action Committee for Women's Liberation) took the floor. This was the first feminist voice to be heard. The committee argued that, despite all the programmatic statements about democratic equality and anti-authoritarian principles, women in the SDS continued to be marginalised and forced into the private sphere. In this first revolutionary phase, which was widely seen as a new departure, the women vehemently challenged the apathy and resistance of their male colleagues. In doing so, they did not model themselves on feminist predecessors or female traditions, nor did they have any well-developed feminist theory. Nevertheless they formulated a few key ideas – most crucially the two slogans: 'The personal is political' and 'Women together are strong'. The first slogan became the basis of a socio-critical viewpoint: 'Women are searching for their identity ... They can only find it if the social conflicts, driven underground into private life, are articulated so that women can show their solidarity with each other and become politicised' (Sander 1975: 11).

Emancipation: Reflecting on Individual and Social Experience

The first stage in the process of feminist reflection and political action was the reconstruction and critical analysis of the reality of women's lives. This was something which had not previously been attempted to any great extent. This concern can be clearly identified in the literature which was produced at the beginning of the 1970s and which called into question the literary concepts of the New Left.[3] The literary devices used were often very different from each other; the subjective-autobiographical approach became as popular as the documentary.

An important example of the documentary trend is Erika Runge's volume *Frauen. Versuche zur Emanzipation* (1970). The author had already achieved a reputation as a documentarist with her work *Bottroper Protokolle*, a graphic report on living conditions and problems in the *Ruhrgebiet*, an archetypal industrial region. The political aesthetic of this work was described by Martin Walser in his foreword as a radical break with traditional literature, which had always subscribed to bourgeois values and had never faithfully reflected the worker's perspective. Walser demanded 'more statements sharpened by bad experiences, more sighs, curses, sayings and contradictions, more testimonies from a class still living with fewer rights' (Runge 1968: 10). In *Frauen, Versuche zur Emanzipation*, Runge turned to another social group, namely women. Here she describes the lives of seventeen women who range in age from fourteen to eighty-four and whose names are changed to make them anonymous. Her subjects, who have different life histories and come from different social backgrounds, some of them prominent, are intended by the writer to be seen not as typical but as representative (1970: 271).

If it was Runge's original intention to collate examples of successful emancipation, ultimately she saw the book as material to reflect on both individual and social experiences (271). For the author the life histories are first and foremost evidence of the crucial influence of social conditions (conditions under which emancipation is unlikely to be achieved). They also, on the other hand, offer a way of defining emancipation. Earning a living and breaking with the subordinate role of the wife in marriage, in other words attaining equal rights, are preconditions of emancipation which the author can conceive of only in the context of the ongoing individual development of both sexes and of social change. Once again Runge concentrates in this documentation on spoken language, wishing to exploit its richness of association and unwilling to fix it in a specific form of literary representation. She hopes to heighten the reader's level of attention by using this unusual mode of expression. A few years later Runge emphasised her personal part in the documentations arising from her role as interviewer and listener and her selection and collation of the material (1976: 114), a factor not brought out at the time of publication.

Over the following years women repeatedly made use of the political effect of documentary texts, frequently in relation to specific topics.[4] This is seen particularly clearly in Alice Schwarzer's controversial and best-selling volume *Der 'kleine Unterschied' und seine großen Folgen. Frauen über sich – Beginn einer Befreiung* (1975), which made Schwarzer the spokeswoman for feminism in the Federal Republic. The book contains reports on sexuality annotated by the editor. In accord with a large section of the women's move-ment, sexuality was represented in the book as central to the women's issue, an area of long-silenced colonisation and violence and at the same time an index of key changes in desires and life plans. It became a central and recurring theme in women's fic-tional and other writing.

For many women the springboard for their writing career was provided by the *Werkkreis Literatur der Arbeitswelt* – a worker writ-ers' circle promoting fiction and poetry about the world of work and founded among others by Runge. The ultimate aim of the group was the emancipation of the workers. It advocated socially effective writing which tackled the issue of oppression and pos-sible forms of resistance and involved group discussion of writ-er's efforts in local workshops. The model, with its emphasis on cohesion and solidarity, proved to be particularly productive for women's writing.[5] Above all the group was receptive to Marxist-oriented demands for emancipation, in which the conflict between the sexes was seen as a 'subsidiary conflict' in relation to the 'class conflict between labour and capital'.[6] For this reason ideas of an autonomous women's movement along the lines of the Anglo-Saxon model was rejected as 'bourgeois'.[7]

In 1975 the first novel to be published in the *Werkkreis* series dedicated to women's emancipation provoked great interest and triggered internal conflicts. In *Ich stehe meine Frau*, Margot Schroe-der, bookseller, wife and mother, uses the realist writing style pro-moted by the *Werkkreis*. The novel is a report by a first-person narrator containing many dialogues and passages which recreate a spontaneous stream of consciousness. In her re-creation of spo-ken language – local Hamburg patois – the author is at times guilty of clichés and laboured plays on words. The protagonist is presented as a positive and heroic figure, a combative woman working as cashier, wife and mother, who grows in self-awareness and assertiveness. The strength of the book lies in its portrayal of the inner insecurity and conflicts of the protagonist – how she drinks to give herself courage, for example. The central issue hinges on the way the protagonist rises above her everyday life to become increasingly politically active, setting up a pressure group among the tenants. Significantly, what motivates her to become involved in the first place are not her interests as a woman but her role as a mother fighting for the rights of children in a modern urban environment. In her second novel *Der Schlachter empfiehlt noch immer Herz*, published in 1976 by the Frauenbuchverlag in

Munich, Margot Schroeder focuses specifically on women's issues: experiences in a feminist group and the battle to save a women's hostel in Hamburg.

For writer Karin Struck the *Werkkreis* also represented a crucial influence in the initial stages of her writing career. In her first book *Klassenliebe* (1973), however, she settles her score with the group's political agenda. The central theme of this autobiographical report, which describes the story of upward social mobility made possible by her studies and literary activity, is the identity problems she experiences as a result: 'I'm cut dead by both sides. No sooner am I an "intellectual" than the workers, anti-intellectual, reject me out of fear and feelings of inferiority, and the others reject me because I'm not a "proper" intellectual and never will be' (49). The author reflects on the inevitable consequences of this problem for her writing: 'What language can I speak? I speak a nobody's language in a half-way place. Neither Bavarian nor Pomeranian, neither Westphalian nor Platt, neither bourgeois nor proletarian' (82).

The search for social identity was an important issue for the *Werkkreis* which sought collaboration between workers and left-wing intellectuals. Struck's text describes the shattering of this hope. Left-wingers of bourgeois origin can provide her with no way out of the crisis; for them 'working-class child' is a term which holds an exotic fascination since they do not know the reality it describes. The identity crisis suffered by the author relates to her gender to the extent that she experiences her conflict in the love for two men from different social backgrounds. She has a child by both of them. She also emphasises her gender in conjunction with the values through which she hopes to find individual salvation and renewal. For the author motherhood, to which she dedicates her second book, becomes the symbol of wholeness and health, both emotional and physical. As Freud observed, a mother's love has the quality of a completely satisfying love affair. The author experiences this feeling in breastfeeding her first child: 'this sucking, then it suddenly falls asleep after all its exertions, lying in your arms, satisfied, nursed as you are nursed. Soothed, Soothed'(24). This apotheosis of old familiar models of femininity, which define women in terms of closeness to nature and motherhood, put Struck's text in conflict with large sections of the women's movement.

A further point of conflict was the liberalisation of abortion, one of the first demands formulated publicly by the women's movement in West Germany in 1971.[8] Nevertheless, in its autobiographical diary form, and its social criticism based on personal experience, *Klassenliebe* represented a milestone in women's writing of the period. Similar elements can be found later in numerous texts by feminist writers, although the specific political climate to which they relate gives these texts a different resonance.

A Woman Is Allowed to Do Almost Anything Today: Until Permission Is Revoked

The three examples presented above come from writers who had their roots in the left-wing literary scene where dominant literary conceptions at this time revolved around documentary and realist forms which came increasingly to stress subjective experience. All three writers soon began to diverge from this path, primarily in their choice of subject matter, but in Schroeder's case, also in her decisions about where to publish. All three, however, focused their interest on the women's movement.

If there were potential conflicts for women in these circles which thought of themselves as progressive, the problem was even more acute where the literary establishment was concerned. The fact that equality was merely illusory was stressed in 1974 by the sixty-two-year old lyric poet, Hilde Domin, who had been part of the West German literary scene since the 1950s. In her theses 'Über die Schwierigkeiten, eine berufstätige Frau zu sein', she writes:

> A woman is allowed to do almost anything today: until permission is revoked. She must always be on her toes; like any social misfit who makes it despite everything, she needs a double helping of luck. If she is ever suspected (of what? of being a woman), she loses her friends and the concession made to her is removed. Because it was only a case of concessions after all. Tolerance is not the same as a birthright. (1974: 45)

In 1977 a significantly younger writer, Angelika Mechtel wrote a polemic in the weekly paper *Die Zeit* entitled 'Der weiße Rabe hat fliegen gelernt'. Like a white raven in a flock of birds women attract attention in the literary world as rarities. This weak position, she claims, makes editors intrusive, and the personality cult created when the private becomes confused with the literary makes it impossible for the works to get a proper reception. She also notes that it had long been necessary for women writers to distance themselves from the so-called 'woman's novel' which was widely dismissed as trivial. It is characteristic of this period and symptomatic of the gradual changes taking place, that Mechtel at this time professes her faith in a newly defined women's literature. She puts her hope in 'women's writing as a generator' and 'women's writing raising questions in a committed anti-traditional way' (1977: 49). She argues that 'the literary world, still slanted towards men, must be made to redefine the rank and status of women writers' (49).

In the following much quoted statement, Christa Reinig attempted to sum up the consequences of this exclusion for women's writing in 1976:

> Literature has been a hard male business for three thousand years. This is something every woman writer must learn if she uses the word 'I'. From this point it suddenly becomes difficult to go any further. The forms and formulae of poetic language are not made for a female 'I' to express herself. One possibility is resignation. The female 'I' of the narrator becomes male. She pretends that the story she is telling under her pseudonym was experienced by a man. (1976a: 119f.)

In contrast to Mechtel, who counted on a re-appraisal of women's writing by the male-dominated literary world, Reinig at this time anticipated that the feminist drive for autonomy would be a much more significant influence in changing the environment within which women writers work.

A Radical Subjectivity, an Autonomous Place

The politicisation and growing solidarity of women in the first phase of the women's movement left its clear mark in the cultural sphere. The mid-1970s saw the growth of an alternative feminist platform which provided women with a place of their own separate from the traditional literary scene. Women's publishing houses and feminist magazines were founded[9] and came to play an exceedingly important role in the development of women's writing in the 1970s. Women's bookshops opened in all the major cities. As well as providing a means of distributing women's books, they acted, along with other venues (e.g., women's centres, women's projects, women's cafés and bars), as meeting places and had an obvious effect on women's writing. The major West German publishing houses also reacted to this new interest in reading and started to extend their lists to include new series of women's books.[10] The commercial potential of women's writing had already been demonstrated by the success of *Klassenliebe*.

In addition to these new concrete conditions, political concepts were no less important for women's writing. In the first half of the 1970s, the North-American model of consciousness-raising groups was adopted by the West German women's movement.[11] These small groups were based on the political assumption that the subjective reconstruction of individual experiences in interaction with other women would give rise to critical analysis and raise the consciousness of members of the group. This new awareness could then be translated into collective political action. A high value was placed on the opportunity for individuals to change and develop. Personal experience was seen as the basis for the development of theoretical concepts. The groups sought to exploit the utopian potential that they saw in the reconciliation of the individual and collective, the subjective and political, theory and practice, communication based on equality, and unrestricted personal development. These utopian aims soon proved to be very difficult to achieve. These experiments in collective communication and understanding provided a starting point for a movement of women writers which was intended as a democratic alternative to the established writing profession. Christa Reinig recorded her impressions of the first meeting of women writers which was held in Munich in 1976. To judge from her report in which she describes her emotions at the end of the meeting, something of the quality of communication which the women desired must have been achieved:

> I'm exhausted in an unusual way. Not as if I'd joined in or been drowned by duels of words for hours or had been receiving, parrying and returning blows to my will power. None of that happened. (Reinig 1976b: 5)

Despite her enthusiasm, Reinig, an experienced writer, was nevertheless somewhat sceptical about the literary fruits of the meeting:

> The right vocabulary is rarer here than gold. There's no bla-bla, no party lingo to help one out of trouble. No one, apart from me, used that expression that I hate so much: 'I would say ...'. There's a way out of the speechlessness. The speaker starts with 'I' and tells of an experience, an event that happened yesterday or ten years ago. From there she hopes to get to what she really wants to say. A long, often fruitless march. (1976b: 5)

In their emphasis on subjectivity, the texts which were produced in this climate cannot be understood in isolation from wider feminist perspectives. These set them apart from those of male writers who opted for 'new subjectivity' (*Neue Subjektivität*) as a literary style at that time. The feminist literary theorist Renate Möhrmann highlighted the following difference: 'This is not nostalgic reprivatisation at work; on the contrary, it is a process of making public centuries-old damage, a retraction of a silence that had become habitual'.[12] This is particularly apparent in the following two books which were linked directly to the women's movement.

The decisive autobiographical text linked to feminist self-discovery was *Häutungen* (1975, *Shedding*, 1978) by Swiss-born Verena Stefan. For the independent publishing house *Frauenoffensive* this first publication proved to be a bestseller. The writer herself was active in the women's movement[13] and wrote her book in the knowledge that she was speaking for many. The reception enjoyed by *Häutungen* in feminist circles confirmed the fact that many female readers identified with the text (more than 100,000 copies were sold in the 1970s). The two central themes of the book are sexuality and language. Stefan formulates her criticism in terms of unfulfilled desires and wishes in private life and in relationships with 'progressive', left-wing men. For her the positive alternative lies in love between women – a form of love as yet undefined and free from the preconceptions imposed by society and gender roles. She has no words at her disposal with which to talk about this love: 'Language fails me as soon as I want to record new experiences' (Stefan 1975: 3). From the perspective of these new experiences she is acutely conscious of sexism towards the female body in almost all areas of life and particularly in language:

> All the slang terms – spoken and written – relating to coitus are brutal and misogynistic (screwing, shafting, poking, etc.) ... when a woman starts talking about her 'cunt', she is simply adopting the manner of speaking of left-wing men. For her, access to her vagina, to her body and to herself remains closed as it was before. (1975: 3)

For the first time in the Federal Republic Stefan had formulated a feminist critique of language which was widely received and provoked an important debate. However, the linguistic alternative that she proposed, in which female sexuality is expressed in traditional and kitschy natural metaphors, was a disappointment. While she was undoubtedly justified in her search for a different female physicality which would be neither sexist nor defined from outside, the results are extremely dubious: there is little innovation in the image of 'pumpkin breasts' or the lyrical descriptions of menstruation. The fact that this successful book provoked very bitter criticism and sarcasm from women is evidence that feminist circles were prepared to engage in serious debate.[14] The discussions and polemics that were triggered by the book confirm its stunning impact, even if the effect it produced was other than the author anticipated.

A further successful book published by *Frauenoffensive* was Jutta Heinrich's novel *Das Geschlecht der Gedanken*. Heinrich had completed this book in 1972 but only one feminist publishing house was prepared to print it in 1977. When the novel finally appeared, it provoked intense discussion in women's circles, coinciding with the new interest in autobiographical texts by women. This was a trend towards identification about which the author herself had misgivings. She saw her first-person narrator as representative of her sex and not as a reworking of her own biography. She was 'a distorted mirror of the structures of power and powerlessness' (Heinrich 1978: 3).

Writing in a style which repeatedly moves into the realms of the fantastic, the novel tells the story of a girl from youth to adulthood. The first-person narrator sees the constellation of power which governs the relationship between her dominant father and meek and oppressed mother repeated again and again between the sexes outside the family. This inescapable power becomes the starting point of her psychological unhappiness. Although it is possible to read Heinrich's text as a psychogram and analyse the work in terms of the psychology of the individual, it is equally important to examine the text in the light of socio-psychological considerations, as the author herself intended. The novel describes a complex problem which was typical for the generation in question. This is the painful process of coming to terms with a mother who embodies the 'feminine mystique' as spouse and housewife and can hardly serve as a role model for a positive female genealogy. At best she manages to maintain a relationship marked by psychological conflict. Her relationship with her father, however, is less ambiguous since she is able to fight against his power and violence. The potential for conflict in the girl's relationship with the father arises from her temptation to ally herself and identify with his more attractive position of power. She sums up the hopelessness of trying to establish her identity as follows: 'I didn't want to be the sex of either of my parents, both revolted me' (1978: 22).

Typically for the period, the author reveals the mechanisms of power in everyday situations. When the father, for example, announces he has a 'treat' in store, the mother and daughter are terrified. He gives a piece of jewellery to the mother, who does not like jewellery, in return for which he demands a whole series of ritualised gestures of submission. The mother accepts her 'obligations': 'Because of the present she felt obliged to endow her actions with a new spontaneity, and when I noticed that she still had make-up on her face in the evening, I realised that she knew she still had to surrender herself'(51). The daughter, empathising with her mother, is constantly aware of the sexuality of her parents, which is depicted as the ultimate expression of the power relations between the sexes.

Faced with this situation, the female 'I' reacts by retreating and adopts the role of a unique avenger. She pursues men as perpetrators but also women who, through their meekness, reaffirm and consolidate the power relationship. The narrator is ruthless in her scrutiny of her own tangled and ambivalent feelings, avoiding a comfortable reconciliation as the way out of her own psycho-social misery. She reacts to external pressure with a cold malice which becomes her instrument of self-assertion and resistance. Her desperate behaviour is a reaction against female subservience which she considers a personal betrayal. The mode of analysis which the author presents is destruction: the literary 'I' acts on the principle of 'destruction in order to get to the core of things' (76).

Provocation and Satire

Christa Reinig is a central figure in feminist literature in the Federal Republic of Germany. This is the case even though she deviated considerably from the dominant pattern of a story of individual development such as depicted autobiographically by Stefan and in a fictional form by Heinrich. Reinig, a highly individual spokeswoman for feminism, has a special place because of long years of previous literary activity. She gave her support to the feminist movement with the publication of her novel *Entmannung* (Emasculation) in 1976.

The title alone was so provocative and offended so many taboos that some of the literary critics never got beyond it in their criticisms. Contrary to the fears of the critics, however, the emasculation refers merely to the decision by the protagonist, surgeon and playboy Otto Kyra, to take up the fight for women. At least this is what he assures Valerie Solanas, editor of the *SCUM* manifesto, who wanders through the book like a form of 'walking paranoia' (Reinig 1977: 58). Even the plans to destroy all women and/or all men incorporated in the fictional text come to nothing. Instead the book is made up of kaleidoscopic scenes which report on the everyday violence perpetrated against women. Even Kyra, the 'softy', cannot do anything to prevent the destruction of the women around him and the fulfilment of the 'world formula for women':

> Madhouse, hospital, prison. That's the rule of three in the world formula for women. If you rebel, you go to prison; if you don't rebel, you crack up and are sent to the madhouse and envy the women who've resorted to the axe. If you give in to someone with lust, you end up in hospital with your womb shot to pieces. And with seven tubes sticking out of your belly, you envy the women who can doze in the madhouse while you have to scream yourself to death. (153)

In contrast to the prevailing trend at this time, the three central female characters have no psychological dimension. In an attempt to provoke analysis, they are stylised figures, governed by traditional patterns of behaviour which the author brings out through historical and present-day references and her use of old and modern myths. There are references, for instance, to the myth of Orestes and the judgment of Paris read with Bachofen: Memmi, the wife and mother, is called Klytemnestra van der Leyden and corresponds to Hera in the judgment of Paris; Thea, alias Aphrodite, works as a prostitute, and Doris, alias Pallas Athene, is a career woman in the male mould. Only one woman in Kyra's circle, Wölfi, who prefers her own sex, escapes a cruel fate.

The many discussions between the novel's characters are based on the thesis that there is war between the sexes, a position which is developed with satirical precision in all its possible and impossible consequences. The category of gender is also questioned in a bitter and playful manner. Thus a distinction is made between masculine and feminine women, namely women who align themselves like satellites with the men, between male and female women impersonators, hermaphrodites and renegades. In the end the author puts forward the theory that 'women and men are two originally separate species who have grown together not quite seamlessly in the course of evolution' (78).[15]

Reinig's provocations met their target and brought criticism from various sides.[16] Explaining her aim, she says: 'In a certain sense Otto's ideological "emasculation" is my own way and Kyra (originally Otto had another name) is Christa. I am examining what elements of "masculine mystique" I can discard in myself … At the end of the book I arrive at much derided feminism' (Reinig 1978: 19f.).

Reinig had already developed her style – with its elements of fantasy – in the 1950s and early 1960s. Living in East Berlin, she had been a member of the avant-garde group of *zukunftssachlichen* (sober futurist) poets since about 1949. Here, as elsewhere, she soon found herself in opposition to the GDR, a position which gave her writing an additional impetus.[17] In a political poem dating from 1951, she speaks on behalf of social and cultural outcasts: 'don't listen, you heroes/ I'm speaking alone/ for anti-social elements'. The last verse emphasises her feelings of isolation and despair: 'I'm talking like mad people talk/ for myself alone and for the other blind people/ for all those in this life/ who can't find their way home' (Reinig 1985: 45). She encodes her criticism in absurd satires, often involving bloodthirsty and monstrous elements, and in the paradoxes of bold, logical people of ideas.[18] In *Der Traum meiner Verkommenheit* (1961), she compares her work with that of a mathematician, defined in terms of the tension between logical rigour and incorrect results, between deviation from the law and responsibility. Reinig's concept of responsibility is also expressed in another earlier text: *Ein Dichter erhielt einen Fragebogen*: 'The questionnaire asked: *What do you consider the most important prerequisite to allow your creative process to function properly?* He answered: the quality of being moved [*Ergriffenheit*] … *Apart from educating the masses, do you pursue any particular personal purpose in your work?* He replied: to gain insight' (Reinig 1985: 11). The satirical reference to the GDR in this passage is clear, outlining the contrasting values of two irreconcilable approaches to art and speech. The continuity leading to Reinig's feminist writing is also apparent: the term 'Ergriffenheit' (the quality of being moved) might be replaced by either 'Betroffenheit' (the quality of being affected or stricken) or 'Parteilichkeit' (partiality, partisanship). But 'gaining insight' remained the main goal in her analytical novel *Entmannung*. It is precisely this critical will to gain knowledge which, in my view, lends power to Reinig's radical way of tackling the feminist issues of the 1970s in her writing.

Paths to 'Female Subjectivity': Self-Doubt, Self-Images

The problem posed by Reinig of searching for a previously denied 'female subjectivity' ('weiblichen Ich'), to which she herself had responded with support for the feminist cause, becomes a thread in the literary production of women in the second half of the 1970s. The search for a new identity, which was part of the political agenda at the beginning of the women's movement, becomes a central issue. Often, though not always, it is presented in bio-graphical-psychological form, using a first-person narrator. The fact that even a writer such as Runge complained of having renounced her 'private and personal identity' in her previously published documentations is an indication that this trend was already apparent in 1976 (Runge 1976: 106). In the following, I will discuss various novels linked directly to the women's movement in which this search for identity manifests itself in different ways.

The texts reveal that the ideal of an autonomous, undivided subject, like that of a direct, authentic mode of speech, became increasingly questionable (Krechel 1979: 80–107). The search for identity manifested itself most prominently in the exploration of personal damage suffered in the private and social spheres, a process which was full of conflict. Here the reconstruction of highly intimate relations is inevitably painful. The beginnings of identity only start to become apparent in a crisis. The element that links most of the texts I have selected is the representation of love, a theme which is held to be the traditional domain of women's writing.

The individual, private, life histories revealed in the texts often provide the starting point for a more general examination of his-torico-political issues. In many of the texts, it is also possible to identify a belief in social change brought about by the commitment demonstrated by the women's movement and the New Left. By this time the women's movement had become a relatively broad-based movement which seemed to have acquired a degree of public acceptance, if one is to believe the fulsome declarations in support of women which were made during International Women's Year in 1975. Nevertheless, women's writing at this time reveals clear signs that the general political climate in the Federal Republic became markedly more conservative again during the course of the 1970s. This was evidenced by campaigns against those on the left which included *Berufsverbot* (the banning of individuals from public-sector jobs on political grounds) following the so-called 'Radikalenerlaß' (law on radical elements) of 1972 and the fight against terrorists and their loosely defined 'circle of sympathizers'.[19]

A revealing example of the search for a female identity in a confrontation with the left-wing political scene is provided by Birgit Pausch's *Die Verweigerungen der Johanna Glauflügel* (1977). The novel describes in the third person the story of a woman who is referred to in the text only by her surname. The distancing effect created by this device is reinforced by the writer's economical, pointed style which incorporates references to the fine arts and visual descriptions. The protagonist gradually breaks away from her conservative boyfriend Ronnen, with whom she lives in a conventional relationship. This relationship is sketched in visual snapshots, e.g., from the point of view of another man, the painter Dortrecht, who becomes progressively more important to the woman. During a conversation with Ronnen, Dortrecht observes her: 'Glauflügel moved him. He had never seen her like this before – obscure, so dull and constricted, her sewing things in her lap, trapped as if in a lead casting, a crawling beetle, cast at the New Year and left there for the year – this confinement and stillness' (7).

The meeting with Dortrecht marks the beginning of change for Glauflügel. He is the agent who allows her to transform her life. Central to this change is her understanding of Marxism, which Dortrecht describes to her as an 'historical and critical tackling, transforming and struggling with the present' (26f.). The changes which result for Glauflügel have relatively little to do with a real love affair with this second man. Her attention focuses now on the injustices and political structures which she perceives in the various areas of her life. Glauflügel's personal life is undefined and emotionally unstable; the radical change in her manifests itself primarily in spontaneous actions – for example, when she is unable to stop herself laughing at her friend Ronnen. She does not go so far as a girl friend who gives up her career as actress because the female roles in the theatre are like 'daily rapes' (74) to her, damaging her emotionally and leading to fantasies of self-abasement. While this woman becomes a terrorist, Glauflügel, on the other hand, puts her trust in step-by-step reforms, confident that people will eventually come to demand their rights with increasing determination.

If Pausch had still expressed a tentative hope of a general process of democratisation, Hannelies Taschau in her novel *Landfriede*, which appeared one year later in 1978, describes the emergence at this critical time of signs of political retreat. In the country area she describes, the signs of the changed political climate are clearly apparent. As Franziska Meyer demonstrated in her reading of Ruth Rehmann's *Die Leute im Tal*, the provinces, when viewed dispassionately, can soon lose all their idyllic charms. The action – described in clipped, barren language – is relatively uneventful.

A young, unmarried couple move to the country, where the man takes up a teaching position. The woman, Anne, is prepared to support her partner in this career opportunity, even though it means that she has to give up her own job as a journalist and work freelance for her newspaper. For her female neighbours in this rural environment, the fact that they are housewives and do not go out to work is neither the result of a conscious decision, nor of a hard struggle for prosperity. Affluence is taken for granted; they live trouble-free lives, making improvements to the furnishings of their well-kept houses and taking the odd drink in secret, sometimes even before lunchtime. 'Nobody tries to hide it, they all admit that they have unending amounts of time' (Taschau 1980: 40).

The peace and quiet appears, at least on the surface, to be idyllic. A recent phase of demonstrations and political action instigated by students and taken up by local young people has been effectively dealt with and is now forgotten, settled by a court case which convicted offenders of breaches of the peace. One of the most active protestors is now the target of hostility from contemporaries and former friends. Disillusioned and isolated, he sinks into depression. Anne's partner, who regards himself as progressive, but avoids potential conflicts at all costs, fails to intervene when the young man is attacked. He has always been cautious where politics are concerned, anxious to avoid the risk of being banned from his job, and now concentrates on his teaching career. As a 'realist' he has come to the following conclusion: 'Adaptation can be vital ... It is a human need.... And politically it can have long-term effects of which we can never dream' (79).

Anne is able to observe the effects of adapting in this particular place. She is also required to be a proper housewife, to fit in and finally to get married. The pressure is clearly palpable, even if living together is regarded with greater tolerance at this time than it was in the moral climate which prevailed before the 1970s. As she is not prepared to fit in, Anne is forced to leave the place and also her partner who has found a lifestyle which suits him. The woman's ideas and hopes remain vague, but with emotions of 'bewilderment, exclusion and mourning', she takes stock: 'Here you have to pretend to think what has always been thought, do what has always been done.' (139).

Both Pausch and Taschau write of love affairs that go wrong. Both male figures, moderate and half-hearted 'progressives', are unsuited to the tough confrontations described in earlier women's writing. However inevitable and unspectacular the breakdown of both love affairs, it nevertheless has a profoundly unsettling effect on the identity of the women. Initially they are sustained only by the will to make their own decisions and hopes for a new beginning in the act of separation.

A separation crisis is also described by Karin Petersen in her novel *Das fette Jahr* (1978), which is an example of the numerous stories of suffering and illness which recur in women's writing. At the beginning the first-person narrator describes how she discovers her identity in her love for her boyfriend. This certainty vanishes in a year of mourning, in which she experiences contradictory emotions, a disjunction of her conscious will and of uncontrollable utterances, and ultimately symptoms of psychosomatic illness. At a social evening with her boyfriend Karl, the narrator longs to be like the other women there: 'Sat there as if I belonged quite naturally to Karl, like these girls to their boyfriends. They were taken along everywhere; they simply sat there dumbly without moving' (53). Her earlier identity with its allusions to gender-specific roles proves to be increasingly less viable. During the course of the year, it becomes clear to the protagonist that she can find a new identity only outside the relationship.

The love relationship between the woman and the man ends unhappily in many texts written by women. The reason has less to do with the psychological problems of modern people and their inability to make a commitment than with the balance of power between the sexes. Svende Merian's *Der Tod des Märchenprinzen* (1980) demonstrates how easy it is for this complex problem to be reduced to a cliché. The fact that this novel, with its tale of disenchantment and separation, became a best-seller seems to me to be due solely to the fact that it inevitably strikes a chord in the reader. In this trivial and stylised text, the pattern of treating separation as liberation finally comes to an end.

It would be premature to conclude that love is generally devalued in women's writing in the 1970s. During this period love between women gradually emerges as a theme which can be more openly talked and written about. Openness of this kind was now being demanded by a feminist-oriented emancipation movement which had emerged from the predominantly male-led homosexual movement. As I mentioned above, Verena Stefan described love between women, as an alternative, feminist hope and the means to the gradual attainment of a personal way of living. Love between women is also shown as an extension of the movement for solidarity between women which had emerged in the political sphere in Margot Schroeder's *Der Schlachter empfiehlt noch immer Herz*.

The exclusion of lesbian literature from mainstream publishing houses is illustrated by the case of Johanna Moosdorf whose novel *Die Freundinnen*, which she completed in 1969, was not published until 1977 although she was already an established writer, with some of her work published under the Suhrkamp imprint. The case of Christa Reinig is equally revealing. She first hinted at the theme of lesbianism in her poem 'Hört weg!' in 1951 (1986a: 38f.) but did not treat it explicitly as a central theme until 1979 in her anthology *Müßiggang ist aller Liebe Anfang*.[20]

Those autobiographical texts which are not dedicated to love affairs and partnerships, but which return instead to the story of childhood, are often classified as either father or mother books.[21] The desperate struggle for individual self-determination is the central theme of Helga M. Novak's novel *Die Eisheiligen* (1979)[22] which I quote here as an example of confrontation with the mother figure. The novel also provides an historical reconstruction of the period from the first year of the Second World War to the first years of the GDR, using the dominant narrative technique of recording the typical language of the time in passages of direct speech.

Throughout Novak's text, the first-person narrator calls the mother by the name of 'Kaltesophie', a reference both to the latter's emotional coldness and to her date of birth, 14th May, the last day of the three saints' days known as the 'Ice Saints'. From early on, the mother negates the daughter's identity. A menacing atmosphere builds up until the mother finally tells the girl she is only adopted, a fact that had been kept secret from her but had always been in the background. The adoptive mother taunts the child: 'Where on earth did they dig you up?' (1979: 37) and 'You crawled from the belly of a whore, you changeling' (303). In reaction to this the 'difficult child' starts to scratch her name on furniture, behaviour that becomes so obsessive that she is turned out of nursery school.

When, years later, the mother wants to cancel the adoption contract, she threatens: 'Then you'll have no name any more, you'll simply be called nothing' (321). For the child, life is a matter of survival which forces her to develop her defences and find at least some sort of self-affirmation in vengeance. The orders, rebukes and insults give a clear idea of the mother's method of bringing up the child. She beats the child without restraint, something that was probably not particularly unusual at the time. In school, too, beating is a normal and accepted method of education. When the pupils are told at the end of the war that beating has been outlawed in schools, the girl finally finds a first convincing basis for her hopes for self-fulfilment, which she links increasingly in her mind with the new political climate. Novak's text recounts political developments through the eyes of a girl, using quotations from everyday speech to reveal contradictions and self-delusions. These are apparent both in the parents' language during the Nazi period and the war, and in that of the girl who has to smother any doubts in order to maintain her enthusiasm for the GDR. The gender identity of the protagonist is not the sole theme of this biography. In her confrontation with the all-powerful mother, the female first-person narrator develops extraordinary strength. This is reflected not in contented stability but in an intractable and 'unfeminine' stance of self-assertion which matches the harshness of the autobiographical novel.

Alongside descriptions of love affairs, depictions of relationships with mothers seem to me to be an indicator of female self-definition. Petersen's female first-person narrator attempts to arm herself against her mother, against 'the mother's preying on the helplessness of her children' (Petersen 1978: 79) (elsewhere the mother is also accused of 'tyrannizing through weakness' 85). At the same time she describes how: 'Her care enveloped me like a scratchy dress, but I feared the icy cold when I took it off' (80). For the girl, it is important to stress that she was not like her mother, whereas Pausch's protagonist comes to the nightmarish insight 'that everything that she had done so far had come from her mother' (Pausch 1977: 52). Thus Novak was not the only woman writer to use hardness and coldness as motifs for the mother, representing the pain of the process of separation which Heinrich also described. Although this process may have been unavoidable in redefining femaleness, it provoked ambivalent feelings and fear of becoming like one's mother, putting a final seal on the loss of childhood security.

Gabriele Wohmann's *Schönes Gehege* (1975), the last novel to be considered here, was written at a clear distance from the women's movement. The novel has obvious autobiographical features even though it does not have a female first-person narrator but is about a male writer and his understanding of literature. A woman writer adopting the proven method of changing sex for the purposes of the story and recounting from a male perspective alienated even male literary critics at the time.[23] It was, however, a logical device for Wohmann's purpose of intentionally omitting the question of gender. The strategy also fits the structure of the text in which elements of autobiography and radical subjectivity, typical of the period, are included but broken up by the distancing effect of the narrative technique.

In the novel, a documentary film about the writer is to be made for television. He is required to reconstruct past phases of his life, including a particular crisis, and to authenticate them in a way which will be comprehensible to the audience. In reconstructing his own past, confronted with the cliché-ridden ideas of the director, he experiences himself from the perspective of an outsider. The dynamics of his relations with the director unsettle and provoke him, but he stays with the project. While he is expected to provide unambiguous information about himself and his writing, it becomes obvious that he is unable to define himself with certainty. This does not mean, however, that the writer is prepared to adapt to the public taste.

With this character Wohmann presents a poetic goal different from that of her previous work. The writer defends himself against the reputation of being an 'angry Cassandra', which Wohmann had herself acquired with her critical literary texts. In his personal life the protagonist strives for individual happiness in retreat from society and likes to be a calm person and as a writer he tries to describe satisfaction (152). This 'programme of friendliness' has its limitations, however: 'A feeling always has two sides, this one or that. But from now on I won't try to suppress the compulsive opposite of being sad, in other words, being happy. I'll even try to emphasise it' (40f.).

'New Women's Writing': Trends and Developments

Wohmann's novel contrasts in almost textbook fashion with certain predominant features of women's writing of this period and thus negatively reminds one of them: the politicisation of virtually all material, the key role of sexuality, and finally the uncompromisingly critical and untypical perspective on traditional preconceived ideas of feminine gentleness and conciliatoriness. Wohmann, together with Taschau and Elsner among others, can be seen as a precursor of this latter perspective. Given the diversity of writing in this period, it is not easy to summarise all the various trends and individual writing styles. Women's themes were taken up by women writers of different generations; some, like Taschau, Novak, Moosdorf, mentioned in previous chapters by Franziska Meyer, had already begun writing before 1968. Others, like Runge, Schroeder, Stefan and Heinrich, found their first inspiration in the specific context of the 1970s.

It is, however, possible to identify lines of development which were linked to changes in the political scene. These encompassed the shifts from the mood of change introduced by the left-wing student movement to the growth of a conservative backlash and the birth of the women's movement to its institutionalisation in autonomous political and cultural institutions as it became more differentiated. As the women's movement developed two main groupings emerged: those who followed broadly socialist lines and those oriented to North American radical feminist models.

In women's writing, realistic and documentary forms gave way to biographical and autobiographical forms. Because politics was specifically conceived as embracing the personal, the emphasis on subjectivity was not in contradiction with the aims of the women's movement. This can be seen from the feminist practice of collective writing, which contrasted with that of left-wingers within the *Werkkreis*. If work and political commitment are the dominant themes of the early years, and the 'private' spheres of love, sexuality and personal relationships those of the mid-1970s, this was understood by women writers not as a process of depoliticisation but a widening of the political perspective. Language itself becomes more politicised: it is used provocatively by Runge and Schroeder to signify class, Struck turns it into a central problem, and in Stefan it is related explicitly to the relationship between the sexes.

A pattern which recurs repeatedly and is somewhat over used, even in documentary and realistic texts with a biographical basis, is the story of a woman's evolution which culminates in an act of emancipation and renewal and then in most cases ends there. (Reinig was an exception to this trend.) The ideal of a politically active and secure subject which predominated in the earlier texts of the 1970s gradually gave way to the depiction of problematic personalities preoccupied with making sense of their own life histories. The concept of subjectivity had obviously become increasingly more complex and contradictory, a trend which would intensify in the following period as the next chapter shows. It seems to me that Mechtel's expectations of women's writing in the 1970s, for example, that it should be a 'committed anti-traditionalist questioning' (Mechtel 1977: 49) were more than fulfilled. The writing of this period shed light on and considerably extended literary representations of female reality. Not only were individual, dominant images of women questioned – women represented in terms of home and family, often in the form of mother figures – but also other images which were anchored in cultural history, such as those examined by Reinig. Over and above this, however, women writers succeeded in banishing the traditional taboos and mystifications, replacing them with undisguised support for their own cause and new aspects such as sexuality and the problems of language.

The texts make it clear that the redefinition of motherhood, going out to work, political activity, and love for men or even for women were possible only at the expense of former certainties and struggles. The extent to which political involvement and the committed writing of women in the 1970s brought about a fundamental liberalisation of lifestyles can perhaps be seen most clearly by the fact that today we take for granted and have lost interest in many of the themes of literature which were so provocative at the time. Nevertheless, each new generation will have to fight their own battles in the process of reflecting on and defining for themselves female concepts of living.

In literary theory and criticism some progress has been made in recognising the value of texts written in the 1970s. The establishment of women's studies in academic institutions from the mid-1970s onwards helped to ensure a continuation of the work of the autonomous women's publishing outlets whose importance had already began to fade by providing an audience for these works.[24] We can only tentatively hope that the anthologies which appeared in large circulation paperbacks in the 1980s are an indication that women's writing can no longer be overlooked and has achieved wider recognition. Then we will be able to say with certainty that writers in this period succeeded in releasing the term 'women's writing'[25] from its old, pejorative connotations and redefining it.

Translated by Elizabeth Doyle

Notes

With the exception of translations from published English editions listed in the bibliography, all translations from German texts cited are by Elizabeth Doyle.

1. Among the socio-historical conditions which helped to bring about the birth of the women's movement at this time, the following are perhaps the most significant. As a result of increased prosperity women had the opportunity to acquire a higher level of education and greater access to the labour market, from which as a group they are displaced at times of economic crisis. Modernisation (together with industrialisation, urbanisation, mobility and social differentiation) inevitably changed the role of women in society. The spread of the contraceptive pill in the 1960s gave women greater freedom to decide whether or not they wanted to become mothers and dissociated sexuality from reproduction. A further specifically German aspect linked to the country's history was the particularly strong need of this generation to dissociate itself from their parents' generation and its links with Nazism; inevitably this affected the image of women.

2. It is obviously impossible here to present a complete account of literature written by women in these twelve years. In particular the restriction to prose writing excludes mention of the relatively extensive production of lyric poetry by women (e.g., Rose Ausländer, Hilde Domin, Renate Rasp, Karin Kiwus, Friederike Roth, Angelika Mechtel, Ursula Krechel, etc.) and drama, a medium in which women were confronted with many obstacles but in which Gerlind Reinshagen was able to establish a reputation for herself in the 1970s.

3. Various studies relating to the literary examples quoted: Ricarda Schmidt 1982/1990, Brügmann 1986, Richter-Schröder 1986, Weigel 1989, Venske 1988, and Renate Becker 1992. These studies also contain further references.

4. For example Hoffmann (ed.) 1976 *Ledige Mütter, Protokolle, Analysen, Juristische Informationen, Sozialarbeit, Selbstorganisation*. The title itself indicates its aim of providing political advice and information for self-help.

5. The *Werkkreis* anthologies *Liebe Kollegin. Texte zur Emanzipation der Frau in der Bundesrepublik*, ed. Noeske, Roehrer et al. 1973, and *Für Frauen. Ein Lesebuch*, edited by a collective of women 1979, were publishing successes.

6. Texts such as Engels' *The Origin of the Family, Private Property and the State* (1972), Bebel's *Women Under Socialism* (1971) and the works of Clara Zetkin (1987) and Alexandra Kollontai (1982) were read. Examples of new studies include Jutta Menschik 1971, articles on central women's issues by Frigga Haug and others published in the Berlin journal *Das Argument*, and Gisela Brandt et al. 1973. The positions adopted by critical theorists, particularly Herbert Marcuse, also found an echo and were taken up by Silvia Bovenschen and others.

7. See chapter 2 note 1.

8. The starting point was a broad campaign of self accusation on the French model which was spread in 1971 by *Stern* magazine. The beginning of the women's movement brought various calls for equality of women within the law (e.g., with reference to labour law).

9. The most prominent of the publishing houses, Frauenoffensive, was founded in 1974 but did not break from the Trikont-Verlag until 1976. The launch dates of

various journals are as follows: 1974 *Frauenoffensive-Journal*, 1976 *Mamas Pfirsiche – Frauen und Literatur, Courage* and *Schwarze Botin*, 1977 *Emma*, 1978 *Schreiben. Frauen-Literatur-Forum*.

10. For example, in *Neue Frau*, Rowohlt and *Die Frau in der Gesellschaft*, Fischer.
11. On the West German women's movement, see Krechel 1975, Dietze 1979, and Altbach et al. 1984.
12. See also Wartmann 1979: 108–132.
13. Stefan collaborated in an earlier feminist educational project 'Brot und Rosen', whose ideas she develops further in her literary reflections on sexuality.
14. See Classen and Goettle 1979: 55–59.
15. This thought was developed further in essays later collected together in the volume *Der Wolf und die Witwen*, Reinig 1980.
16. Criticism from the feminist side is found, for example, in Bammer 1986: 107–127.
17. Although despite her proletarian origins, Reinig was able to take her 'Abitur' in the GDR and to study, she reported problems with her first attempts to find a publisher. In 1964 she was awarded the Bremen Literature Prize for her lyrical poetry published in the West and moved to the Federal Republic at that time.
18. As an example of encoding criticism, Reinig cites *Japanische Bittschrift* (1949) in which a prisoner demands the death penalty by way of a pardon (Reinig 1986a: 38f.).
19. The 'Radikalenerlaß' provided a legal basis for excluding citizens from holding jobs in public service on the grounds of their political convictions. Within the left-wing, splits had begun to appear with a crucial dividing line between those who sought to bring about social change the long way round through institutions and those who, disillusioned and radicalised, opted for terrorism. The name of Ulrike Meinhof, who was a member of the Red Army Faction, crops up repeatedly in literary texts.
20. One impetus behind the writing of *Entmannung* was the trial of two lesbian women in 1974. This was sensationalised by the press and made the writer aware for the first time of the political dimension of the subject.
21. A few examples of father books: Plessen 1976 (trans. 1979), Rehmann 1979 (trans. 1995), Bronnen 1980.
22. Novak had been published since 1965 and gained a reputation in particular for her poems. In 1966 she was stripped of her citizenship of the GDR.
23. See Heinrich Vormweg, 'Das Gehege der mittleren Jahre', in *Süddeutsche Zeitung*, 6/7 September 1975, reprinted in Scheuffelen 1977: 97ff.
24. In 1976 the first Berlin Summer University for Women brought calls for women's studies to be included in literary theory and criticism. In the same year a discussion was launched on the question: 'Is there a feminine aesthetic?' by Silvia Bovenschen, Elisabeth Lenk, Hiltrud Gnüg and others. A survey of the first developments in this field can be found in Möhrmann 1979: 63–84, and Heuser 1983: 117–148.
25. See Serke 1982, Jurgensen 1985, Puknus (ed.) 1980. The latter has useful bio- and bibliographical information.

Chapter Seven

WOMEN'S WRITING OF THE 1980S AND 1990S

Margaret Littler

Feminism and Postmodernism

Within the broad spectrum of recent West German women's writing there are elements of both continuity and change, but if the 1980s bears a distinctive mark, it may be seen in the emergence of what can be termed 'postmodern' feminist literature. By 'postmodern' I mean literature which reflects a sceptical attitude to the existence of general, all-encompassing principles governing our natural and social reality. For feminism this implies avoiding the construction of theories of women's oppression which merely generalise from the experience of white, Western, middle-class women. To this extent, there is less evidence of the lack of simultaneity (*Ungleichzeitigkeiten*) which, Sigrid Weigel argues, separated feminist theory and much textual practice in the previous decade (Weigel 1989: 25ff). Whilst many of the older generation of post-war writers – Ingeborg Drewitz, Luise Rinser, Johanna Moosdorf and Eva Zeller – produced significant mature works,[1] the work of several authors who began to publish in the 1980s reflects contemporary theoretical debates within postmodern feminism. This is not to imply a consensus on the definition or usefulness of categories such as *Frauenliteratur* or *weibliche Ästhetik*. Liberal and Marxist feminist voices in particular continued to protest against the 'ghettoisation' of women's writing, whether self-inflicted or imposed by a critical establishment which effaced the individuality and plurality of their literary production through their summary classification as women writers.[2]

Notes for this section begin on page 127.

Whilst attempting to do justice to this diversity, for the purposes of this chapter, the focus will be on the various ways in which recent German women's writing reflects what might broadly be called the 'postmodern condition'.[3] This is seen in new ways of conceptualising subjectivity, sexual difference, historical progress, and the literary tradition. The very notion of 'femininity' as used in its political context by the women's movement has acquired a broader application in postmodern discourse. As identity has been variously theorised as a complex effect of culture rather than an 'essence' at the heart of the individual, so the cultural suppression of the feminine may be understood as much more than the exclusion of women from positions of institutional power. It is manifested in all attempts to marginalise difference in the increasingly homogeneous, market-orientated societies of the capitalist West. The collapse of the Communist régimes of Eastern Europe and the emergence of East European writers on the West German literary scene such as Libuše Moníková and Herta Müller, has brought with it a new diversification of women's writing. Just as the integrative socialist and radical autonomous impulses of 1970s feminism gave way to more pluralistic concerns with *otherness* and with the *differences* between women, some of the most prominent new voices of the decade came from the German-speaking enclaves of Romania and Czechoslovakia, with their own specific histories of marginality and oppression. These writers became popular as a result of a new interest in the 'national question' and were marketed as Germans from abroad (*Auslandsdeutsche*) rather than women writers.

The Decentred Subject

As the previous chapter shows, it was important for the politicised feminism of the 1970s to emphasise women's shared experience in the interests of female solidarity. In contrast, in the 1980s, 'femininity' came to be associated by some with all forms of resistance to the history of women's exclusion which underpins Western culture. From a position of marginality in this culture, femininity came to represent the urge to transgress all boundaries set up to perpetuate hierarchical, normative categories of existence. The acknowledgement of multiple, interpenetrating and colliding realities brought with it a shift of focus in literature from 'epistemological' to 'ontological' concerns, that is, from the text as representation of reality or expression of a subject's psyche to the text as the site on which difference is articulated.[4] Instead of being the originator of the text, the subject was generated by it, hence the focus of much of the discussion that follows will be on the diverse approaches of women writers to the construction of subjectivity. These range from the more traditional autobiographical narratives such as Maria Beig's anti-idylls of a Swabian rural childhood, *Rabenkrächzen* (1982); *Hochzeitlose, komm* (1983b); *Urgroßelternzeit* (1983c), to those texts which abandon linear narrative along with the notion of an integrated, continuous subject.

Many contemporary women writers represent the impulse to challenge the repression of the feminine in Western culture by affirming 'abject' forms of subjectivity. These are forms of subjectivity which might be deemed 'psychotic' because they lack the coherence and stability of identity normally associated with the speaking subject. The interest in that which the dominant patriarchal norm excludes is itself a critical moment of feminist analysis of that norm, and opens up alternative potential ways of understanding the self. This trend can be related to the revival of interest in 'pre-feminist' writers of the 1950s and 1960s whose representation of femininity failed to answer the need for positive role-models in the 1970s (Anne Duden's interest in Marlen Haushofer is a case in point[5]). There has been a similar revival of interest in the work of female surrealist writers and in surrealist aesthetics, with its questioning of the autonomy of the creative subject, and challenge to the primacy of consciousness in literary production.[6] The marginality or exclusion of the feminine has been represented variously in topographical metaphors of the self, notably in the large number of 'city' novels, which, unlike their modernist forerunners, suggest a fragmented rather than an alienated self.[7]

The feminisation of the city in European literature has been seen as paradigmatic for representations of the relations between the sexes in the cultural history of the West. From the domestication of the feminine in early allegorical personifications of the city to the sexualisation of urban space in the modernist 'city novel' (*Großstadtroman*) and beyond, the underlying structure of domination and subordination may be linked to the anxiety of male subjectivity which constitutes itself in opposition to the city as the place of the 'other'.[8] In the urban landscapes of much recent women's fiction there are attempts to appropriate and reappraise this tradition, whether in criticism of the city as an emblem of masculine culture, or in affirmation of the city's subject status and its 'otherness'. Gisela von Wysocki has applied the image of the city with its artificial neon lights to patriarchy itself, oblivious to the crumbling of its own foundations in the 'dialectic of progress' (Wysocki 1980a: 8–9).

Ulla Berkéwicz's *Michel, sag ich* (1984) depicts a 'winter of man-kind', associated with the evil influence of the city, which eventu-ally destroys itself in an apocalyptic catastrophe. The constant sun, heat, and noise are symptoms of the corruption of urban life, placed in simple juxtaposition to the wholesome rural values of the female protagonist's home village, which she leaves to search for her lover. A thunder storm is an early warning of nature's revenge for the city's ravaging of the land: 'The city, the city is breaking through, devastating the land, replacing summer with wintertime, transforming the world, by the force of the city alone' (Berkéwicz 1988: 43). Her search for Michel takes her to a subter-ranean world of opposition and dissent, and the novel ends with her Orpheus-like escape back across the Main, not daring to look at the infernal conflagration behind her. The novel's cultural cri-tique (with recognisable references to 1970s urban terrorism) sits rather uneasily with the unquestioning citation of Romantic folk-song topoi, archaisms, and the idealisation of a pre-industrial world.[9] However, there are parallels with Anne Duden's *Das Judasschaf* (1994) in Berkéwicz's representation of death, which remains present in the intact bodies of the city's victims, as a form of irrepressible, destabilising memory.

If the dichotomy of natural and urban world is somewhat schematic in Berkéwicz's novel, the depiction of the city in Libuše Moníková's *Eine Schädigung* (1981/1990) is more sinister in its brutalising, depersonalising effect on its inhabitants. The rape of the young woman protagonist by a policeman, whom she then kills in self-defence has been criticised as mere reversal of the victim-oppressor opposition.[10] However, the rape and mur-der occur at the start of the novel, and thus suggest not a solution to, but rather the logical outcome of the city's culture of violence and anonymity. Jana experiences her rape as an obliteration of self, which sharpens her awareness of the transformation of the city crowds into a faceless, undifferentiated mass. The violence begins with the assault on the buildings of pollution emanating from the streets, and is transmitted to the fearful pedestrians, dodging the traffic: 'Pedestrians walk awkwardly, nervously among the trams and the carriageway, from above she can see the danger ... The hostility rises from the paving stones with the traffic fumes right up to the highest windows in the ornate turn-of-the-century plasterwork. The façades with angels over the front doors ... are blackened with the daily devastation' (Moníková 1990: 27). The remainder of the novel is devoted to Jana's problem of finding a way to inhabit the city. The position of the feminine 'other' is epitomised by Mara, the friend who lives on a houseboat on the city's canals, constantly moving from one prohibition to the next, the spaces between them becoming ever narrower. Jana resists the mere reversal of existing power structures, rejecting courage as an alternative to fear, to the debilitating terror which besets her after her rape. She becomes acutely aware of the mechanisms by which women are marginalised and turned into victims, by fashion, hierarchical relationships, mythology, and by language itself, and her escape from the 'pressure of language' is found in back street cinemas and in 'secret places in the midst of the city' (103). By a process of reinstating her senses (notably those of taste and hearing), she achieves a protective, perceptual distance from the city, gaining particular comfort from the sound of incomprehensible languages from foreign radio stations at night, communication from beyond the boundaries of the city and its language: 'She searches for a woman's voice, for a language which reminds her of nothing, in which she will hear nothing but its soothing, calming sound' (101).

Karin Reschke's *Dieser Tage über Nacht* (1984), depicts a woman's desperate, helpless flight from relationships of sexual dependence on men, as she is pursued through the threatening, surreal streets of Berlin by the spectre of repetition in the form of the ubiquitous 'Albert': 'That was what I'd been afraid of. Him and me. Then him. Then him again, and in the end only him. And I the air he breathed. I didn't have the right words to shake him off once and for all. He raced alongside me and retained the upper hand' (Reschke 1984: 11–12). Like Jana in Moníková's novel, she feels an affinity with the waterways of the city, identifying with the fish and waterfowl. She also finds refuge with a series of women, Mathilde, Isolde, Lore, and Frieda, sometimes adopting their identities, occasionally betrayed by them. The fluidity of her identity is symbolised by her changing of clothes and shoes, the subordination of women in patriarchy encapsulated in the motif of stilettos on the asphalt. She eventually buys trainers, which represent at least the potential to escape from whichever new snare encloses her.

She begins to regard trappings of her femininity as a deliberate masquerade rather than an oppressive straitjacket: 'Show myself as I was? How *was* I, though? With a few strokes I painted myself a new face' (33). She repeatedly falls back into complicity with the patriarchal, capitalist manipulation of women, but retains her trainers to facilitate her next escape. The Berlin of Reschke's novel is represented in an allegory at the end of the book as a city governed by a régime of terror, where the mildest eccentricity counts as insanity and leads to incarceration or even death. It is policed by 'trappers' whose murderous activity is justified by the city itself: 'The city, all cities, in fact, virtually require that insanity and difference are hunted down' (89–90).

If all of these novels depict the city as a hostile environment in which the female subject must be constantly on the move in order to survive, Herta Müller's *Reisende auf einem Bein* (1989) goes further toward constructing the city as a feminine space. Irene comes to Berlin as an exile from the dictatorship in her own country and remains a perpetual visitor, a foreigner abroad, resisting all temptations to assimilate to her new environment. Coming from a German-speaking minority in Eastern Europe (Müller herself is Romanian), she is doubly alienated on arrival in Berlin to hear her 'mother tongue' being spoken by people who do not share her nationality. However, she begins to identify with the city in preference to national identity of any kind, a fact which is underlined in her estrangement from her German lover, Franz from Marburg. Irritated by his own sense of disorientation in the unfamiliar Berlin, he invokes the notion of 'fatherland': 'Since the city resisted his advances, he needed the state ... A state. And Franz, and at the centre of it all his ribcage' (Müller 1989: 124). Irene's scepticism about this ego-centric notion of national identity merely intensifies her identification with the city, confirmed in a letter from Franz after their separation, in which he quotes from Italo Calvino's *Le città invisibili* (1972, *Invisible Cities* 1979): 'Irene is the name of a distant city which changes as you approach her. She is one city if you pass by without entering her, another if you are possessed by her and cannot leave; she is one city when you enter her for the first time, another when you leave her, never to return' (Müller 1989: 94).

Even more pronounced than in Reschke's novel is Müller's use of clothing, and especially shoes, as metaphors for identity. Fashion both denies individuality and allows for a multiplicity of selves, and the sight of poor immigrants rummaging for pairs of matching shoes in a bargain basket represents their desperate struggle to regain an intact identity. Irene, who left her homeland 'in her stockinged feet', resists conformism to this 'logic of the same'. Like Moníková's Francine Pallas in *Pavane für eine verstorbene Infantin* (1983), who develops a physical limp in resistance to the pressure to adapt to her German environment, Irene settles for an asymmetrical, provisional self. Maria Kublitz-Kramer identifies the novel's main theme as the preservation of difference wherever it is suppressed. She sees this as a characteristic of femininity: 'If difference [*Fremdheit*] is an integral part of female identity, then it is extended in Herta Müller's text to an essential feature of all relationships between the sexes. Difference is inherent in all phenomena which purport to belong together' (Kublitz-Kramer 1993: 26).

'Writing the Body'

The concern with difference underlying eccentric modes of subjectivity has its roots in the formal experimentation which arose out of psychoanalytical theories in the 1970s and linked symbolic language to a masculine libidinal economy (Lacan, Kristeva, Irigaray, Cixous). New impulses from postmodern thinkers (Derrida, Foucault) prompted women writers to question not just individual linguistic structures, but also the underlying logic of discourse, and to explore modes of extra-symbolic signification. Foucault's influential theory of discursively codified power, and the body as the only irreducible site on which that power is registered, has had its impact on the 'corporeal' feminisms of the 1990s.[11] This can provide a productive framework for the interpretation of many German women's texts of the 1980s and 1990s, such as Jutta Heinrich's 'extreme Texte', *Alles ist Körper* (1991).[12]

Still known mainly for her feminist novel *Das Geschlecht der Gedanken* (1977), Heinrich's more recent writing is particularly interesting as the response of a materialist feminist to contemporary developments in feminist theory which challenge any simple 'constructivist' notions of gender. Although she resists the idea of language specific to women, in her 'extreme texts', she focuses on embodied sexuality as well as gendered socialisation.[13] So, for example, in the story 'Doppelbett' (1991), she condemns the damaging effects on the female body of the absence of symbolic constructions of female sexuality. In the distressed thoughts of a young woman waiting for her lover in the bedroom, sexual intercourse is presented as an invasion of her body, the 'murder' of her desire, and losing her virginity as 'the murder of my first life'. She reflects bitterly on the distortion of her sexuality by language, and defiantly on the recalcitrance of the body: 'In the beginning was the lie, then came the word. Silence, the only place free of untruth ... The skin treats language with surly contempt' (Heinrich 1991: 23).

'Die Stunde des Hahns' (1991) focuses on male sexuality, which is caricatured in the minute observation of pubescent male 'display' at the public swimming baths. The middle-aged female narrator looks on with mock-sympathy: 'Oh, how exhausting it must be to become a real man, and as such, the OTHER, and I wonder whether puberty actually means: conscription into phallic service' (36). In a comic reversal of cultural stereotypes, the female gaze objectifies and mystifies the male body as a 'magic dragon', capturing women irresistibly in its supernatural power. Adult masculinity appears almost a burden too great for young men to bear, putting them in deadly competition with each other and in a restless 'battle with the self'.

A more serious note is struck in 'Vermächtnis des Körpers' (1991), which captures the obsessive stream of consciousness of the anorexic/bulimic woman. The breathless lines and repetitive patterns of the narrative demonstrate her tormented resistance to imperatives to consume, whilst also showing that her physical self-hatred is the sign of inner pain: 'I only wake up in order to discover myself in my body again, nothing but the body, the scales, and the burden of my inner world' (11). Driven by a relentless logic, self-annihilation seems to her the only way to accede to identity: 'To be perfectly slim one must disappear. I won't be really me until I disappear completely' (17). This can be read both as a condemnation of the self-destructive nature of socially constructed femininity, and as a vision of emancipation from the tyranny of her imaginary feminine identity, represented here by the detested mirror image. This fictionalised account of anorexia clearly follows on from the documentary 'illness chronicles' of the 1970s, and may be compared with Ulrike Kolb's novel *Idas Idee* (1985), with its female protagonist who chooses extreme obesity as a means of liberation from the cultural constraints of femininity. Damage to the female body, self-inflicted or otherwise, can be read as a metaphor for feminine alterity in Libuše Moníková's *Eine Schädigung* (1981) and *Pavane für eine verstorbene Infantin* (1983), as also in Anne Duden's *Übergang* (1982, *Opening of the Mouth*, 1985a). This volume of short prose texts arranged around the autobiographical title story reflects Duden's interest in the psychological and symbolic construction of the subject, in contrast to Heinrich's more materialist and satirical approach. In Heinrich's story 'Zerstören, denkt sie' (1991) the insomniac fantasies of the female protagonist reveal a subject crippled by the enforced passivity of femininity and fragmented by the endless implosions of her 'bottled up energies'. Although she drugs herself with sleeping pills and alcohol, at night she is unable to ignore the turmoil raging within her: 'The bursting, shattering in a preserving jar ... bursting and reflected in a thousand inner mirrors of her own self, dismembered and splintering ... not developing or projecting outwards' (92). For the female narrator of Duden's 'Tag und Nacht' (1982, 'Day and Night' 1985b), in contrast, the night and sleep bring a liberating state of 'skull and skeltonlessness' in which the boundaries of the self become fluid, as do those between inside and outside, presence and absence, darkness and light. Waking puts a violent end to this state, in an enforced splitting and reimposition of boundaries, an eruption without transition. An uncomfortable awareness of her body accompanies the onslaught of consciousness and return to the spatio-temporal world, and survival of daily life requires a repeated effort of self-reconstruction.[14]

It is the transition between these two states (absent in 'Tag und Nacht') which is the theme of the title story 'Übergang', when the damaged female body becomes the site for the articulation of a radical female subjectivity.[15] The female protagonist's face is badly injured as she escapes from the scene of a fight in a Berlin bar, but the ensuing medical intervention to restore her mouth and jaw is depicted as a still worse act of violence. Once released from the constraints of language and her visual image, she regains access to the repressed chaos which guarantees the stability of individual identity and human culture. Instead of a frightening state of disorientation, however, this state of painful vulnerability brings with it an intense, somatic encounter with the world, and the reconciliation of the discrepancy between perception and expression:

The hole, the trap was to be stopped up, scarcely had it been ripped open. Yet in fact I could consider it fortunate that now, finally, my anatomy too had cracked, that my body could begin to catch up on what had until then been reserved only for my brainhead: following the limitless chaos of the world along all its secret pathways and everywhere where it made itself noticeable, to let it break into me then, and rage in me. Basically, I was relieved. (1985: 63)

If the protagonist's injured mouth and wired jaw represent the silencing of the feminine in patriarchal language, the significance of music as an alternative signifying system is that it allows the female subject to exist in a state of mobile, osmotic relation to the world. In *Das Judasschaf* the critique of the logocentric subject – that is, the stable subject founded on the real presence of meaning in language – is articulated in the protagonist's encounter with paintings. Duden's recent volume *Steinschlag* (1993) departs from the representation of a single subject altogether, whilst still revolving around the themes of embodied subjectivity, cultural identity, and history. It is more aptly designated as prose-poetry than prose, subordinating the referential, symbolic function of language to its rhythmic, associative patterns, in a convergence of content and form.

Reinstating the Subject

Whilst many of these texts construct radical models of decentred subjectivity, even of states of 'dereliction' (Irigaray 1985), others are concerned to establish a *viable* position for the female subject in a cultural order which can be co-habited with men.[16] Brigitte Kronauer first attracted widespread critical attention with her novels of the 1980s, *Frau Mühlenbeck im Gehäus* (1980), *Rita Münster* (1983) and *Berittener Bogenschütze* (1986), but has found mixed reception among feminist critics. The self-conscious artistry of her narratives, the defamiliarising focus on the minutiae of everyday experience, and renunciation of interpretative intervention (all reminiscent of the French *nouveau roman*) clearly struck a chord with an enthusiastic readership in the 1980s, as Regula Venske notes: 'In the trivial, the whole world comes to light, so to speak … This seemed to hit the nerve of the 1980s, indeed, to expose it, as seen in the effusive tributes of the literary critics' (Venske 1991: 130). One reviewer of her latest novel *Das Taschentuch* (1994) was irritated by 'an excess of uneventfulness, of elaborately contrived chat, of familiar flirtation with the reader' (Höbel 1994: 36). Some of her most vehement criticism, however, has come from women who object to her representation of femininity, whether because it panders to popular clichés or is too uncompromisingly critical. She has also been accused of stylising, even idealising masculinity, and exemplifying a 'masculinisation' of women's narrative style.[17]

Implicit in much feminist criticism of Kronauer seems to be an assumption that radical women's writing is incompatible with the category 'subject', which is irretrievably linked to a patriarchal system of dominance and exclusion. This is arguably an unnecessary narrowing of the criteria used to evaluate women's writing, and there may be a place for writing which is critical of traditional gendered definitions of subjectivity without abandoning the notion of the subject altogether. Kronauer's protagonists resemble force-fields rather than stable identities, all of whom experience some sort of 'epiphany' which projects them beyond the banal repetition of their everyday lives, whether this is through an aesthetic relationship with the world (*Rita Münster* 1983), or in a productive, enabling relationship with language (*Frau Mühlenbeck im Gehäus* 1980).

The role of language in constructing the world is construed by Kronauer in positive terms: 'We have to … give shape to the outside world, order it according to our needs and furnish it with meanings – fictional narratives provide the model for this' (Kronauer 1993: 121–122). Above all, this process is crucial for the consolidation of a viable subject: 'The "I" consolidates itself by attaching itself to ready-made categories, patterns, models of world-interpretation, if not it will disintegrate' (123). Far from offering such pre-formed explanatory models in her own narratives, however, she merely demonstrates the (often quite eccentric, individualistic) ways in which people adopt and adapt the interpretative structures available to them:

> The central character describes a circle around her/himself, erects a construct of individual or adapted connections and inferences, whether gradually or suddenly, plausibly or in obvious error. S/he inserts what happens to her/him into a framework which is meaningful for her/him, however arbitrary. And the world appears to yield to this effort, at least in the consciousness of the 'I', and this is no small achievement! (122)

The 'shelter' (*Gehäus*) of Kronauer's Frau Mühlenbeck (1980) is an excellent example of this. In a complex four-stranded narrative the lives of two women of different generations are juxtaposed: Frau Mühlenbeck, a housewife in her sixties, and a young teacher of about thirty. So understated is the relationship between them that the reader is left to reconstruct the objective circumstances of their encounter and to draw conclusions from the parallels in the two women's experience and the contrasting manner of their narration. Frau Mühlenbeck narrates her own life story, her frustrated youthful ambitions, marriage, motherhood, stoical survival through the Second World War, then renunciation of her unaccustomed autonomy on her husband's return from the war, to allow him to resume his traditional role. Viewed through the eyes of the teacher, her days are dominated by the senseless repetition of domestic tasks, but in her own narrative, her life assumes the contours of a meaningful and purposeful existence.

In contrast, the disjointed narrative of the young teacher's life hardly depicts a viable subject at all, despite her youth, career, and financial independence. She is unable to formulate her experience into a coherent biography, and is clearly struggling to cope with a crisis in both her private and professional life. One could read the contrast between the two women as a demonstration of the potential hazards inherent in theories of the subject which threaten its integrity. Whilst the teacher remains a diffuse figure, apparently immobilised by the bewildering onslaught of her perceptions, Frau Mühlenbeck constructs a narrative which makes sense of the mundane repetitiveness of her daily chores in iterative patterns of 'always', 'never', and 'everytime'. She emerges as an assertive individual with indefatigable optimism, able to confront authority in the form of neighbours, employers, and institutions, whilst the teacher (in a position of *real* authority) can have her confidence undermined by an insolent schoolgirl. Indeed, this novel offers a challenge to precisely the sort of feminist reading which looks for positive role models, presenting one here in the most unlikely of figures. The reader is precariously positioned between identification with and distance from the two principal characters.

Frau Mühlenbeck might well be subjected to a feminist critique, as a woman who is complicit in her own oppression to the point of wilful self-deception. Furthermore she is incapable of female solidarity, and bases much of her self-esteem on the respect of men. Magdalene Heuser has drawn attention to the ambiguity of both women figures in the novel: 'The housewife's chores and everyday reality become the object of literature, in all their excessive detail; they are taken seriously whilst also being viewed with a critical eye. On the other hand there is the younger woman, the I-narrator, trying to lead her life in the areas of love, work and leisure in such a way that she emerges as a person as well'.[18] The teacher becomes increasingly indignant at Frau Mühlenbeck's voluntary blindness to the futility of her tasks, such as the washing-up ritual (156–161), whilst also detecting moments of barely suppressed anger which temporarily disrupt the 'stubborn inevitability of repetition' (Kronauer 1991: 161).

In Frau Mühlenbeck's narrative, 'distance', 'borders' and 'connections' are crucial concepts, but these are precisely the qualities which are lacking in the teacher's private and professional life. With her pupils, for example, she is unable to distance herself adequately from them to fulfil her pedagogical duty to them. If read as a metaphor for the subject-object relationship, that between the teacher and her pupils illustrates amply the dislocation of social interaction where the boundaries between the two are not clearly defined. She is aware of failing to treat the pupils as subjects in their own right, because her empathy with them is too strong and her own sense of self too fluid.

Gradually, however, Frau Mühlenbeck's narrative style begins to influence that of the younger woman, who becomes increasingly coherent, even taking pleasure in tying together the various strands of the narrative in the final chapter. She returns repeatedly to three phrases, which both formulate her dilemma and seem to offer a way out of it: 'I can't go on', 'There's no going back', and 'The only way on is forward'. At the end of the novel, the narrative structure itself has provided her with a stable framework for her life: 'I won't deviate from it, it's something to hold onto, a painstaking investment, it gives me a beginning, or at least, an end' (236). If the end of the novel perhaps fails to convince, implying that practical, social agency can be effected by means of a textual strategy alone, the depiction of Frau Mühlenbeck remains a narrative tour de force. It illustrates Kronauer's concern to affirm a positive position for the female subject, whilst also demonstrating the inadequacy of existing social definitions of femininity. Her positive conception of language, as an enabling structure of subjectivity, rather than a 'castrating' force, is also in line with a distinct trend in feminist thinking which emphasises the strategic necessity of positive female subjecthood.

The Historical Subject

Even for those writers who depict a fragmented feminine subject, this subject is neither unequivocally a victim, nor does it lack an historical perspective. Indeed, the necessity to confront in particular the National Socialist past is as evident in recent women's writing as anywhere in post-war German literature. This is seen in

the relatively conventional search for the father in Sibylle Plogstedt's *Niemandstochter* (1991), or in Eva Demski's thriller *Hotel
Hölle, guten Tag* (1987), in which a Jewish woman takes revenge on
an old Nazi for the murder of her father. Grete Weil combines a
Jewish perspective with a cultural critique in *Meine Schwester
Antigone* (1980), in which the female survivor of the holocaust
rejects Antigone's model of martyrdom. In *Generationen* (1983),
Weil explores the problems of a community of women of different
generations in living together, their struggles for sympathy and
affection foundering on the historical specificity of their experience. A more ambivalent relationship to Jewish identity is seen in
Barbara Honigmann's *Roman von einem Kinde* (1986), whilst the
Jewish/German, victim/oppressor dichotomy is suspended altogether in Anne Duden's *Übergang* (1982, *Opening of the Mouth*,
1985a) and *Das Judasschaf* (1994). Other writers illuminate the past
from uncomfortable or unexpected angles: Karin Reschke's *Mem-
oiren eines Kindes* (1980) and Margaret Hannsmann's *Der helle Tag
bricht an. Ein Kind wird Nazi* (1982) both present a child's view of
National Socialism. Ulla Berkéwicz has received mixed critical
response for her provocative *Engel sind schwarz und weiß* (1992),
with its vivid evocation of the 'seduction' of the German nation
and lack of moralising commentary.

Two common concerns of much recent women's historical writing are with the departure from the 'history of the victors' and
from the notion of history as a linear, progressive phenomenon.
These are often found in texts in which works of art play an
important role. Whether they signal an historical narrative or act
as the repository of a collective unconscious, they can provide a
link with the past for those who are absent from the written histories of the dominant culture. A useful conceptual framework
within which to look at such texts is that of the 'dialectical image'
in Walter Benjamin's 'Theses on the Philosophy of History'. For
Benjamin, an historical consciousness is not a case of factual
knowledge, but rather an ability to recognise where the present
'quotes' images from the past, reopening the potential for change
(realised or not) in historical events, and infusing them with present significance: 'To articulate the past historically does not mean
to recognise it "the way it really was" … It means to seize hold of
a memory as it flashes up at a moment of danger' (Benjamin 1973:
257). Sigrid Weigel has demonstrated the potential of Benjamin's
ideas in exploring the usefulness of painting and myth for opening up 'alternative' histories.[19]

One of the first historical novels of the 1980s to break with the pathos of 'New Subjectivity' (*neue Subjektivität*) – writing which concentrates on internalised subjective experience – and explore new ways of confronting the past was Birgit Pausch's *Bildnis der Jakobina Völker* (1980). This novel is the story of a female victim of the *Berufsverbot* policy of the 1970s which sought to exclude radical political elements from the public services in the Federal Republic. Yet the text has perspectives that reach back to the early nineteenth century and to the Italian Renaissance through works of art incorporated into the narrative. These are 'dialectical images' in as much as they take on an immediate and urgent significance in the life of the protagonist, and play a role in encouraging her resistance to the stultifying political conformism of her time. The name Jakobina Völker itself, with its populist, revolutionary connotations, derives from a sixteenth-century portrait of a young girl (*not* actually featured in the text), whose wooden pose and earnest expression belies her evident youth. Like her modern namesake, she is a victim of a suffocating cultural pressure to conform.[20]

Having lost her job in a state school due to her political radicalism, Jakobina teaches in a private boarding school and is invited to give a talk on the history of the school's benefactors as part of its bicentennial celebrations. Instead of a story of benevolent philanthropy, as anticipated by the headmaster, her research in the school archives reveals a grim saga of the brutal suppression of an uprising of migrant textile workers on the van Löring estate. Between the lines of the 'heroic deeds and silent lies of the van Löring family' in the official family chronicles, she sees the roots of the economic exploitation and social alienation which she is combatting in her own time (Pausch 1985: 11–12). Although well aware of the precariousness of her situation at the school, which is always looking for grounds to dismiss her, when standing in the school hall beneath the large fresco depicting a revolutionary scene, she is unable to resist telling the story as she sees it, and loses her job as a consequence.

Inspired by an 1849 woodcut by Alfred Rethel entitled 'Auch ein Totentanz', which was a working title for Pausch's novel, this fresco depicts a bloody scene from the 1848 revolution. Although she is aware of the anti-revolutionary sympathies of the artist, for Jakobina the fresco revives the moment in which the status quo was threatened and change possible. She later explains the power of Rethel's graphic political metaphors to a group of decadent, complacent, young art-lovers: 'And tell me … is it not the same again today, might there not be a knock at the door any minute announcing the grim reaper's return?' (77).

In this novel the paintings function precisely as described by Benjamin, reopening history for those who have been excluded from it and who feel the urgent need for change: 'In every era the attempt must be made anew to wrest tradition away from a conformism that is about to overpower it … Only that historian will have the gift of fanning the spark of hope in the past who is firmly convinced that *even the dead* will not be safe from the enemy if he wins' (Benjamin 1973: 257). Jakobina Völker is one such writer of history whose loss of her teaching post leads her into an exploration of her own family history: her Nazi mother's flight to the West after the war, the inexplicable taboos of childhood, the failure of 1968, and estrangement from her lover, Richard, whose political disillusionment is channelled into resignation and a devotion to his career which merely reproduces the pattern of his father's life. Yet it is Richard's father who articulates the view of history to which Jakobina clings. When explaining to his young son the concept of history, he had used the statue of a mounted hero, viewed from the position of the slave, cowering under the horse's hooves: '"That's history", he explained to his son who was peering through from the other side underneath the horse, "we're the ones lying or standing below and looking on, the others are the ones sitting up on top"' (Pausch 1985: 87). Klaus Briegleb has described Jakobina's struggle as the attempt to salvage the story of the defeated in Germany's history of counter-revolution, oppression and submission to authority (1992: 139).

It is notably *not* in the art of the contemporary avant garde (represented by Steller, the caricature of a Joseph Beuys figure), but in the dialectical images of previous ages that Jakobina finds hope for the future, first in the social content of nineteenth-century woodcuts and etchings, then in sixteenth-century Venetian art, encountered in Venice at the end of the novel. Here, she is transfixed by the art of the Italian Renaissance, 'when a new world was created in paintings, lending new forms to old dreams' (Pausch 1985: 110). Pausch focuses in particular on Tintoretto's depiction of the rescue of the body of St Mark in the Venice Academia, a work which is also prominent in Anne Duden's *Das Judasschaf* and which offers an illuminating point of comparison between the two writers. In both novels the painting is evoked when the protagonist is in St

Mark's Square and the boundaries between reality and representation become blurred. As Jakobina contemplates the storm-ravaged scene and the body of the saint being carried by disciples away from the waiting funeral pyre, she is struck by the redemptive aspect of the scene: 'Weren't we all secretly susceptible to the vision of being swept away from the years of torment as if by some miracle or of being dragged back from the edge of despair by helping hands' (106).

For the most part, Pausch's novel reaffirms a humanist, universal, aesthetic view of art as the repository of truth, in contrast to Duden's more complex relation to the cultural heritage of the Renaissance. In place of Pausch's nostalgia for lost revolutionary causes and the hope for deliverance from institutional brutality and legitimate violence, Duden's protagonists inhabit a reality where war and violence is the norm, peace always just a temporary respite, and the repression of this knowledge part of the conspiracy of exclusion which perpetuates the status quo.

The itinerant female subject of *Das Judasschaf*, who is variously 'I', 'she', and 'the person', encounters five works of Renaissance art in her travels through Berlin, Venice and New York. If Jakobina Völker sees in art a way to combat the forgetfulness and conformism of contemporary German life, the evocation of German history in Anne Duden's writing encompasses a much broader cultural critique. Rather than alienated subjects in a hostile social environment, Duden's protagonists might be termed what Rosi Braidotti calls 'nomadic subjects', whose resistance to 'settling into socially coded modes of thought and behaviour' extends to the renunciation of metaphysical, fixed identity (Braidotti 1994: 5). Duden's critique includes not only the 'secondary repression' of the holocaust, but also the 'primary repression' which brings the stable subject into being. Thus the memories evoked by paintings in *Das Judasschaf* are not those of an individual 'I', but 'structures of *cultural* memory, the *traces* of which are to be seen on the female body and in the paintings'.[21] Thus the significance of the Tintoretto in her novel lies in the irreducible physical presence of death in the saint's body, representing figuratively a knowledge which is repressed in the rational logic of language. Similarly the camel depicted behind the group of men in the foreground represents all that exceeds the abstract rationality of human culture (Duden 1994: 23). Paintings not only open up alternative narratives in this text, they contain knowledge which cannot be articulated in any other way.

The Relationship of Women's Writing to the Literary Tradition

> There are just as many voyages of discovery to be made in the history of women as there are on the wide, green-brown surface of the Earth. (Steinwachs 1992: 154)

A crucial aspect of women's relationship to history remains their absence from it. The 1980s saw no reduction in the fascination with women's literary history and the urge to give voice to female victims of male criticism. This enterprise ranges from the realm of academic research[22] to imaginative reconstructions of the obscure lives of women on the margins of German male literary history.[23] Ria Endres, whose doctoral thesis on Thomas Bernhard was a feminist critique of patriarchal aesthetics, is concerned in her novel *Milena antwortet. Ein Brief* (1982) to give voice to one of literary history's silenced women, known mainly for her correspondence with Franz Kafka.[24] Like Libuše Moníková, Endres is fascinated with Milena Jesenská's (1896–1940) life and work. This interest encompasses her radical political journalism, her Communist activism, her humanitarian commitment to the plight of German and Jewish exiles from Nazi Germany in Eastern Europe, and her own arrest and death in Ravensbruck concentration camp, where she was ostracised by other Communist women prisoners for her outspoken condemnation of Stalinist terror.[25]

Endres does not set out to construct a coherent biography – much of the sparse detail known of Jesenská's life is incorporated in the fragmentary reminiscences of her imaginary letter, addressed to Kafka after his death. In keeping with Endres's view of human beings as 'subjects which are constantly beginning again and never come to an end' (Endres 1989: 105), Jesenská is depicted on a train journey to Vienna, beginning and ending in Prague. The protagonist is both 'I' and 'Milena' and the addressee either 'you' or 'Franz Kafka'. The fluctuating narrative voice suggests that she is no longer the 'Milena' who translated Kafka's early work into Czech and corresponded with him in the early 1920s. The letter, like the journey, is used as a way of distancing herself from Kafka, 'each letter written during the train journey as a solid little distance' (Endres 1982: 23). Using images such as that of his hand on her hair, it tells of her pain and resentment at the way in which he had diverted his love away from her person and into his writing: 'You traced my parting, as if out of curiosity, a straight line through my landscape. But from your hand it is not far to your handwriting and to your letters which lie open before me' (27). Their love was always subordinated to his work and subject to the barriers he erected via language (28).

Her own desire, in contrast, overflowed not only the boundaries he imposed, but also those of language: 'There were always reasons for not being close. You had to exert all your energy against the desire on the paper, which was my desire, bursting out over the edges of the paper' (31). All the time he had 'directed' their intimacy from behind his writing desk in what she describes as 'a present absence' (32), his writing functioning as a voluntary banishment from life. Yet he had revealed to her 'the heart and soul of words … their meandering, their cruelty and clarity, their contradictions and the unexpected flashes of fire in them' (59).

However, it is her sensitivity to language and its corruption by National Socialism which informs the novel's devastating critique of the structures of authority and oppression persisting in German culture: 'The German language is foreign and boiled dry. Again and again the guard and controller-mentality comes to the surface. I won't be deceived by it again as I once was' (59). In a relentless litany on the verbs 'to execute' (*hinrichten*) and 'to keep back' (*zurückbleiben*) (59–61) she demonstrates how the language has lost its innocence and where the structures of inhumane, bureaucratic power are alive in the German language today. With her experience of helping the victims of Nazi persecution and becoming one herself, she is all the more contemptuous of Kafka's use of language to immortalise himself in the future by protecting himself from the dynamic, dangerous engagement with life: 'You wrongly spared your own life, when our love was at stake. You avoided that movement by which we are emotionally moved. A cursed stability; your dangerous retreat and your dangerously calm equilibrium' (120).

If Endres presents Jesenská as a 'subject in process' (Kristeva), then a similar notion is suggested by the title of Ginka Steinwachs' play *George Sand. Eine Frau in Bewegung. Die Frau von Stand* (1980).[26] In fact, Steinwachs is much more radical in her theoretical utterances on the 'schizophrenic' nature of the subject, saying of her character George Sand: 'She is split between the woman who once belonged to her husband, but who she no longer is, and the woman writer, who she is yet to become, between a "no longer" and a "not yet"' (Steinwachs 1989: 113). Like Endres, her interest is not in reconstructing George Sand's life 'as it was', but rather in envisaging 'borderline states' (*Grenzzustände*) which might have arisen out of Sand's defiance of convention, and in blurring the boundaries between fantasy and history, past and present: 'George Sand ... protests against any socially determined norm, just as I have always protested against any form of norm or exclusion. In this sense my theatre is an attempt to transgress the threshold separating dream and waking, madness and sanity, i.e., to protest against all forms of exclusion' (Roeder 1989: 115). The play is an attempt to understand George Sand better than she could have understood herself, by incorporating into the historical figure the needs, desires, and insights of modern women. Thus early in the play she is depicted straddling an abyss, her right leg in her aristocratic marriage to Baron Dudevant, her left in Paris with her lover. She is suspended between 'THE INSTITUTION OF MAR-RIAGE (MARRI-ARCHY) BY EXTENSION THE CHURCH, MIL-ITARY AND FATHERLAND' and 'SO-CALLED FREE LOVE (AMOUR-ARCHY) BY EXTENSION ANARCHY, DEBAUCHERY AND EXCESS. RIGHT LEG: TRADITION IN THE SENSE OF HOW IT HAS ALWAYS BEEN. LEFT LEG: UTOPIA IN THE SENSE OF NOWHERE AND NEVER. RIGHT: YESTERDAY'S ETERNAL FEMININE OF THE SELFSAME SEX. LEFT: THE NOVELTY OF HAIR-RAISING DARING' (Steinwachs 1992c: 31, use of upper and lower case as in original in this and all subsequent quotations). This signals early in the play the poles of desire and disappointment, of aspiration and frustration between which the heroine of the title moves.

Whilst she sees the uncovering of women's suppressed creativity in history as an important voyage of discovery, she is also concerned to liberate the theatre from its traditional role of edification, according it rather 'the task of ecstasy', to compensate for the failure of the Enlightenment to satisfy the human need for happiness (Nowoselsky-Müller 1989: 17). To turn the theatre into this sensuous experience, she seeks to release language from its denotational function, liberating its musical qualities, its 'musical excess'. She also describes *George Sand* as a good example of her 'oral theatre', privileging the sense of taste over the sense of sight: 'For me it is the mouth and not the eye which is *the* organ through which we experience the world. The mouth is a site of transformation, as in alchemy' (32).

The result is not a play in any traditional sense. The stage directions are separate chapters in their own right, and entirely capitalised, in contrast to the unorthodox mixture of upper and lower case in the main dialogue. The effect of this is to make the stage directions more suggestive of an imaginary space than descriptive of any real theatre. Similarly, directorial comments appear unexpectedly in the dialogue, underlining the self-conscious artifice of the action, as in Balzac's lines: 'Prolopussies come jumping from the circle. MES ENFANTS DU PARADIS' (Steinwachs 1992c: 63). There is no attempt at naturalistic characterisation, indeed, in the divorce court the presiding officials are donkeys and the proceedings accompanied by a rhinoceros orchestra, with catfish as drum-majorettes. Elsewhere the press barons and newspaper proprietors are portrayed as crocodiles. It is perhaps hardly surprising that the play was first staged eight years after its publication (not until 1988), although Steinwachs toured with it as a one-woman show, played in miniature on a small mouth-shaped stage. The first of a projected trilogy of plays, *George Sand* was intended to challenge in particular the unity of place, whereas *Erzherzog Herzherzog* (1985) has at its centre an androgynous figure with multiple personalities. The Gertrude Stein project (working title: 'Sappho in Palma') is to challenge the linearity of time, creating a 'futory of histure' (Nowoselsky-Müller 1989: 34).

George Sand is depicted as a woman of insatiable desire, larger than life and hungry for experience, an *Explora-Terra-ristin*, a piratical, marauding figure: 'It is a fundamentally terrorist act for someone of the female persuasion to dare as much as George Sand did and to want to indulge her greed for life in the middle of the nineteenth century, with its belief in progress, but its aversion to the satisfaction of human needs' (Steinwachs in Nowoselsky-Müller 1989: 32). She is seen in the play leaving her aristocratic estate for an impoverished bohemian existence as a writer in a Paris garret; travelling to Venice with her lover Alfred de Musset, dressed as a man; caring for the consumptive Frederic Chopin in the inhospitable Mallorcan winter; defending herself in court against the unfair divorce settlement with the Baron Dudevant, and taking a leading role in the political ferment of 1848 as 'FOSTER-MOTHER OF THE REVOLUTION'. In the filmic interlude which follows the revolutionary scene, the utopian social order is one of hedonistic, sensuous self-interest as well as social justice: 'HUMAN BEINGS ARE PLEASURE MACHINES/ALWAYS AFTER ENJOYMENT/ORAL GREED/SHEER LUST/BEASTS' (Steinwachs 1992c: 138). History fails to deliver satisfaction, however, appearing personified as a young virgin with flowing hair and a zigzag gait, going one step forward and two steps back. Yet, just as the first part of the play ends with the words: 'ART SETS THE COURSE', so the prophetic, utopian dimension of art is evoked again near the end: 'MESDAMES MESSIEURS, THE END OF THE PERFORMANCE WEIGHS HEAVILY BECAUSE WHAT IS ALREADY POSSIBLE ON STAGE IS NOT YET REALITY IN THE WORLD. THEATRE CAN FLY: FOLLOW ON, FOLLOW ON, FOLLOW ON' (127).

During the farcical divorce proceedings, counsel for Dudevant articulates the real nature of society's rage against George Sand: 'WOMEN IN TAILCOATS CHASING AFTER THE MUSE, WOMEN WHO BOLDLY FLAUNT THEIR ARTISTIC AMBITION are and remain … repulsive to us. long live the PHALLUS. three cheers for the PHALLUS. down with the mannish women'. She responds in her own defence: 'THE MEASURE OF A WOMAN'S FREEDOM IS THE MEASURE OF A SOCIETY'S FREEDOM. it's all over with the MYTH OF VAGINAL ORGASM, and with the dominant male idea of the cunt' (Steinwachs 1992c: 118).

George Sand certainly appears here as a 'premature feminist', but she is also a hermaphrodite figure, the site of a continuous dialogue between the sexes, which is presented in the play as the prerequisite for artistic creativity. In a scene in which French literature features as an express train pulling into the foyer of the Paris Opera, Flaubert announces to Balzac: 'THE ARTIST MUST HAVE BOTH SEXES'. Steinwachs considers one of her positive messages to be the future emergence of a third sex, 'a neuter', which will banish the antagonism between the sexes once and for all.

There is clearly much more to Steinwachs' play than her interest in women's suppressed creativity. She also calls into question the very notion of the modernist 'aura' of the artist as producer, the idea of the creative genius whose appropriation of tradition always invests it with a unique, innovative touch. The complex relationship of contemporary women writers to a tradition which has excluded them is compounded by postmodern questioning of the traditional criteria of aesthetic value (notions of innovation, authority, universal and timeless significance). For Steinwachs this is also related to her fascination with surrealism, and its notion of art as 'discovery' rather than invention.[27] Thus Steinwachs uses collage, montage, mimicry, and citation in ways which dismantle altogether notions of originality and historical authenticity. She uses the term 'original copyist' to designate her own status as a writer, and has George Sand flout the taboo of creative originality in calling her work, 'TRANSCRIPTS OF SCRIPTS' (1992: 53). Similarly, the novel *G-L-Ü-C-K* (1992a), with its generic designation 'original fake', demonstrates in a self-conscious gesture the construction of romance in literary discourse.[28]

In spite of the greatly increased access of women even to the institution of the theatre in the 1980s, they are still debarred from certain modes of literary production due to outdated notions of female sexual passivity, as seen in the lack of critical recognition of a writer of female erotica such as Elisabeth Alexander. A relative outsider on the literary scene (publishing mainly in underground journals and editions), her controversial novels treating female sexuality include *Die törichte Jungfrau* (1978), whose naive sexual heroine, Josephine Bähr, offers a positive alternative to the female pornographic heroine, *Sie hätte ihre Kinder töten sollen* (1982), an outspoken attack on the marginalisation of women as mothers, and *Bauchschuß* (1992), the articulation of an older woman's revenge fantasies. Critical censure of women's writing on sex was also seen recently in the shocked reception of Ulla Hahn's first novel (dealing with a man's sexual humiliation) *Ein Mann im Haus* (1991).[29]

Women's art and women *as* artists and writers are in themselves perennial themes, but often ones treated with an ironic or satirical tone which suggests that the artistic persona can be read as a metaphor for the social construction of femininity itself. Thus Gerlind Reinshagen's play *Die Clownin* (1985) depicts an actress's disillusionment with the roles written for her by men and her decision to seek artistic autonomy in the circus ring instead. In Angelika Mechtel's novel *Gott und die Liedermacherin* (1983) the singer-songwriter protagonist turns into a sort of modern Scheherazade, re-casting the mythological and biblical tradition in the interests of arresting man's self-destructive urge.[30]

The problematic relationship of women to their literary heritage is seen also in the very different responses of poets such as Ulla Hahn and Anna Jonas to the lyric tradition of Goethe and the Romantic folksong. Whilst some critics have derided Hahn's 'derivative classicism', Jonas seems to represent a radical break with the hermetic tradition of poetry, along with all notions of originality and artistic truth.[31] Ulla Hahn is something of a publishing phenomenon, her success initially due largely to the enthusiastic reception of her poems in the pages of the Frankfurt daily paper the *Frankfurter Allgemeine Zeitung (FAZ)*, and to the unqualified praise of Marcel Reich-Ranicki.[32] This began with the appearance in the *FAZ* in August 1979 of 'Anständiges Sonnett', which exemplifies precisely those qualities praised by her admirers: the use of traditional verse forms, whilst referring to contemporary reality and the characteristically punning title (it combines strictly observed metrical sonnet form with erotic subject matter). In addition, the formal control, emotional sensitivity, and avoidance of political subject matter no doubt corresponded to the gendered expectations of a conservative critical establishment.

Hahn's first three anthologies *Herz über Kopf* (1981), *Spielende* (1983) and *Freudenfeuer* (1985), whilst enjoying a popular success, were increasingly criticised for their apparently unquestioning appropriation of literary tradition (love lyrics in closed, harmonious forms, the use of nature imagery, assonance and rhyme, and the explicit, un-ironic references to the poets of romanticism and courtly love).[33] There is little evidence of awareness of the modernist crisis of the lyric subject, the caesura of the Holocaust and much else which has raised problems for late-twentieth century poets. A programmatic poem in *Herz über Kopf*, 'ars poetica', offers a resolute response to this criticism: 'Thank you but I need no new/ forms, I stand on/ firm verse feet and old/ norms give rhymes aplenty'. It ends with a defiant Heine quotation, 'and that is what the Loreley has done with her singing' (Hahn 1981: 79). The ironically titled 'Gibt es eine weibliche Ästhetik' (26) is concerned rather with the blindness of a woman in love to her (male) lover's flaws than with questions of female artistic production.

Love and the loss of love are the central themes, especially of Hahn's fourth anthology *Unerhörte Nähe* (1988), the title of which encapsulates both longing and inevitable disappointment (*unerhört* meaning both 'incredible' and 'unrequited'). However, there is also a response to her critics in this volume, where she mentions models such as Nietzsche, T.S. Eliot, and Mallarmé, and insists that the poetic conventions of past ages serve her merely as a source of productive resistance.[34] Many of the love poems in this volume, such as 'Irrtum' (7), 'Vorfreude' (9), and 'Nie mehr' (12) rely on quite simple devices of ambiguity and reversal to suggest the delicate balance between modern cynicism and rediscovered hope. Desire is ever present, but not generally problematic, even where there are echoes of C. F. Meyer's poem 'Lethe' in 'Ein Netz' (28) in a muted archaism and the motif of the shared goblet of love, the poem lacks any of Meyer's dark despair.

The response to the poetic legacy of past ages offers a useful point of comparison between Ulla Hahn and the relatively little-known poet Anna Jonas. Jonas' writing is much more clearly politically motivated, radically rejecting the hermetic tradition of poetry which accords a separate status to life and art. Her relationship to the literary tradition is best characterised as pastiche, as in the self-ironising parody of the mediaeval courtly love poet Walther von der Vogelweide in her first anthology *Nichts mehr an seinem Platz* (1981), 'Im Wasser gefallen' (61). The poem from which this volume takes its name, 'Meine Insel' (11–12) is a mocking comment on the transcendent solitude of the lyric subject (who appears as the captain of a leaking submarine). It evokes the devastation of a poetic landscape, ending on an unexpectedly positive note, this disfiguration affording a new clarity of vision: 'As night falls/ the moon melts/ the trees fall/ to the ground/ and the clouds turn/ into greenish streaks/ as the wind comes up/ I can see more clearly/ because nothing is in its place any more' (Jonas 1981: 12).

Romantic 'Inwardness' (*Innerlichkeit*) and the use of nature as the mirror of the poet's soul are exposed as meaningless for the modern self who ascertains, 'my soul is/a gap between heart/ lungs and stomach' (65). The discrepancies between language and meaning, conceptual thought and experience, are central themes, for example in poems which explore the inadequacies of structures of binary opposition, such as 'for' and 'against' in 'Ich für mich' (19), and 'true' and 'false' in 'Wiegenlied für meine Mutter' (95). Her poetry constantly raises questions of authorship and of the arbitrary nature of signification. Jonas' response to Goethe's *Über allen Gipfeln* (Over All the Hill-Tops) in 'Subkultur' can usefully be contrasted with Hahn's 'Spürest du' as an index of their degree of questioning distance from the lyric tradition he represents. The content of 'Spürest du' appears to negate the very mood of evening peace and tranquility of Goethe's poem with its evocation of disturbance in nature: 'the wind shrieks in the tree tops/ splaying their crowns no nesting place/no resting place no peace' (Hahn 1988: 72). In its brief, five-line lyric form, however, it draws much of its effect from association with Goethe's poem, also using euphony, assonance and onomatopoeia. Jonas's 'Subkultur', in contrast, opens with an interrogation of Goethe's poem: 'If peace is over all the hill-tops/that says nothing about the undergrowth' (Jonas 1981: 21). The poem, which makes no attempt to mimic the short lyric form, raises questions of difference and positionality which make all such universalising utterances problematic, indeed, suspect, for the way in which they condition our perceptions and patterns of thought. Whilst Hahn would probably agree with Jonas's statement that 'any questioning of forms can make new forms possible', there seems little doubt that Jonas conducts a more radical confrontation with past poetic forms than does Hahn (Jonas 1985: 44).

Anna Jonas's prose debut, *Das Frettchen* (1985a), is an unconventional 'autobiography' which defies all notions of linear development of either time or the subject. Developing a spatial notion of time already present in her poetry ('Sie können' in Jonas 1981: 37), the novel opens with a statement of the cultural specificity of concepts of time and self: 'The Aymara [an Amerindian people] say: I can see my past, it lies before me. I cannot see my future, it must lie behind me. Whether my past lies before me or behind me, I now realise, depends on where I grow up' (1981: 6).

The historical specificity of knowledge and perception is also a concern of the more recent poetry of Karin Kiwus. Whilst not explicitly feminist or political in her poetological statements, her poetry of the 1970s (the volumes *Von beiden Seiten der Gegenwart* [1976] and *Angenommen später* [1979]) reflected an acute gender awareness ('Entfremdende Arbeit', 'Hommes à femme') and the disillusionment of a whole generation with New Left politics ('Darum').[35] Many of the poems in her recent anthology *Das chinesische Examen* (1992) take paintings or film/photographic technologies as the basis of philosophical reflections on time and memory. So, for example, 'Anfang, Abbild, Retrospektive' juxtaposes the timescales of inner memory, photography, and artistic representation, and explores the grey areas where they overlap: 'Two images approach each other, one/from outside, the other from within:/the photograph in my hand and the memory in my body. How/will they come together?/Synchronised, in perfect focus? True to life?' (Kiwus 1992: 9). The 'immortality' of artistic representation, however, has become crucially historically specific: 'Art, so we once thought/made its/objects immortal. In this century, in the middle/of this century they reached for their revolvers' (10).

The sense of having only culturally mediated access to our world, or indeed our 'self', is explored and positively affirmed in 'Selberlebensverjährung' (71–72), whilst the surreal play on the metaphor 'einen Blick werfen' (to cast a glance) in 'Blendend ersetzt' suggests the need for a new kind of vision, akin to that of the hunted animal, to replace the 'ordinary desolate/blind days/ staring into emptiness with eyes wide open' (63). This raises the theme of occupying the position of the 'other' of human culture, which Kiwus develops in her introductory essay to a volume of animal photography with accompanying literary texts, *Tiere wie wild* (1994). Recalling the theme of the city, the retreat into the zoo is presented as, 'a place for resuscitation and convalescence in the midst of a sick world', which leads to reflections on freedom, confinement, civilisation, and the wild (1994: 13). In contrast to the photographic images in the text she learns to see all that exceeds the momentary image, 'habits', 'movements', 'emotions'. However, far from an anthropomorphic gesture, her observation does not diminish the 'otherness' of the animals, instead it teaches her to respect their highly differentiated systems of life and interaction. What also emerges is the illusory nature of human freedom, and the insight, common to so much contemporary women's writing, that the dominant culture of the West is based on conflict, exclusion, and subordination: 'All things struggle, conquer, are defeated, stake out their boundaries, and die. This freedom is an illusion, invented by the few, coveted by the many' (19).

Notes

Translations from German texts are my own except where published English editions are referenced. See the bibliography for details.

1. Such texts include Drewitz 1978, Rinser 1981, and Moosdorf 1989.
2. See Demski 1992b and Elsner 1983.
3. For further discussion of postmodernism and feminism see Braidotti 1994 and Nicholson 1990.
4. See Lersch 1988. For further discussions of feminine aesthetics see Othmer-Vetter 1988 and Ingeborg Weber 1994.
5. See Anne Duden in Duden, Ebner, von der Lühe et al. 1986: 108–114.
6. Scholl 1990 and von Wysocki 1980. Ginka Steinwachs's doctoral thesis (1985) combines her interest in structuralism and surrealism.
7. In addition to the texts discussed here, see Steinwachs's 'city-tetralogy' 1978, 1979, 1992, and the Barcelona project, *Baranella*. In *marylinparis*, the myopic female protagonist both inhabits and embodies the city which functions as the repository of male 'master discourses' from the Enlightenment to poststructuralism. In Gerlind Reinshagen's *Die flüchtige Braut* (1984) the bride is Berlin, the mystical scenario for the convergence of an anachronistic group of Romantic intellectuals, artists and drop-outs. Undine Gruenter's *Ein Bild der Unruhe* (1986) presents the surreal urban landscapes of Berlin, Brussels and Paris as the backdrop for the male protagonist's compulsive wandering.
8. This is indebted to Sigrid Weigel's wide-ranging exploration of the city in literature in Weigel 1990.

9. Mörike's 'Das verlassene Mägdlein' is echoed in the protagonist's dream: 'Früh, wann die Häher krähn, sing ich mein trauriges Lied. Ich steh am Herd und ich muß weinen' (Berkéwicz 1988: 44).

10. See Venske 1992.

11. See, for example, Butler 1993, Grosz 1994, and Braidotti 1994.

12. The awareness of specifically feminine structures of desire and its incompatibility with culturally codified 'love' finds expression in the work of Renate Schostack (the prose collection *Heiratsversuche oder die Einschiffung nach Cythera*, 1985), Friederike Roth (*Das Buch des Lebens*, 1983), Angelika Klüssendorf (*Sehnsüchte*, 1990), and Christa Reinig's *Die Frau im Brunnen* (1984) which focuses on lesbian love.

13. In her essay, '"Männlich schreiben – weiblich schreiben" oder "gibt es eine Geschlechterspur in der Gegenwartsliteratur?"', Heinrich states her view that the difference between women's and men's writing is due entirely to their relative access to the world (Heinrich 1986: 219).

14. Rosi Braidotti has a similar view of the postmodern subject, forcibly unified by language and consciousness: 'The subject … is a heap of fragmented parts held together by the symbolic glue that is the attachment to, or identification with, the phallogocentric symbolic. A heap of rubble, calling itself the center of creation; a knot of desiring and trembling flesh, projecting itself to the height of an imperial consciousness. I am struck by the violence of the gesture that binds a fractured self to the performative illusion of unity, mastery, self-transparency' (1994: 12).

15. See Sigrid Weigel's discussion of the text in *Die Stimme der Medusa* (Weigel 1989: 123–129).

16. Luce Irigaray uses the term 'dereliction' in her *Éthique de la différence sexuelle* (1985) to describe the state of women 'abandoned outside the symbolic order', and lacking the 'mediation in the symbolic for the operations of sublimation' (Whitford 1991: 78).

17. See Venske 1991: 132. Elsewhere, Venske has detected a 'masculine' narrative stance in the writing of Kronauer, Libuše Moníková, Angela Praesent, Karin Struck, and Undine Gruenter, in Briegleb and Weigel 1992. Sigrid Weigel sees in Kronauer's writing an example of 'eine ästhetisierte Variante weiblicher Subjektivität … die eher durch das Feuilleton gefördert wird' (Weigel 1989: 97).

18. Magdalene Heuser, '"Die Gegenstände abstauben" und "Mit Blicken wie mit Pfeilen und Messern": Brigitte Kronauer im Kontext der Gegenwartsliteratur von Frauen lesen', Knapp & Labroisse 1989: 345.

19. Weigel writes: 'Während sich die am Entwicklungskonzept orientierte Geschichtsschreibung über weibliche Subjekte, Autoren, Künstler etc. weitgehend ausschweigt, eröffnet sich bei der Lektüre von Mythen, Gemälden und anderen imaginären Quellen eine Fülle an Korrespondenzen zu den Erfahrungen und Situationen heutiger Frauen', Weigel 1990: 35.

20. In his 'Nachwort' to the 1985 Ullstein edition of Pausch's novel, Uwe Schweikert describes the portrait which appears on the cover of this edition: 'Ihr Leben hat noch kaum begonnen und ist doch schon an sein Ende gekommen', Pausch 1985: 116.

21. Sigrid Weigel, '"Es war ihr nicht zu teilendes Wissen, auf das sie ununterbrochen zustürzte". Zum Bild- und Körpergedächtnis in Anne Dudens *Judasschaf*' Weigel 1994: 24.

22. See Behrens 1981; Edschmid 1990 and 1992; Endres 1992; Ursula Krechel's essays on Irmgard Keun and Elisabeth Langgässer, and Ulla Hahn's work on Else Lasker-Schüler, Gertrud Kolmar, Gertrud von Le Fort.
23. Carola Stern, *Der Text meines Herzens* (1994) on Rahel Varnhagen; Karin Reschke, *Verfolgte des Glücks. Findebuch der Henriette Vogel* (1982); Christa Moog, *Aus tausend grünen Spiegeln* (1988) on Katherine Mansfield; Ursula Krechel's *Hörspiel* on the position of women writers, *Der Kunst in die Arme geworfen* (Südwestfunk 1982); Sibylle Knauss' historical novels *Ach Elise oder Lieben ist ein einsames Geschäft* (1981) about Elise Lensing, lover of Friedrich Hebbel, and *Charlotte Corday* (1988).
24. Ria Endres, *Am Ende angekommen. Dargestellt am wahnhaften Dunkel der Männerporträts des Thomas Bernhard*, Frankfurt am Main: 1980. See also her essays on women writers (Endres 1992).
25. See Moníková's essay on Milena Jesenská in which she writes: 'Sie war ein freier Mensch, "ein lebendiges Feuer" – nicht nur für Kafka' (Moníková 1994: 44-55).
26. In *The Revolution of Poetic Language* (1974: English 1984), Julia Kristeva develops a notion of the subject which is not fixed once and for all on the acquisition of language, but which is constantly recreated in each new utterance. See Moi 1986: 89–136.
27. See Steinwachs' doctoral dissertation (1985).
28. Mimicry is also a key technique in the following dramas: Jutta Heinrich, *Männerdämmerung* (1989), Friederike Roth's *Das ganze ein Stück* (1986) and *Erben und Sterben*, premiered October 1994 in Berlin.
29. Compare Joachim Kaiser's outraged review of this 'rückhalt- und rücksichtslose Weiberphantasie' reprinted in the Reclam *Jahresüberblick 1991*, (Görtz 1992: 162) with Regula Venske's more measured critical response (Venske 1991: 94–95). See also Karin Struck's comments on the subject of female erotica (Struck 1983).
30. See also Ellen Widmeier's first novel *Eis im Schuh* (1992), and Gisela von Wysocki's drama, *Schauspieler, Tänzer, Sängerin* (1988) for further examples of the thematic treatment of women's creativity.
31. For a more detailed discussion of women's poetry, see Krechel 1978. Krechel invokes Cixous, calling for a poetic style which articulates specifically female desire.
32. See Wittkowski 1991.
33. Ulrich Greiner has expressed growing reservations about Hahn's work: 'Schön sind diese Gedichte, aber ihre Schönheit ist restaurativ, nämlich gegenwartsabgewandt, vergangenheitsselig', quoted in Braun 1994: 7.
34. Hahn compares lyric rules with the air which is so essential to the bird's flight: 'Wer sie abschaffen will, gleicht der Kantschen Taube, die glaubt, im luftleeren Raum besser fliegen zu können' (Hahn 1988: 90).
35. These poems are reprinted in Kiwus 1981.

Chapter Eight

ORIGINAL DIFFERENTIATION
The Poetics of Anne Duden

Johanna Bossinade

The Key Episode

One key experience informs the work of contemporary author Anne Duden. Appearing in many guises, it is the driving force behind her texts and strengthens their internal coherence. The basic idea is always the same: a brutal event ruptures the everyday life of the narrator. This event takes the narrator by surprise and henceforth, she is only able to react in a disturbed fashion. The text 'Tag und Nacht' ('Day and Night') from Duden's volume of prose *Übergang* (1982, *Opening of the Mouth* 1985a) contains just such an event. It will serve to introduce a work which relocates common motifs in a linguistic world peculiar to the author.

At the opening of the story the narrative voice relates how she was submerged one morning in a 'wave of sound':

> I was woken up by this still distant, but already at that distance, threatening wave of sound coming steadily nearer, a wave taking possession of all space. Arriving like a world-wall. Filling everything, catching everything up in it, flushing away what was thinkable and imaginable and conceivable at a distance. Trains, cars, dogs barking. (Duden 1985b: 97)

It is evident what causes the surprise: the self has been sleeping and only comes round at the point when the wave of sound can no longer be stopped. Duden's narrator recognises the intense noise of an aircraft, which, approaching from the distance, tears the distance apart as it comes nearer. The disturbance occurs with sudden violence and, although it is part of the 'normal' world, it cannot be integrated into the narrator's reflections. The distance between internal and external space collapses, the wave of sound fills the entire space. Everything which had helped to maintain the distance is 'flushed away' (97).

If Duden had said 'washed away', the proximity to Freud's semantic field would have been more apparent. Shortly after the First World War, in *Beyond the Pleasure Principle* (orig. 1920), Freud described the incursion of a traumatic disturbance as the flooding of the mental apparatus with large amounts of stimulus (1984: 301). According to Freud, such inundations would occur when the individual's psychological defences were destroyed as the result of a shocking event. The ego then had to muster all its reserves to preserve the mental system 'against the effects threatened by the enormous energies at work in the external world – effects which tend towards a levelling out of them and hence towards destruction' (229). In order to signify an event which itself erases all signifiers, Duden takes precisely this effect as her starting point. The narrator is affected by an immense anxiety just as the psyche is affected by 'extreme' excitement.[1] Her field of perception, including her understanding of time, is at risk of being levelled out.[2] In the noise episode this field is differentiated in acoustic terms. Animal sounds (dogs barking) exist alongside the noise of civilisation (trains, cars). The sensory organs can anticipate both types of sound. Within the area dominated by the aircraft, however, the creature loses its right to speak; it has submitted this right to the 'higher' power of the sound. According to the text, the aircraft 'made it clear that there were no spaces anymore ... but only an everywhere, spinning' (97).

When one concentrates on the descriptive level, the threat to space is apparent too. It is as if the semantic differentiations, as well as the individual noises, are to be erased. On the other hand, it is precisely the narrow grid of the words which reveals the semantic differentiations. The effect is intensified by a rhythmic acceleration. The sentences become shorter and shorter, until one is left with 'trains, cars, barking dogs'. The narrative therefore develops a descriptive mode which, in its use of linguistic material, addresses the theme of violent reduction.

The noise episode leads one to expect that it will be repeated. The incident related in the text is in fact itself the recurrence of an earlier event. The narrative voice changes from the past tense 'I woke up' to the present tense, which is an iterative present. The laconic remark 'arriving like a world-wall' acknowledges that the 'wave' is familiar, since its influence already has a name. Referring to the traumatic deluge of stimuli, Freud emphasised that the psyche tries to absorb it by repeatedly imagining the situation which caused it. In a similar fashion, the narrative voice tries to cope with the incursion of the 'wave', by continually finding new names for it. However, since the 'wave' itself is already one of those names, the incident is presented as basically incomprehensible. Each word simply replaces another.

In this chapter, I will examine the constant indicative character of the presentation of events in Duden's work – a feature inherited from the modernist narrative tradition, a tradition which, in my opinion, she develops with her own specific accents.[3]

'Original Differentiation': Perspectives for a Reading

It is now over fourteen years since Anne Duden's first book *Übergang* was published in Germany. In this chapter I will focus on two problems in Duden's work and I will attempt to subject these problems to an exemplary analysis in order to contribute to a solid critical perspective on her work and its poetic achievement.

The first problem is the motif of mental trauma which appears in Duden's work in relation to 'history', 'art' and 'the body'. Historical experience is characterised above all by the trauma of the Third Reich, as for example in Duden's second volume of prose *Das Judasschaf* (1994, orig. 1985). In this text the artistic themes result from the description of pictures, which the author constructs according to established patterns.[4] She tries to connect the individual and general levels of violent history by establishing a dialogue with the picture.

The theme of the body is almost omnipresent in Duden's work. 'My memory is my body' is the programmatic announcement in the epilogue of the volume *Übergang*. The title story in particular is an account of an attack in which the lower part of the female narrator's face is destroyed.[5] This attack could be a prototype for the motif of the violent incident, which on the other hand also touches upon the author's own experience. She describes the broader connection between her life and her work thus: 'Everything is broken and fragmented, here as it is there' (1985a: 142).

The second problem is Duden's style of writing.[6] As detailed as her descriptions are, they do not seem to refer to any one particular

object. Movement within the text also seems to be a very important feature. Extreme situations are described in great detail, and
yet remain decidedly indistinct. As her third, and as yet most
recent, publication *Steinschlag* (1993) suggests, her poems are
dominated by the free, episodic moment. In this chapter, however,
I will concentrate on the prose style of *Tag und Nacht*.

The 'wave of sound' episode points to a dilemma. On the one
hand, the individual's personal space is threatened by a trail of
sound, whilst on the other, it is individual noises which maintain
this personal space by creating internal differentiations. Accordingly, the same form of sensory perception, in this case hearing,
can be connected with very different qualities of experience.
Duden's narrative voice reacts to this dilemma in a disjointed
fashion. It flees the experience of difference as much as it pursues
it. The enemy is also the object of desire. Without a divisive cut,
the individual can literally not be 'there'. At the same time however, this incision exposes the individual to destructive influences.
Duden herself says that her text-person is situated in an 'endless
field of conflict' (1985a: 147).

At this point the question of methodology becomes pertinent. My
method suggests a fresh approach to the concept of differentiation:
it should be understood in the way that it is used in the work of Derrida. Normally 'differentiation' means that prescribed units are
divided up according to a simple set of alternatives, for example
genre. The underlying assumption here is that one can know what
'person', 'gender' or 'literature' actually are. The picture changes
however, if 'differentiation' is related to 'differential'. For now it is
the divisive moment itself which creates the differences, so that
apparently autonomous units become recognisable as part of a
structure. This shift in perspective draws on the concept of *différance*
posited by the French philosopher Jacques Derrida in 1968. The concept of *différance* implies both 'differing' and the deferral of meaning.

To support his theory, Derrida refers amongst other things to
Freud's theory of psychic life. Derrida claims that Freud always
explained this life using two concepts: condensation and dis-
placement in the primary processes, which correlate with the secondary processes, just as the reality principle correlates with the
pleasure principle, and so on. Derrida regards *différance* as the
motivation behind such correlated doubles. He names the mark of
this *différance* 'trace', since it lays routes and diversions for differential incision: each one of these diversions postpones the point of
exhausted immobility.

From this dynamic of *différance*, which propels the process of differentiation, Derrida has developed the option of reading psychic symptoms as if they were a text. In epistemological terms, this means that textual theory and psychoanalysis share some common ground. This is not so much a system of concepts or motifs, so much as the line of a differential incision, which lets such symbolic formations appear in the first place.

Hence *différance* functions as a collective term for the constant correlation of 'otherness' and 'postponement' in the pattern of signifiers which emerges from the text. Since this correlation is not immediately apparent, Derrida distinguishes between this and 'determined differences', which for their part, are only possible as a result of *différance*. At this point I am translating Derrida's word *différance* as 'differentiation', in order to distinguish between the concepts of difference and differentiation. Differentiation indicates the level of the continuous process of linguistic division, of which difference is a more clearly defined product.

With the help of this methodological division, culturally determined patterns of difference can be traced back to the process from which they originated and the subject who speaks can be traced to a position within that process.[7] In this context 'originated' does not mean that the process of differentiation provides a simple basis. It is rather the division providing the signifier with a basis in the first place, which is original.

The figure of 'original differentiation' allows historical and psychoanalytic motifs to be considered on a text-specific basis.[8] Interrelated motifs, such as those of the body, gender and history, can now appear in a relation which is differentially fragmented from the very beginning. This means that the textual signifiers are divided by points of intersection, which relate the signifiers to each other to the same extent that they are divided from each other.[9]

Owing to the dynamic sketched above, the signifiers can form larger units of meaning, but can never form a complete whole. When viewed in its entirety, the division of differentiation transcends the restrictions of determination. The analysis of the text must, therefore, begin precisely at the point where the work *in* the text begins, namely, at the point where the motifs of the text are lifted out of the differential context of linguistic signifiers and reunited in specific projections. This level must be taken into account both before and in order that the text can be accommodated in a particular interpretative perspective.[10]

My interpretative perspective on Duden's work begins here. For the figure of 'original differentiation' does not seem to me to be exterior to Duden's text, but on the contrary, to provide the basis of its poetics. The narrative 'Tag und Nacht' for example, thematises a 'real' perceptive space, that of hearing and seeing. At the same time this narrative challenges the reader to acknowledge the internal functions of these senses. Linguistic material is processed in this interior space: it is divided up, categorised and rearranged. This becomes apparent when one examines the patterns of sentences such as 'trains, cars, dogs barking'. A more definite perceptual context could not be produced without differentiating incisions, but these same incisions prevent closure. Apt as the words 'wave of sound' are, they do not exhaust the possibilities of 'what is', because they also indicate the other places in the text to which they can be related.

Anne Duden herself defines this suspended certainty as an effect of the 'intervening space' (*Zwischenraum*). She explains that it is this 'gap' (*das Zwischen*) which creates and preserves space in artistic creations (1985a: 124–125).[11] The author's poetic principles correspond to a textual practice which reflects, amongst other things, the distinction between difference and differentiation. The gaps in texts can evidently be arranged in such a way that things and people within them appear as if in fixed patterns of relation. When Duden speaks of the 'positioning' of language, she is touching upon this point.[12] On the other hand, the work of differentiation becomes apparent in images, which have the effect of creating space.

'Tag und Nacht': Between Comfort and Trauma.

The narrative voice in 'Tag und Nacht' can be identified as female: '... do I have to wash my hair yet again, will my beloved be in a better mood today ...' (105). No attempt is made to avoid stereotypical topoi of femininity, such as the maintenance of one's appearance and relationships. At the same time, however, this statement is not a definite identification of the narrative voice; the statement seems rather to indicate the all-embracing problem of linguistic categorisation.

The narrative is barely ten printed sides in length and is divided into three numbered sections. It is structured by three episodes, which scan disturbances in the everyday life of the narrator. The first section deals with the incursion of aircraft noise, the second with an arguing couple and the third with the mechanisms of the world of work. The period of time indicated in the title 'Tag und Nacht' is tightly compressed in the first section. The time span runs from 'seven o'clock in the morning ... until darkness falls late in the evening' (97, 99). The two other sections each present day and night separately.

The thematic discourse of the narrative is surrounded by descriptions which seem to have little to do with the theme itself. In the first section, the description is that of the undulating movement of noise, in the second it is the alternation of sleeping and waking, in the third the circumstances which underpin everyday life. These passages cannot be distinguished in a precise manner: they run through the whole text, like walkways. Different emotional levels become apparent as well. The couple's argument in the second section, for example, leads to a reallocation of rooms which initially relaxes the situation. This double orientation is characteristic of the text as a whole. Every event which overstretches the individual's perceptive ability changes state from time to time. The basic motif of the text is being between comfort and trauma and I use the discursive themes *noise, conflict* and *work* to trace the development of this motif.

'The quicker the cut, the more painless it is' (98). This is the stoic reaction of Duden's protagonist to the threatening wave of sound which tears her out of sleep. The 'ultimate attempt at flight', hiding her head, does not help at all (97–98). As is often the case in Duden's texts, a type of guillotine seems to be at work, carving up an organic whole. What makes this divisive 'cut' essential can only be deduced indirectly.

The trauma motif gives rise to an initial perspective. For if one examines the text more closely, the incursion of the wave of sound is described in images which are reminiscent of physical and sexual actions. Events which Freud credited with a tendency to induce trauma are signified in the text: birth, weaning, the loss of one's object of desire. Phantasmagorical scenes such as copulation or castration are also signified in this way. All of these images and imaginings connect the development of the individual as a linguistically and sexually differentiated being, with the resolution of separation experiences. The ego is forced to develop defence mechanisms and strategies of repression to prevent itself from being exposed to an excess of stimuli. The basic form of this 'traumatic situation of helplessness' was described by Freud as 'primary repression'.[13] Strictly speaking, nothing is actually repressed at this point, since the ego has not yet begun to develop. What actually takes place is a rupture in the attainment of basic needs, which initiates the function of suppression *per se*. At the same time an insoluble dilemma appears: for the shock of exposure is just as much part of the experiences which continue to affect the ego at an unconscious level as is the initial absence of defence, in other words, openness and receptivity.[14]

For the textual 'I', lying in bed, the wave of noise is linked to the phallic body of the aircraft. A penetration is imagined, which attacks space in its cosmic dimensions: 'The airplane bores into it, regardless of whether paths and tunnels exist'. The room takes on the form of a pregnant body without really having received a 'gift'. Inside, it remains empty: '… now a giant blown out stomach, and still the iron fuselage presses and drills on steadfast and unswerving' (98). The distended stomach is not prepared to take something other into itself. The image of a violent deflowering follows: 'The tissue tears, shreds in all directions, finally gives way. What remains is this wound, one wound after another, a chain of wounds …' (98). The word 'chain' suggests that the overpowering can be repeated infinitely.

From a historical perspective, the motif of the modern world suggests itself. In Duden's work the ears perceive the task of making obvious the demands of a highly technologised 'inhumane' society. The body, the more so the female body, becomes the 'essence of the experience' in which the perceptive integrity of the individual is under threat.[15] The threat emanates from machines which can just as easily connect social spaces as destroy them from above. In words such as 'air ruins', 'top alert' or 'all-penetrating bugling' (98–99), fragments of memories of the nights of bombing in the Second World War are juxtaposed with the contemporary state of unrest. This recalls issues found in Ingeborg Bachmann's writing.[16]

Another of Freud's observations can be applied to that layer of the motif which produces images. Freud established that, in the context of traumatic experiences, a wound suffered at the same moment is able to bind them together. Admittedly the 'anticathexis' results, according to Freud, in the obstruction of other psychic functions. As if in a tactical application of this discovery, Duden's narrative voice imagines that her ears have been injured. The incursion of the wave of sound is thus contrasted with a suitable image.[17] It ought to be remembered that the Greek word trauma means 'wound'. As in the case of the psychological anticathesis, however, there is a price to be paid for focusing creative energy. The narrative self is unable to address any other theme. The involuntary perception of stimuli by the ear is translated into an image of rape:

> For a few moments the wave rushes booming close past me, as though it wanted to go through there too, sweeps up to the membrane, forces and thrusts itself in, but this time doesn't make it. The next time the blood will be running out of my ears. (99)

Although the membrane is not penetrated, it is indicated that penetration is possible. This type of evaluation, clarifying the situation, is a common feature of Duden's work. These evaluations obstruct the eruptive changes which are characteristic of the 'language of the body' used by Antonin Artaud or Elfriede Jelinek. The narrative voice recognises physical symptoms better than she does her own psychological ones, although she is still capable of a certain amount of irony. 'The next time the blood will be running out of my ears'. The matter-of-fact tone of this prediction makes it appear both dramatic and comic. Duden presents the long-term effects of this reality as destructive. The ego risks losing its aptitude for differentiated orientation. The points which create spatial and temporal distance in the everyday world collapse under the 'spinning omnipresence' of the noise:

> So it goes. Every few minutes until darkness falls late in the evening. Flow and ebb, flow and ebb, ebb and flow, flowebbflow. The intervals are so brief I no longer know whether it's still ebbing or the flood has started up again. (99)

On balance, the unprotected openness of the ears proves to be indispensable. They have to keep the ego informed of the circumstances in which it is embroiled. But, as the 'cosmic' rape clearly demonstrates, this same openness makes the ego vulnerable too. In the most extreme case the whole existential space is threatened with collapse: 'There noise and silence and absolute speech – and soundlessness become one' (98). The grid of words 'flow, ebb, flow' indicates the threat presented by the reduction of distance, whilst at the same time indicating the intricate work of differentiation.

A new field of conflict opens up in the second part of the text. The narrator has a partner whom she introduces in the first sentence: 'In my bed, he was already sleeping' (100). In addition to her partner, the house is shared with a second couple, who live on the floor below and are presumably also a woman and a man. The narrator eavesdrops undetected on the 'lower' couple's argument, since her own partner is already asleep. In the narrator's relationship there also seems to be an upper and a lower, a sleeping and a waking half. Furthermore, what is described as 'the madness on the floor below' (100) appears to be a projection: the narrator projects her own unresolved conflict onto other people. According to Freud, the psyche does this when disturbed by strong inner drives. He maintained that the psychological upheaval is projected onto external objects, 'so that it may be possible to bring the shield against stimuli into operation as a means of defence against them' (1984: 301).

Thus the situation is reversed. The 'enemy' now lurks within the narrator herself. Duden's narrative voice actually emphasises how quiet her external environment is. Even commonplace noise has ceased: 'The daytime noise was over. The gas heating finally quiet, the neighbour was no longer listening to Bob Dylan, and over the whole country there was no television programme any more' (100). But what is being fended off by the defensive construction of the second couple?

Let us return to the opening sentence, which is inverted. The definition of the voice's 'own' position precedes the subject: 'In my bed …'. This indicates that the partner is occupying a place which belongs to the narrator and which is not big enough for two people. Meanwhile Duden's narrator tries to avoid the already present 'other': 'I sat down in the other room and tried to read' (100). The sleeping lover is not supposed to notice that his partner feels disturbed by his presence and goes into another room. Only once she thinks of him as a 'sympathetic body' is she prepared to 'go and lie down beside him' (100). Yet she is absolutely unable to lie still next to another person.

Her flight is not caused by a 'real aching': 'It's more a tearing and straining, coming from an undetectable centre, a stretching and overstretching, that then always shoots into my consciousness when the relevant part of the body comes into contact with the sheet or even with certain parts of the pillow' (100). Consequently the contact of a 'certain part of the body' with other parts is to be avoided. Apart from the reversal of interior and exterior, a parallel can be drawn with the previous episode. This parallel centres on an invasive proximity, in the first case that of sound, here that of another body, both of which threaten the distance with which the narrator needs to surround herself. However, unlike the 'wave of sound' which has to break in to the narrator's proximity in order to 'rush booming close' to her, the body is always

already there. Therefore its proximity results in a more subtle torment than that of the wave of sound.

Is the 'undetectable centre' of this torment located in an earlier
period? Freud considered the 'loss of love' suffered by the child at
the hands of its parents as one of the deeply painful experiences of
childhood, which left an impression like a narcissistic scar. The
events which bring about this experience, the birth of a sibling for
example, are as unavoidable as the child's own recognition that
love can come to an end.

The former victim of rejection has now turned this experience
into a strategy. Duden's narrative voice tries to hurt the object of
her love by withdrawing, although ironically, her partner is sleeping so soundly that he does not notice. The narrator's flight from
being touched represents a defence mechanism against an earlier
experience or, more precisely, the return of an earlier desire.
Painful scars are involved which the author describes elsewhere
as the 'memory of earlier wounds'.

However, the conflict extends even further into the past: in a
figurative sense right back to the parents' bedroom door. This is
implied by the lower couple's scene. At the level of the 'I', an additional element is present, which could be described in Freudian
terms as a 'preparedness for anxiety' (1984: 303). The fear is supposed to compensate for a previous failure to prepare for a traumatic intrusion and make a cathexis possible. The narrative voice
must have reached this conclusion herself for she develops a
readiness to be on the alert, if not to be frightened. She is determined not to let the 'madness' of the lower couple take her by surprise: 'I knew the madness of the floor below was lurking; it was
wide awake, although its partners lay stiffly in bed and had even
switched off the light' (100).

There is apparently nothing she can do, except to stay wide
awake, to lurk and wait until the partners made a move. '... I
couldn't read because the whole time I was trying to decipher the
madness on the floor below' (100). This effort is eventually re-
warded: 'Then on the floor below the bedroom door flies open.
The sudden surge of air, the pressure wave drives right under my
skin. So the madness has exploded' (101). The surge is probably so
sudden because the relationship which preceded it was so stiff
(100). Thus the 'pressure wave' explodes a problematic proximity
rather than causing a damaging collapse. The narrator eavesdrops
on a movement of violent repulsion as if two animals were fighting: 'A few snarling sentences jerked out – from which of the

opponents, female or male? Then, over the tiled floor into the kitchen, rapid, determined little steps. Female then' (101).

The bodies of the opponents recoil from each other as these sentences are jerked out. A sexual act or violent birth is implied by what appears on the surface to be an argument. The couple's difference arises from their everyday differences. The narrator now identifies with the emotional upheaval of the female partner from the lower floor. The sound symbols emerging from there are spelled out emphatically:

> Now she is sitting there, blowing her nose and coughing alternately, one hour, two hours, three. Her heart is racing, her tearducts overflow. Again and again the one drop to make them brim over. (101)

The occupant of the house is relieved when she settles down to sleep. Her position, cleanly divided from that of the 'madness', appears safe for the time being. But even the retreat into sleep can not take place straight away. First another, more distant, neighbour must return home. He is a taxi-driver and a bachelor and lives alone – the exact opposite of the other characters. The narrative voice envies him: 'I think how wearily he must climb into bed now' (101). The thought of the distant loner is comforting, for a new type of perception is initiated, apart from that caused by the narrator's own return to bed. The time before the 'wave of sound' returns, as though its destructive 'incision' has been invalidated along with the 'madness'. In a parallel development, the process of differentiation becomes more apparent. Traffic noise and animal sounds, birdsong this time, are registered as they reach the listener from afar and maintain the distance:

> A train passes through. Goods train at this hour. The window frames beat rhythmically against one another. Past. And that? My hearing is a fully extended antenna, ready to transmit the most sensitive sounds. Yes, the customary first bird, still half asleep, blurred, as though it were sitting behind thick curtains in its nest or in a tree. (102)

Freud described the sensory organs as 'feelers', 'which are at all times making tentative advances towards the external world and then drawing back from it' (1984: 299). In the same fashion the narrator's hearing serves her as an 'antenna', which tests out stimuli. Behind the protection of 'thick curtains' the sounds are bearable. Even physical proximity is no longer threatening, as the expression 'in the nest' indicates. It has almost become a matter of indifference: 'The body next to me, yes all right, but without him it would be the same now. Redemption falls upon me' (102).

'Without him' – this could indicate a state beyond physical determination, a state of 'indifference'. Yet the opposite image is also present. The distance from the 'other body' can only be ensured in an active fashion, by means of conflict. In the final analysis it is distance which provides an answer to the question 'female or male?' The fact that the female partner rushes straight to the kitchen may be regarded as an example of subtle irony. In any case without this event the narrator is literally not in a position to tolerate being touched. Before this event takes place she is also unable to find 'salvation', the ability to sink into a peaceful sleep.

At this point, the dilemma which dominates the central part of the narrative has come full circle. The narrator tries to submit to a state of mind, which has evolved with the different phases of the night and which is open to suggestion.[18] As in the case of the ears, however, openness appears to entail danger, for at the same time she seeks the security of difference. This difference in turn, makes access to that 'other state' difficult. The 'partners' have now been slotted firmly into a pattern of gender. Just like opponents, they can now only pursue one of two directions.

The motif of limited direction is over exaggerated at the end of the text. Again the action begins with an awakening. This time it is not one event which forces itself into the narrator's perception, but the 'day-shape' itself. Just like the wave of sound it 'approaches violently' (103) and even looks like 'a gigantic flying object' (104). But now the narrator must follow the path of the 'orbit' which has been established. This obligation to follow a predetermined course is decisive.

The 'mundane terror' of coping with everyday life is a recurrent theme in Duden's work. The difficulty is not getting into the 'other state', but getting out of it. The narrator is not permitted to remain 'in the condition of that skull- and skeletonlessness' beyond the dawn (103). Duden's narrator is summoned to work (105).

The work which has to be performed involves two steps. Once again, the beginning creates an incisive division. The narrator has to 'tear herself away' (104) from the feeling of 'without me' (102). According to Roland Barthes, the feeling of 'without me' arises from time to time in love and at work. It frees the individual from responsibility and decision-making: '… like the worker in the electronic age or the lazybones in the back row at school, all I have to do is *be* there: the *karma* (the machine, the class) is making a noise in front of me, but without me'. Duden's character is not permitted such a 'little *corner for slackers*'.[19] She has to face up to decisions. An initial success in her conformity is indicated by the fact that the violence now originates with her actions:

> With a brutality that constantly astounds me, I just swiftly deal the other state a powerful, irreparable kick, usually with my left foot, because it never disappears of its own volition … (104)[20]

The second step is the connection with the 'day-shape' (105). By now there is no mistaking the success of the narrator's attempt to conform: 'I'm locked into position in the right place and have inserted, anchored and riveted myself in the prescribed way' (105). If the 'connection' is not missed 'quite simply … through oversleeping' (105) – the narrator will end up in the 'normal orbit' (106). This is her only chance to defend herself against the new day. If she misses this, she will be left behind, 'flattened and squeezed dry' (104), as she was by the 'wave of sound'.

Words such as 'flattened and squeezed dry' give one the impression of a thoroughly organised system, but one which predates the technological revolution. After the preceding episodes, it is off-putting that the day's 'enormity' (103) lies in its mechanical regularity, relieved by Chaplinesque idiosyncrasies. The narrator also seems to have noticed the farcical element in this type of technology. She uses everyday expressions such as 'falling down' or 'missing the boat' (105). Her own efforts are described in the style used by sports commentators: 'A certain current of air now, a precisely known noise level, and there – yes – I'm hanging fast, rather my hands are holding fast to it' (104).

Both the comforting and the frightening sides of existence have now been dulled. On the one hand the 'frame' (*Halterung*) protects the narrator from the temptation of going back to sleep. The question 'whether I can get back in the old condition or not' (105) seems to be academic. As if to compensate for this, the intricate work of differentiation now retreats behind the obvious difference of 'light and dark'. From now on only familiar circumstances return: 'Everything is there again and switches itself on and functions smoothly …' (104). Accordingly, the physical encounters which caused a restless night are no longer a problem. The body next to her has now taken on the more familiar form of 'my lover' (105).[21] The flight into another state would not even be possible now: 'The day now takes its course in a straight line' (105). On this straight line, there is now only the 'right moment' and the 'right place'. Everything else finishes up in 'the motionless and airless space' in which one can not 'hold out' (106). The straightened and corrected day turns out to be a construct, in which 'everything already conceived and suffered and divined as unthinkable has its place' (104). Thus there is room, but no unoccupied space.

The mechanical regularity of the day therefore represents the narrator's lack of free space. She is ruthlessly exposed to the routine questions and the facts: 'putting some verve into it, as though I were on the parallel bars – I hurl my body against the flat surface above me; it cracks and slaps and jolts and creaks' (104–105). And yet the 'levelling' influence is really starting to have an effect at this point, for the rhythm of the sentence is as monotone as the noises which the body is making. The representation is drastic, yet its sting is removed by the comical precision of the description. Duden's utopian horizon seems to have been so radically reduced that the narrator is just left with a type of home-made 'shelter' (106). Her closing remark is that she keeps a 'hammock' to hand for real emergencies, 'to get on an even keel with … if need be' (106).

Space Within the Text

In a manner exemplary of Duden's work, the text 'Tag und Nacht' takes as its theme space which is doubly threatened: whether by collapse or by over-regulation. The individual's perceptive abilities are so closely connected with the space, that any threat to it also endangers the individual. In Freudian theory, the psychic system forms a surface which is turned towards the exterior world and which is itself differentiated by its position. As if commenting on this insight, Duden's text reveals what dangers are involved in the formation of difference between the self and the world. Either a very rigid pattern of difference is established, sexual relationships on one side and the workday routine on the other or the ability to differentiate is itself threatened.[22]

By the end of the text, it is apparent that the initial scene is the most traumatic moment. In the aeroplane episode, it is not only involuntary perception, but perception as such which is at risk. Only the work of linguistic transformation can keep pace with events, and even this possibility is quite explicitly undermined:

> What is happening there, for that no experience, no language is adequate. The torn up space itself would have to speak. After this type of violence, though, there is nothing left to be said. There noise and silence and absolute speech- and soundlessness become one. (98)

The choice, therefore, is that of inflexibility or destruction, and Duden does not show the reader a way out of this dilemma. However, she does indicate to what this dilemma may be attributed. This occurs expressly in the descriptive passages which leave open to question what alternative will eventually be reached: that of the 'normal' everyday differences, which impose severe limitations on the female subject, or that in which nothing is left except 'torn up space' (98). The passages deal with internal as well as external spaces, birdsong as well as states of consciousness, although the latter are not attached to a particular subject. Although they are linked thematically, these spaces open up the linguistic material, rather than giving it a particular direction. This is where my reading starts to work upon the most essential level of the text. The signifying principle of the text is not only practised, but also symbolised here as the effect of differentiation. In the second section of the text, for example, the arrival of the 'most sensitive sounds' is preceded by a widening of vision: 'Is it becoming light or has my eye only cleared paths through the darkness?' (102). In the third section, the 'other state' is captured in the image of flowing alternation:

> The condition is connected with movements that jar against nothing, with light conditions in which there is no separation between light and dark, with notes without scales, and colours that are always running into one another so that I never manage to name them. The best thing about it though is its facelessness and the total absence of thoughts. It is crossed neither by streets nor by borders, it has no walls or roofs and no separate organs with individual functions. (103)

It is as if the narrator is calling up a fragment of the openness which forms the basis of her more conscious existence.[23] It has now become apparent that this is an ambivalent openness: its other side is characterised by the extreme situations, verging on attacks, which fill the individual with panic. Once again she lacks the necessary defence mechanism. Yet even these fearful situations still retain the trace of a movement which has neither sense nor meaning outside itself. For example, the incursion of the noise leaves behind it 'one single groaning and bellowing field of ruins,

over which the wildly bugling and then ebbing echo of the remaining eddies and whirlpools still sloshes away' (98). If it was
not for the semantically determined words 'field of ruins', the violent motion of the action could supplement the modality which
reigned before the incursion of the noise, described as 'the even-
ness of movement: no wing-beat, no speeding up or slowing down,
no curve, no turning off' (97).

Duden inscribes the already opening path of the movement of
signs in a variety of contexts, in urban and artistic landscapes, in
natural and meteorological conditions. 'Music settles over the sea,
wind, that first went through the poplars, in summer there are also
the flight lines of swallows too and elongated strands of cloud'
('The Art of Drowning', 1985d: 124). Yet Duden's main example is
'music'. The text 'Das Landhaus', also from *Übergang*, reveals the
space-creating effect of musical compositions more clearly:

> At first it opened up a chamber, then a room which led to another
> larger room, and so on and on, until half-dreaming, half-waking,
> the awareness emerged that meanwhile one had been channelled
> and carried onward through all the rooms and walls and roofs by
> one single, great gathering and uplifting movement, a surge of air
> which finally caught one up into the open and there gently and
> evenly restored one's breathing. (1985e: 21–22)

Thus the arrival of a 'wave' opens up two possibilities. As above,
it can be a musical 'surge of air', but it can also be a 'wave of noise',
as in 'Tag und Nacht'. Where the latter destroys, the former 'channels and carries onward' whatever its 'great movement' picks up
and carries 'into the open'. In the latter case, no 'I' is involved,
only a quasi-neutral 'one'. Yet as another text by Duden shows, it
is precisely the more closely defined subject which is 'driven into
the open' by the essential level of in-depth differentiation:

> An impetus took her away from something in which she urgently
> belonged, a type of suspended fauna and flora with which all the
> threads of her connective tissue were interwoven. The connection
> was cut from behind by a sudden event from above. A call, a
> scream. Much of her remained below, torn away, torn out, all the
> peace of which she was capable, so that she was dragged up com-
> pletely. (1985e: 12)

Does this describe – not without pathos – the birth of a female individual from the 'suspended fauna' of signs? And at the same time
the beginning of her disturbance whose two-fold outline 'Tag und
Nacht' lays bare. In an extreme case the individual is completely

cut off from those parts of her that remained 'below'. In a normal case they are forced into restricted paths 'above'. Over and over she searches for the way into that 'connective tissue' which is the basis of her subjective and textual existence. The mode of representation points beyond the 'real' perceptive space of the subject to the text as such: to its grid of words, to its semantic field, to its cuts and suspended connections, in short to its process of 'original differentiation'.

I see this bringing together of represented and representing space as the particular feature of Duden's aesthetic. The gender-specific dimension of her work is affected by it. For while traditionally 'spaces' only have female connotations, in Duden's work a female subject is caught up in them.[24] It establishes the space of the psyche and the space of the text. The latter interweaves the former with itself as a layer of motifs which have many points of reference in history and cultural history. It is an intimate symbiosis of space which encourages an openness to the 'original' effect of signs and a retaining of this effect in wider contexts. Not as a sign of an ideal world, but rather of a structure broken from the beginning, open to movement full of relish, but also to catastrophes. Even when these catastrophes, seen structurally, are merely possible, they are in the foreground in Duden's work. Her writing forms a chain of repeated traumatic situations. Yet as her mode of description shows, something else is also involved from the start. And this something else is what gives individual texts their range – between consolation and trauma. In this way Duden develops the starting point for a poetics which provides the immanent standard for her own work. This way of seeing can be taken further. For from this same starting point a further step could be taken which would be to place Duden's work more precisely in its literary historical context.

Translated by Caroline Bland

Notes

Except for translations from published English editions listed in the bibliography, all translations from German texts cited are by Caroline Bland.

1. See Duden and Weigel 1989: 120–148.
2. 'Perception' is used here to mean a system for the reception of stimuli which emanate from the exterior world as well as from psychic phenomena. The system works with movable/temporary interpretations, although the permanent trace of the stimuli remains in the unconscious. See Freud 1982b: 495–516, esp. 511–514.
3. For this text's place in literary history see also: Menke 1986: 279–288; Brügmann 1989: 253–74; Briegleb and Weigel 1992: 117–150.
4. See Dieterle 1990: 260–283.
5. See, for example, Allerkamp 1991: 35–44.
6. See Greuner 1990 and Schnell 1986: 312–313.
7. The subordinate status of the subject in Derrida requires more careful thought. A critique is to be found in Kristeva 1977: 55–106. See also Kristeva 1980: 187–221. According to Kristeva, if a sensual subject is not recognised in principle and regarded as essential, the anti-metaphysical critique of sense and subject is merely 'negative theology'. A critique from the perspective of the philosophy of consciousness is provided by Frank 1988: 7–28.
8. In this reading psychoanalytical motives do not merely reflect the psychic 'reality' of literary figures, as was the case in the old school of literary psychoanalysis. They are signifiers which structure the text, just as the literary characters do. A similar reading is offered in Winkels 1988b: 42–58. However, Winkel's analytical process seems to have been drastically curtailed. To illustrate the themes of the body and narration in Duden's work, he compresses Lacan's theory of signification, Derrida's grammatology and Kristeva's cultural semiotics into a few sides. Thus the title of his essay ('Silenced') unintentionally gains in significance.
9. When Sigrid Weigel asked her about the diachronicity of conscious and unconscious, perception and permanent trace, Duden outlined her literary project as follows: 'It deals with the impossibility of bringing something together which does belong together in principle, and to do so in a way which reveals internal difference. It deals with the alleged impossibility of expressing and representing these things; allegedly a problem of literary form and expression' (1989: 146). With her postulation of the concepts 'together' yet 'different within themselves', Duden appears to be approaching the idea of 'differentiation' which I have tried to develop from Derrida's philosophy.
10. The task of analysis and interpretation which takes into account the openness of basic relations within the text can only ever lead to partial results. Yet these rest on a basis which does allow for further development. For this type of analysis avoids the double dead-end which obstructs literary analysis in general and gender-specific analysis in particular. No assumptions are made on the basis of fixed differences which could be read into the text later on. Nor is it suggested that the text is somehow 'beyond the difference principle' where it would be limited to a merely nominal form of variety. For further consideration of these problems, see Bossinade 1993: 97–120.

11. Duden also refers to the 'gap' as an 'empty space', a 'hole' or 'in between' and emphasises its meaning with references to artistic and religious history. About the figure of Christ 'writing on the floor', the text says that he is making a 'hole' for the reader: 'For it is precisely in this hole that fixed images have the possibility of dissolution and disappearance. And only from there is it possible for the new moving images to re-emerge'. ('Zeichen auf der Erde', 1990; Column 3).

12. See Anne Duden 1986: 112.

13. See Freud 1982d: 233–308, (303). Freud postulates that 'quantitative moments, such as the excessive strength of the stimulus and the penetrations of the defensive layer, are the most likely causes of the initial repressions' (240). The psychic helplessness, Freud argued, corresponds to the period of life when the ego is still immature (218), yet adulthood also does not offer sufficient protection from traumatic experiences of fear (288). For further reading on the effects of trauma, see Freud 1982a: 517–543.

14. See Lyotard 1991: 671–708. The author determines the inexplicability of the traumatic impression as analogous to the effect of 'primary repression', i.e., as a '"presence" without representation' (688). Then he emphasises the continuation of early helplessness (which he refers to as a 'childish emotional phrase'): 'In adulthood this appears as a sensitivity to the "presence", to an occurrence which is both temptation and threat, because when confronted with it, one's "defences" collapse'. This model explains why situations of extreme danger in Duden's work are connoted with equanimity or dream-like states, as well as with fear, rigidity or death.

15. The use of the female to represent 'general' experience of suffering in Duden's work has often been criticised. For an example of this see Dangel 1990: 80–94. In principle I feel this criticism is justified, but doubt whether it is based on adequate analytical consideration of the text. In addition, the stereotypical category 'women's writing' seems to hinder a more precise definition of, for example, Duden's development of the elegiac genre.

16. See especially Bachmann 1964/1982: 278–293. Bachmann describes Berlin as a place of 'sick people', who constantly have to put up with aircraft 'thundering' through their rooms (280). The city suffers from the 'suppressed pains' of its historical memory, which emerge abruptly in words such as 'Plötzensee' (292, 288). When compared with Bachmann's direct approach, Duden's text seems restrained, probably also because little has changed since Bachmann wrote her description. The world which is inhabited by the self becomes louder as its silence increases, in other words as the opportunities for discussion of the terrible facts of German history diminish. Aptly enough, Bachmann says that: 'the thundering noise of Berlin includes the frightened silence of Berlin in its prayers' (286). On the theme of 'traumatic structure' and 'the poetics of perception' in Bachmann's work, see Höller 1987: 146–147, 150. The posthumously published poem 'Schallmauer' is printed on p. 219; its motif of noise pollution seems to anticipate Duden's text.

17. In other texts by Duden injury is presented in a more obvious fashion. In the narratives 'Herz und Mund' and 'Übergang', the area around the mouth is affected. In the first text Duden even uses the phrase 'rape of the head' (1985a: 42). On the other hand the alleged aggression of wild animals, here that of the dragon, is revealed as a convenient projection: 'And there – ah – now they too are being attacked by the beast, having their bellies torn apart, just as one might expect' (1990a: 85).

18. Deep darkness is more likely to be a site of fear in Duden's work, as Adelson 1988: 234–252 has indicated.
19. Barthes 1988: 235–237; both quotations from 236.
20. Allegorical figures in Duden's work, such as the 'other state' referred to here, have not yet been examined in sufficient detail. Instead of investing a female character with allegorical status, Duden creates partial figures which conform with the subject of the text. For example, in the story 'The Mission. The Love', love is presented as the female narrator's notoriously querulous chaperone.
21. On this point see Venske 1988: 260–270.
22. With the terms 'day-shape' and the 'madness of the floor below', Duden is describing disturbances which can be personified or presented as concrete objects. The events surrounding the 'wave of sound' are less tangible. They appear in an allegorical field of reference: that which threatens the narrator to her very core, threatens space itself in a similar fashion. The seriousness of the danger varies, and this is reflected in Duden's work, by the difference between allegorical and parabolic forms. Comic ruptures on the one hand are matched by a more hermetic style on the other hand, which consistently postpones the incomprehensible event.
23. This 'internal' description of an extreme situation is reminiscent of the possibility of self-observation in a semi-recumbent state. According to Freud the translation of thoughts into images can be directly observed in this state, although it is primarily the sleeper's own situation which is represented in these images. See Freud 1982a: 41–68. This quotation is from 63f.
24. On the special significance of psychic space for women, see Jessica Benjamin 1990: 122–130. According to Benjamin, the symbol of space offers women the chance to relate their own subject positions to those of other subjects. I do, however, have reservations about the fact that the author determines the point of closure for this project. Benjamin states that 'differentiation' is 'the development of the individual to a self, which is conscious of its difference from others' (15, cf. 22). I find attempts to talk about 'psychological differentiation' in direct relation to Freud's work equally problematic (for example Fast 1984).

Chapter Nine

SEARCHING FOR INTERCULTURAL COMMUNICATION

Emine Sevgi Özdamar – A Turkish Woman Writer
in Germany

Isolde Neubert

This chapter offers a tentative approach to reading texts by Emine
Sevgi Özdamar, a Turkish woman writer in Germany. Its aim is to
encourage further studies of a most thought-provoking and exciting
author who raises fundamental questions about multi-culturalism.

In order to contextualise discussions about multi-culturalism I
will make a few general remarks about the present situation in
Germany.[1] There have been waves of Turkish immigration into
West Germany since the beginning of the 1960s. The economic
upturn following the 'economic miracle' demanded labour mainly
in the mining and car industries and in branches of the public services. Immigration was promoted by the government, emigration
encouraged by German officials in Turkey who propagated the
economic benefits for both sides. However, the history of foreign
employment in Germany shows that since then the 'guest workers', as they are called, have been the scapegoats in economic crises
and a decisive factor in periods of economic growth. Reports and
statistics about unemployment and legal discrimination speak for
themselves. Many immigrants have left Germany again because of
prolonged periods of unemployment or because of restrictive
immigration policies. Some have made a little money for a new
beginning in Turkey. However, many immigrant families founded
small private businesses, predominantly in the service sector
and settled down in Germany. Their children are already the
second generation and have grown up and been educated in a

Notes for this section can be found on page 168.

multi-cultural environment with all its discrimination, social conflicts and cultural richness.

As far as the average German is concerned, 'integration' and 'tolerance' may be acceptable solutions to existing problems. Yet in their German usage the two words have discriminatory connotations because they mean adaptation to 'German norms' or living next door to one another without real communication. However, arguably the very words have degenerated into empty phrases in the face of the riots and the hatred against foreigners which have followed the unification of East (GDR) and West (FRG) Germany.

These are the result of a failed policy in both parts of the country. In the East, the people had hardly any contact with foreign people either at home or abroad because of the closed border to the West. However, this cannot be the chief reason for the persistence of racism, since it is also a strong feature of West German society and West Germans were allowed to travel everywhere. Those foreigners who came to the GDR as students or workers (mainly from Vietnam and Angola) on exchange schemes were not looked upon as competitors, as everybody had the right to work and to social security. Although the educational system taught all children the value of solidarity and the equality of the human race, national stereotypes and exotic clichés continued to exist at many different levels. Unlike in West Germany, neo-fascism and right-extremism were suppressed in the GDR, but their roots were not publicly discussed. The increasingly self-righteous course of the Communist Party largely prohibited a critical approach to social questions. Research into the roots of nationalist and racist thinking in both the former GDR and the FRG still needs to be done.[2]

Turkish women writing fictional texts in or about Germany is a relatively recent phenomenon. Their presence is minimal in bookshops yet, except in the women's and feminist sections. A childhood in Turkey, emigration, a Turkish-German young adulthood, the shaping Islamic traditions and values, and the sensitive and challenging artistic presentation of different cultural experiences are the main topics of this writing. One of the writers is Aysel Özakin (b. 1942) who came to West Berlin in 1981 after the military had come to power in Turkey in 1971, and who now lives in London and writes in both the Turkish and English languages. Another author who should be mentioned is Renan Demirkan (b. 1955) who has lived in Germany since her childhood and who is also an actress. In this chapter, however, I focus on Emine Sevgi Özdamar.

To speak of Özdamar (b.1946) only as a 'woman writer' would not do her justice because she is an experienced film and theatre actress, director and writer. She won the Bachmann Prize for literature in 1991. Such a career is rare enough both in Turkey and Germany and one might be tempted to speak of her as an 'exception'. The very word itself already denotes marginalisation. Often 'exceptions' are not noticed by the cultural establishment at all, more rarely they are offered token inclusion in a patronising cultural 'canon'.

My intention is to avoid categorising and labelling, although I am aware that I might not be free from internalised or unconscious Eurocentric clichés. Reading Özdamar's narrative texts – texts which refuse to be put into a pre-fabricated genre system – was enlightenment without a capital 'E' for me and stimulated a learning process. This was all the more the case since my East German background has suddenly thrown me, following unification, into a net of cultural irritations and alienation. As for her immigrant characters, so for me, too, the experience of what the words 'Arbeitsamt' (labour exchange), 'Fremdenpolizei' (police department dealing with aliens) or 'Lohnsteuerkarte' (income tax card) really mean was new. In the following, I focus my analysis on literary images which offer an exciting challenge to the reader to move between cultures. The metaphorical presentation conveys meaning in a global, liberating context and thematises the 'self' and 'other' from many different perspectives.

Özdamar came to Germany for the first time in 1965 when she was nineteen years old. She found work in a pipe factory where she remained for two years. Afterwards she studied at drama schools in West Berlin and Istanbul. At twenty-four she experienced the military coup in Turkey. Theatres were closed, careers ruined. In 1976 she came to Germany (the GDR) with a recommendation to the Volksbühne in East Berlin where she became an assistant to Benno Besson, then manager and artistic director. She went with him to Paris and returned to Bochum to work with the directors Thomas Langhoff and Manfred Karge. She now lives both in Berlin and Düsseldorf. Her first text was the play *Karagöz in Alamania*, performed for the first time in 1986. Only two books written by her have appeared to date in Germany: the collection of stories *Mutterzunge* (1991), which includes a prose version of *Karagöz in Alamania*, and the novel *Das Leben ist eine Karawanserei, hat zwei Türen, aus einer kam ich rein, aus der anderen ging ich raus* (1992). This novel is about Turkey and a Turkish childhood in the 1950s and 1960s.[3]

Mutterzunge

Mutterzunge is both the title and the opening short poetic piece in Özdamar's first collection of texts written in German and originally published in 1990. Each text in this collection combines a plurality of voices, views, questions. They include autobiography as well as fiction, poetic writing and documentary as well as mythology. But above all they are aesthetic presentations of political and social questions written with great insight and sensitivity. The author uses concise and complicated imagery which shows her ability to distinguish clearly between denotative and connotative meanings. Places and experiences in Turkey and in both parts of Germany, past and present, overlap, contract, expand and mix in a uniquely textured language. It is a stream of cultural and political consciousness, a free flow of thoughts provocatively organised. Fragmentation seems to be a means to master the abundance and density of the signs by which we are surrounded. However, this never means dislocation or disintegration. The fragments assemble, form chains, become knots in a net of human experience.

The opening sentence already suggests bi-culturalism: 'In my language tongue means: language'.[4] Since this is true of many languages, a basis for symbolic communication is created from the very beginning. Yet in the German language the immediate relationship is lost in every day usage: *Sprache* (language) and *Zunge* (tongue) are separate signs. The beginning of the text is archaic and thus has a poetic effect, hinting to the German reading public at an originality and individuality still characteristic of other languages.

Özdamar's mother tongue is the Turkish language. In this first sketch, which is surely partly autobiographical, she complains that she has lost her mother tongue. She asks where this could have happened, trying to remember possible places. She is sitting in a Berlin café, 'Negro café' (*Neger-Cafe*), she calls it, using an insulting and discriminating word to point to the extreme mental strain caused by her loss. Her feet have metaphorically lost touch with the ground, she is psychically and physically uprooted: 'I sat with my twisted tongue in Berlin city. Negro café, Arabians as guests, bar chairs too high, feet waggle'. The mental and linguistic journey between the two countries becomes a search for cultural identity.

She remembers vaguely glimpses of intimate dialogues with her mother, as if they were spoken in a well-learned foreign language. In her memory Turkish newspaper headlines change into

German sentences: 'Arbeiter haben ihr eigenes Blut selbst ver-
gossen' ('Workers spilled their blood themselves', 1991: 9). Even
the story of a Turkish mother whose son had been hanged for 'anarchy' after the military coup seems to her as if it had been told in
German. The story is written in broken German, effecting a sense of
closeness and local presence as well as alienation. The place, the
house and garden, the policemen, the court become unconsciously
both Turkey and Germany. The two languages and places are no
longer clearly separated. The artistic style creates an immediate
sense of coherence when the next place mentioned is evidently in
Germany – a Stuttgart prison. Here she caught a few words spoken
by Turkish prisoners out of the window. The most significant word
she remembers is 'görmek', which means 'to see'. The word works
like a vital signpost on her way to her cultural origins.

An incident in her dream produces the words 'kaza gecirmek'.
A Communist friend had told her that one has to 'experience the
accidents of life' to avoid superficiality and achieve depth when
telling stories. The friend did not smile, whereas all the others told
their stories with the 'corners of the mouth' – smiling, lying, pre-
tending, imitating, mimicking?

The third word is 'isci' (worker). It is the profession written in
her passport. She had once wanted to hide it when the train she
was travelling in was inspected at a check point and people were
arrested. At the check point a photocopying machine produced a
large picture of her as 'isci'. This machine, a symbol for repression,
also had its place in Berlin, at Check Point Charlie (or Friedrich-
straße station) between the two parts of Germany.

Özdamar mentions two places where she assumes that she
could have lost her mother tongue: 'I once sat in an intercity train
restaurant at a table. At another one a man was reading a book
with delight. I asked myself what he was reading. It was the
menu. Perhaps I lost my mother tongue in the IC restaurant' (10).

Reading is an intellectual effort because it means decoding language and meaning. Here this process is opposed to reading as
eating or consuming. In the text, marginal but decisive events are
magnified. The scope of the text and the language used are limited, restricted by a one dimensional theme. This, like the normal
indifference of Western standard behaviour, is criticised by a very
simple but effective antithesis and it is intensified because it is
related to the 'loss of language'.

The train arrives at Cologne central station. The cathedral is the
building next to the station. At first the narrator is not able to look

at it. Then, one day, she opens one eye and 'a razor blade entered my body and was cutting inside, suddenly there was no longer pain, I opened the other eye. Perhaps, I lost my mother tongue there' (10). The cathedral, patriarchal sign of a different religion, monumental, threatening, is sucking the identity out of her body. The cultural shock leads to speechlessness. The train scenes have a general significance. Being exposed and checked, crossing borders, leaving and arriving, moving, being on the way – these are painful experiences at both primary and secondary levels of significance.

Her first attempt to rediscover her language involves crossing the border to East Berlin. The intellectual impetus is Bertolt Brecht. So the starting point is the language of art which is not seen as confined to a particular cultural background. In the canteen of the Berlin Ensemble she feels at home as 'isci' because it is normal that everybody is talking about work. The words 'görmek', 'kaza gecirmek' and 'isci' attain a meaningful depth. There is the mainly receptive 'to see' (watching, observing, standing outside), the mainly passive but already personal experiencing of the accidents of life, the feeling with all your senses that something bad is being done to you, and the connotation of 'working' as being active, productive. Losing includes the possibility of finding. It is as if she is finding a new language, words which are of general human significance begin to form a meaningful pattern. Words assemble anew.

'Großvaterzunge'

'Großvaterzunge', the second story in *Mutterzunge,* is about the search for the Arabic origins of Turkish culture. After the breakdown of the Ottoman Empire Atatürk wanted to transform the Turkish state into a modern European Republic. The use of Arabic letters was prohibited in 1927, the Latin alphabet introduced. The law, the constitution and the educational system were reformed according to European models. Secularisation was also carried out by force. Mosques were closed, religious education forbidden. To wear Islamic dress, the fez and the veil, was made a punishable offence.

The narrator would not have been able to communicate with her grandfather – that is her roots, her origins – if they had both been dumb. That is why she goes to an oriental scholar in Wilmersdorf – Ibni Abdullah – to learn Arabic letters. In this section the language of the text embarks on a journey through Arabian mythology and religion. The voice of the Koran and the language of ancient sagas, sayings and fairy tales confront the reader with the elaborate symbolism and poetic richness of a different culture. One might feel excluded by the language and imagery on a first reading. The text is waiting to be deconstructed and leaves much room for interpretation. The whole text is a balancing act between the language of love and tenderness, mainly materialised by mythological signs and signifiers, and that of down-to-earth metaphors of violence reflecting global reality.

The seven brothers of Ibni Abdullah died in the conflict between Palestine and Israel. Ibni Abdullah himself, who opposed the government, was accused of being an Islamic fanatic. The narrator experienced both the death of people in Turkey and the death of the student Benno Ohnesorg in Berlin during the students' revolts of 1968. 'Paradise and hell are two neighbours, their doors opposite each other', her grandmother once said (13). Abdullah feels free to say what he thinks in Germany but the narrator remarks that 'money has no fear here, it has teeth' (15). Money is dangerously strong. It does not fear words. It is money that will finally win.

The Germans' attitude towards their political past is reflected in one episode. Friends are showing private holiday films of 1936. The Germans react with a nostalgic sigh :'Well, those aluminium cups of the 1930s!', whereas the narrator's glance is caught by the 'flags of the time clashing on the city hall' (18) that make her feel as if she were in a fever. The overtly political, but unobtrusive, judgement is omnipresent.

The conflict between East and West Berlin is effectively reduced to observations that ridicule the artificial scar between the two parts of the city as expressed in everyday human life. As a frontier commuter, she is able to comment on the strange signs that she comes across in form of dialogues and situations, for example, the old and the sick, who were allowed to cross the border. Seemingly real details are always presented as having many levels of meaning. There is the handicapped, fat, young woman from the East, who is (metaphorically or ideologically) sedate (in case of an attempted flight easily caught) and blind(ed), so that she will not see the tempting signs of the West. She is mothered and spoken to by her companion as if she were a child. The tempting attraction that they want to visit is Aldi, the cheapest Western supermarket chain. On the other hand, Özdamar feels like a thief in an East German vegetable shop because of the poor supply. Yet it is more important that souls are impoverished, values have degenerated into the desire for mere consumer goods. She wishes that the statue of Brecht might come to life again, standing there with a cap and a flute, simplicity and art united.

In 'Großvaterzunge' the Arabic language becomes the language of love and suffering. Together with the narrator, the German reader discovers, almost unconsciously, the richness and potency of a foreign culture. Learning becomes a playful experiment of thoughts, as reader and writer share almost the same innocent perspective. Learning the letters, their shapes acquire meaning. They become both local and global images of great depth: birds, a heart with an arrow in it, a caravan, sleeping camels, a river, trees uprooted by the wind, slithering snakes, pomegranate trees that are freezing in the wind and rain, evil-looking eyebrows, wood floating on a river, a fat female bottom on a hot stone in a Turkish bath, eyes that cannot sleep. In certain situations the letters conquer the human body. Ibni Abdullah's face becomes a scornful letter or a begging letter on its knees, the narrator's hand becomes letters without a tongue. The Koran still has letters with a mystic quality, the meaning of which has not yet been deconstructed. So the author's aesthetic approach is also one of exegesis.

The Koran is the textual and emotional body of her learning. It is seen as a symbol of diversity and unity. Her reception of it goes beyond a merely spiritual interpretation. The text is law, culture, religion and history.[5] Literal knowledge mixes with new ideas of love and suffering which seem not necessarily to contradict the basis from which they have arisen. The text questions whether the religious roots are anti-women or have only been interpreted in that way during the course of history.[6] Liberating thoughts are very often equated with the simple metaphor of a flying bird. Sometimes these have blurred shapes, they can hardly be caught, not steady, rising and stooping. In Islamic culture, birds embody fate as well as the souls of the dead believers living in the tree of life. Above all the cultural search is a new emotional and intellectual experience, far removed from a fundamentalist Islamic approach.

Özdamar's sexual frankness is remarkable. Physical love and desire are written about without taboo. The narrator is sexually much more emancipated than her teacher. She leaves him in the end because he demands 'pure and holy love', feeling that he can not cope with the passion that has engulfed him. He is still trapped within the patriarchal religious tradition. Her sexual freedom and demanding unrest is too quickly equated with unbelief.

He is not yet able to master the contradiction intellectually. Love becomes a reward for good learning: 'The scripts will not forgive you' (30) or 'If you will learn that with patience today, I will spend the night with you' (31). These words are like self-defiance. The narrator becomes more and more the property of her teacher – she is shut up behind a veil in the room of the scripts. The veil is, of course, ambiguous in a larger context. It is both the Islamic sign and another Berlin Wall, a forcibly erected barrier defying communication. These outward signs contradict the interior states of the protagonists. Their feelings for each other are honest, but tradition prevents them from realising them. But the final conclusion is again political. It is money that has teeth. Ibni Abdullah says: 'You are beautiful, I want holy love, pure love. If I go on sleeping with you, my body will change, I will lose my work … My body has gone crazy. If you will go on coming into my body, in a month I will have lost my work, and I am a poor man' (40). The author remembers old sayings of her grandfather which have proved still to be true: that the one who wants the treasure (love?) has to hit the dragon (tradition, one-dimensional discourse?) and that the beloved, who has shown no patience in suffering while put to the test, will sleep alone under the tree of love. At the end of their affair, both are victims. On the surface nobody is verbally assaulted or blamed. Every line that is written is a subtle balancing act with a liberating potential sometimes very difficult to decode and far from the labels 'right' or 'wrong'.

Reality breaks into her world again. When she says that words of love have a childhood and that in a foreign language words do not have one, she confesses to the life she has lived. It is hers with all the feelings of alienation and sorrow. Historical deficits can be compensated for intellectually, though sometimes under great emotional strain. Ibni Abdullah's letters and words have become guardians with bows and arrows killing the heart and the bird. She leaves the room of scripts in which she has been locked for forty days. She throws the scripts on the motorway. She denies their implications for the present which seem to be violent interferences in life. This need not necessarily be so. History and modernity, tradition and social and technical advance are questioned in the claims they make for automatic acceptance.

The first news headline that she reads is about death in Rio. The political motif merges into a private one: the suicide of a young German artist whose girlfriend she meets on a bench. The young woman tells her story. The narrator, introducing herself as a 'collector of words' tells her that *Ruh* in her language means *Seele* (soul) in German. The translation shows the ambivalence. *Ruh(e)*, which is also a German word, means in this context 'peace'. So the Turkish and the German woman share the fate of lost love and find a common language. Soul means peace. Both repeat the sentence. A few words express a common desire, a state of mind, a non-verbalised agreement, a similar experience of the 'accidents of life' without their having had a common childhood. Life can start anew.

'Karagöz in Alamania'

This narrative text, also published in *Mutterzunge*, was originally written as a drama which was performed for the first time in 1988 in Frankfurt. It is the story of a Turkish emigrant seeking his fortune in Germany. The frame is a political satire, a fable in which the donkey, accompanying the peasant Karagöz, becomes an intellectual, a philosopher, commenting on the events. His intrusive remarks provide the framework of the text and the political commentary. Quoting Marx's *Capital* on labour and production, freedom and alienation, he, the intellectual, clearly confesses to being a Marxist. But at the end he does not get any responses from the peasant, who has been betrayed, despite the accumulation of pseudo values such as a big car, a diplomat case, cassette recorder and a pocket calculator. Karagöz is no longer free and proud, but he tries to live up to a fake ideal, restlessly commuting between the two countries, feeling at home nowhere.

The donkey – and thus his criticism – is only understood by the female donkey and the young peasant descending from an apple tree and leaving together with him to an unknown place. Might this signify an awakening of the marginalised, the women and the young? The donkey's counterpart, a young Turkish scholar of the new generation referred to as 'the enlightened one' enters the stage sitting with a typewriter in a bath tub. The reference to the Roman stoic philosopher and writer Seneca, who committed suicide in the bath, and his questions about how to live is clear. The young man's ideas reflect the various approaches found in trends of modern philosophy. His language is interspersed with Western catchphrases such as 'culture shock' and 'guest worker'. Half of his words are in English, even in the interview with a fellow Turkish youth at an immigration check point. Clichés about cultural identity are revealed by a sewing contest of Turkish dresses made with German fabric.

However, the philosopher of this younger generation also offers different approaches which Marxism has neglected. He suggests that both a Turkish and a German goddess should comment on history from the Crusades to Bismarck and on a Greek and a Turkish statue from Pergamo. The donkey sees the economic roots of the connection between the Baghdad railway and ancient Pergamo, given as a present to Berlin in the last century.

In the end there is still a communication barrier between the old and new generation. Their views of the world still disintegrate, they do not listen to each other. But Özdamar seems to be painfully aware of the necessity and possibility of assembling experience and knowledge anew. In the story old Turkish folk motives, fairy tales and religious and worldly wisdom mix with Western postmodern experience. Both cultures are reviewed from an ironical distance. One seemingly subordinated sentence in the middle of the text becomes a motto of the author's work in general: 'Should we claim that we really understand all we perceive by listening and watching?' (69). The question could be a starting point for a more sensible and non-prejudiced approach to multicultural societies.

Özdamar's mainly Turkish protagonists give an explanation of the world from their perspectives. They all believe that they know the answers, at least for themselves. Özdamar sympathises with the common sense of her people, with their cleverness, wisdom and irrepressible humour. But they are also partly ridiculed – but not betrayed – by the unmasking of their uncritical acceptance of given standards and their inability to communicate in a wider cultural context governed by both tradition and change.

Women suffer the most, waiting for their husbands for a long time, if not in vain. If they join their families in Germany, they become entangled in the social network of tradition and new experiences. They experience patriarchal sex and gender relations both at home and in Germany, racial and class discrimination in German cities.[7] Özdamar's female voices describe their position with a good deal of realism and human insight.

Clichés on both sides are satirised. The universal applicability of the sacred values of our postmodern society are questioned: 'The minaret now had a tape recorder. The Hodscha was not to be seen any longer. But the Ezan rang out at the wrong speed' (84). Another example is that of the old man who is blow-drying his beard before wetting it again and again, drinking at the well.

Özdamar uses her sharp critical techniques to reveal the motives behind the recruitment of foreign workers in Turkey, the proceedings of immigration controls and health checks, the effects of family separation and generational conflicts, the ridiculous instructions about behaviour for guest workers, language problems – in short all the burning socio-political and cultural issues of the present which are not only confined to one or two nations.

Let us have a closer look at some allegorical images. On their way to Alemania, Karagöz and the donkey meet a lion with a plastic bag. The bag contains the bones of a man and some coins. Suddenly two tombstones grow out of the soil and start a religious dispute. It is an adaptation of the Grave Diggers' Scene in *Hamlet*. The tombstones ask the bone man about his God, Faith and Prophet and whether or not he observes the religious rites. As he cannot answer, they speculate and try to remember what they have heard from other people about him (a would-be immigrant to Libya who was waiting in vain for an answer to his application). However, in the end it does not matter whether he was eaten by the lion (killed by 'plastic bag modernity', the rich, the strong, the touts) or whether he had committed suicide because he was eaten away by life itself. Believer, non-believer, heretic, in the end they are all equal. The tombstones do not mind burying him with dignity since he is a human being. In addition, the lion himself is imprisoned for life, if not hunted in Africa for the sake of money which is the declared aim of a young man in a different context of the same story.

Money is the God by which the new generation's thinking and acting is determined. It intervenes in areas of intimacy and privacy, it erodes human values. Thus the changing attitude towards the dead is a striking example. Two old men, whose sons have been killed in an accident on the motorway, are discussing the problem of how to transport them back to Turkey by plane in a decent coffin. Money is not the object. What matters is the dignity of the dead. Their opposites are two sons who do not want to pay the price. They put their dead father in a television box and transport him back on top of their new status symbol, a Ford car. On the way back the television box is stolen because of its valuable original contents. The open ending of this incident of black humour speaks for itself.

The text clearly reveals Özdamar's skills as a woman of the theatre. The dynamic sequence of the scenes and fragments, both comic and tragic – in some cases even absurd – and the almost unlimited possibilities for props may be more suited to a play. Nevertheless the prose text conveys its message impressively and powerfully.

Career of a Char – Memories of Germany

> I am the char, if I do not clean, what else shall I do? In my country
> I was Ophelia. (Özdamar 1991: 102)

'Karriere einer Putzfrau. Erinnerungen an Deutschland', which is
also included in *Mutterzunge*, is a rigorous reckoning with a female immigrant's fate which is partly the author's own, as well as
that of many women with different social backgrounds.[8] It also
has an overtly feminist tone. The Ophelia image, which is central
to the whole text, has many layers. The Shakespearean character,
Ophelia, was a victim of class hierarchy and of a man's lust. In the
end she went mad and drowned herself.

Özdamar's protagonist gets divorced in Turkey. Her modern
Prince Hamlet, a rich man with an 'only child complex', and his
mother point out the class differences between them and denounce
her. As it is the husband's declared aim to be 'silent' and build up
democracy (and climb the political ladder) – a very abstract male
construct in the text – he feels that his wife talks too much. (Here
politics connect past and present). This is considered dangerous
(quite realistically, because a friend's wife has died in police cus-
tody) and so he, like Hamlet, advises her to go to a nunnery, not to
save her own but his life. However, she does not go mad nor does
she commit suicide. If she stays, she is sure that 'they will find her
body' sooner or later. So she decides to leave for Germany.

Unlike Ophelia, she is able to face life, even if it is depraving
and degrading at the bottom of the social ladder. She develops her
own view of the world from her new perspective – 'from feet to
knee' – as she is mainly on her knees or bent down while working.
She is full of bitterness that she has to clear up the excrement of a
man's beloved dog called Prince (again a Hamlet?). When the dog
eventually dies, she has to leave. The intercity motif from 'Mutterzunge' appears again. Between sleeping and wakening she
experiences a vague scene of sexual harassment of a woman by a
drunk man. The woman pretends to have cancer which the man
interprets as her sign of the zodiac.

She arrives in a city where she continues her career as a charwoman, cleaning a block of flats where the tenants again leave 'piles
of shit' on their doorsteps. She becomes a witness of the solitude of
the German high-rise flat dwellers. From her perspective they are
imprisoned between dirt, carelessness, trivial talk, sexual desire and
brutality. She listens to the sounds of loneliness. The voices of the

city, television, toilets, birds, trivial German pop songs expressing meaninglessness – they are all symbols of a failure to communicate.

The text is full of sexual allusions. There is a man who committed suicide, apparently because of venereal disease – at least, the trouble for which he has to go to hospital is his 'broken cock'. The woman in the dustbin with her legs stuck up in the air is also ambiguous. That two immigrant workers refer to her as 'standard' and say that they could have used her for the next thirty years, leaving the impression of an inflatable sex doll. It does not matter whether the 'body' is real or not. It is the symbol of a dead female, abused and thrown away. Violence as normality. As in T.S. Eliot, the city is still a 'waste land', raped, barren, numbed, indifferent.

She finds the antithesis to this, 'cleanness', with a simple woman, a junk-dealer. In her role as charwoman, she was accused of having spoiled the linen. She decides to buy a new set. The vulgarity of language which has characterised the text so far, is gone. The dialogue which follows reveals much of a sympathetic mother/daughter relationship and becomes political once again. It is about the war, loss, psychic strain and a deep longing for peace. The old woman will not experience the next war. As she feels that the danger has not disappeared, she has bought 'good pills'.

The linen is clean and cheap. It is as unspoiled as the woman's character is honest and dignified. She is able to communicate without signs of alienation or discrimination. Recognising the charwoman's beauty, she suggest that she should have been a theatre actress. This is like a revelation to her. She confesses to an intellectually active life: 'In real life the bad win. But the dead are allowed to make their nonsense on the stage' (111). She was 'killed in her own country'.

Now the betrayed and drowned Ophelia comes to life again and with her, many personalities, mythological, literary and historical characters as well as bystanders. They all meet in an absurd Pinteresque stream of consciousness. Among them are, for example, Medea, Cleopatra, Richard III, Nathan the Wise, Robespierre, Caesar, Rimbaud, Woyzeck, Van Gogh, Hamlet, Artaud, all grave diggers, all Shakespearean Fools, Horatio, sailors, all dead messengers, Eva Braun and Hitler. Although it is referred to as 'nonsense' – perhaps the modern Ophelia's madness – the text demands to be read as a network of intertextual postmodern allusions, meaningful on the political and cultural level.

As it is overcrowded with symbolist associations, the text refuses to be comprehended on a first or second reading, and it leaves much space for polysemic interpretation. Behind each character lies a period of human or cultural history. Here are some examples of Özdamar's literary imagination. The stage (the world?) where they all meet is a men's urinal painted black by Van Gogh. Ophelia, Cleopatra, who took her own life to escape being carried off as a captive by Octavian, and Medea, the magician in Greek mythology friendly and helpful to strangers who killed her own sons to take revenge because of her husband's betrayal, have to clean it. Ophelia has to clean away the semen of a masturbating clerk and pours it on the blue skirt of Hamlet's mother. Later she appears as a Latin American whore. Medea, a militant feminist, wants women to have access to the urinal, too, and is stroking the balls of Brutus.

Hamlet, Horatio, Medea's children and a number of extras are occupying the urinal and are threatened by Hitler and Eva Braun. Hitler says that their place is 'behind the wall'. East Berlin is a punishment (or refuge?) because it has no 'beautiful motorways'. But, on the other hand, it can also be a prison wall. They are bitten by Eva Braun's dog (Hitler himself?) who decides who is 'the Jew'. Nathan the Wise, with his plea for religious tolerance, now a Nobel Prize winner for Peace, is also bitten.

Hamlet is also corrupted by modernity. He has not fulfilled his potential. The modern Hamlet's philosophy is linked to the delicatessen, telephone, cheese and Coca-Cola. Caesar sends him to 'Third World urinals to teach humanism' because he is no longer 'really political'. So-called plastic snakes, modern devils, are omnipresent. They bite, they have boxing gloves and they want to kill Woyzeck's mother.

At the end of this literary fantasy Caesar demands obedience from his subjects, otherwise he will kill them. Despite the negative frame of the interlude, the end of the text itself is structurally both open and closed. We find the protagonist at the stage door with the plea to act. The scene reminds one very much of the fate of Shakespeare's fictitious sister Judith in Virginia Woolf's *A Room of One's Own* (1929). Judith was as gifted as her brother but was laughed at by the men of the theatre and seduced. Finally she killed herself.

Özdamar's heroine is given a floor-polishing machine. The stage has to be polished every day. 'That was it' (118) is the final statement. A char remains a char? This would be too simple a conclusion. Despite its seemingly closed ending, the final image is ambivalent in a deconstructive sense. In one reading she remains a char, kicked around in a place where as a Turkish woman she is as skilled and knowledgeable as her German colleagues, if not more so because of her experience. She remains a victim of race, class and gender oppression. In a second reading she gets a subaltern job in the place where she wants to find professional fulfilment. Actually, while cleaning, she is already on the stage waiting for her time to come. In a third reading she clears away the remains of the dead making space for a metaphorically new beginning. In a fourth reading, if the stage is too slippery because of her polishing, she will symbolically cause some actor's, manager's, official's or character's (Caesar's and Hitler's?) downfall ...

Emine Sevgi Özdamar's literary work is a multi-faceted play with artistic images and the subtleties of language. Often she conveys her profoundly political messages through complicated artistic structures. The level of secondary signification is important. Deliberately subversive, she challenges short-sighted thought and behaviour in a world which is now multi-cultural. Superficially one could define the dynamism of her ideas as an imaginary chaos which is equivalent to the confusion of our time. Her approach is historical, but she questions old explanations. She neither promises a better future nor romanticises the past. She is very realistic about the possible prospects of our planet. Allegorical, anticipated and real death play a central part in all of her texts. There are moments of deep pessimism and doubt in her work. However, she refuses to forget, to obscure facts, to repress experience. She is aware of a movement, full of energy, with the capacity to change the existing limits and to bring about better communication and mutual acceptance. This movement includes resistance to the existing patriarchal and discriminatory power structures in Germany and elsewhere in the world.

Notes

1. See Schulte et al. 1985.
2. See Elsner and Elsner 1992.
3. See Pfister 1992: 1–2.
4. The English translations in the text are my own.
5. See Rudolph and Werner 1984: 5-38.
6. For a deeper understanding of sexuality and the Islamic tradition see Heller and Mosbahi 1993; Minai 1981; Minces 1992.
7. See Franger 1990.
8. See Pfister 1992: 2. Özdamar mentions in an interview that she smuggled herself into the plays in the dumb role of a cleaning woman, at first with a rag, later with a polishing machine.

Chapter Ten

WOMEN WRITERS IN THE GDR, 1945–1989

Eva Kaufmann

Introduction

Since the 1970s literary works by East German women writers have become increasingly well known both inside and outside the former GDR. Abroad, it was primarily German specialists who recognised the value of this writing and it was highly valued on all sides during the lifetime of the GDR. It was not only women readers who found works by women writers good reading – appealing to the head, the heart and the senses in equal measure. This type of literature interested readers both for its discussion of real life problems and for its aesthetic qualities.

Very few of the writers were (or are) prepared to use the term 'women's writing' to describe their work. This term has various connotations which are not applicable to the lives and work of these writers. For one thing the term has pejorative connotations where aesthetic value is concerned. Since the second half of the nineteenth century 'women's writing' has been understood to refer to inferior fiction which was produced en masse by women, about women and for women. It was all classed as shallow, kitschy, stereotyped and trashy. All these traits, which describe popular fiction, including that written by men, were readily applied to novels written by women. Secondly the term 'women's writing' has been linked to feminism, in particular, since the end of the 1960s, to the autonomous women's movements in Western Europe and in the United States. This concept of 'women's writing', as it was developed systematically by Sigrid Weigel in her book *Die Stimme der*

Medusa (1989), does not include all women authors; it only applies to those who support the aims of the women's movement and communicate its ideas. In this type of writing, which began with Karin Struck's *Klassenliebe* (1973) and Verena Stefan's *Häutungen* (1975, *Shedding* 1978), artistic merit is not the primary concern.

It was not possible to talk about 'women's writing' in this second sense in the GDR because the GDR had no autonomous women's movement. The only legal women's organisation in the GDR, the Democratic German Women's Federation (*Demokratischer Frauenbund Deutschlands,* DFD) had no independent policies of its own. The DFD was one of the large mass organisations of the GDR. Like other mass organisations, its task was to influence as many women as possible to accept the policies of the ruling elite and to encourage them to become involved in a wide variety of useful activities. Courses on child care, running a household and on popular scientific and cultural topics were most popular, in particular among older women. They were also social events. The state's policies on women provided the framework for the organisation's work down to the last detail. As far as history and tradition were concerned, only the women's section of the Marxist workers' movement was recognised as important. Feminism was held to be a spectre and was ignored by the DFD.

Whenever women writers in the GDR acknowledged feminist ideas and literature from the West, they interpreted them in the context of their own lives and used them in their writing in ways that corresponded to their own experience. They tended to place specifically female interests in the context of the general interests of mankind (e.g., against war and power politics).

These writers did not want to be evaluated differently from their male counterparts; they did not want to be judged according to special criteria on account of their gender. To see their work labelled as 'women's writing' would have seemed to them like ghettoisation.

For all these reasons I avoid the term 'women's writing' where GDR women writers are concerned and only use it in inverted commas. The following study deals with more than just feminist-oriented writers. It is selective in so far as it discusses or mentions those texts which, in their day, achieved special literary historical importance. It also includes other texts which, in spite of artistic quality, gained little recognition. Almost without exception these are texts which are still worth reading today. They depict the experiences of women in an historical period which is now past and in situations never to be repeated.

The lives of women writers in the GDR, the conditions under which they lived and wrote, differ in certain ways from those of German-speaking women writers in the FRG, Switzerland, and Austria. This is a result of differences in public, cultural and literary life, in the economy and in the social structure. In short it is due to differences in their respective social systems.

The appeal and dynamism of the literature written by GDR women writers are based not least on the fact that it reflects the changes which characterised the lives of the younger generations of women. New opportunities, and especially new needs are highlighted, together with new conflicts, for which there are no answers or solutions in sight. Women's writing depicts how both the old and the new roles assigned to women become entangled. Moreover, their texts are frequently very emotional since they often address destructive contradictions.

The biographies (and the texts) of GDR women writers have a lot to do with what can be described as the normal life stories of women in the GDR: learning a trade or profession, marrying at an early age, having children early on, working with short interruptions and then picking up their career where they left off. This life pattern is depicted in many texts and is increasingly questioned – a factor which contributed much to the popularity of this writing.

In the GDR over 90 percent of all women had mainly full-time, paid jobs and, at the same time, almost all had one or more children. Highly subsidised child care facilities were provided: crèches, nursery schools and after-school care. Women received training as skilled workers, studied at technical colleges and universities. All careers were theoretically open to them. Yet despite this there was a sexual division of labour and despite the principle of equal pay for equal work, correspondingly less favourable rates of pay for 'woman's work'.

On the whole the husband's income was not sufficient to secure the desired standard of living for the family. Being economically independent from one's husband became the common experience. This was particularly important if the husband wanted a divorce, or (as became increasingly the case) when women initiated divorce proceedings, or when women ruled out marriage altogether, doing without a 'breadwinner' for themselves and their children. Women were very heavily burdened with responsibilities, especially as the service sector was underdeveloped, and a chronic shortage of all sorts of goods meant that satisfying everyday needs was in general stressful and time consuming. In spite of all this it was not considered desirable to be only a housewife; women were supposed and wanted to be employed, independent of men, and have a life outside of the home.

The equal-rights policy implemented by the state was based on ideas and theoretical precedents developed in the German Workers' Movement in the nineteenth century by Marx, Engels, Bebel and Clara Zetkin. It was also influenced by the policies on women in the Soviet Union, which were based on the same theoretical principles, but started from different material and cultural conditions. Women did not have to fight for new opportunities; they were granted them quasi-historically and legally 'from above'. The negative effects of this historical advantage are particularly evident in the fact that women developed hardly any awareness of themselves as women. They had no experience of what women could achieve when they worked together. Things that are freely available seem to be worth less and to be less worth defending than those which one achieves through one's own efforts. This applies in particular to attitudes towards paragraph 218 which criminalises abortion. Immediately after the end of the war, paragraph 218, which was infamous in Germany, was relaxed and abortion made easier. Yet by 1950 this progressive measure had been rescinded. This directly contradicted the traditions of the Workers' Movement and left-wing progressive writers in the 1920s, who had fought passionately against paragraph 218. In the GDR there was no public discussion of any of this, not even in fiction or poetry.

When, in 1969, the contraceptive pill was introduced and, in March 1972, abortion was legalised (women were allowed free access to abortion within the first twelve weeks of pregnancy) women saw these important measures as a free gift. They were not conscious of the really historic dimensions of this new law, which was introduced in a suspiciously quiet way. They used the opportunity to take independent decisions about the birth of children and thus about their own bodies. However, even on this occasion, there was no public discussion of the issue. This is evident from the lack of space devoted to it in women's writing. After 1972, it became increasingly hard to imagine that paragraph 218 would be re-introduced. Twenty years later, after the demise of the GDR, the new ruling elite could rescind the progressive laws without much resistance from women in the former GDR.

Even if the idea of self-determination did not exist in the GDR with its generally authoritarian living conditions, the majority of women felt that their situation was incomparably better than that of their mothers and grandmothers. The common experience of millions of women of being on an equal footing with men in qualified jobs increased self-esteem. Yet as long as male standards were tacitly regarded and accepted as the norm, very little sense of female self-awareness could develop. From the beginning of the 1970s 'women's writing' was particularly important in developing such awareness.

Women did not find it any more difficult than men to have texts accepted by publishing houses in the GDR. The restrictions with which they had to contend were of a general political or cultural political nature and were equally applicable to both sexes. Nevertheless, independent ideas, which went beyond the official equal-rights policy, put forward by women writers were judged to be political and were treated in a correspondingly restrictive manner. (Compare, for example, the experiences of Irmtraud Morgner with her stories of gender swapping discussed below.)

Like the majority of their male counterparts many women writers decided after only a few publications to become freelance, giving up their previous profession, prepared to earn a living by their pen alone. This income was composed of fees from publishers, from editing magazines and from radio programmes. Fees from publishers were important in making possible work as a writer insofar as one third of the agreed royalty sum was paid out when the contract was signed, another third on the submission of the manuscript and the rest on publication. As a rule, a percentage royalty was worked out in the case of further editions. A striking number of women writers of the middle generation, who were born in the 1930s and 1940s, were single parents. In this respect their biographies very much resemble many ordinary women's lives. Many women writers, some divorced, some never married, provided for themselves and their children with their income from writing. In the GDR it was possible, thanks to lower rents and other subsidised necessities, to live from a monthly income of 500 Ostmarks, even with a child – provided one had very modest aspirations where one's apartment, food and clothes were concerned. This also explains why some writers who increasingly came into conflict with the political system of the GDR did not want to 'go West'.

The Cultural Political Context

Like all writers, women writers also had to deal with cultural policy. Culture, too, in the GDR was centrally planned and directed.

The role of culture and art was to bring about the central, if distant, goal of a classless society. All members of society were to be taught enthusiasm for this goal. Since art and culture were given an important role by the state apparatus in the shaping of political ideas, they were simultaneously promoted and strictly controlled.

From early on in their artistic careers writers came into contact in different ways with the cultural political institutions. There were 'Writers' Seminars' and working groups for young authors in which up and coming authors of both sexes could exchange ideas, under guidance, about each other's work. Women writers whose work revealed talent could study for one or more years at the Johannes R. Becher Institute of Literature in Leipzig. A large percentage of the women writers, whose work is discussed below, studied at this institute.

There, as in other cultural political institutions and committees, much depended on how the current director and his or her staff applied the mostly very narrow official party line. With the passage of time, however, staff and students in particular used the often very restricted space for free expression to develop a creative atmosphere. During their study the students received grants. If the women brought children with them to Leipzig, they were taken care of. On the whole such facilities, from which many women of the middle and younger generations benefitted, were full of contradictions. Yet in principle they neither tolerated political criticism nor refusal to conform.

The same was true of the Writers' Union, to which writers could be admitted after making an application with the support of sponsors and following a trial period. In each case, the precondition was publications. The Writers' Union of the GDR held conferences approximately every four years, at which it would take stock of its work and lay down the new literary political line. The choice of the union's president and its committees were watched closely and with growing suspicion by the party and the government. The work took place in regional branches. In the smaller ones, for example Weimar, Neubrandenburg and Cottbus, practical work played a large role. There were discussions of new manuscripts by members of the group or of new publications which were considered to be important to the literary life of the GDR.

The central concept governing cultural policy was 'Socialist Realism' and its most important components were loyalty to the party and 'closeness to the people'. As the years passed the interpretation of these concepts changed and they became broader and ultimately meaningless. They had a practical importance insofar as they could be significant in the assessment of a literary work, and at the decisive stage of obtaining permission to print a text. State control of literature was not known by the name 'censorship'. That only made things worse. The system worked more or less as follows. A writer submitted a text to a publisher. The publisher ordered one or two external assessments of the text from academics, critics or from other persons with a literary background. In the publishing house one editor was given the task of producing an internal assessment. These assessments were passed on to an office which either granted or refused permission to print. This office had the innocuous name 'Central Office for Publishing in the Ministry for Culture'.

On the long path which a text had to travel, it could come up against diverse factors which could be either beneficial or obstructive. Which referees were chosen depended on the understanding of art and on the courage of the directors of a publishing company. If the publishers really wanted to get a book approved by the authorities, they needed strong arguments in the assessments. Even within the Ministry there were employees who covertly gave helpful tips. Here, too, the individual enjoyed a certain amount of freedom.

It quite often happened that even with all-round positive assessments from the publishers permission to print was denied. Sometimes months or even years would go by without a response. If those responsible for granting permission thought that the political dimensions of a text were too hot to handle, then the manuscript would be passed up the bureaucratic ladder until it reached Ulbricht's or, later on, Honecker's desk. This of course, sounds absurd. Could a book really undermine the state? The result of this was that literature (as well as theatre, films, art and sculpture) came to have an inappropriately high significance for the general public and the artists themselves. Even if one ignores the grotesque overestimation of their importance, it is still the case that art and above all literature had a far higher status in the GDR (and in other socialist countries) than in bourgeois democratic countries with market economies. For this reason book publishing was also highly subsidised. Books were extraordinarily cheap. Even books which were neither outright bestsellers nor especially recommended by cultural policy had relatively high print runs.

In the GDR, literature and art were the only media through which public discontent and criticism could be articulated and abuses of the system exposed. In many ways literature took over the functions which the press, the radio and television should have fulfilled and in this respect performed the much quoted role of a substitute for the media.

In the cultural policy of the GDR, extremely restrictive phases alternated with phases of relative liberalism. At times strongly restrictive tendencies contended with those which saw a slackening of the reins or opening of the vents as a better tactic. One could suppose that struggles between different factions in the leadership of the SED (Sozialistische Einheitspartei Deutschlands, the Communist Party), as well as differing views of economic or foreign policy, lay behind these swings in policy.

Literature is now free from censorship and other similar state-imposed constraints. It must now deal with market forces. The tactics with which women writers used to outwit the old powers are no longer of any use.

From the 1940s to the 1960s: Beginnings

After the end of the war it was women writers of the older generation who first came to the fore. These women, who had already begun to write either during the Weimar Republic or even earlier, and who had either gone into exile or 'inner emigration', had returned to Germany after the end of the Second World War from the countries to which they had emigrated either in the East or the West. The decision to set up home in the Soviet zone or in one of the Western-occupied zones depended to a large extent on the basic political credo of the writer. As a rule, those women writers who prior to 1933 had been members of the Communist Party or its associated literary, cultural, and theatre movements moved to the Eastern zone irrespective of their former place of residence.

Yet there were hardly any traces of any kind of feminism in the writing of these women. An important reason for this lay in the Communist movement's belief that women's interests should not and must not be represented separately. Everybody's energy, including that of women, should be concentrated on the principal conflict between capital and labour, and not be deflected and split by giving attention to a 'secondary' conflict between the sexes. In addition to this, it was considered superfluous to want to make a separate case for women's interests since the emancipation of women would be realised through the state's equal rights policy and the building of socialism – simultaneously and automatically. Emancipation would also be promoted by more progressive writers.

For these reasons there was also little interest in feminist literary traditions dating from the pre-1933 period. Everything that took place prior to the Nazi régime and the war appeared, in the light of the ravages of Nazism, as a lost world. Twelve years of fascism, which is really not a lengthy period of time, had for the time being completely wiped out the memory of past literary traditions of women writers. So at this historic turning point, as so often in the history of woman's emancipation, the lessons of earlier emancipation struggles, which had often also been fought out in literature, were not passed on.

Apart from the indifference shown towards feminist traditions of thought, little emphasis was placed on women writers from the past either in the editing programmes of publishers or in literary history. Else Lasker-Schüler, Franziska zu Reventlow, Lou Andreas-Salomé or Irmgard Keun remained unknown for a long time in the GDR. This 'amnesia' of female traditions in literature was, amongst other things, economically motivated. The publishing rights to such literature lay, for the most part, in the hands of Western publishing companies and would have had to have been purchased with hard currency. In order for this to happen, there would have had to have been a strong lobby for literature written by women. This only came into being with the new interest in emancipation developed by women writers in the 1970s. Women's achievements during the course of history in male-dominated literary institutions remained buried. The presence of significant individual women writers such as Marie von Ebner-Eschenbach or Ricarda Huch did not have the effect of raising the question of the literary role of women more generally. For this reason, too, the pejorative concept of 'women's writing' discussed above remained tacitly in place.

A relatively large number of works by Ricarda Huch (1864– 1947) were published in the post-war years. This grand old lady of German literature was also celebrated because she was one of the first women to study in Zürich, where she obtained her doctorate in 1891, an achievement which at that time was still impossible in Germany.

Anna Seghers

The woman writer who in East Germany ranked alongside the great male names of Brecht, Becher, Wolf and Weinert was Anna Seghers. She had been known in the literary world of the Weimar Republic since the end of the 1920s, winning the Kleist Prize in

1928. Her worldwide renown came with her novel *Das siebte Kreuz* (1942, *The Seventh Cross*, 1987). Born in Mainz, she had returned to Germany in 1947 from exile in Mexico and had settled in East Berlin in 1950. Her works, including those written in the GDR in the 1950s and 1960s, offered little reason to look for specifically female qualities in her writing. The interests of women in her work are totally subordinated to more general historical problems: overcoming fascism and the consequences of the war, and the building up of a more just social order. In the short story 'Die Tochter der Delegierten' (1951b) and in the prose-cycles 'Friedensgeschichten' (1953a, orig. 1950) and 'Der erste Schritt' (1953b) the question of what women have to struggle for as women appears to be almost out of place. Nonetheless many of Segher's female characters demonstrated exceptional human achievements and will-power. Thus in the story 'Die Umsiedlerin' (1953c) from the cycle *Der erste Schritt*, a woman who is accustomed to patiently accepting all sorts of injustice and strife becomes a heroine. In the face of traditional feminine reserve this leopard learns how to change her spots. She becomes involved in a debate over village affairs and in this way provides an impetus to others to defend themselves against injustices. Anna Seghers created a particularly impressive female character in the poor Mexican girl Crisanta (in the story of the same name of 1950). Her fate is actually quite without hope. With hardly any resistance she adapts to the eternal sacrificing role of the maternal woman. At the outset the narrator emphasises that she particularly does not want to tell the story of the grand men of the Mexican struggle for independence from the Spanish, not the story of Hidalgo, Morelos or Juarez but of Crisanta, who is everything but a Mexican Joan of Arc. Differences between the sexes are very prominent in this story. Crisanta's boyfriend, who is just as poor and uneducated as she, works his way out of misery by getting to know and joining resistance groups. He initially wants to take her with him, but she is unable to join him. She would have had to transcend female norms of behaviour which would have taken double the effort. In spite of this, she summons up the strength, like millions of women in similar positions, to earn a meagre living for herself and her child.

The interpretation of such a text depends a great deal on the way in which it is read. Anyone who misses the reproachful and angry pathos could think that Anna Seghers is casting women in the old role of the silent sufferer. It is important to me that this story shows the true position of the sexes: the inequality between men and women in what they give to others and what they receive, especially in the Third World.

As the years went by, Anna Seghers's interest in women and their unequal share in the opportunities for happiness increased. In the volume of stories *Die Kraft der Schwachen*, published in 1965, half of the stories have female protagonists. No matter what they achieve, they receive no thanks. It is left to the female reader to draw the conclusion that the world needs changing. As far as history is concerned (particularly the First and Second World Wars and the Spanish Civil War), this is a product of man's doing; women help but have no independent influence over the chain of events. Anna Seghers increasingly stresses the unjust position and relationship between the sexes as she loses hope that socialism is the alternative to the destructive tendencies of mankind's development.

After the novels *Die Entscheidung* (1959) and *Das Vertrauen* (1968), Anna Seghers wrote no more novels, just long and short stories, for example, *Das Licht auf dem Galgen* (1961), the collection *Die Kraft der Schwachen* (1965) and *Das wirkliche Blau* (1967). Many of these stories, which deal with history and philosophy, are as beautiful as they are disturbing. Their plots are almost always situated in other countries and continents. The GDR did not really seem able to inspire poetry in Anna Seghers.

The Old, the Young and the Emergence of the Younger Generation

As far as the number of book titles and sizes of print runs are concerned, some of the older women writers were very successful in the 1950s and 1960s. Such women were Elfriede Brüning (b. 1910), Marianne Bruns (b. 1897), Ruth Kraft (b. 1920), Margarete Neumann (b. 1917), Hildegard Maria Rauchfuß (b. 1918), Inge von Wangenheim (b. 1912) and Hedda Zinner (b. 1907). Their success was based in part on the fact that they wrote in a style that was accessible to all, in accordance with cultural policy as well as with their own their convictions and literary inclinations. Preferred genres were the novel and short story based on conventional models with a chronological plot and an omniscient narrator. They also chose themes which were of interest to larger sections of the public, thereby satisfying needs both for education and entertainment. Especially popular were stories from the past, even the recent past. An example of this is Ruth Kraft's novel *Insel ohne Leuchtfeuer*

(1959) which is about the development of missiles during the Second World War. It sold 450,000 copies and is now being reprinted. Hedda Zinner and Berta Waterstradt (b. 1907) were successful with plays for the theatre, radio and television, for example, about Dimitroff and the trial following the burning down of the Reichstag.

It was precisely those women writers who were associated with the workers' movement and the struggle against fascism who, just like their male counterparts, undertook to write about those subjects which were important for political developments in Germany. Limiting themselves to specific women's themes was out of the question for them. Yet since it was in the interest of the state to win over as many women as possible to socialism, they also took up the theme of the development of women from old-fashioned apolitical housewives to modern, emancipated women. Often they used the novel of development, a form which is rich in tradition in Germany, in order to present the path of the heroine from a middle-class or lower middle-class background to socialism.

These books were willingly devoured by women readers. Older women especially, many of whom had been left without a husband after the war, who often had children to care for, and were forced to lead lives of privation and work, found self-confirmation, encouragement and practical knowledge in these books. This 'useful' literature, which reveals contemporary public thinking about equal rights, is far removed from the feminist tendencies which began in the 1970s. These tendencies come from another generation of younger women – above all from Christa Wolf, Irmtraud Morgner and Brigitte Reimann – who experienced war and fascism either as children or teenagers and who, after 1945, threw themselves into the 'new life' with enthusiastic commitment. They availed themselves of the opportunities which the equal rights policy opened up to young women as regards schooling, higher education, having a profession and working as a writer. Their early literary works from the end of the 1950s and beginning of the 1960s belie their later rebellious attitudes.

Feminism, too, was non-existent for these writers in the 1950s, unfamiliar even as concept. The first prose works of Brigitte Reimann and Irmtraud Morgner are marked by established patterns of thought and aesthetic form. They show how the fate of women has taken a turn for the better under the new socialist relations, provided they follow the path mapped out for them to a career. This makes them feel as if they have done better than their mothers. Although during the war and in the post-war period many women worked outside the home, this was considered to be merely an emergency solution, made necessary by the lack of a male provider. It was seen as a temporary diversion from a normal way of life as a housewife and mother, forced by circumstances. The next generation of women, feeling themselves equal to men in their education and career choice, polemically distanced themselves from this stance. This is demonstrated by Irmtraud Morgner's early novel *Ein Haus am Rand der Stadt* (1962). From such a standpoint history seemed to have taken a great leap forward. The lives of women seemed to have changed more visibly than those of men. Yet women had problems believing in their up-until-now unknown, because untapped, strengths and talents.

In the first half of the 1960s, these three young women writers, who started out as 'good girls', developed independent ideas and approaches to writing surprisingly quickly. This transformation is particularly noticeable in the case of Irmtraud Morgner. One of her books and a confusing leap forward in time demonstrate this. In 1992, a year after Irmtraud Morgner's death, the unpublished novel *Rumba auf einen Herbst* appeared. It had been found among her papers. The title was familiar since it had been mentioned in the novel *Leben und Abenteuer der Trobadora Beatriz nach Zeugnissen ihrer Spielfrau Laura*, published by Morgner in 1974, where long extracts had been quoted from it. It was not known, however, that it concerned a novel which had been suppressed by the censor when Irmtraud Morgner submitted it to be published in 1965. When the novel appeared twenty-seven years later, it did not seem outdated, but rather, its form and narrative technique gave the impression of being decidedly modern. Gone is the didacticism which was prevalent in the previous book *Ein Haus am Rand der Stadt*. Its distinctive characteristics are the joy of story telling, fantastic ideas, humour, terseness, a subjectively tinted involvement with social issues (the Cuban Crisis in 1962, a politically motivated generation conflict, and bold ideas about love and marriage). This novel, which is full of utopian elements and hopes for a sensible development towards socialism, does not give the impression of being anachronistic even today. In *Rumba auf einen Herbst* Morgner had broken away from the prevailing canon of ideas about form, exploding chronology and setting the course for a new form of narrative. A few years earlier, Christa Wolf had gone beyond the formal limitations of her first work *Moskauer Novelle* (1961) and in her important story *Der geteilte Himmel* (1963, *Divided Heaven*, 1976) set off a controversy among critics. In the middle of the

1960s Christa and Gerhard Wolf's film project *Fräulein Schmetterling* became the victim of the campaign which was conducted during and after the infamous XIth Plenum of the Central Committee of the SED at the end of 1965. It targeted all artists and writers who did not present the development of socialism in a purely positive realist manner. The film tells the story of two adolescents, orphaned sisters, who have difficulties in developing their talents and finding their niche in life. This process is both helped and hindered by the state welfare services. As a fairy tale about reality, this film project demanded a style which combined realistic plots with documentary elements and poetically heightened dream sequences. Simultaneously it required both sympathy and distance in the way the characters were portrayed. Such sophisticated cinematic language was new to GDR film production and was for this reason open to all imaginable sorts of misunderstandings and ill-meant misinterpretations. Morgner's, Reimann's and Wolf's encounters with the censors clearly changed their world-views, understanding of emancipation and their conception of literature. Believing in a real alternative, they had endorsed the socialist ideals and early development of the GDR with conviction. Now they regarded the situation and developments in their society increasingly critically. The gap between ideals and reality became more and more perceptible, especially since the hopes of a fundamental renewal of socialism, raised by the Twentieth Party Congress of the Communist Party of the Soviet Union (1956), were not being fulfilled. The invasion of Czechoslovakia by Warsaw Pact troops in August 1968 deepened the disillusionment.

Rigorous state intervention was supposed to apply a brake to the tendencies – perceptible everywhere – of artists to develop an independent interpretation of history and new concepts of art. The opposite happened. The process of emancipation from dogmatic ways of thinking could not be stopped. This was also true in the case of certain women writers' understanding of women's emancipation. In the meantime, more than one generation of women had experience of GDR equal-rights policies. Such experiences were contradictory. Women showed unreserved approval for the possibility of leading a life economically independent of men. For the vast majority of women, this was an imperative, but still only a first step on the long road to emancipation. This historically exact but critical evaluation starkly contradicted official policies for women. These saw women's emancipation as already realised and considered critical discussion of it to be harmful.

In the novel *Hochzeit in Konstantinopel* (1968), Irmtraud Morgner raised the question of whether it would be better for a woman
simply to leave a relationship with a man in which she was unable
to develop and realise her individuality. She tells the story of how
the protagonist, who cannot accept how her boyfriend thinks,
feels and acts, literally gets out of the relationship, en route to the
wedding, by getting out of the car. She considers her own behaviour to be necessary and justified. The heretical tendencies of this
book are conveyed in a lively, playful, yet effective way. Unusual
humour, and many fantastic ideas camouflage the bitter gravity of
the message. The critics did not react. They ignored the book
because it was not immediately evident what was serious in the
book and what not.

The underlying theme of Morgner's novel *Leben und Abenteuer
der Trobadora Beatriz* also has its genesis at the end of the 1960s. It
combines its plot with an appraisal of the history of the female sex.
Thus the French student revolution, the left-wing movements, and
the nascent women's movement in Western Europe set the scene
for a fantastic event. In 1968 Beatriz de Dia, a courtly love poet
from the middle ages, wakes up from an eight-hundred-year sleep.
She wishes to ascertain whether or not the situation of women has
improved over the past eight centuries, and she undertakes her
investigation in the GDR, the country which proclaims itself in
official reports as a 'wonderful place' for women.

Brigitte Reimann too, gains a new profile for herself as a prose
writer in the latter half of the 1960s. She tells the story of her novel
Franziska Linkerhand, which she began in 1963 in a new subjective
style. The writing of this novel, whose form runs counter to standard canonical norms, took many years to complete due to cancer.

Among the younger women writers born around 1930, Christa
Wolf soon became highly respected. Letters show how much her
artistic achievements and attitude, for example her objections to
the notorious XIth Plenum in 1965, encouraged other women to
trust their experiences and to discover their own view of reality
and their own way of presenting it.[1] Both the content and the style
of Wolf's work and her ideas about writing changed radically as
can be seen from her important novel *Nachdenken über Christa T.*
(1968, *The Quest for Christa T.* 1982) and her theoretical essay *Lesen
und Schreiben* (1972, *The Reader and the Writer*, 1977).

In both her narrative style and in her conception of the individual and individual expectations, Christa Wolf differs markedly from
Anna Seghers. As a young woman writer in the 1950s, she had felt

close to Anna Seghers. This relationship between women writers and Wolf's subsequent cutting of the umbilical cord is noteworthy insofar as it differs from the male practice of the 'sons' breaking forcibly away from their 'fathers', and in a manner of speaking killing them. Christa Wolf's relationship with Anna Seghers came to an end in a friendly and supportive way, despite their differences.

When compared with prose, poetry plays a less important role in the literary works of women. At the beginning of the 1960s, Sarah Kirsch (b. 1935) became famous as part of a young literary movement known as the *Lyrik-Welle*. Her poems, which were collected in *Gespräch mit dem Saurier* (1965, written together with Rainer Kirsch) and *Landaufenthalt* (1967), draw on everyday life in their choice of objects, language and in their perspective on the world. The mix of emotionality, wit and vividness give them a fresh and unconventional touch. Sarah Kirsch's influence increased with her later poems in which she exchanged her youthful carefreeness for a painful sensitivity which, however, never sank into sentimentality. The poets Christa Reinig and Helga Novak, who emigrated to the Federal Republic in the 1960s, were never published in the GDR.

The 1970s: A Profusion of Work

In the first half of the 1970s there was an amazing increase in work produced by women writers born between 1930 and 1940. At no other time did women publish so many books of such a high literary standard. Hence the following list:

1971: Helga Schütz (b. 1937)	*Vorgeschichten oder schöne Gegend Probstein (prose)*
Anna Seghers (b. 1900)	*Überfahrt* (short stories)
1972: Helga Schütz	*Das Erdbeben bei Sangershausen* (prose)
1973: Sarah Kirsch (b. 1935)	*Zaubersprüche* (poetry)
	Die ungeheuren bergehohen Wellen auf See (short stories)
	Die Pantherfrau (interviews)
Anna Seghers	*Sonderbare Begegnungen* (short stories)
Helga Schütz	*Festbeleuchtung* (short stories)
Eva Strittmatter (b. 1930)	*Ich mach ein Lied aus Stille* (poetry)

Christa Wolf (b. 1929)	*Unter den Linden* (narratives)
	Lesen und Schreiben (essays)
Christine Wolter (b. 1939)	*Meine italienische Reise* (prose)
1974: Irmtraud Morgner (b. 1933)	*Leben und Abenteuer der*
	Trobadora Beatriz nach
	Zeugnissen ihrer Spielfrau Laura
	(novel)
Brigitte Reimann (1933–73)	*Franziska Linkerhand* (novel)
Gerti Tetzner (b. 1936)	*Karen W.* (novel)
1975: Elke Erb (b. 1938)	*Gutachten* (poetry and prose)
Helga Schubert (b. 1940)	*Lauter Leben* (prose)
Eva Strittmatter	*Mondschnee liegt auf den Wiesen*
	(poetry)

Generational Differences Among Writers

The age difference between Christa Wolf and Helga Schubert is small, yet it was experienced as a generational difference. Anyone born in 1929 or 1930 could still have very vivid impressions of the war and of fascism, could also have been influenced by the Nazi ideology, and could have experienced the defeat of Hitler's Germany as ignominious. Later this might be experienced as failure or even guilt and lead to a desire to make good through active involvement in the reconstruction of Germany. Christa Wolf brought out a child's feelings of guilt in her novel *Kindheitsmuster* (1976, *A Model Childhood*, 1980) on which she was working intensively at the beginning of the 1970s. It portrays the autobiographically inspired development of a girl called Nelly.

In contrast, a few years later Irmtraud Morgner, in her novel *Amanda* (1983), writes in relation to her heroine Laura, who was born in 1933, of 'the regalia of innocence', of the luck of being in 1945 'no older nor younger than 12 … For if I had been older I would have been mixed up in that mess, and if I had been younger, I would not quite have realised what was going on and, as a consequence, I would not have understood my luck' (Morgner 1983: 27). In her story 'Innenhöfe', Helga Schubert ponders on the particularity of her generation: 'The year 1940. The first new school intake in Germany who did not begin the lesson with "Heil Hitler". Innocent at that time' (1984: 9). Yet, in retrospect, this did not seem like luck. The narrator sees her generation as standing in the shadow of the older generation:

After the war they were our new nineteen-year-old teachers … At seventeen they had still been at war, but they had killed nobody … For us they were the more experienced ones, the more mature ones, the ones more aware of responsibilities. Clever older brothers and sisters … But from the very beginning they were already grown up, they dived head first into new responsibility and beliefs … Now they are our headmasters, our chairmen, our party secretaries, our teachers, our mayors, and our renowned authors. (13)

No more than seven years separate Morgner and Schubert's views, yet they are worlds apart. Their different perceptions of chances and obstacles are succinctly expressed in Schubert's words: 'Enthusiasm ended before our time' (10).

Those few writers of the older generation had not only experienced this enthusiasm, as many of their earlier texts demonstrate, with their strong conviction; they had taken it further. The enthusiasm of the early years of reconstruction and the belief in the possibility of eradicating war, need and oppression for ever, through the new social order, were genuine. All the work and privation that people took on seemed meaningful; the removal of the right of dissidents to decide things for themselves and their disadvantage seemed justified.

Christa Wolf, Irmtraud Morgner, Brigitte Reimann and Eva Strittmatter had to work hard to free themselves from this enthusiasm. The contradictions in socialism, which could no longer be explained away as teething difficulties, demanded sober criticism. With changes in how writers felt about life and their understanding of society, new aesthetic norms were called for. A critical examination of their own lives and artistic development became for many the source of inspiration for new work. In 1974 Christa Wolf publicly expressed the painful insight that she 'should and could have known better' in 1959, when, at the age of thirty, she made her literary début with *Moskauer Novelle* (1974: 170). The experience of being able to change their views of important, existential questions, and the need to do so, became a constant impetus to see, think, and feel in a more truthful way.

This was also true in a different way for younger women writers, for Helga Schütz, Helga Königsdorf, and Gerti Tetzner who, in later texts,[2] reflect critically on their youthful commitment. As they only began to write or publish at the end of the 1960s, they had the great advantage of avoiding the literary cul-de-sacs encountered by older writers in their first works. They were also free of the strong feelings of bitterness, which are expressed in the above-quoted text by Helga Schubert and others of her works which were written after the autumn of 1989.

Visible Undercurrents from the 1960s

The profusion of books published in the first half of the decade, in an abundance not to be seen again, has various causes. Strikingly, three books appeared by Sarah Kirsch in 1973, two of which are prose. Both the fictional and the documentary text bear witness to her interest in the lives of women.

As a film producer and screenplay writer, Helga Schütz had direct experience of the repressive nature of cultural policy. She began to write prose, at first only for herself and her children. As part of a series of literary events in which older women writers introduced younger ones to the reading public, she was presented and encouraged by Christa Wolf. After the publication of her first book *Vorgeschichten oder Schöne Gegend Probstein*, the publishing company asked her to write more. This was a strong stimulus in the extremely inconsistent and in many ways negative cultural political context. In 1971, 1972, and 1973 she brought out three small books of prose, one after the other. This explosion in literary output, which was not unique to Helga Schütz, grew out of the friction created by coming to terms with both positive and negative experiences.

The extensive novels by Morgner, Reimann and Tetzner, all of which appeared in 1974 and which had cost their authors many years work, had their origins way back in the 1960s. In contrast with Reimann, Wolf, Morgner, and Strittmatter, all of whom had entered the literary world at a very young age after studying German literature and working as editors or critics, Gerti Tetzner had studied law. Her experiences during her time as an articled clerk in legal practice in the GDR led her to abandon the profession. She began to write, as can be seen from the short exchange of letters between her and Christa Wolf (1965–1969). She had the patience, as an up and coming writer, to go back and study at the J. R. Becher Institute for Literature. She worked for so long on the novel that it was not until she was in her mid-thirties that she felt ready to hand over the manuscript to a publisher.

In a completely different, historical and literary moment – in 1956, at the mere age of twenty-two – Brigitte Reimann had easy initial success. In 1961 her book *Ankunft im Alltag*, which kept to conventional formal principles, was praised by the critics as an important work for the younger generation. This success in the official literary world proved more of a burden than encouragement. Brigitte Reimann needed a long time before she could bring her critical unease to bear on her own work and was able to start writing again.

Eva Strittmatter emerged late onto the literary scene. She became publicly visible as a writer with her volume of poetry *Ich mach ein Lied aus Stille*. At that time she was forty-three and had been writing for years. It obviously cost her dearly to free herself, even partially, from the role of wife and help-mate to the renowned author Erwin Strittmatter and to dare to emerge with a literary profile in her own right. To do this she not only had to fight against her own scruples but also against the mentality of publishers.

The development of women writers of this generation was varied, yet they all worked with great energy and a sober sense of their own worth. They made constant new demands on themselves. They did not make writing any easier for themselves than their male counterparts. At the same time their working and living conditions were often more difficult. Often they had children and for the most part they were single parents. Of the above-mentioned writers only Brigitte Reimann was childless. The others had children long before the advent of the pill, not to mention legal abortion. What all their biographies show is that for these women art and children went hand-in-hand. It must be said, however, that this depended on particular socio-economic conditions which are now history. The stubbornness with which they remained true to their path was, in part, a reflection of their conviction that they had important things to say about their experiences to others, especially to other women.

Key Works and Stories of Gender Role Reversal

In the following section some texts will be identified that in their time were innovative and of consequence for broader literary developments in the GDR.

Brigitte Reimann was not able to finish her novel *Franziska Linkerhand* before her death at the beginning of 1973. She had changed her ideas countless times and was constantly tormented by the worry of failure. This writer, who had become used to literary fame early in her career, published only one piece of work in the intervening years, a description of a journey through Siberia, *Das grüne Licht der Steppen* (1965). After an operation for cancer in 1968, she worked with reduced physical energy but with unparalleled seriousness. Writing became the main occupation in her life. With increasing self-confidence and awareness of difficulties, she paid less attention to the question of whether or not her work would fit in with the line laid down by current cultural policies.

At the centre of the story is a young female architect, who – full of ideals about beautiful modern buildings for workers and ordinary people – is confronted with the obligations to design cheaper and often ugly mass-produced housing. The story relates the everyday struggles which a women has to endure in a predominantly male working environment. In the construction industry, her youth and beauty come to her aid in disparate ways. Work and being in love bring her constant confusion and conflicts, as do the strains of searching for an identity. These are intensified by her painful experience of the deep-rooted cultural differences between her solid middle-class origins and the foreign, proletarian world of the building site and the workers' hostel. The official theory of the disappearance of class differences and the prospect of a classless society in a historically foreseeable time, appear an illusion in the face of the communication problems which the cultivated daughter of the middle class and the young female workers have with each other.

There are many autobiographical elements in the characterisation and development of Franziska Linkerhand. At the beginning of the 1960s and in response to new cultural policies, the writer moved to the town of Hoyerswerda. It had been built on a greenfield site in the vicinity of huge lignite mines and coal-fuelled power stations. Thirty years later its name would resound around the world in connection with attacks on foreign workers. The novel tells how the heroine gives up love and marriage in order to realise her identity through her work. Feminist influences play no part in this scenario. Reimann draws solely on her own experience, for example her horror at the lives led by housewives. She shies away from generalisations.[3] She tells her extensive (five-hundred-and-eighty-page) story from the subjective perspective of the main character. She felt constricted by the officially sanctioned and supposedly objective form of third-person, realist narrative.

Gerti Tetzner's novel, whose title *Karen W.* clearly alludes to Christa Wolf's *Christa T.* and which also contains many autobiographical references, caused a sensation in its day simply because of its open ending. The situation of the protagonist is more difficult than that of Franziska Linkerhand in so far as she not only leaves her unsatisfying marriage, but also gives up her career. Whilst Linkerhand found a meaningful life in her work building homes, however difficult this was, Karen W. gives up a legal career, which she had initially chosen out of a desire to support anti-fascist policies. She leaves the law because she realises that in the justice system she has to do things which run counter to her ideals of and objectives for a new society. Equal to men, Karen W. can gain experiences at work and learn in the process about herself. At the end of the day she knows what she does not want, but not what she can do about it. She has – together with her young daughter – in any case, made a start.

Morgner's novel *Trobadora Beatriz* is, in many ways, more radical than Reimann's. Whilst Reimann adheres to 'the forms of life itself', Morgner uses the fantastic and mythical on a large scale. She allows legendary goddesses to appear in the book and turns a resurrected courtly love singer from the middle ages into one of the two principal female characters. She quotes and brings together authentic texts, for example extracts from the speech by the Minister for Health on the legalisation of abortion. This seven-hundred-page long montage novel, with its bewildering amount of material, is provided with a table of contents with more than one hundred and fifty chapter headings which covers over ten pages. In the complicated structural framework she can inconspicuously insert the one hundred and sixty pages from the Rumba novel which the censor had previously suppressed.

Morgner loved transgressing boundaries in every respect. She was ruthless in her analysis of the relationship between the sexes and their respective roles. At the same time she insisted on presenting her protagonists as lovers of men. They openly express their sexual desires and precisely because of this, they avoid the risk of becoming subordinate to men through love. They set their own female standards against the all prevailing, male norms which supposedly represent general human standards. Laura, the train driver, when looking for a lover, first examines a young man for his fatherly qualities. The novel is peppered with utopian elements. In it we are confronted with a varied and colourful female world. At its centre is a fantastic duo of female figures who are at the same time 'feminised': a troubadour and companion, Beatriz and Laura. Around these two, the narrator positions countless minor or well developed women characters and their destinies. Like the novel as a whole, the ending is left open. Laura's mother,

Olga, who remains tied to her role as a housewife, asks the goddess Persephone to send her to sleep for as long as possible. Her request is granted for three hundred years. The troubadour mysteriously falls from a window whilst cleaning it. Laura, however, seems to have found a partner in Benno who is just as interested in an equal relationship as she is. In the concluding first story of the 'thousand and one' stories, there is talk in the penultimate sentence of a massive innovation: the overcoming of the 'barrier' of the family through proletarian solidarity. In a reversal characteristic of Morgner's work, this is told by a man. Everyone can derive something appropriate from this massive book today, yesterday and tomorrow.

With its calculated unsurveyability, this montage novel is full of allusions, cunning humour and irony. Morgner had learnt from her experience with the censor and with her readers. She counted on the deep and long-term effects of her multi-layered and plural texts. Here time proved her to be right. During the lengthy period that she spent writing the book – she, too, was a single parent – she did little to publicise it. There was a large time gap between it and the publication of its sequel *Amanda* (1983).

At the beginning of the 1970s the American woman writer Edith Anderson, who was living in the GDR, encouraged her fellow writers to write stories about gender role reversal. The subject lent itself to the examination of the relationship between the sexes, especially when they were undergoing such changes as in the GDR. The project touched the nerves of cultural functionaries and it was years before the volume *Blitz aus heiterm Himmel* appeared in 1976 with contributions from both female and male writers. The women writers used this imaginative topic to take a closer look at GDR equal-rights policies. In the stories by Christa Wolf, Irmtraud Morgner and Sarah Kirsch, all the protagonists are highly qualified and extremely capable scientists. They easily accomplish work previously reserved for men. This is the basis for asking further questions about the emancipation of the sexes.

When as part of a scientific experiment, the protagonist of Wolf's 'Selbstversuch' (1974, 'Self-Experiment', 1978) is changed into a man, she experiences emotional impoverishment. As a result she finds that she does not want to be (like) a man. She stops the experiment prematurely in order to become a woman again. The story denounces the limits of existing ideas of equal rights, but the narrator does not conclude the story with a negative ending. There is a final utopian twist. The protagonist counters the abandoned experiment of the man with her own: a 'love experiment' which leads to a fantastic dis-covery, 'the discovery of what one can love' (82).

Irmtraud Morgner's story 'Gute Botschaft der Valeska' – writ-ten for the anthology – was rejected by the publishers. It found cover under the wide umbrella of the Trobadora novel where it was less noticeable. In Morgner's 'Gute Botschaft', sex is dis-cussed bluntly and taboos are violated with cheerful innocence, one after the other. Morgner writes with ease about lesbian rela-tionships, something which the censors found particularly offen-sive since they are set in Moscow. The lively story, so full of allusions, is developed from a utopian perspective. Sexual roles and sexual hierarchies are mixed up and deconstructed. The pos-sibility of love and friendship between people of the same and different sexes is portrayed with charm and humour.

Sarah Kirsch presents deep-rooted sex roles by focusing on seemingly banal everyday issues: the uneven and unjust division of household chores ends at the moment when the woman changes into a man and confronts her lover as a friend. Among 'equals' the division of domestic labour is only natural. The original husband does not find his increased workload a burden. He now listens with interest to the other's account of the everyday world of work as is usually the case between friends. Sarah Kirsch's irony is as gentle as it is biting.

Beyond the book on gender role reversal, Christine Wolter ex-plores the idea of equality in the home. Her story *Ich habe wieder geheiratet* presents a harmonious home life. Both partners take care of the children and housework through a sensible division of tasks. They are both women. They have both left their respective mar-riages. Reasons for this are not given, they are only too well known. The characters mature in every way, even as women, for they sup-port each other in their relations with men. All these stories show the importance of the equality of women in education and professional employment. It is the necessary prerequisite for emancipation, but no more than this. Once it has been achieved, then it is possible to begin the process of the human emancipation of both sexes.

Innovative Forces

The work produced by women writers at this time was both new and unheard of. The demands made by the female characters had implications for society as a whole. This was no thin-blooded pamphleteering. The visions of change are also aesthetically very attractive. Unconventional ways of looking at problems and unconventional styles of writing are mutually dependent. It is clear from many of the texts that women who have become self-confident may wish to go along with men, but also to do without them, or even to go against them. This sort of literature offers both sexes dialogue and communication as equals. Women articulate their interests in order, at the end of the day, to make possible better co-existence between the sexes. This is the real driving force behind their utopian approaches.

This point demonstrates what this GDR literature has to do with *Frauenliteratur* as it is understood by the feminist movement, and how it differs. In the GDR, the critique is of patriarchy as a structure and it does not deny men the possibility of change. This literature is marked by a zest and exuberance, full of hope, which might be characterised by the questions 'if not now, then when?' and 'if not us, then who?'. It is an obvious source of pleasure for the writers to express thoughts and feelings in an original way and not repeating what others have already said. It is the joy of creating something new from their particular circumstances.

Although these prose works were written and, in part, published at the beginning of the 1970s, the legend persists that in comparison to women writers in the West, women writers in the GDR were way behind. This is the opinion, for example, of Margarete Mitscherlich who said at the beginning of the 1990s that GDR literature 'was given a feminist hue by women like Maxie Wander and Irmtraud Morgner much later' than in the West (Mitscherlich and Burmeister 1991: 102). In fact GDR women writers were stimulated by Western feminist classics such as Virginia Woolf or Simone de Beauvoir, as well as by the new women's movement. They made their own use of these ideas. Personal experience remained the touchstone and this experience was in many ways different to that of Western women writers. Feminist writing from the West encouraged the conscious working through of empirical experiences. Feminist theory was able to help women not to become irritated by accusations of feminine spontaneity, subjectivity and formlessness. It helped writers appreciate open styles and forms which could be found in the existing, mostly male, Western artistic canon.

Some women writers (for example, Morgner, Wolf and Königsdorf) considered the question of feminine writing in relation to their own lives and styles of writing. Irmtraud Morgner, for example, traces her turn to the montage novel primarily to her life as a single parent. This meant that she could only write short pieces when time allowed. This lifestyle favoured the concentrated shaping of individual parts and their montage. As much of her work shows, Christa Wolf had an intensive relationship with the work of Ingeborg Bachmann before it was included in the feminist literary canon. Christa Wolf felt strengthened and encouraged by Bachmann's aesthetics, by her open, subjective forms of the narrative, in her search for new styles of prose writing. Wolf's sensitivity towards both female achievement and the obstacles to it increased with the years, as can be seen, for example, from 'Von Büchner sprechen. Darmstädter Rede' (1980), 'Berliner Begegnung' (1986a) and 'Krankheit und Liebesentzug' (1984b). Women writers in the GDR often found that their insistence on female self-determination, even if it did not refer to the public domain, was judged as a political issue. Anyone who went a single step beyond the officially recognised and prescribed policies on the situation and wishes of women, found themselves, usually unintentionally, in conflict. On the other hand, however, general critiques of society did not automatically lead to a clearer perspective on women's problems. To do something for women through writing meant, for writers like Irmtraud Morgner and Christa Wolf, participating in the necessary changes in literature and, above all, in the development of society. This type of writing, which focused on intervention, took for granted a certain belief in the ability of socialism to change. This belief dwindled away as the 1970s progressed. The feeling of loss that remained marks, for example, Christa Wolf's *Kein Ort. Nirgends* (1979, *No Place on Earth*, 1982).

Writing was not something these authors could take or leave. Under the existing, unsatisfactory political conditions, it was not easy to be productive. The conviction that readers were waiting for new works helped to some extent. The feeling of being needed also motivated renewed involvements with the censors and attempts to get round them. Yet the most important thing was the inner drive to write. It was connected to the wish to articulate the fullness of the experiences which distressed the individual.

Worsening Conflicts

The phase of cultural policy following Walter Ulbricht's replacement by Erich Honecker in 1972 had brought with it a cautious relaxation of censorship. It came to a sudden end with the deportation of Wolf Biermann in 1976. This measure, a warning to artists and intellectuals, deepened the divisions between critically minded writers and those who toed the line or helped to implement it. A range of writers – amongst them Sarah Kirsch, Christa Wolf, Helga Schütz and Elke Erb – protested in writing to the government about the expatriation of Biermann.

Three years later the situation deteriorated again when writers who were not published in the GDR and had therefore given their manuscripts to publishing companies in West Germany – in particular Stefan Heym – were prosecuted and fined for violating the laws on hard currency. This led to renewed protests and was followed by a new round of expulsions from the Writers' Union. Sarah Kirsch left the GDR in 1977. Christa Wolf was publicly treated as a non-person. The media kept to the ban on giving her air time or column space and on talking or writing about her. So for example, her fiftieth birthday was ignored, with the exception of the journal *Sinn und Form*, which published warm birthday wishes from Anna Seghers. The effects of this cultural policy, which was aimed at safeguarding power, on the younger generation are discussed below.

Late Débuts

Despite the many interventions by the state and the faltering inconsistencies in cultural policy, the development of female talents was not to be stopped. New women arrived on the literary scene – many of them because they had been encouraged by the literary achievements and successes of other women. Often they were women in their middle years, with long years of career and marriage behind them, who had brought up children and who had felt the need to write about their experiences for others. Some of them said all they had to say in one book.

Others proved to be mature 'late developers', who after their début made their way in the literary world. In 1978, for example, Helga Königsdorf (b. 1938) became famous with her well written, laconic volume of stories *Meine ungehörigen Träume*. With Königsdorf, a woman from a scientific background entered the literary scene. Science, a domain which had previously been reserved for men, had been introduced into literature in the gender reversal stories of the early 1970s. Up until then Königsdorf had worked as a mathematics professor – an area far removed from the literary –

and had published papers on the problems of mathematical statistics. In her stories, she introduces the world of the 'exact' sciences and scientists in a duly disrespectful way, using Brechtian ideas of alienation.

In the late 1970s one book above all achieved a large circulation and a great effect both inside and outside the GDR. It was Maxie Wander's volume of taped interviews, *Guten Morgen, du Schöne*, which appeared in 1977. It was also well received among those sections of the general public who had little access to complicated artistic language. With it, a completely unknown author articulated issues which had occupied and tormented women of different ages and backgrounds. For years to come this book served as an important medium for public discussion. It was the subject of countless literary discussions, parts of it were staged by many theatres and enjoyed great success.

Maxie Wander, who was born in Austria, but who had lived in the GDR for years, was already forty years old when she became well known. As the wife of the renowned author, Fred Wander, she too spent a long time gathering the courage to write in her own right. In the middle of her work, she fell ill with cancer. Terminally ill, she finished her work and saw the publication of the book a few weeks before her death. The great impact which this book made in the GDR had much to do with the interest of the reading public in works which provided relatively 'pure' reality, unmediated by literary conventions. Maxie Wander's book had important predecessors. In the Federal Republic there were, in particular, the taped interviews by Erika Runge, *Frauen. Versuche zur Emanzipation* (1969) and by Alice Schwarzer, *Frauen gegen § 218* (1971). In the GDR there was Sarah Kirsch's 'Fünf unfrisierte Erzählungen aus dem Kassetten Recorder' which were published as *Die Pantherfrau* in 1973. The unusually lively appeal of this documentary literature can be explained by its difference from earlier reportage, published by the Aufbau Verlag, which had taken a predictable form. This new documentary literature valued the unvarnished expression of reality and because of this, it was subject to stricter controls. This trend will be discussed further in relation to the 1980s.

The Older Generation Speaks Out

Woman writers of the older generation who came from the Marxist workers' movement had held ranks for a long time and had not publicly expressed doubts about socialism. It was, therefore, all the more interesting when they, encouraged perhaps by younger women writers, began cautiously to change and to adopt new tones when speaking of the relationship between the sexes. This was particularly true of Anna Seghers. In the 1970s, with deteriorating health and a limited capacity to work, she used her authority to counteract anachronistic theories of realism and narrow-minded concepts of art. Such ideas still haunted the minds of many people, who, employed as teachers and cultural workers of all sorts and at all levels, did as much to hinder as to promote culture. In the story *Reisebegegnung* (1973), she presents, alongside Gogol and E.T.A. Hoffmann, Franz Kafka (who had long been condemned in the GDR) as an author who had created evocative images for the twentieth century and its fantastically distorted social relations. In her own way – for example in a quite different way from Irmtraud Morgner – she showed herself to be completely at home with fantasy. In *Sagen von Unirdischen* (1973d), which – reading between the lines – is about the relationship between art and war, she depicts a rebellious woman for the first time. And it is not coincidental that the word 'witch' is used in connection with this character. The plot revolves around a young woman who at the time of the Thirty Years' War rebels against all earthly and heavenly authorities, fearlessly becomes involved with the envoy from another planet and becomes the founder of a new race. Such a positive figure of a woman is the exception. In her last work, the cycle of stories *Drei Frauen aus Haiti* (1980), women appear throughout as those who in the course of bloody historical battles must always endure a double burden of suffering.

In the 1970s and 1980s a few new writers of both sexes discovered this great author for the first time. They were mostly attracted by Seghers' later texts with their marked mythical and fairy tale elements. Works by Heiner Müller and Volker Braun, writers of the second generation, have direct links to Anna Seghers' texts: Müller's play *Der Auftrag* (1979) to Seghers' story *Das Licht auf dem Galgen* (1961), and Braun's play 'Transit Europa' (1989) with Seghers' novel *Transit* (1944).

In her memoirs, published in 1977 as *Sonjas Rapport*, Ruth Werner (b. 1907) tells of her long years of service as a spy for the Soviet secret service in China in the 1930s. What is unusual about this is her unauthorised behaviour. Against orders she manages to have three children. Even this is not enough; they are by three different men. Some readers found this authentic proof of independent female self-determination in a situation which demanded utmost obedience disconcerting or even improper.

The 1980s: A Time for Cassandra's Prophesies

The 1980s, the last decade of the GDR's existence, were marked by social stagnation, decline and worsening of crises in all areas of life. At the Xth Congress of the GDR Writers' Union, held at the end of 1987, political differences could no longer be hushed up, even with exceptional efforts on the part of the authorities. For the first time at an official literary forum censorship was named as such by Christoph Hein. Gorbachev's policies of *Glasnost* and *Perestroika* made the state of affairs in the GDR seem all the more anachronistic and unbearable. Even in those literary texts which were published legally, not least by women writers, there were warnings of doom.

Several generations of women writers were effective in the 1980s. Women writers born in the 1930s and 1940s were at the forefront. Increasingly, women born after 1950 or even 1960 who had grown up in the GDR took up the pen. Many of them saw no reason to judge the conflicts and deplorable state of affairs caused by 'developed socialism' lightly, or to use the Cold War or other such arguments to make excuses for them. They did not identify with the state and so they did not work to change things for the better, as did many older women. They felt no responsibility for conditions which were there before they were born, not even to the extent of criticising them. In addition to this young writers who were as yet unknown in the West were treated more ruthlessly by the authorities than established writers. State power handled them without kid gloves.

Christa Wolf juxtaposed these different attitudes in a scene in her book *Was bleibt* (1990) which takes place at the end of the 1970s. The female protagonist, a semi-autobiographical figure, meets a young woman who has served a prison sentence in the GDR for a political offence and despite this does not mince her words when she writes. The older woman is obviously unsettled by this uncompromising style.

During the 1980s several women writers left the GDR. Bettina Wegner (b. 1947) left in 1983; Barbara Honigmann (b. 1949), Katja Lange-Müller (b. 1951) and Christa Moog (b. 1952) in 1984 and Gabriele Eckart (b. 1954) in 1986. In 1988 Freya Klier (b. 1950) was deported and Irina Liebmann (b. 1943) and Monika Maron (b. 1949) obtained long-term visas. Heike Willingham (b. 1962) left in 1988. It was no longer possible to define what was GDR literature and what was not. Alongside those who lived in the GDR and were also published, in part, in the Federal Republic, there were those who had long-term visas and who lived and were published in different places. In addition, there were women writers, resident in the GDR, who were only published in the West, and young women writers who could only publish in semi-legal magazines in the GDR. Some wanted to emigrate because they could not get their work published in the GDR, whilst others did not want to be published in the GDR in order not to fall under suspicion of conformity. To stay or to leave was a contentious issue among dissidents.

On the one hand the authorities were keen to see dissidents leave as they believed it would reduce the chances of potential unrest. On the other hand they wanted to keep the younger generation in the country, in accordance with the principle that the future belongs to those who have youth on their side. Gerhard Wolf was able to exploit these inconsistencies in policy and to use the series *Reihe außer der Reihe*, founded at the end of the 1980s, to publish young writers of both sexes who had been silenced for years. These included Gabi Kachold's first book (published in the summer of 1989). Ines Eck and Heike Willingham were being prepared for publication when the situation changed radically in the autumn of 1989.

Many writers had their work censored. Christa Wolf, for example, allowed sixty-four lines to be deleted from her *Cassandra* lectures. Helga Schubert sacrificed some critical stories in her collection entitled *Blickwinkel* (1984), which had appeared in 1982 in a western edition under the title *Das verbotene Zimmer*. She replaced them with other texts. Gerti Tetzner's novel *Die Oase*, which was rejected at the beginning of the 1980s, still remains unpublished today.

The question of whether women writers should compromise with the censor was, and is, difficult to answer. Many factors need to be taken into consideration. Compromises seemed justifiable on condition that the message, which was the most important thing for the women writers, was not affected by the changes. To be published with some parts cut seemed to be the lesser evil when faced with not being published at all. At least then the text was 'officially' available even if for the most part only in a small print run. This made it harder for the public to come by a book unless they had a special relationship with a publishing house or book store. Those books which the public really wanted to read were never on the shelves in the book shops. They were kept under the counter and so became known as 'bent goods'.

At a time when critical dramatists were finding it difficult to have their work staged, women had little hope of getting their foot in the door of an institution that the 'father state' was watching particularly closely. Yet, it was a woman, Irina Liebmann, who seized the initiative to found a theatre for authors, something which under the circumstances stood little chance of survival. The contradictions in society had taken on grotesque and sometimes absurd features even in the literary world. In this area, too, the overriding impression was that things could not carry on as they were.

Tendencies Among the Forty- and Fifty-Year Olds

After the literary successes of the 1970s, Christa Wolf and Irmtraud Morgner once again published key works at the beginning of the 1980s. Wolf produced *Kassandra* (1983, *Cassandra. A Novel and Four Essays*, 1984a) and Morgner *Amanda*. That both were published in the same year, 1983, is not the only point of similarity. Both react – independently of each other – in an unusually urgent fashion to the threat of nuclear war and both link this theme to an equally sharp analysis of gender relations.

Irmtraud Morgner once again adopts the figure of the Berlin local train driver and relates her life history from the cradle onwards, at times with explicit sarcastic self-criticism. She embeds the everyday existence of Laura, a single mother, in a network of old and new poetic motifs, many profoundly historical. These include the 'devilish' division of women into sexual beings and caring workers; witches complete with unconventional Brocken mythology; female rascals and fools, and many, many more. Men are systematically questioned about their ability to form alliances and since the corresponding results are overwhelmingly negative, countless strategies are sketched for women – sometimes even using magic – to help each other confront the dominance of a patriarchal system which is constantly reproducing itself. In this 'witches' novel' we are shown how the female sex, whose situation has not improved since the *Trobadora* volume, learns to mobilise all sorts of spiritual and emotional strengths.

In the 1970s Helga Schütz recounted her childhood memories of the last years of the war and the first few post-war years in several thoughtful volumes of prose. Again and again the central theme was the relationship between the Germans and their Polish neighbours. Her stories were calculated to promote a long-lasting and peaceful co-existence between Germans and Poles by linking relations officially sanctioned from above by the state with life as experienced from below, with the everyday lives of ordinary people. In the 1980s Schütz's views became more radical. In *Julia oder Erziehung zum Chorgesang* (1980) she subjected the early history of the GDR and the life story of her semi-autobiographical heroine to sharp criticism. She could no longer identify herself with events in the GDR and so she distanced herself from the 'chorus'.

Following her first publications in the 1970s – *Gutachten* (1975) and *Der Faden der Geduld* (1978) – Elke Erb (b. 1938) brought out several volumes of prose, in particular *Vexierbild* (1983) and *Kastanienallee* (1987). Having begun with poetry and prose, she began to turn more and more to short stories. These are often anecdotal, trenchant texts, which lay bare language and show it in motion. They reject description and explanation and so demand the full cooperation of the reader. Discussions of cultural history and linguistic philosophy are always linked both to everyday life and the subjectivity of the writer.

Helga Königsdorf continued her precise analyses of how things were, often setting them in a scientific milieu. Short, anecdotal, exaggerated, ambiguous stories – collected in *Der Lauf der Dinge* (1982) and *Lichtverhältnisse* (1988) – point to the destructive effects of the busy idleness and non-productivity that were gaining the upper hand. As the years went by, her talent for humour became blacker and blacker. Cheerful humour retreated behind malicious irony, the grotesque and black comedy. Women characters, too, are affected, particularly when they allow themselves to become integrated in the dominant structures, and resemble men in the means that they choose to their ends.

Charlotte Worgitzky's (b. 1939) *Meine ungeborenen Kinder* (1982) is of interest insofar as it dealt for the first time with the problems of women in the GDR up until the legalisation of abortion in 1972. This topic was still tabooed. In public readings and discussions it became clear just how much women, even belatedly, needed the opportunity – with help from fictional examples – to talk openly about their traumatic experiences. This book divided the public, not for any artistic shortcomings, but because of the challenge that it offered to existing and unquestioned ideas about motherhood. Worgitzky defends the right of women not to have their value as human beings defined by reference to their biological nature and their child-bearing capacity. Ideas like this had, up until then, not been openly expressed.

In the 1980s women also began to publish who, at about forty and with ample experience in professional life, finally considered their work worth publishing. In her second book *Alpträume aus der Provinz* (1984), Rosemarie Zeplin (b. 1939) took up the problems of growing up in the 1950s in the GDR in a similar way to Helga Schütz. She uses a mixture of precise matter-of-factness and enigmatic irony to tell her story. Brigitte Struzyk (b. 1946) has a completely different temperament. She first attracted public attention as a poet with her book *Leben auf der Kippe* (1984) and in 1988 she published the novel *Caroline unterm Freiheitsbaum*. Brigitte Burmeister's (b. 1940) first novel, *Anders oder Aufenthalt in der Fremde* (1987) shows mature artistic talent. This specialist in romance languages, who had a doctorate and had already proven herself a keen analyst and theorist in the area of literary criticism, became increasingly involved in the writing and production of literature. Since she could not reconcile her artistic and academic interests in the long term, she decided in favour of creative writing. She gave up her secure position in the Academy of Sciences and became self-employed. She emerged as both an intellectual and an original story teller. She knew how to disguise her message and to handle the most sensitive issues such as the 'Stasi' and informers in a playful manner.

The New Young Generation

Gabriele Kachold (b. 1953) is, judging from her biography and her temperament, a particularly rebellious writer of the second generation. In her angry address to the 'forty year olds', she presented older writers with a negative balance: 'We will not keep to your deals, your laws are nothing to do with us, you did not ask us, you always spoke for us ... we stand on the periphery of your world. We find and seek no admission' (*zügel-los*, 1989: 80). Here a 'we' speaks and makes clear it has neither fear nor courage, neither place nor hope nor aim. Kachold's generalisation is aimed at fundamentals: 'We are a generation of hybrids, we are hermaphrodites ... we do not need you, for you live without us, we are infertile, born to no purpose ... you cannot forget us, for we are another form of hope for you' (81). She deals with the topics of women, gender relations, love and sex in the same radical style. Of all the young writers a feminist critique is most marked in her work. She tries to write in an unconventional style which corresponds with her uncompromising, independent view of life. She recognises no rules unless they are themselves unconventional like those of automatic writing. However interested she may be in critical analysis, she is also committed to synthesis, both of poetic and epic forms and in the wide-ranging women's groups in which writing, painting, fashion, film-making, and performance have all had their place for years. Art and life should be united. In 1977 she was sentenced to one year's imprisonment for political reasons. This imprisonment was the reason for her writing and her single-mindedness. After her spell in prison she not only remained in the GDR, but in the Thüringian town of Erfurt with friends and enemies alike.

Katja Lange-Müller and Christa Moog, who had both left the GDR in 1984, depicted the different social worlds of the GDR in their first volumes of stories, which were published in the Federal Republic as *Wehleid – wie im Leben* (1986) and *Die Fans von Union* (1986) respectively. These were images which would not otherwise have appeared in their literary works. They wrote about people who had been removed from public consciousness and who had disappeared from normal, respectable life: people in care homes and psychiatric institutions, especially old women; alcoholics and loners of all sorts. The texts are derived from first-hand knowledge. For a long time before her emigration, Moog had to live from casual work and Lange-Müller had worked for years in clinics and homes as a carer. In their larger scale prose works, both these writers, whose styles are very different, tell of their lives after the GDR, of experiences of new opportunities and new burdens, of old characteristics and new inner conflicts. In both books, Lange-Müller's tale *Kasper Mauser – die Feigheit vorm Freund* (1988) and Moog's novel *Aus tausend grünen Spiegeln* (1989), the autobiographical background can be clearly felt.

Compared to Kachold-Stötzer, Lange-Müller and Moog, Kerstin Hensel's (b. 1961) entry into literature was free of controversy, especially since she was extremely reserved about revealing her own biography. She began as a poet and was successful as a prose writer, in part because she followed the tradition of comic-grotesque writing. She does not use an 'open visor' or direct polemics to engage with existing reality. She creates suggestive images, metaphors and plots. This is the case, for example, in the story

'Gruß' (in the 1989 volume *Hallimasch*) in which she paints a seemingly unreal yet precise panorama of the decay of old blocks of flats in Leipzig and the inability and/or unwillingness of their tormented tenants to fight back. Hensel feels a close affinity with Irmtraud Morgner, primarily because of her comic viewpoint (which in Hensel's opinion is typical of people from Saxony). Like Morgner, Hensel understands female self-confidence above all else in terms of the self-confidence of the artist. Perhaps this is also due to the fact that she began to publish early in life. In contrast to the older writer, she does not engage in an explicit and programmatic confrontation with patriarchy, neither in her polemics nor in her utopian vision. Yet Hensel deals in some of her stories with unresolved issues which affect women's real lives, especially the relationship between the sexes. These include not only the inequalities of opportunity facing women, but especially the question of women and men's ability to love (for example, 'Lilit' and 'Veilchen im Knopfloch' in the collection *Hallimasch*).

Like Hensel and Lange-Müller, Angela Krauss (b. 1950) also studied at the Johannes R. Becher Institute for Literature in Leipzig (1977–1979). The official cultural policy that writers should get to know conditions in the factories and among workers and introduce the world of work into literature, bore unexpected fruits in her prose work *Das Vergnügen* (1984) and in stories in the volume *Das Glashaus* (1988). Here she told stories of the everyday life of working-class women and men in a way which differed starkly from the official image of the worker. With increasing experience of life and writing, Krauss arrived at an uncompromising way of presenting even autobiographical material. In 1988 she was awarded the Bachmann Prize for her story *Der Dienst*.

The small amount of background material given here on those writers who were born after 1950 shows how varied their experiences and careers were. Charges against the older generations, like those raised by Kachold, are not found in the works of Hensel, Krauss and Moog. It is inappropriate to talk of generation-based similarities between these writers. This is true whether one looks at their use of literary forms or at their views on feminism and its failings. This is due to deep-rooted differences between openly expressed dissidence and the discrimination, including imprisonment, that followed from it, and partial, often ironised, conformity to the circumstances.

In Search of a Feminine Tradition

The 1980s saw an increased interest among women writers in uncovering the intellectual and cultural achievements of women in their work. Morgner and Wolf had already begun this process in fine style. In her *Trobadora* novel, Morgner dealt not only with the awakening of the poet Beatriz de Dia from the Middle Ages, but also with goddesses from various mythical circles. Christa Wolf had recreated Caroline von Günderode in her novel and written an essay about her happier sister Bettina von Armin. In the 1980s several women writers in the GDR became interested in women from the eighteenth and early nineteenth centuries, their great literary predecessors.

Caroline Schlegel-Schelling's biography became a focus of attention for several writers. Sigrid Damm published a selection of her letters with a detailed study of Schlegel-Schelling's life (1980). In 1988 Brigitte Struzyk's prose work *Caroline unterm Freiheitsbaum* was published. It was a great success as a depiction of the life of a self-determined woman who tries to achieve the impossible in the face of all the concrete difficulties of her age and pays a high price for it. Struzyk's Caroline transgresses all norms and roles. She has several children by different men, she is as much the passionate mother as she is the lover, and in the wake of the 1789 revolution, she gets involved in the political, intellectual and artistic concerns of men as an equal. The narrator focuses on the unruly and the creative, greatness in giving and taking, and pride in preparing for oneself all joys and pain.

Renate Feyl's book *Idylle mit Professor* (1986) is much more modest. It is about the wife of the prominent enlightenment writer Johann Christoph Gottsched, a woman to whom literary history has not been kind. With monotonous irony Feyl describes the discrepancy between the achievements of the talented wife and her jealous exploitation and neglect by her 'great' husband. Another wasted female talent of the eighteenth century who stood in the shadow of a great man, Goethe's sister Cornelia, was 'exhumed' in 1987 by Sigrid Damm.

In 1981 Renate Feyl published a volume of portraits, *Der lautlose Aufbruch. Frauen in der Wissenschaft*, which traces the difficult scientific careers of women from the seventeenth century onwards. Here Feyl revises her first work devoted to scientists *Bilder ohne Rahmen* (1977), which included only one woman, Lise Meitner, alongside eleven men. Helga Königsdorf made the very same Lise

Meitner the heroine of her story *Respektloser Umgang* (1986). Not only did this woman have to sacrifice to science everything that brings fulfilment in life, but her achievements in the field of atomic physics were 'forgotten' by history after she was forced to leave Germany in 1938 because she was a Jew.

One of the oldest women writers, Hedda Zinner (b. 1907), showed an enthusiastic understanding of the female tradition in politics and in feminism in the work of the Russian Alexandra Kollontai (1982). Kollontai should have been known to women interested in feminism in the GDR who would have regarded her as an important role model. In the GDR Kollontai – for years a close colleague of Lenin – had been, until the 1980s, largely forgotten and not simply for political reasons. In 1982 her volume of stories *Wege der Liebe* (first published in German in 1925) appeared. In the afterword Zinner praises Kollontai because she was a century ahead of her contemporaries where gender relations were concerned. Both as a theorist and a story teller she represented the 'sexual morality of tomorrow' (*Die neue Moral und die Arbeiterklasse*, 1918). This was late recognition for a neglected inheritance!

Fact and Fiction

Women – both newcomers and established writers – appeared strikingly often as authors of the different forms of documentary literature which were much in demand in the 1980s due to the public's 'hunger for reality'. Documentary writers had a particularly hard time since the censor paid a lot of attention to these works which did not use subtexts but decoded texts, facts, and 'names and addresses'.

Precisely those authentic reports from the world of work, which for decades had been propagated as the most important subject for literature, were particularly scrutinised and blocked because they often revealed facts which the state authorities did not like. The store of taboos in this area was immeasurable. Gabriele Eckart, a young writer (b. 1954) who had already published successful poetry and prose, got involved in a confrontation over her reports about the fruit farmers of Werder. After the publication of two articles in the prestigious literary journal *Sinn und Form* (1984) which caused the utmost indignation, the publication of the book was stopped. The edition published in Cologne by Kiepenheuer &

Witsch appeared in 1984 under the title *So sehe ick die Sache. Protokolle aus der DDR*.

Daniela Dahn (b. 1949) was prevented from doing research in industrial plants. In 1987 her book *Prenzlauer Berg-Tour*, which presents a differentiated portrait of the East Berlin district which had become an 'in-place' in the meantime, was only published after arduous discussions with the censors.

In part, writers of documentary literature dealt with themes and problems that were normally dealt with by journalists. Since they could not be openly discussed under the prevailing conditions by the media, the domain of literature offered a certain amount of limited freedom. In the publishing houses, placed between novels, documentary texts acquired a literary aura. For this reason they may have seemed less dangerous to suspicious officials, less 'dangerous' because less reliable.

In a few cases women who originally wanted to write factual reports about social injustices and bring them to the public's attention, changed to fiction because of endless problems with the censor. Thus Lia Pirskawetz, who for years had tried in vain to discuss ecological problems, eventually published a novel (*Der stille Grund*, 1984) about them. Monika Maron on the other hand did not even get this far. As a journalist for the magazine *Wochenpost*, she had written articles about the ecologically devastated region of Bitterfeld, the site of many chemical factories. They were not printed. From the material she had gathered she wrote a novel and was even given a large grant to do so. Accepted by the publishers, the novel *Flugasche* was refused printing permission by the Ministry for Culture. It appeared in the Federal Republic in 1981.

Women wrote countless accounts of basic human needs which should really have been dealt with by the media: for example, alcoholism or physical and mental disability. In part these were self-portraits for which the demand was huge. Print runs of 10,000 copies sold out in no time at all. Women also wrote sober accounts of their experiences which brought to light neglected chapters of history. For example, Veronika Friedländer wrote about the childhood of a Jewish girl in Berlin (*Späte Notizen*, 1982) and Ursula Höntsch-Harendt about the refugees fleeing Silesia in the wake of the Second World War (*Wir Flüchtlingskinder*, 1985).

In view of the long-term effects of Maxie Wander's interviews with women, there was also great need for interviews with men. For years no man took up this challenge, so eventually two women occupied this space, Christine Müller with *Männerprotokolle* (1985) and Christine Lambrecht with *Männerbekanntschaften. Freimütige Protokolle* (1986). These authentic reports from the world of men had a twofold effect. There was little trace in them of the 'new man' and some critics blamed the women writers for this, claiming that they had unfairly manipulated their material. Such debates revealed the suppressed tensions and inconsistencies in the relationship between the sexes. Despite censorship these books can be read today as an extraordinarily rich historical source about life in the GDR. Women in particular, with their critical eye on everyday life, raised a lot of issues in these books which otherwise would have been lost. However, these book do not contain anything which might have threatened the structures and practices of 'socialist patriarchy'.

Postscript

The list of books which appeared in the 1980s is lengthy both in spite of and because of the crises and the sense that an era was coming to an end. The well-known writers from the 1970s were joined by many new ones. The wave of writers who began forcefully in the 1970s did not disappear. They marked the beginning of a tendency which continued to consolidate itself. The next chapter will consider whether or not this trend continued after autumn 1989 when the social conditions which gave rise to it changed radically. Until the autumn of 1989 literature written by women gained increasing influence within the GDR. Evidence of this were the numerous contributions to discussion made by women at the Xth Writers' Congress of the GDR at the end of 1987. Most of the contributions were critical and demanded change. Theirs was a thoroughly committed literature. Since the majority of writers, in spite of predictable difficulties with the censor, dealt with contemporary themes, they had to proceed with cunning. In order to write what they and their readers wanted them to write, they used and developed modes of representation which allowed their message to be read between the lines. Literature by women shows an exceptionally wide range of traditional and modern techniques. It is particularly noticeable that comedy appears in endless shades and variations. Laughter did not desert the women writers, it was used as a weapon to facilitate change.

Women – like their male colleagues – wrote under the pressure of high expectations. Under such circumstances their commitment had its costs. Many texts have a polemical force that is perhaps sometimes even intense. Foreign readers tend to see this as a typically German deficiency, overburdened with problems and lack of ease. Whether or not that is true, literature written by women played an important, if immeasurable, part in the events of autumn 1989 that have been called a 'bloodless revolution'.

Translated by Chris Weedon

Notes

Except for translations from published English editions listed in the bibliography, all translations from German texts cited in this and the following two chapters are by Chris Weedon.

1. See the correspondence between Gerti Tetzner and Christa Wolf in Liersch (ed.) 1975 and Reimann and Wolf 1993.
2. In Mudry (ed.) 1991: 15ff, 78ff and 30ff. See also Schütz 1980.
3. Reimann's letter to Wolf 1.6.72. in Reimann and Wolf 1993: 14.
4. Gabriele Kachold changed her name three times. At first she published under her married name Kachold. Later she added her maiden name, Stötzer, to it and then finally reverted to her maiden name.

Chapter Eleven

 DEVELOPMENTS IN EAST GERMAN WOMEN'S WRITING SINCE AUTUMN 1989

Eva Kaufmann

Positions During and After the *Wende*

The crisis situation in the GDR in the autumn of 1989 was brought to a head by the mass emigration of young people via the West German embassies in Prague and Budapest. At this point GDR women writers took the initiative. They drew up a resolution which rejected any condemnation of the refugees and called both for a discussion of the causes of the situation and for change.[1] This resolution was signed by Dahn, Damm, Königsdorf, Schütz, Tetzner, Wolf, Zeplin and it was presented to a full meeting of the Berlin Writers' Union by Christa Wolf on 23 September 1989. It received majority approval. Dissidence was now public.

With the demonstrations at the beginning of October, the GDR government began to fall apart. There were calls in the media, in public meetings and in democratic organisations for more openness, and women writers, too, began to make their views known, both in what they said and wrote. Groupings formed among both men and women writers. These had their roots in the deep, mostly politically motivated polarisations of the 1970s and 1980s. They came to a head once the question of the removal from power of the governing forces of the old state and SED-leadership had been solved. Both had been completely unwilling to undertake any reforms.

Now the question of how the GDR should develop in the future was at the centre of debate. Those who were in favour of thoroughgoing reforms in the GDR, and opposed to it's 'annexation' by the

Federal Republic and the re-establishment of capitalism, became marginalised. This could be seen from the replacement of the original slogan at the mass demonstrations 'Wir sind *das* Volk' ('we are *the* people') by the slogan 'Wir sind *ein* Volk' ('we are *one* people').

This change could be seen most clearly in the reactions to the proclamation 'Für unser Land' ('For our Country') of 26 November 1989.[2] This urged resistance to any selling out of the material and moral values of the GDR and the retention of its independence. The proclamation was initiated and signed by the writers Stefan Heym and Volker Braun but also Christa Wolf. After the election of 18 March 1990, which signalled the end of GDR sovereignty, the various media condemned those writers – male and female – who had argued against the incorporation of the GDR into the Federal Republic calling them dangerous utopian dreamers, alienated from the ordinary people, intellectuals whose words should be disregarded.

From the early summer of 1990 onwards, an increasing number of articles appeared in various West German newspapers which attacked Christa Wolf in connection with the publication of her book *Was bleibt* (1990, *What Remains*, 1990), denigrating her politically, morally and as an artist. Nothing should remain of the authority which she had gained for herself since the 1960s. Of course the attacks were not only directed at her. Yet they escalated at the beginning of 1993 when Christa Wolf made public her short-term connection with the Stasi in the late 1950s. She had come across documents relating to this as she had looked through her own comprehensive Stasi files.[3]

Irmtraud Morgner, who had been severely ill with cancer, lived just long enough to experience the euphoria over the collapse of the old power structures. In an interview with Alice Schwarzer in the feminist magazine *Emma* in the November/December 1989 issue, she complained that she was tied to her sick bed and had passively to come to terms with her own responsibility for the demise of the GDR. 'For in spite of everything, I have always supported this country in principle because, as far as I am concerned, capitalism was and is no alternative and this is particularly true in the case of women'.[4] She died in May 1990.

The differences between the political positions of women writers, which had formed over a long period, now came out into the open. Above all they disagreed about how to judge the imploding system: should the whole of the past be rejected *carte blanche* as unjust and a catastrophe, or should it be looked at in an historically specific way. These viewpoints were irreconcilable because, as a rule, they involved individual decisions about life and individual attitudes. It seemed as if all those writers who had not left the GDR had to justify themselves in intense discussions. In this situation there were very few opportunities to publish open to women writers where they did not feel that they were already in the dock. What was needed in the turbulent process of the collapse of the old régime was that culture of dialogue that had developed during the last years of the GDR under the heading *Neues Denken*.

The conversation between Margarete Mitscherlich and Brigitte Burmeister *Wir haben ein Berührungstabu. Zwei deutsche Seelen einander fremd geworden* (1991) is an example of this. In this book the two women objectively discuss many topical contentious issues. Among them is Helga Schubert's view that life in general in the GDR over the previous forty years should be seen as life in a psychiatric institution.[5] Helga Schubert also developed her position in a book of dialogues between herself and Rita Süssmuth, a leading CDU politician from the old Federal Republic, which was published in 1992 under the title *Bezahlen Frauen die Wiedervereinigung?*

A Necessary Supplement

At this point I am discussing texts which, seen historically, should have been handled in the previous chapter. A publication date of 1990 or even 1991 is misleading. They are texts that had already been completed and handed in to publishers before the autumn of 1989. Yet when they came out into a fundamentally changed historical landscape, their effect was anything but anachronistic. The fact that they were written in an earlier period is barely noticeable since their subject matter, themes, motifs and tone unmistakeably point to the crises and decay of socialism which were becoming apparent.

Rosemarie Zeplin's novel *Maulwurf oder fatales Beispiel weiblicher Gradlinigkeit* (1990b), which deals with denunciation, reveals the extent to which relationships between people had been poisoned down to the very details of everyday life and how the apparently intact mechanisms of public and private life had long since been undermined.

Helga Schubert's book *Judasfrauen* (1990), which she spent many years writing, is concerned with women denouncers of the Nazi period. Using archive material the book attempts to show the degree to which repressive state structures based on spying and denunciation led exclusively female characters, who were not criminal by nature, to deliver other people, in particular men, to the Nazi authorities.

The question of corruptibility and resistance is the central motif of Helga Königsdorf's epistolary novel *Ungelegener Befund* (1990b). Set in the present, the novel depicts a scientist who, following the discovery of a letter, has to find out whether or not letters about the writer's activities as a racial biologist between 1938 and 1945 were written by his own dead father. This was a man who, after the war, gained undivided respect over many years as the director of a children's home. These attempts to discover the truth about an evil past are made between 1986 and 1988, an historical moment characterised by extensive motifs of decline and depicted as an intense period of crisis. It is a period of deceptive calm in which a storm could break out at any moment and things could be turned on their heads.

In 1990 the extensive narrative *Das Stendhal-Syndrom* written between August 1987 and September 1989 was published. It was written by Christine Wolter, who had been living in Italy since the mid-1970s following her marriage. Wolter continued to publish regularly in the GDR. In this book she captures the atmosphere in the GDR using the image of a secret disease. The gap between the generations is deep.

Written into these texts is the more or less urgent warning: if things carry on as they are, they will give rise to irreparable damage with unpredictable consequences. These Cassandra-like prophecies were disregarded like those of the mythological figure. When these books appeared in 1991, they disappeared into a void. Everything had changed at breakneck speed, more radically than these authors – or anybody else – had predicted. In the ensuing turmoil these books were neglected.

After the introduction of hard currency in July 1990 and the establishment of a market economy, which brought with it a complete change in established patterns of living and consumption, hardly anybody wanted books by GDR women writers. In addition to this, they were either absent from or difficult to find in bookshops, which had switched to selling the products of Western publishing houses. Books had risen steeply in price and demand now focused on practical publications: on tax guides and travel books and literature by writers who had not been published in the GDR. The reading of literature declined considerably from autumn 1989 onwards. People were turning to newspapers and magazines. They were following the public discussions in the media so as not to feel completely overtaken by the quick pace of events. Most women writers were also desperate for news, trying laboriously to come to terms with daily events, intellectually and psychologically. They involved themselves to some extent in public debate through their own journalistic contributions, but only while it still seemed possible to contribute to an open exchange of views.

Journalism and Documentary Literature Under New Conditions

According to their individual disposition, women writers made varying use of the opportunities to express themselves openly in public on political issues. They were often invited to take part in public events and talk shows and they were approached by newspapers, magazines and editors of all types. The list of competent topical contributions which women writers wrote during and after the *Wende* is long. In 1990 Christa Wolf's *Reden im Herbst*, which included pieces written between 1988 and 1990, was published. Helga Königsdorf, who was the woman writer most active in journalism, published two collections of her work in 1990: *1989 oder ein Moment Schönheit* and *Aus dem Dilemma eine Chance machen*.

In 1991 a book was published with contributions by women writers from different generations with the evocative title *Gute Nacht, Du Schöne*. These were writers who had stayed in the GDR, had been published and who now felt the need, partly in response to external pressures, to explain themselves. They wrote about their relationships to the past, present and future, mostly in a subjective and relaxed form. The original plan was for groups of two women writers to enter into dialogue. The fact that this idea could only be partially realised in the book points to the changes and violent breaks with which everybody, including women writers, had to deal.

Under these new conditions women writers undertook to represent the views of ordinary people who could not write for themselves. Examples of this are Helga Königsdorf's interviews about the immediate present in the volume *Adieu DDR* (1991) and Elfriede Brüning's – a writer born in 1910 – book *Lästige Zeugen* (1990). This is a documentation of the fate of women who, as German emigrants to the USSR, became victims of Stalinist cleansing and, if they survived, remained silent as the state required. Eva

Maria Stege, who was deported to Siberia at the age of sixteen by the Soviet occupying forces and was released after five years, had lived in the GDR ever since and also remained silent. The book *Bald nach Hause – skoro domoi* (Moser 1991) provides a detached insight into the lives of these women who had been raped in every sense. Two other women were involved in its creation and 'female style'. It was the starting point for a film about Eva Maria Stege made by Freya Klier, a drama producer and writer who had been expelled from the GDR in 1988.

Regina Scheer (b. 1950) investigated a part of the GDR's repressed history in her book *Ahawah. Das vergessene Haus. Spurensuche in der Berliner Auguststraße* (1992). In it she follows the traces of the Jewish school which existed in the district of East Berlin known as the *Scheunenviertel* until 1944. Scheer objectively documents the difficulties that she had in persuading contemporary witnesses, inhabitants of the area and neighbours to talk. Her book, which is based on years of careful research, shows awareness of how to handle history – including one's own history – critically.

Changed Conditions for Writing

Most women writers only saw a point in becoming involved in new committees and organisations or in day-to-day journalism while social developments still seemed open. *Die Geschichte ist offen* is the title of a collection of essays published in 1990 in which, among others, Elke Erb, Helga Königsdorf, Katja Lange-Müller, Monika Maron and Rosemarie Zeplin are represented. The title of the book refers to Rosemarie Zeplin's essay. The introduction of the Deutschmark on 1 July 1990 and the treaty of unification, which came into effect officially on 3 October 1990, consolidated social relations on the model of the old Federal Republic. Following this, women writers changed the focus of their interests, attention and work. Once again they orientated themselves more towards their own literary work – now under fundamentally changed economic and social conditions. They had to adapt to a market economy, to conditions under which their Western colleagues were used to living and working. Those writers who were young found this easier than the forty, fifty or sixty-year-olds. Whereas their work had previously been subject to 'cultural political requirements', the most important question now was whether publishers would find their work economically viable.

Above all, a literary industry regulated by a market economy demanded mobility and flexibility. Women writers now felt they had to be continuously looking for opportunities in the market and the literary world and making offers. 'Today taste rules everywhere. Fashion (which determines whether or not you are paid) dictates taste. Fashion is censorship. What we do today has an uncertain future and can easily disappear.'[6]

As far as I can see, the market has not led to a decrease in standards of writing. With a few exceptions, women writers are not concentrating on fashion and the market. In order to be able to afford the 'luxury' of being independent of market forces some women writers have decided to secure their living completely or partly through paid work, even if it has nothing to do with literature or culture. For example, Zeplin has been working for years in a foundation for the compensation of political victims. Tetzner worked for some time as a qualified legal expert in one of the newly founded advice centres for people with debts. And Struzyk worked in a local Berlin office of the Department of Family, Sport and Culture. Schütz and Hensel were lucky enough to get teaching appointments in art schools and are thus able to finance their own artistic work. Some of the younger women writers have had employment on job creation schemes (*Arbeitsbeschaffungsmaß-nahme-Stellen*) for one or two years. Here they can work on projects that they find meaningful. Only a few women writers are able, as does Christa Wolf, to live from freelance work. They include Burmeister, Dahn, Damm and Königsdorf. Prizes, grants and positions as 'writers in residence' help to secure precious time to write for a few months at a time. Since writers cannot live from book sales alone, they have to undertake extensive reading tours which are difficult to organise for women which children.

Despite the choice provided by free abortion from 1972 onwards, the majority of young women writers chose to have children. Many of them were single parents from the start: Gröschner, born 1964, has one child; Hensel, born 1961, has one child; Eck, born 1956, has two children; Moog, born 1952, has two children; and Schmidt, born 1958, has four children. For most women writers, adaptation to hard-hitting market relations did not mean any significant change in standards of living. Writers living in the GDR had learned to reduce their expectations and get by on DM 400–500. This put them in a position where they could afford to take as little notice as possible of the censors. Living on such a small income was possible because rents and other basic living costs were low. Such people could also adapt to a frugal way of life under the new conditions.

New Texts

Those volumes of poetry published since 1989 mostly include poems written both before and after the *Wende*. There are hardly any noticeable breaks in the texts since they do not foreground political reflections and the poets' worldviews and attitudes to life hardly change. This is particularly true of younger writers, for example, the volumes *Herzdame Knochensammler* by Annett Gröschner (b. 1964), *vom fegen weiß ich wird man besen* (1992) by Heike Willingham (b. 1962), and *Gewitterfront* (1991) by Kerstin Hensel (b. 1961). Barbara Köhler (b. 1959) achieved higher acclaim internationally with her debut *Deutsches Roulette. Gedichte 1984–89* (1991). Her poems are marked by strength, simplicity, depth, sharpness of thought and emotional and sensual flair. With astonishing independence she also reflects in her prose on both intimate and large-scale historical themes.

Some of the prose works that appeared after 1990 also have their roots partially in the time prior to the *Wende*. In some cases the epochal change that was the *Wende* is clearly marked, in others this is not the case. Renate Feyl's novel *Ausharren im Paradies* (1991) is a GDR family chronicle which stretches from the postwar years to the present. It is framed by pieces of text which reflect upon life after the *Wende*. As if under pressure to justify herself, the narrator tackles the question of why people did not leave the GDR when – up to 1961 – the borders were still open or when they had chances later. It seems as if her characters were punished for enduring the 'GDR paradise' in so far as they themselves were damaged and their lives substantially impoverished.

Ines Eck's (b. 1956) first work, the novel *Steppenwolfidyllen* appeared in 1991. She had been writing it for a long time. The malicious irony of the title corresponds to the misery and inner conflict which determine the life of the young woman. Gabi Stötzer-Kachold's book *grenzen los fremd gehen* (1992) contains texts written between 1988 and 1991. Among them is the autobiographical sketch 'Erfurt – mein Mittelalter' in which – with laconic objectivity – she tells her own story up to her imprisonment. In so far as her biography is not affected by the events of autumn 1989, her prose is also free from breaks. In its form it resembles her first book *zügel-los*

(1989), which was constructed from a bringing together of fragments. Elke Erb's book *Winkelzüge* (1991) also contains texts from both before and after the *Wende*. It contains an extremely rich picture of a woman's work, based on the life of the author herself. She sees her various types of work – housework, her child, literature – as of equal value and mutually affecting each other.

Brigitte Struzyk's long story *In vollen Zügen – Rück-Sichten* (1994) extends further back. It sketches a differentiated picture of the complicated relationships in which people who wanted to live an alternative lifestyle in the GDR became involved. The text is extremely dense and powerful. Both its starting point and goal is the suicide after the *Wende* of the daughter of the first-person narrator. She has despaired of a world which has been ruined by male power. The opportunities available to women of different generations to realise their longings and needs are scrutinised with ruthless openness.

Helga Königsdorf's volumes of prose *Gleich neben Afrika* (1992) and *Im Schatten des Regenbogens* (1993) are highly topical in their approach. These two books are also linked directly to the contemporary events with which Königsdorf had become actively involved. The second book is about the major social changes caused by German unification, above all the 'disbanding' of the old GDR intelligentsia. In a variety of ways the book shows how people behave who, at a mature age, lose almost everything: profession, worldview, material security, friendships and family ties.

In 1992 Helga Schütz published *Heimat, süße Heimat*, a travel diary from Kazakhstan. It documents the weary search for traces of a man, a German emigrant to the Soviet Union, who lived for many years in Kazakhstan as a result of Stalinist repression. Helga Schütz was preparing a film script based on his memories. The radio play *Ein holdes Liebkerlchen* (1990a), which Rosemarie Zeplin wrote about the German actress Carola Neher who met her death in the Soviet Union, deals with similar material and a similar problem. Schütz and Zeplin treat their 'cases' without sensationalism, making clear references to the present and the contemporary concern with repressed history.

Brigitte Burmeister completed a novel *Unter dem Namen Norma* in 1994. It follows the lives of mostly ordinary people who live in an old, dilapidated, four-storey block of apartments in East Berlin, dating from before the war, and who have to come to terms with living conditions in the old GDR and the new Federal Republic. The theme of Germans from East and West growing closer together is handled with exact social detail, curiosity and humour. As the title *Auditorium Panoptikum* signals, Kerstin Hensel's novel, which was published in 1991, is not totally serious (1991a). As it happens, it is the youngest of the women writers who reacts to recent history with humorous distance, creating, with grim pleasure, fantastic and grotesque characters and events which throw sharp light on the absurdity of reality.

Perspectives for Feminism

After the fall of the Berlin Wall women writers did not express any increased interest in feminism. This, however, tells us very little about their support for women's interests. Just as women writers – with a few exceptions – kept away from political parties and other organisations with new democratic aspirations, so they also kept their distance from the Independent Women's Organisation (Unabhängiger Frauenverband). This organisation was founded in the GDR in December 1989, yet soon after its enthusiastic beginnings it began to stagnate.

A few women writers became active when concrete solidarity was needed. For example, Brigitte Struzyk organised an exceptional series of literary events under the title 'Scheherazade. After the Gulf War'. It regularly invited women writers from various countries and regions of the world – in particular crisis regions – to read from their works. These texts have been prepared for publication but have not yet found a publisher. Christiane Barckhausen founded the women's centre Susi (Solidarisch-Unabhängig-Sozial-International) in Berlin – a multi-cultural information and meeting centre.

Women writers' attitudes to feminism are no different now than they were in the time of the GDR. At that time they developed a marked distaste for ideology and this gave rise to a dislike of all theoretical and practical tendencies which led to separatism and dogmatism, exclusiveness and narrowness. They tend to avoid anything that hinders communication between women, between the sexes, and between different social strata. On the other hand, a feminist perspective is unmistakable in many literary texts. In contrast to previous times, women writers are hesitant towards utopias, yet do not share the general fashionable denial of them. Writers have a sharp eye for structural inequalities between the sexes – economical, political, cultural and personal – under both the old and new régimes. Their analyses are precise but hardly

polemical. Thus the pronounced polemics against patriarchy articulated by Gabi Stötzer (she gradually gave up her married name
Kachold) in her essay 'Against the Leading Role of Men'[7] is all the
more striking. Women writers who had shown interest in feminist
questions since the 1970s and gained important knowledge about
sex roles and relationships reject none of it. These analyses find
even more concrete confirmation in capitalist patriarchy than in
patriarchy under socialism.

Future Perspectives

After unification women writers did not move either from East to
West or from West to East. Those who had left the GDR for the
Federal Republic before autumn 1989 stayed there. In a few individual cases, especially among younger women, writers moved to
other countries, partly for family reasons (Köhler went to the
Netherlands, Moog went to Sweden). Even though communication between East German women writers and women writers
from the old Federal Republic, Austria and Switzerland is no
longer prevented by barriers such as borders and currency, closer
relationships between them have not developed since the *Wende*.
There do not seem to be any important reasons for closer contact,
such as, for example, exchanging ideas about questions of writing.
Everyday experience does not draw them to one another. The key
ideas in the book of conversations by Mitscherlich and Burmeister,
*Wir haben ein Berührungstabu. Zwei deutsche Seelen einander fremd
geworden* (1991) still seem to be valid.

Yet this does not mean that the women writers whose work I
am discussing here feel themselves to be especially responsible
for the *Neue Bundesländer* (former GDR). Nor had they previously
understood themselves to be writers whose voices were limited to
the GDR and could not be understood elsewhere. Disinclined
towards a narrow-minded nationalism, they direct their attention
to the whole world. Their personal experiences of the collapse of
a world system has given them a lively sense of global questions.

As published and unpublished texts of the last few years show,
neither younger nor older women writers lack the impetus to
write. Nor do they lack ideas, material or artistic ability. They continue to write even when, in contrast to before, they get little feed-
back from their reading public about what their texts mean to
other people. There can be no talk of a paralysis of productivity,

even in the face of the arbitrary nature of the literary industry. Despite their objectivity and lack of illusions about what literature can achieve, their conviction that they have important things to say about the state of the world, about the huge breaks and shifts in the structures of human relations, social and national groups, gives them a firm basis from which to live and write. Their view of life and the world lacks cynicism and perhaps for this reason might be characterised as an *indispensable* 'feminine' view.

Translated by Chris Weedon

Notes

1. The resolution is reprinted in Königsdorf 1990.
2. Reprinted in Wolf 1990: 170f.
3. Wolf's Stasi file and the debate that it provoked are published in the comprehensive volume of documentation edited by Vinke 1993.
4. Morgner 1990: 32.
5. See Mitscherlich and Burmeister 1991: 50.
6. Kerstin Hensel 'Ohne Angst und an allen Dummköpfen vorbei', in Mudry 1991: 212.
7. In Naumann 1990.

Chapter Twelve

 READING CHRISTA WOLF

Chris Weedon

To fail is to have no crises, but rather to go through life, hard and undeviating, untrue to oneself. With or without crises, to walk alongside oneself to the end of one's life. One can achieve enormous success in this way. One can become president or anything else, but cannot be a writer. But that would be to fail.

Berliner Zeitung, 27/28 February 1993[1]

Christa Wolf ranks among the most controversial and highly respected writers from the GDR. Born in 1929 in Landsberg, she studied German in Jena and Leipzig. Subsequently she worked as a editor, critic and from 1959 onwards as a freelance writer. A committed socialist, Christa Wolf was also an unremitting critic of many aspects of GDR society. The quality of her novels, short stories and essays, which were published in both East and West Germany and were widely translated, earned her international respect. From the early 1960s onwards her criticisms of socialism as it existed in the GDR led to conflicts with censors and cultural functionaries. Meanwhile West German critics sought to use her writings as a weapon in the ideological struggle against East German Communism. Yet despite problems with the GDR state, Wolf remained committed to the GDR and to the construction of better forms of socialism.

After the fall of the East German régime, following the opening of the borders with the West in 1989, Christa Wolf found herself under attack from the West German media. She had published her essay *Was bleibt* (1990, *What Remains* 1990) on 6 June 1990. In this text, originally written during the summer of 1979 and revised in November 1989, Wolf analyses the reasons why the narrator, a writer like Wolf, seemed to lack the courage of the younger generation and had not gone further in her literary and political opposition to the SED régime. The response of the West German press in 1990 was to accuse Wolf of trying to present herself as both victim and resistance figure, while having failed to contest the régime and fight on behalf of persecuted writers. Moreover, critics not only attacked Wolf's integrity and that of other key GDR writers, but sought to question the literary merit of her work.[2]

In 1993 Christa Wolf's brief connections with the Stasi came to light. In the wake of revelations about the dramatist Heiner Müller's links with the Stasi, Christa Wolf published a statement in the *Berliner Zeitung* (21 January 1993). Here she recounts how, when in May 1992 she gained access to her Stasi files, she discovered – in addition to forty-two volumes on her and her husband covering the period 1968–1980 – a further file. This was:

> A thin manuscript, from which I learned that the Stasi were using me from 1959 to 1962, first as a 'social informer' [*GI: Gesellschaft-licher Informant*] and then as an 'IM' [unofficial collaborator]. I was completely unprepared for this. I only remembered being visited by two men from the 'Firm' in 1959, when I was editor of NDL [*Neue Deutsche Literatur*]. They knew about my connections with a West German writer who had just made strong critical statements about the GDR. Intimidated by this, I said that I was prepared to meet them again.

Her further contacts with the Stasi, in Berlin and Halle, were few and far between. Seemingly they damaged no one, and in 1962 Wolf was dropped as an 'IM' and herself became the subject of constant surveillance. Wolf's statement created a furore in the West German press. Her account of her repressed involvement with the Stasi was viciously attacked as untrue, particularly in the weekly news magazine *Der Spiegel* 4/1993, and her reputation rubbished to the point where she concluded: 'I don't think that anything can hurt more than this' (*Berliner Zeitung*, 27/28 February 1993).

Part of the West German press reaction to revelations about the past of GDR intellectuals can be traced back to lack of knowledge about the GDR, its history, development and institutions, particularly in the early years. Yet it is also a political question. Unification has, in practice, implied attempts to obliterate anything that might have been good about the GDR from public consciousness. Forty years of history have been reduced to a single narrative of repression. The 1990s have seen a climate in Germany in which little space remains in which to consider GDR history in a differentiated way and not simply to dismiss the state as an *Unrechts-Staat*, that is as both unjust and unconstitutional. Thus the political choice of critical intellectuals to remain in the GDR has been interpreted by many as proof of unacceptable complicity with a monolithically repressive régime.

To a large extent, the attacks in the West German media on Christa Wolf's record as a critical writer in the GDR fail to take account of the historical and political context of her work, or to recognise as legitimate any belief in the moral and social superiority of socialism. The importance of reading historically is one of the central focuses of this chapter. The other major focus is on Christa Wolf as a woman writer.

In a chapter of this length, it is impossible to cover all of Wolf's work. I have chosen to concentrate on three important literary texts which, in effect, represent different decades in GDR history and cultural politics: the 1950s, the 1960s and the 1970s. They also represent changes in Wolf's aesthetics. This has meant excluding such important works as *Kindheitsmuster* (1976, *A Model Childhood*, 1983) and *Kein Ort Nirgends* (1979, *No Place on Earth*, 1983), as well as Wolf's shorter prose and essays.[3] In the first part of this chapter I will examine two early novels, read in the context of GDR society and cultural politics. I look in particular at Wolf's innovative role, politically and aesthetically, in extending and transforming ideas about literature in a socialist society and the nature of socialism itself. I concentrate on the novels *Der geteilte Himmel* (1963, *Divided Heaven*, 1965) and *Nachdenken über Christa T.* (1968, *The Quest for Christa T.*, 1982).

In the second part of the chapter I look at Wolf's novel *Kassandra* first published in 1983 (*Cassandra. A Novel and Four Essays*, 1984). *Kassandra* is a novel that examines the causes and effects of the Trojan War as symptomatic of war more generally, raising questions about gender, power and violence. I analyse the main themes of *Kassandra* and look at how the novel might be read in relation to questions raised by recent feminist literary theory.

In the brief conclusion I consider how Christa Wolf's work depicts the relationship between female subjectivity, identity and language, the role of patriarchy in this process and writing as a form of resistance.

Christa Wolf: Committed but Critical Socialist

As we have seen from chapters 10 and 11, an important ideological role was attributed to literature by the state in the GDR. Its official role was to help the construction and consolidation of socialism. It was to do this by helping to form 'all-round developed socialist personalities' via its ideological and moral power to influence the consciousness and values of individual readers. As the years went by, its actual role was closer to that of critical commentator on the problems besetting the development of socialism in the GDR. The ideological importance ascribed to literature by the state brought with it a significant level of both support and policing. As the previous two chapters suggest, writers received substantial levels of subsidy and sponsorship. In return they were expected to serve the 'interests of the working class' who, it was argued, created the economic basis to support their art. The Socialist Unity Party claimed to represent the interests of the working class and, as such, legitimately to determine what artists and writers might do. In practice writers were expected to conform to a centralised set of norms about their role and responsibility and to follow Central Committee guidelines on how they should write and what they should write about.

In the first two decades of the GDR these centralised norms also covered the aesthetics of writing. The theory of Socialist Realism, derived from cultural policy developed in the Soviet Union in the 1930s, defined how texts should be written and their supposed effects on the consciousness of the reader.[4] While prescriptive aesthetic norms were successfully challenged from the 1960s onwards, new works were consistently subject to political scrutiny and censorship.

Christa Wolf's early work is marked by both current cultural political thinking about literature in the GDR and a critical extension and eventual reworking of established aesthetic norms. Moreover, her early novels played a central role in extending the limits of what it was possible to say in the GDR in literary texts at this time.

Christa Wolf's first novel, *Der geteilte Himmel* published by the Mitteldeutscher Verlag in 1963, is a story of a young GDR couple in the years leading up to and including the building of the Berlin Wall. It is narrated from the present of 1961, in the months following the closing of the border with the West. The novel's central character, Rita, is at first in hospital and then in a nursing home following a nervous breakdown caused by the emotional effects of choosing to remain in the GDR and foregoing her relationship with her fiancé Manfred, who has left for a life in the West.

The novel tells the story of Rita and Manfred and their relationship and life together in the GDR. This personal history is part of a broader social history which deals with social, ideological and economic aspects of GDR life. Manfred, born and educated under the Nazis, comes from a petty bourgeois background. His cynicism, the novel suggests, is a response to his father's collaboration with both régimes. Manfred is rescued, temporarily, from this unhappy state by his love for the young and idealistic Rita. His new love encourages a new perspective on life, but one that proves vulnerable to problems at work. The inadequacies of the system, with its petty corruptions and tendency to value ideology over professional skill, eventually lead to the triumph of Manfred's old cynicism and his decision to leave for the West.

For Rita, new love at the outset of the plot coincides with the beginning of a new life which takes her to the city for work experience in heavy industry and teacher training. Rita – an idealistic child of the immediate post-war years of reconstruction – finds herself confronted by a series of demands and difficulties. In the factory these include problems in the workers' brigade caused by different attitudes and levels of commitment on the part of individual workers. They further include breakdowns in the production process caused by failures in the supply of raw materials – a result of the Western economic blockade of the GDR. In the classroom, Rita is faced with dogma coming not from lecturers but from fellow students. She sees how individuals can be forced into impossible positions by the emotional effects of stigmatisation. At home she has to cope with the effects of Manfred's difficulties at work. Unlike Rita, he refuses to endorse the system on the basis of its aspirations rather than the reality with which he is confronted on a daily basis.

It is not only age and experience that place Manfred and Rita differently in relation to the GDR. Crucially, Rita is a working-class girl who is offered new possibilities beyond her expectations by the new educational structures of the GDR. She is portrayed more positively than Manfred. The text stresses her sensitivity, which is contrasted with Manfred's acquired indifference. She is committed to the goals of socialism whereas Manfred is committed only to his work. Her integrity, stressed on various occasions in the narrative, is contrasted with Manfred's holding apart and remaining an onlooker rather than becoming a committed actor. While the contradictions and choices with which she is faced drive Rita to a nervous breakdown, she recovers from it ready to resume her life as a committed socialist.

Der geteilte Himmel takes on and transforms official socialist realist aesthetics. The novel was in part a product of Wolf's own experience with a brigade of workers at the railway carriage factory, VEB Waggonbau Ammendorf, near Halle. The cultural policy that came to be known as the *Bitterfelder Weg* was put into practice in 1959 and encouraged professional writers to spend time in factories and on collective farms. The aim was to promote new literature of direct relevance to working people, which spoke to their experience in industrial and agricultural production. Wolf's novel offers realistic portrayals of town and country, the factory and the teacher training institute. It does not paint an idealised picture. One is struck by the images of grime, pollution in the city and of the material and social problems of the workplace – whether factory or college.

The material and social problems faced on a day-to-day level in the process of constructing a new socialist society are depicted as they affect individuals. The novel depicts a wide canvas of characters, who, in the socialist realist tradition, represent different ideological positions. Apart from Rita and Manfred, whose characterisation is developed most fully, we encounter Mangold, a petty-bourgeois party hack masquerading as a true Communist, Meternagel, a worker who struggles constantly, makes mistakes but never gives up, Schwabe a well-meaning party dogmatist, who highlights the limits of such a position, Wendland, who is ideologically sound, perceptive and totally for the system, Schwarzenbach, who is committed to socialism but also against dogmatism, and Manfred's father who is a petty-bourgeois fellow traveller, who only acts in his own interests. In a break with conventional socialist realism, description and characterisation in the novel are complexified by shifts in the narrative into a stream of consciousness mode, which allows the main protagonist, Rita, to comment directly on events.

The reception of the novel in the GDR points clearly to the ways in which Christa Wolf went beyond the literary norms acceptable to party functionaries. This was true both of her use of aesthetic form and of the content of the novel. Between August and November 1963, various critical articles about the novel appeared in the party newspaper *Freiheit*, published in Halle.[5] The voice of the official party line can be heard clearly in a piece by Dietrich Allert and Hubert Wetzelt. They define the project of the book as the author's concern to smooth a path for the 'Manfreds of this society' into accepting the GDR way of life and way of thinking:

> The author is concerned with the Manfreds – this is the name of the main hero – who do not yet believe in our future, but who have to find

their way here and work with us. She wants to smooth a path for them
to our way of life and thinking. (Quoted in Fischbeck 1979: 61–62)

Already this interpretation suggests more about what party critics
thought the book *should* be doing than about the actual message of
the text. Wolf's text might more reasonably be read as showing
why people like Manfred cannot become committed socialists and
what social changes would be necessary to bring this about.

Allert and Wetzelt choose to focus on the supposed transforming power of love, rather than the depiction of the shortcomings of
GDR society, particularly in the industrial sphere, which drive
Manfred away. In doing so, they set the novel up to fail. Rita is
unable to change Manfred's consciousness and values, and her
love is not enough to keep him in the GDR. This lead the critics to
attack the novel for its inadequate non-socialist portrayal of love.
In a similar vein the article reads Rita's breakdown as an effect of
the realisation that she cannot succeed in convincing Manfred of
where he must live and fight.

Allert and Wetzelt also accused the novel of not being positive
enough in its representation of the forces changing society. Yet
Wolf's focus is arguably on the shortcomings and difficulties of
this process of change. At stake here is the very role of literature,
and whether or not it should be allowed to criticise failings in the
system. The review is also critical of the characterisation in the
novel, particularly of party members, who are seen as insuffi-
ciently positive. Where characters are clearly good people, the critics argue, they are depicted as good individuals rather than as
committed party members and good socialists. Conversely the
petty bourgeois characters are read by the critics as too positive.
Applying classic socialist realist norms, Allert and Wetzelt accuse
the positive figures in the novel of not being 'typical' enough,
something that leads to a distortion of reality.[6]

In the debate over the novel which ensued, other critics questioned the appropriateness of this reading and made a plea for the
legitimacy of showing *part* of life, rather than the supposed total-
ity demanded by socialist realist theory. They argue that the articulation of negative criticisms does not equal decadence, and that
it is important to depict problems in the construction of socialism.
They insist on maintaining a distinction between the author and
characters and on not collapsing one into the other.

Ultimately the debate over *Der geteilte Himmel* was of considerable significance in the development of the politics of literature in

the GDR. It marked a successful attempt to articulate alternative criteria for assessing texts, other than those of a narrowly defined socialist realism. It signalled a move into an acceptance of 'constructive criticism' as a legitimate theme for literature.

Nachdenken über Christa T.

Der geteilte Himmel is a good example of how Christa Wolf took on, and began to extend, socialist realist literary theory, laying down in the process some of the key issues that would inform her subsequent writing. Of all the issues raised in *Der geteilte Himmel*, it was the role, nature and status of the individual in the construction of a socialist society that would become central in Wolf's subsequent work. Questions of individual responsibility, of the individual versus the collective, of social versus individual interests and of the contribution that individuals could make to the construction of socialism are the key themes of Wolf's then controversial and now classic novel *Nachdenken über Christa T.*

Written as a reflective reconstruction of the life of the central character, Christa T., *Nachdenken über Christa T.* broke radically with the aesthetic norms of socialist realism. Rather than portraying a broad-ranging canvas of everyday life in the years following the Second World War, it focuses on the assumptions and values that underpinned the construction of the new German state as they affected individuals. The text is written from the perspective of a woman narrator who has known Christa T. since childhood and who feels that her own life has been profoundly influenced by Christa T.'s questioning approach to life. The novel seeks to demonstrate what was important about a woman who, although committed to the goals of socialism, did not conform with her peers. It is an argument for valuing those dimensions of individual people which did not fall within the remit of what was officially deemed useful and desirable in the first two decades of the GDR.

From her very first encounter with Christa T. in a school classroom during the Nazi period, the narrator finds her own conformist attitudes challenged as the new girl both questions and humanises established norms and authority:

> I could see the gym teacher with the marker pennons marking out her everlasting ball-game field; it was more pleasing to look at than at the way this newcomer treated our teacher. The way she kept the

reins on her, turning the interrogation, which would have been statu-
tory, into a conversation, and how she even decided what the class
was to talk about. I couldn't believe my ears: the topic she suggested
was 'The Forest'. The whistle was blowing for the start of the new
ball game, but I turned my head and stared at the newcomer, who
had declined to name a favourite school topic because her favourite
activity was walking in the woods. So that was how the teacher's
voice sounded when she was giving in: wasn't it the limit? (1982:7)

The effect of the narrator's ensuing friendship with Christa T. is to
make her realise that conformity at the expense of discovering
individual needs and potential is dangerous, '… that you'll come
to a bad end if you suppress all the shouts prematurely' (11).

Although radically different in their value systems and political
structures, both Nazi and early GDR society are shown to share a
tendency to insist on one single way of understanding events, and
to have quite clearly defined expectations of how people should
think and behave. To challenge this, the novel stresses the importance of recognising that events and people can be seen in different ways. It questions the status of 'facts' as given, rather than
produced and open to question.

For Christa Wolf, the formation of the individual is of central
importance, as indeed it was in official GDR policy. Yet she insists
on attention to dimensions of the individual that the state ignored
or even suggested were undesirable. Christa T. refuses to accept
the equation of the individual with the individualism of bourgeois
society and its suppression in the interests of an increasingly hollow collectivism.

The development of the individual, like that of society, is rooted
in her own history, which encompasses the Nazi period.[7] The
novel stresses the importance of not simply suppressing the past
but of coming to terms with it – a process which is fraught with
difficulties since people have a psychic and emotional investment
in not being part of that past:

But to make the precise and sharp cut-off separating 'ourselves'
from 'the others', once and for all, that would save us. And secretly
to know: the cut-off very nearly never came, because we ourselves
might well have become otherwise. But how does one cut oneself
away from oneself? … (27) This terrible gratitude for the lack of
opportunity isn't something to be forgotten. (28)

The question of brutality is central to the question of coming to
terms with the past. Exposed to extremes of brutality under the

Nazis and during the final stages of the war, when the German population flees westward in the face of the Soviet army, during the post-war period, Christa T. refuses to accept or play down minor everyday, brutal acts, even by children. Moreover, the novel suggests that the desire to repress the past leads to the failure to recognise implicit parallels with the present. It offers the example of Horst Binder who was praised by a Nazi functionary (*Bannführer*) for delivering his father over to the authorities for listening to an enemy radio station. Parallels with East Germany in the immediate post-war decades would not be lost on GDR readers.

The novel is, in part, a history of individual development, rooted in the experience of a particular generation of people who were at school under the Nazis and experienced war and flight as refugees. We are told how, after the war, Christa burned her old diaries with their enthusiasm, Nazi pledges, sayings and songs which were now a source of shame. We are told how reading material provided by the Soviets gave her a new sense of purpose:

> Gorky, Makarenko, the new pamphlets which everyone was given, as important as one's daily bread, unless one's hand was shut. Curiously enough, she finds some of what she reads familiar: it dawns on her that such thoughts are possible; she doesn't understand how, after all this rational clarity, the uttermost unreason could still have been possible. She jumps up: yes, that's how it will be, this is the way to ourselves. (30)

Yet her whole-hearted endorsement of the new socialist ideas on which the construction of the GDR in the immediate post-war years is founded does not lead Christa T. to give up her questioning attitude to life. Gradually this crystallises around one central question: the relationship between stated goals and aspirations and the reality of life in the GDR. Goals and aspirations, the novel suggests, must not be allowed to become a substitute for individual critical engagement with reality.

The question of critical engagement with socialism as it actually exists is, the novel suggests, a question affecting language and subjectivity. It involves a refusal to see things as static, as achieved once and for all. Fixing – whether of the individual in the mould of the required committed socialist or of social aspirations in official slogans – runs the risk of reducing people and policies to hollow shells. Christa T. reacts against much-used words like 'complete' (*vollständig*), constantly comparing rhetoric with reality. She privileges the movement towards a goal over the goal itself and moves on when no longer challenged. The concern with shifting meanings and forms of subjectivity is reflected in the narrative style which is radically subjective. The position of author and narrator seem to merge. Even the very title of the novel points to the need to reflect carefully before making apparently 'true' statements about people and social relations.

Unlike her fellow students, who are full of certainty, she is unable to name what she will become. Moreover she doubts the reality and fixity of language:

> What she doubted was the reality of names, though she had to deal with them; she certainly felt that naming is seldom accurate and that, even if it is accurate, name and thing coincide only for a short time. (35)

Unlike her fellow students, who work hard for the good of their particular collective, she follows her own path. Instead of preparing for her exams, she reads Dostoevsky and considers matters of substance that others pass over.

The detailed portrayal of Christa T.'s values and attitudes is set within the context of the *Aufbauphase*, the phase of post-war construction of the new state in the GDR. The effects of this phase in GDR history on individuals is described by the narrator as a conformity to dogmas based on insecurity:

> The truth is: we had other things to do. We were fully occupied with making ourselves unassailable – perhaps the sense of that can be felt. Not only to admit into our minds nothing extraneous – and all sorts of things we considered extraneous; also to let nothing extraneous well up from inside ourselves, and if it did so – a doubt, a suspicion, observations, questions – then not to let it show. (50–1)

Questioning, the admission that one might not be sure of the truth of one's dogma and the rightness of one's actions, was seen at this time as a sign of vulnerability. No vulnerability could be allowed in the face of the Cold War against the new socialist state. 'The idea of perfection had taken hold of our minds, had passed into us from our books and pamphlets; and from the rostrums at meetings came in addition a great impatience: verily I say unto you, you shall be with me today in paradise' (51–52).

Rather than certainty, Christa T. sees conscience and imagination – both important dimensions of the individual – as crucial to the building of a new society. In the absence of a genuinely critical approach to socialism, she notices how names gradually become mere surface and individual qualities irrelevant. When she is called upon to do things she does them but wonders if it is really *she* who is meant when her name is called or just another name. Would anyone notice her absence? She notices how names are increasingly becoming empty shells as people go through the motions without conviction. The sense of the growing inauthenticity of official rhetoric alienates her and she loses 'the capacity to live in a state of rapture':

> The vehement overplayed words, the waving banners, the deafening songs, the hands clapping rhythms over our heads. She felt how words begin to change when they aren't being tossed out any more by belief and ineptitude and excessive zeal but by calculation, craftiness, the urge to adapt and conform. Our words, not even false ones – how easy it would be if they were! – but the person speaking them has become a different person. Does that change everything? (56)

The increasing hollowness of official propaganda – its loss of a sense of reality – has negative effects on the subjectivity of individuals. People no longer feel part of what they do. They find it impossible to live up to official role models and to sacrifice themselves to the greater goal of socialism. This leads to an increase in conformity which reduces the creative contribution of individuals to society. The vigorous debates of the early years shift into unanimous monologues. Where individuals speak out against this process they are dismissed as cases 'of subjectivism'.[8]

Christa's inability to conform takes its psychological and emotional toll. Unable to doubt the world, she doubts herself: 'I don't know what I'm living for. Can you see what that means? I know what's wrong with me, but its still me, and I can't wrench it out of myself!' (70). When she becomes ill she is told by the doctor that with her intelligence she will learn to conform.

In her non-conformist questioning, Christa meets either non-comprehension or cynicism. Occasionally her work gains recognition, for example, her dissertation for her diploma which proves much more thoughtful, personal and self-critical than that of other students. In contrast her critical attitudes to her role as a teacher meet with cynical responses from both pupils and headmaster. The pupils write unrealistic, yet strategically conformist, essays to ensure good marks. When Christa confronts the headmaster with this problem she finds little support. He has left idealism behind and has trained himself to want only what he can achieve. Later in life a former pupil accuses her of having made impractical demands on them, telling her that conformity is the key to good health.

Yet conformity in this society rests not only on an implicit acceptance of things as they are, but on an explicit endorsement of how things are officially said to be. The discrepancy between the two highlights the precarious status of so-called 'facts'. Towards the end of the novel the narrator comes across a piece of Christa's writing entitled 'The Big Hope, or The Difficulty of Saying "I"' (169). These words are followed by '"Facts! Stick to facts." And underneath in brackets: *But what are facts?'* (172).

The novel is a plea for valuing authenticity. The individual, it argues, should value his or her self and should on no account give up her or his own identity in an effort to conform. Moreover, the individual needs constantly to question the degree to which official policies and the rhetoric of socialism are realised in actual day-to-day practice. These are the values which Christa T. embodies. By the end of the narrative she is dead. Leukaemia has killed her, a disease in which the *white* blood cells in the blood stream kill off the *red* blood cells. This disease was read by both GDR and Western critics as a metaphor for GDR society. Christa T., they argued, was destroyed by the social structure, and her truly socialist principles could not survive the pressures of the GDR state. This was a reading contested by Christa Wolf, who maintained that Christa T. was not destroyed by this society but, on the contrary, had lived her life to the full.[9]

Wolf's use of a female central character in the novel is important. It could be argued that official ideology in the GDR, and the social institutions and organisations which help give structure and content to people's lives, focused on a public sphere which was shaped by what might be described as traditionally male values. In its critique of GDR society, the novel makes a case for the valuing of what have traditionally been seen as feminine qualities of the individual, sensitivity, emotionality, lack of certainty, mothering and the concerns of the individual, private sphere. The polarisation of gender attributes and the marginalisation of 'feminine' qualities would become a key theme of Wolf's novel *Kassandra*.

Kassandra

Christa Wolf's story of Cassandra and the course of the Trojan War was first published, together with four lectures, in West Germany in 1983. The West German edition was followed by a slightly censored East German edition in 1984 and the lines cut from the GDR edition received widespread coverage in the West German media. Located as it is in the ancient world, *Kassandra* uses a past setting to raise profound questions about the nature of our present. This strategy, which many East German writers have used, offered the possibility of saying things which, if set in a contemporary context, would incur further censorship.

The narrative opens in Mycenae as Cassandra awaits her immanent execution. As she faces her death, she reflects on past events and concludes that more than any other feeling, deeper even than her fear, it is the indifference of the gods to mortals that affects her most. As the favourite daughter of King Priam of Troy and the priestess of Apollo, given the gift of prophecy by the god, Cassandra has been forced by events to question both the social structures and belief system which, before the war, offered her privilege and security. Finally she has come to realise that man's and woman's future lies with themselves.

The Analysis of War

Kassandra raises fundamental questions about the causes and effects of war, questions which are as relevant to the present as to the fictional Troy of the novel. While the Trojan war has underlying economic motives, for example, the Greeks' wish for free access to the Dardanelles, these could be resolved by treaty. War becomes a more intractable problem once it has been transformed into a question of 'honour'.

Gender is central to the analysis of the causes and conduct of war in *Kassandra*. Masculinity, in particular, plays a central role. Both the world of politics at the court of King Priam and the waging of war are depicted as male concerns. While women – Queen Hecuba and her daughter Cassandra – are tolerated by the state council while they offer no challenge to the policies pursued by the men, they are excluded once they begin to question the need for the war and its conduct. It is male pride which prevails despite rational arguments against war which invariably come from the women. Although abducted by the Spartan Telamon, King Priam's sister Hesione has actually – as Hecuba points out – been made queen by him. This cannot pacify Priam's pride. He insists that this is not the point: if he does not act, he loses face. Similarly, it is feelings of inadequacy and the need for recognition as a hero that motivate Paris's abduction of Helen, whom he subsequently loses to the King of Egypt. The abduction of women by men lies at the root of the war. Cassandra urges a settlement with the Greeks, but for the men of the court this would be an impossible admission of failure.

Masculine weakness and the pride which accompanies it also govern the behaviour of the Greeks. *Kassandra* links Agamemnon's 'exquisite' cruelty in battle to his impotence. Achilles' extreme brutality is tied to his homosexuality. Achilles, whom Odysseus 'dragged into the war by the scruff of his neck ... was after everyone in sight: young men, whom he genuinely desired, and girls, as a proof that he was like everybody else. A fiend in battle so that everyone would see that he was not a coward, he did not know what to do with himself once the fighting was done' (1984: 83).

Cassandra analyses the first sign of war as 'letting the enemy govern our behaviour' (64). War – for example the Cold War in the early years of the GDR – soon leads to a siege mentality in which questioning is suppressed. As Cassandra comes to realise, events can always be interpreted in different ways. These interpretations are invariably both politically and personally motivated. For a long time Cassandra:

> ... still believed that a little will to truth, a little courage, could erase the whole misunderstanding ... After all, we need only call to mind our Trojan tradition. But what was that tradition? What did it consist in? When I understood: In the Helen we had invented, we were defending everything that we no longer had. And the more it faded, the more real we had to say it was. (85)

Thus, as the war progresses, concern with truth becomes redefined as either treachery or madness.

It is Cassandra's concern with truth, in the face of a war based on a falsehood, in a court governed by the wish to avoid the truth, that gradually alienates her from her family. 'The same old story: Not the crime but its heralding turns men pale and furious. I know that from my own example. Know that we would rather punish the one who names the deed than the one who commits it' (14).

War imposes unity by polarisation. 'Child', Priam tells Cassandra, 'anyone who does not side with us now is working against us' (70). This taking of sides, forced by the men of the court, produces an ambivalence in the women: they both hate Troy and wish it victory. Unity is also imposed by deflecting differences onto the enemy: internal conflicts are projected onto the Greeks as the Trojans close ranks against them.

Cassandra sees herself as different from other members of the court. Yet as the war progresses, she is forced by circumstances and by the insights of other women to recognise that the difference she 'took such pride in amounted to nothing more than my inner reservations' (87). Thus Arisbe interprets one of Cassandra's dreams as complicity with the powers of the court: 'faced with a completely perverted question, you nevertheless tried to find an answer' (87). This complicity makes the powers behind the war stronger. Yet as the situation becomes more polarised, inner reservation is no longer possible. When Cassandra finally takes a stand and refuses to agree to the court using her sister Polyxena as bait to kill Achilles, she is imprisoned.

The novel stresses the difficulty and importance of self-recognition:

> We had believed that the terror could not increase, but now we had to recognise that there are no limits to the atrocities people can afflict on one another; that we are capable of rummaging through someone else's entrails and of cracking his skull, trying to find out whatever causes the most pain. I say 'we', and of all the 'we's' I eventually said, this is the one that challenges me the most. It is so much easier to say 'Achilles the brute' than to say this 'we'. (119)

For Cassandra, the discovery that the enemy and her own people are alike is both shocking and undermining. To be alive, the novel suggests, is 'not to shrink from what is most difficult: to change one's image of oneself' (21).

Women and the Patriarchal Order

Even before the war Troy is a city run on patriarchal principles. In this context, Cassandra is depicted as a woman unwilling to conform to traditional gender roles. Intelligent and interested in politics, she becomes her father's favourite child. Yet as her views diverge from those of her father and their closeness gives way to distance, Cassandra realises that her relationship with her father was 'based, as is so often the case between men and women, on the fact that I knew him and he did not know me' (50).

The role of priestess is one of the few recognised forms of power which women can exercise in this society. Yet even the role of priestess has become male-defined. The religion in which Cassandra is brought up has excluded older female goddesses. 'I saw Apollo bathed in radiant light the way Panthous taught me to see him. The sun god with his lyre, his blue although cruel eyes, his bronzed skin. Apollo the god of the seers. Who knew what I ardently desired: the gift of prophecy, and conferred it on me with a casual gesture which I did not dare to feel was disappointing; whereupon he approached me as a man' (15). At this stage Cassandra – like many committed but critical socialists in the GDR – 'did not want the world the way it was, but I wanted to serve devotedly the gods who ruled it' (40).

For Cassandra a sense of sovereignty, of having a voice in the male-defined world of the court is central: 'Why did I want the gift of prophecy, come what may? To speak with my voice: the ultimate' (4). Yet, ironically, she is not the source of the prophecy and from the start, her prophesies are destined not to be believed – a punishment from Apollo for her resistance to his sexual advances.

Cassandra's position as the daughter of the king and priestess creates a barrier between her and other women at the court. As an agent of patriarchal structures – both religious and secular – she does not behave like other women. Her distance from them is only finally overcome when she abandons the court's values and its version of the truth and joins the community outside the city.

In the besieged Troy existing patriarchal sexual divisions in Trojan society become harsher and more exaggerated. As even privileged women's positions change and they are excluded from all decision making, they find no space for the expression of doubts or critiques. Female resistance to events and the changes in values that war brings can only find expression in the alternative communities which exist beyond the walls of Troy.

Cassandra's access to an alternative world outside the city comes through her wet nurse Parthena and Marpessa, who is Parthena's daughter and Cassandra's servant. Beyond the walls of Troy a counter-world proliferates 'like a plant, lush, carefree' (48). Women from both camps, and some of non-conformist men, live or meet regularly here throughout the war. Many live in the mountains, the forest, in the caves along the Scamander river, demonstrating that 'between killing and dying there is a third alternative: living' (118).

Female deities, like hidden and tabooed forms of female power, have been excluded by the Trojan patriarchal order. Yet they continue to exist on the margins outside the city and are still called upon in moments of crisis. When first introduced to this alternative female religion, Cassandra is shocked and terrified by it. Cybele, a forbidden goddess, has a sanctuary on Mount Ida beyond the walls of Troy. Here women from both the Greek and Trojan camps continue to worship her in ways that are tabooed by patriarchal religion. They dance with abandon, giving expression to female sexuality:

> They gradually increased their tempo, intensified their rhythm, moved faster, more demandingly, more turbulently; hurled individual dancers out of the circle, among them Marpessa, my reserved Marpessa; drove them to gestures which offended my modesty; until, beside themselves, they shook, went into howling contortions, sank into an ecstasy in which they saw things invisible to the rest of us, and finally one after another sagged and collapsed in exhaustion. (20)

The residual, feminine religious practices that survive outside the city walls privilege female sexuality and sensuality in ways that are impossible within the patriarchal order of Troy. Here young women – who are still virgins – wait passively in the temple for men to select them and initiate them into heterosexuality. Love and sex are important to Cassandra but can only be realised by her in equal relationships. These are possible with other women, but also with men in so far as they elude the power relations of patriarchal society. Thus Cassandra's love for Aeneas keeps her going during the war, bringing new life to the 'husk' of her body. Yet as the war ends, Cassandra refuses to flee with Aeneas since a traditional relationship with him, dictated by society, would be contrary to what she sees as her nature. Cassandra reflects that she cannot love a hero. She does not want to see him 'transformed into a statue' (138).

Kassandra offers a complex and sophisticated account of the interrelationship between war and patriarchal institutions, norms and values. It illustrates both how patriarchy works under the extreme conditions of war and offers an image of female resistance which incorporates alternative values and ways of living which might offer hope for a different future. Though set in the ancient world, its message is one equally applicable to our nuclear present.

Conclusions

Among the key lessons to be learned from a reading of Christa Wolf's work is the centrality of history to an understanding of literary texts. This is all the more important in the case of texts written in societies different from those with which we are familiar as readers. Neither *Der geteilte Himmel* nor *Nachdenken über Christa T.*

can be adequately understood without knowledge of GDR history and cultural politics. *Kassandra* addresses a less GDR-specific agenda: the question of war and its connections with patriarchal structures and values. These are questions which became part of a broader feminist agenda in both East and West, particularly in the context of the escalation of the nuclear arms race under U.S. President Reagan. They remain central questions even after the end of the Cold War.

It is possible to identify certain key concerns which surface in different ways in Wolf's writing over more than three decades. These are also questions which have preoccupied recent feminist literary theory. Among other things, writing, for Christa Wolf, is a way of exploring the relationship between subjectivity, identity and language. This was a key theme of both *Nachdenken über Christa T.* and *Kassandra*. In both the former GDR and in Wolf's ancient world, official public language privileged traditional masculine norms and values. In both cases this had dire effects on the society in question. For women who find themselves marginalised by the existing patriarchal order, literature offers a site for the expression of new and more open forms of subjectivity and different value systems. Increasingly in Wolf's work this exploration of the relation between subjectivity, identity and language takes us into questions of the relationship between language, culture and patriarchy.

For Christa Wolf, the exploration of the relationship between subjectivity, identity and language is integrally related to questions of aesthetic form. Her writing is, in part, a questioning of authoritative forms of narrative. It produces new forms of subjectivity which are marked by lack of certainty, questioning and openness to change. This agenda is realised in novels with female protagonists. Whether or not critics would want to identify this aspect of Wolf's work as a kind of 'female' aesthetic would depend very much on their own political agenda as well as their conceptions of 'female' modes of writing.

Whatever the context – the GDR, the ancient world or post-unification Germany – writing, for Wolf, is a site for questioning existing power relations and the forms of subjectivity which they produce. In this respect it is ultimately a site of resistance and transformation.

Notes

I would like to thank Eva Kaufmann for her helpful comments on this chapter.

1. This is a published version of a television interview with Günter Gaus.
2. For an account of the ensuing debate see Anz 1995.
3. For a comprehensive bibliography of Wolf's work see Drescher 1990.
4. For more on Soviet socialist realism see Gorky et al. 1977.
5. A selection of these are reprinted in Fischbeck 1979.
6. For the principles of socialist realist writing, including the theory of 'typicality', see Lukács 1963.
7. This is a key theme of Wolf's *Kindheitsmuster* (1976).
8. See the case of Gunther 1982: 67.
9. For more on the writing and reception of *Nachdenken über Christa T.* see Drescher 1992.

Chapter Thirteen

POST-WAR AUSTRIAN
WOMEN WRITERS

Allyson Fiddler

Women in Austria

In 1988 one critic of Austrian women's writing noted rather wryly
that 'because the recent feminist movement has had minimal
impact on conservative Austrian society and on the Austrian consciousness, Austria and feminism appear to many a contradiction
in terms' (Vansant 1988: 1). For Ruth Pauli, a journalist working in
Austria and the author of a book on women's emancipation there,
the situation is even more acute. She comments that:

> Austria, together with Iceland and Switzerland, form a strange trio
> among the industrialised countries. While, in the early 1970s, Wom-
> en's Liberation Movements everywhere were trying to get hold of
> the tiller, there were no acts of female disobedience in these three
> countries. They were the three most traditional and hierarchical
> societies in the West. (Pauli 1986: 7)

That Austria is indeed a conservative country with a small 'c' is
beyond doubt. The political history of post-war Austria has been
determined by the principle of consensus rule. Through the establishment of institutions such as the Parity Commission (Paritätis-
che Kommission), which ensures compromise and negotiation in
political and industrial disputes, and with frequent coalition governments, Austria has been subject to a philosophy which tries
hard to avoid conflict. While promoting peaceful co-existence and
stable economic growth, this strategy has also helped form a typically static and conservative attitude of mind.[1] Moreover, the
influence exerted by the church in Austria is substantial and it is

certainly true that Catholicism is one contributory factor in the slow pace of change in women's lives and in the traditional attitudes to gender and family life which prevail.[2]

However, the situation for Austrian women is not quite as desperate as Pauli's statement suggests. The 1970s saw a great deal of progressive legislation from the legalisation of abortion during the first three months of pregnancy in 1975, to the establishment of marriage based on the principle of partnership (*Partnerschaftsehe*) with the improved ease of divorce and provision for divorcees with children which this entailed (1975). This process culminated in the Equal Treatment Act, passed in 1979.[3] Austria also has a secretary for women's affairs (Bundesministerin für Frauenangelegenheiten),[4] many of its political organisations have introduced women's quotas and it has a very generous state provision of maternity and paternity leave which permits receipt of a state benefit for up to two years with the guarantee of being able to return to one's job.

This is how things seem on paper. The reality of women's 'emancipation', however, looks very different. According to research documented by Gudrun Biffl, women's participation in the labour market since the 1970s has rocketed in most Western countries but not grown massively in Austria. More to the point, perhaps, the differential between men's wages and women's wages has been eroded more slowly in Austria than in other European countries.[5] Women politicians, as in most other Western European countries, tend to be concentrated in areas which are seen as some sort of extension of their 'natural' domain – health and education, for example. While there is provision for both maternity and paternity leave, the number of men taking advantage of this is negligible. In practice, of course, it is usually the man's wage which is much higher and which constitutes the income from which a couple can more probably live. Cynically, one might argue that the emphasis on the importance of child care by the child's parents (usually the mother) in fact reinforces traditional family and gender roles. The idea of 'packing one's kids off to a childminder' is without doubt still tabooed to a much greater extent in Austria than, for example, in Britain.[6]

As far as the cultural life of contemporary Austria is concerned, women have a high profile and have attained a certain success in some areas. In literature, for example, Elfriede Jelinek and Ingeborg Bachmann certainly have the same high stature as Peter Handke or Thomas Bernhard.[7] However, women are still very much under represented in music, surely the most prestigious of arts in Austria. To this day, for example, women are not allowed to play in the Viennese Philharmonic Orchestra!

For decades the debate has raged as to whether there is such a thing as a distinct Austrian literature. It is not my intention here to duplicate this debate for women by asking 'is there a distinct Austrian women's writing?'. In her study of post-war Austrian women writers, Jacqueline Vansant picks up on Egon Schwarz's perspective that 'there is an Austrian literature because there is an Austrian historical reality. Every work of literature emerging from this reality reflects it in some way and is bound to be impregnated with elements of the Austrian experience' (Schwarz quoted by Vansant 1988: 13). Similarly, then, there is an Austrian women's writing, because elements of Austrian women's experience are expressed in writing by Austrian women. In the following discussion I have attempted to draw attention to Austrian-specific references and qualities where they are relevant. The writers I have chosen for my discussion all began writing after the war and most of them may be termed proto-feminist (writing before second-wave feminism) or feminist. Erika Tunner has noted that there are numerous Austrian women writers such as Enrica von Handel-Mazzetti (1871–1955), Gertrud Fussenegger (b. 1912), and Paula Grogger (1892–1987), who remain bound by tradition. Tunner talks of the gentle sense of tolerance and tradition which characterises these authors' works and those of Christine Busta and Christine Lavant, whose writing deals with Christian themes (Tunner 1988: 405). There is not so much of the 'radical' or abstract feminism as seen in West German women's writing, and it may be due to this broadly political attachment that Austria has not produced feminist thinkers such as Sigrid Weigel and Silvia Bovenschen.

The writers in the present chapter could all be termed 'critical' writers. All of them take issue with the existing 'order of things', many use wit and irony to point out the patriarchal fabric of the society in which they live, many write in ways which are experimental and challenging. I would maintain that the writing of these Austrian women is in the main linked to a political critique of societal structures, a characteristic which is not held to be a characteristic of mainstream writing by Austrian men. Clearly, the writers discussed in this chapter represent only a small selection from a very wide range of Austrian women writers. I have chosen only one or two representative writers from each decade in order to discuss one text by each in some detail. This means that it has not been possible to mention the work of such important writers as Elfriede Gerstl (b. 1932), Marie-Thérèse Kerschbaumer (b. 1936), Friederike Mayröcker (b. 1924), Erika Mitterer (b. 1906), Christine Nöstlinger (b. 1936), Hilde Spiel (1911–1990), Dorothea Zeemann (b. 1909), to name but a few.

The 'Infancy' of Women's Writing: Childhood Themes in the 1940s, 1950s and 1960s

In her article 'Deutschsprachige Literatur von Frauen nach 1945', Sigrid Weigel argues that:

> The link to the trauma of National Socialism is closer in women's writing than in other literature. It seems that women have a lesser investment in that illusion of a historical zero hour which otherwise marks post-war literature. (Weigel 1984b: 63)

While it is not possible here to test in detail Weigel's thesis, it is certainly true that Ilse Aichinger, one of Weigel's examples, in fact played a strong part in trying to destroy the illusion of a 'zero hour' in post-war literature in German. Aichinger's impact on post-war writing and on the famous opinion-building literary group, *Gruppe 47*, is well-documented (see chapter 4). In 1952 she won the Group's prize for her short story, 'Spiegelgeschichte', a story which was so radically new and stylistically interesting that it initiated a move away from the aesthetic programme previously espoused by the *Kahlschläger*. (*Kahlschlag* literally means 'deforestation'; in the 1950s it became a slogan for writers demanding a complete break with literary tradition.)[8] The reverberations caused by the reception of this story have been cited by one critic as one of the reasons why Aichinger's only novel and first publication, *Die größere Hoffnung* (1948) has not received due attention and why, as late as 1980, it constituted 'a book which is waiting patiently for us' (Härtling 1980).[9] This thesis has, to my mind, been justifiably refuted by Gisela Lindemann, and more recently Sigrid Schmid-Bortenschlager has suggested that Aichinger's non-realist mode of writing made her something of an outsider in the post-war tradition of writing in German (Lindemann 1988, and Schmid-Bortenschlager 1991). Numerous important literary prizes, texts printed in anthologies and school books, indeed complete new editions of her work seem at first sight to contradict Aichinger's position as a relatively unknown writer. More important for feminist literary history, however, is the fact that Aichinger 'appears in the accounts, but then after a mention usually connected to her "breakthrough" in the Gruppe 47, she is dutifully ticked off the list and forgotten'. Although this important début with *Gruppe 47* should have set up Aichinger for 'a discovery by feminist literary studies', this perspective has surfaced only briefly in the rather sparse collection of secondary literature (Schmid-Bortenschlager 1991: 86).[10] If, against this background, I nevertheless now turn my attention to Aichinger's earliest work, her novel *Die größere Hoffnung*, it is not with the intention of ticking her off 'dutifully' as a writer who was important in *Gruppe 47*, but with the aim of presenting a woman whose work has been of paramount importance in the context of Austrian women's writing.

For Austrian women, as for women in other previously Nazi-occupied countries, the immediate post-war years were a period when mere survival and the physical and emotional rebuilding of society and of individual lives was an all-consuming activity. It is perhaps not surprising that issues of sexual equality seemed relatively unimportant and that literature by women only began to deal directly with gender issues in the late 1950s and apply a feminist understanding to these in the 1960s and 1970s. Aichinger's novel, set in a city which is easily identifiable as Vienna, though this is never explicitly stated, is not specifically 'Austrian' in its relevance.[11] Equally, though it is important to locate the novel in its historical context – that is, against the backdrop of the persecution, oppression and massacre of Jews by ordinary people, by soldiers and by the Gestapo during the Third Reich – *Die größere Hoffnung* has a resonance beyond that of a mere war novel. Aichinger's text does not deal with or depict the bloody violence of war, instead it focuses on the lives of children, who, having been stamped by Nazi racial classification as Jewish – in the language of the children they have 'the wrong grandparents' – are left to try to make sense of their lives as outcasts and ultimately to wait to be taken away by the secret police.

The novel consists of a series of episodes in the life of the central character, a half-Jewish girl called Ellen,[12] and her group of Jewish play-mates. In the last four chapters of the novel, Ellen is left completely on her own as all her friends are taken away to concentration camps, and her grandmother, unable to cope with the fear of being taken by the Gestapo, swallows poison. The sheer horror of Nazi ideology and the Holocaust is made all the more horrific and poignant in *Die größere Hoffnung* by not being put in the 'adult' terms of politics, death and destruction. The children playing on the canal bank want nothing more than to be allowed to do such simple things as play football, sit on the park benches and have a ride on the merry-go-round.

The way in which the children's natural innocence is assaulted by the demands and harsh realities of wartime is one of the central frictions of the novel. This, however, is a principle which applies both to the thematic and aesthetic concerns of the text. As the critic Lawrence Langer has stated, in Aichinger's style 'image collides with concept instead of reinforcing it'. Aichinger's style is a mixture of realism and fantasy. The reader is often deliberately confused and the world of dreams and reality conflated, such that in Langer's terms: 'the action repeatedly trembles on the edge of dissolution and the attentive reader must struggle perpetually to reorient his [or her] confused sensibilities to these alien but coexistent worlds' (Langer 1975: 149, 136). Although the fantastic mode is partly inspired by the choice of children as characters – games, dreams and fantasy are the means they use to try to cope with and understand their situation – it is also part and parcel of Aichinger's poetic language. Fantasy in Aichinger's work does not, however, signify escapism or an unwillingness to deal with reality; in fact the word does not do justice to the strange, allegorical parallel worlds created by Aichinger or to the highly developed personifications which she employs. 'I hated the word fantasy even as a child', Aichinger comments. 'I didn't want fantasy, I wanted reality, as precise a reality as possible.... Fantasy, that sounds too much like a cherished collection of private poetry, like rapturous prose, or bursting into unsolicited meanderings' (Aichinger in Steinwendtner 1993: 12). But then Ilse Aichinger has always known how treacherous words can be.[13]

One example from the chapter 'Der Tod der Großmutter' must suffice here to illustrate the collision between expectation and reality which so often confronts the reader. Night, personified by Aichinger, hears a child crying, and trying *not* to fall asleep:

> At times the March night felt like crying, but tears were not in her brief. Thus she tried to cheer herself up and put nightcaps on the heads of the sleepers ... Through the half-open window they [the night and persecution] heard the sobs of a child resisting sleep. (156–157, 159)

The chapter begins much as a fairy tale might, but the situation in which the little girl finds herself is very real indeed and it has no happy ending: Ellen has hidden her grandmother's poison and after much protest finally agrees to give it to her grandmother if she tells her a story. But grandmother cannot get past the empty beginning, 'Once', she stammers, 'once upon a time', and Ellen has to take the task upon herself and become the story-teller (170). She, too, stops in her tracks once she has asked the ominous question of why her grandmother's hands are so cold (174).

The tone of the narrative is not moralising, nor does Aichinger try to explain or blame someone for the children's plight. She refuses to paint a black and white picture and remains true to the principle of searching for the human qualities in both victims and perpetrators (Lindemann 1988: 21). Faced with confusing moral dicta, presented to her by the adult world in terms which are strongly reminiscent of Kafka, Ellen manages to hold on to her hope in the face of each and every blow. At the beginning of the novel, she tries to obtain a visa to follow her mother to the United States, but is told by the consul that, 'Anyone who does not give herself a visa … can travel the whole world and yet never get there' (20). In the symbolically charged final chapter, after having undertaken something of a spiritual journey with her friends, and having physically roamed the streets, Ellen heads geographically and spiritually towards home. She sees the blue sky behind the hills and declares, in an imagined dialogue with her friend Georg, a hope, which is now stronger than ever. Ellen rejoins her dead friends as she is blown to pieces by a grenade. Her final words, 'I see the star!' (269) reaffirm the paradox of her symbol of hope, the Star of David, meaning death for many who were forced to wear it, and meaning hope and joy to Ellen, who was envious of those who were allowed to wear the pretty, shiny star, since *they* had the required number of 'wrong grandparents'.

The stories in Marlen Haushofer's collection, *Wir töten Stella* (1993) also deal with the innocence of childhood, and the title novella (orig. 1958) concerns its abuse by the adult world. Stella's innocence is stolen in a way radically different from Ellen's: her guardian father first has an affair with her, then discards her cruelly. The resulting severe depression eventually leads her to run in front of a lorry and kill herself, an incident which the adoptive parents and even Stella's real mother welcome and can conveniently pass off as an accident. Stella's inheritance from her dead father can now pass on to her mother and her mother's new boyfriend, and the foster family can return to its former acceptable, if uneasy, family life.[14] This title story is recounted by a first-person narrator, the mother and wife who has silently looked on in full knowledge and recognition of what was happening to poor, unwanted, and unloved Stella, without intervening or providing much-needed support, advice and affection. This accounts for the narrator's status as accessory to the crime and her admittedly understated regret as she writes down her story, in order not to forget Stella (54).

Incredible as it may seem, the radical and critical tone in Haushofer's writing has been overlooked, indeed ignored by many critics. Regula Venske reminds us that 'the arts pages read Marlen Haushofer's novels as affirmative "women's" novels, that is to say, as novels about marriage and families, and they recommended them particularly to "single women" or to "ladies with psychological interests"' (Venske 1991 a: 102–103)![15] Haushofer's work, like that of other now highly regarded women writers such as Ingeborg Bachmann, belatedly received critical acclaim. She has, however, been emphatically labelled 'a feminist from Austria' (Lorenz 1979). This description seems apt given the fact that relations between the sexes form one of Hauhofer's central concerns and are illuminated from the woman's point of view, if perhaps without the broader societal or political perspective of later writers, such as Brigitte Schwaiger. Her writing and central character in *Wie kommt das Salz ins Meer* (1977, *Why Is There Salt in the Sea?* 1988) definitely bear the mark of a feminist consciousness. Sexual relations are formulated by Haushofer in similarly radical terms to Bachmann and Elfriede Jelinek, that is, as antagonistic and warring. In a much-quoted passage from her novel *Die Tapetentür* (1957), the narrator comes to the following recognition: 'I always used to find men's blindness and clumsiness touching, but now it begins to frighten me. Their apparently so endearing awkwardness conceals something monstrous and inhuman, a lack of interest in organic life. . . The enemy is hiding in them, in these people we must love' (quoted in Venske 1991b: 26).

Women are not exempt from blame, however. Anna describes herself as a kind of fellow traveller at man's side: 'I have lived the life of a well-to-do woman, I've stood at the window and breathed the scents of every season, while all around me people have been killed and injured' (1993: 71). The tone of Haushofer's novella, 'Wir töten Stella', is on the whole pessimistic and resigned, and her narrator seems only dimly aware of the potential and power of hope, so cherished by Aichinger's protagonist: 'It is true, human beings can endure a great deal, not out of habit, but because they nurture a faint glimmer of hope which helps them to believe secretly that one day they'll be able to break out of the habit' (1993: 55).

A further Austrian writer to take up the theme of childhood in her work is Barbara Frischmuth. Like Haushofer, Frischmuth has written many children's books, though neither author has limited her thematisation of childhood to this genre. The distinction is for Frischmuth, in fact, a rather fluid one.[16] Frischmuth's concerns in her first novel, *Die Klosterschule* (1968, *The Convent School* 1993) are with the process and instruments of gender inculcation and religious upbringing and she uses the story of a teenage girl in a convent boarding school to exemplify their mostly harmful effects. The novel is made up of fourteen short chapters which form not a chronological plot, but a collection of narrated experiences presenting a representative picture of what everyday life is like for the girls of the convent. The tone of Frischmuth's text is quietly satirical. The narrator recounts to us all manner of routines and regulations, prayers, punishments and moral lessons, sometimes in a straight but lengthy verbatim fashion, emphasising the dulling effects of these strictures on the girls, and sometimes in a confused or slightly distorted form which ironises the brainwashing being carried out in the name of religious upbringing.

Gaps appear between what the girls are taught to believe and what they in fact fantasise, dream, and giggle about. The girls are linguistically 'programmed' on the one hand by a range of sayings and proverbs with which most readers will identify, ('The sleep you get before midnight is the soundest. Early to bed, early to rise' [51]), but which are repeated *ad nauseam* and in such a monotonous way as to reveal both the narrator's disaffection and the ineffectiveness of this as a pedagogical method. On the other hand, the girls' moral and religious instruction is also designed to make them conformist, chaste, and pious and to erase any tendencies towards individualism. Their confusion over this is also expressed in their language, whether in jumbled parables and inverted religious imagery, as in the nightmarish enactment of the parable of the sheep and the goats, where in her fantasy it is the kindly devil who cares for the narrator when she lies ill in the sick-bay; or in the hollow repetition of learned regulations: 'We are supposed to keep our columns straight; we are told to hold hands, to speak English, not to leave the group ... Whether we want to or not, we are to submit our will to a Higher Will because it was That Will which willed our Being, and we are constantly to desire That Will with our own'. The insertion here of 'whether we want to or not' and the inclusion of the phrase 'we are to' in the final clause, reveals the narrator's disquiet and mental, if not physical resistance. The first-person narration is almost entirely conveyed through this unauthentic 'we'. The only places where Frischmuth employs 'I' are in the narrator's fantasies and dreams, in the chapter where she explores her image in a mirror,[17] and in the final chapter when she composes a letter to a friend outside the convent. In this she expresses openly her doubts, while retaining a more muted, for her perhaps a more tenable, more acceptable conception of faith.

Frischmuth's linguistic experiments in this novel, her attempt to show how an understanding of the world can be transmitted through language structures, and her calculated playfulness with these structures, place her in a very Austrian tradition of linguistic scepticism (*Sprachskepsis*).[18] *Die Klosterschule* puts into practice her central line of enquiry: 'For me, children mean a lack of inhibition, they mean spontaneity. I want to know how the world finds its way into children's language' (Frischmuth in Ester 1982: 7). The author herself has tried to play down the important position which religion occupies here, glossing it as a 'quite specific manifestation of power' (Frischmuth in Sauter 1981: 100). Patently, there is far more to it than this, and critics have not been slow to pick up on the feminist implications of Frischmuth's critique. Arnold Blumer points out how the system or form of human behavioural organisation embodied by the teachings of the convent, is a thoroughly patriarchal one; it is one in which 'being part of mankind means being male'. Religion is merely one of the discourses – in the case of the convent girls, of course, the primary discourse – which contributes to women's oppression, to their self-understanding as servants, their submissiveness and, indeed, to their status as passive, sexual partners (a theme of the chapter entitled 'Lessons in Deportment'). Blumer emphasises how 'it is equally clear right from the start that this male order is supported by the church and by Judaeo-Christian traditions and that its most intricate linguistic structures have been marked by them' (Blumer 1983: 187). It should not be forgotten that shaking the pillars of Catholicism and calling into question its dogma and its legitimacy is a bold venture, given the power and importance of the Church in Austria.

The Period of Feminist Consciousness in Austria

Against the background of 1968, the year Frischmuth's first book was published, the religious upbringing of the convent seems very remote and out-of-touch with reality. However, the student protest movements and the feminist groupings that the era spawned had much more muted and belated reverberations in Austria, whose counterparts played a less urgent role in generating a counter-culture than they did in West Germany. The autonomous women's movement which emerged in Austria in the early 1970s was called AUF (Aktion unabhängiger Frauen, Campaign of Independent Women) and there is still a feminist magazine with this title.

Austria's feminist publishing house, the Wiener Frauenverlag, was also founded in the 1970s. With a population of around eight million and a very much smaller publishing industry, however, it has always been more difficult for alternative presses to establish themselves in Austria.[19] Gudrun Brokoph-Mauch may be right when she says that at a time when East and West German writers (men and women) were openly writing auto-biographically, Austrians such as Barbara Frischmuth and Elfriede Jelinek persisted in a more distanced approach. However, it should be stressed that the subjective, feminist consciousness so prevalent in the *Beziehungsliteratur* (novels about relationships) of West Germany never really established itself in Austrian women's writing. 'Movement literature' (*Bewegungsliteratur*), that is writing which openly thematised the concerns of the women's movements, often using autobiographically inspired characters active in feminist groupings, is notably absent (see chapter 6 above). Verena Stefan's *Häutungen* (1975, *Shedding* 1994), Margot Schroeder's *Der Schlachter empfiehlt immer noch Herz* (1976), even Svende Merian's 1980s blockbuster, *Der Tod des Märchenprinzen* (1980) stand out as curiously 'German'. Brokop-Mauch comments in this regard that 'above all it [the literature of Austrian women] lacks the effusive urgency, the excessive narcissism and self-revelation of a West German [sic] Verena Stefan or Karin Struck' (Brokoph-Mauch 1989: 1,201).[20] One has to search to find lesbian sexuality and politics in texts by Austrian women. Klaus Zeyringer has noted, 'that the starting-point of Ingeborg Bachmann's "Ein Schritt nach Gomorrha" has hardly been developed in the 1980s, at least not significantly' (Zeyringer 1993: 272). Jelinek's lesbian vampires in *Krankheit oder moderne Frauen* (1987) are one 1980s manifestation that he has overlooked, although Carmilla and Emily admittedly represent a more humorous critique of heterosexual relations than Bachmann's, and function more as a political cum philosophical argument, than as erotic beings.[21]

The self-experiential literature (*Selbsterfahrungsliteratur*) of the 1970s did have its equivalent in Austria, however, and Brigitte

Schwaiger's novels are a good example of the move towards subjective, autobiographically based writing, which, in the case of
women writers, centred on everyday experiences and themes. Her
novel, *Wie kommt das Salz ins Meer*, has been described by Sigrid
Weigel in relation to Stefan's *Häutungen*, as 'the counterpart for the
middle-class reading public' (Weigel 1984b: 71). Certainly, it is the
nearest thing that Austria has to Stefan's novel: both texts sold
massively and undoubtedly promoted a great degree of 'consciousness-raising', as thousands of women recognised their own
experiences of heterosexual (sexual) relations (in the case of *Häutungen*), or marriage and social conditioning (as in *Wie kommt das
Salz ins Meer*). Stefan's project was explicitly political and openly
autobiographical – she invites recognition of her attempt to
explore language and relationships, to redefine and in some cases
reclaim language for feminist purposes. In contrast Schwaiger's
critique of bourgeois society and its central means of perpetuating
its own patriarchal values through the institution of marriage, is
undertaken without a programmatic 'call to arms', but with a considerable amount of wit. The narrators' explorations of self in both
Wie kommt das Salz ins Meer and *Lange Abwesenheit* (1980) are motivated partly by the author's own biography, and it seems almost
unintentional, therefore, that Schwaiger should have laid bare
recognisable patterns of behaviour and oppression with which
women could all too readily identify.[22]

Wie kommt das Salz ins Meer is the story of a middle-class woman's loveless marriage to a man with a good, solid job and thoroughly traditional middle-class attitudes. The novel recounts how
the narrator's marriage breaks down and ends in divorce, a conclusion which, while not presenting an up-beat ending to the novel,
does at least show the narrator's germinating desire and ability to
take control of her own life. All her life she has been defined by others, by her father and the values of 'keeping up appearances' which
the family has instilled into her, and by her husband, Rolf, who
takes on the role of determining for his wife how she should behave, what she should wear, talk about and cook.

To today's feminist reader, the first-person narrator may seem
irritatingly manipulable, but Schwaiger grants her an enquiring
mind, and uses the narrator's child-like desire to question basics,
symbolised by the title question – Why Is There Salt in the Sea? –
to provide an apparently innocent but cleverly calculated political
critique. Thus, for instance, Rolf is lulled into a false sense of security as his wife panders to his sense of self-importance by asking a

range of simple, uncontroversial questions about his job, leading up to the crunch question, 'Does VÖEST supply steel for weapons to Africa?' (94).[23] Ultimately, it is not the narrator's apparent naivety but Rolf's blind acceptance of the status quo and lack of plausible justification for accepting things the way they are which is made laughable. After Rolf has criticised the Church for being too politicised, the narrator asks him why, then, did they get married in church, upon which he silences her, saying: 'As an Austrian you are Catholic, and you wear that like a national costume. And that's it now' (1988: 24).

Political enquiry in the national sense, such as in the sale of arms example above, is the exception rather than the rule in Schwaiger's novel. Although her narrative does not break the taboos targeted by Stefan, (there is no detailed discussion of menstruation or sexual intercourse, for example), the political critique, like that of *Häutungen* conforms to the same 1970s insistence that 'the personal is political'. During the course of the novel Schwaiger exposes a range of 'do's and don'ts' constituting the values of middle-class Austrian, Catholic society, but many of the attitudes which stifle the narrator cut across conceptions of class or country and account for the wider appeal of the novel. Arguably, Stefan's preoccupation with the individual's sexual emancipation and quest for a more authentic relationship with nature, appear intrinsically 'bourgeois' when contrasted with Schwaiger's focus on societal forces.[24]

The narrator of *Wie kommt das Salz ins Meer* knows that she has internalised the middle-class values which have trapped her, a sentiment which is well illustrated in her particularly black humorous reason for not committing suicide: 'one doesn't kill oneself' (86). The theme of psychological complicity is taken much further in Schwaiger's *Vaterroman*, *Lange Abwesenheit*. In this address to her dead father, the first-person narrator explores her own relationship with him and reminisces about her childhood and the power which the father wielded over her and the entire family. The novel is one of many autobiographical German-language novels of the late 1970s and early 1980s whose authors delve into the biographies of their fathers and question the latter's roles in, and culpability for, the atrocities perpetrated in the Second World War.[25] Far from being detached from her father's anti-Semitism, the narrator finds herself reproducing her father's prejudices. In an act of revenge and futile self-assertion she takes an older Jewish man as her lover to spite her father, but despises him for being Jewish and finds herself thinking the most hateful, anti-Semitic thoughts. Michael Schneider observes that 'in her hate-filled fixation on her father, Schwaiger never once becomes aware of the extent to which her hatred binds her to him and makes her like him while she actually wants to rid herself of him at any cost' (Schneider 1984: 39). It is the act of writing, however, and indeed the reading of the text which makes possible this awareness for the reader. Arguably, the narrator (Schneider's simple reduction of the narrator to Schwaiger, the *author*, is regrettable) is still caught up in the process of recognition, in the very recounting of her story, a narrative which is largely told in the evocative present tense.

On a human or psychological level, the novel shows the pain of the narrator whose love for her father, a love which shines through despite her hatred of him, is never reciprocated by him. This novel is an example of the specific kind of *Vaterroman* where the relationship between daughter-narrator and father is set in the context of war guilt. There are numerous other texts written by women which take as their central theme a father-daughter relationship. For example, in the German writer Jutta Heinrich's *Das Geschlecht der Gedanken* (1978), the strong father is the parent with whom the daughter finds she can identify; Jutta (now Julian) Schutting's novel *Der Vater* (1980) is an Austrian novel which deals with the difficult process of a daughter's bereavement.[26]

Perhaps more important for feminists have been the explorations of *mother*-daughter relationships which have taken place both in theoretical feminist texts and in novels by women writers, in particular since the mid-1970s. American theorists such as Adrienne Rich and Nancy Chodorow were read widely in Europe and helped to form a new context within which the ideological, psychological and sociological meanings of motherhood could be investigated. In her aptly named book, *The Reproduction of Mothering*, Chodorow set out to analyse the reproduction of mothering as a 'central and constituting element in the social organisation and reproduction of gender' (Chodorow 1978: 7; Rich 1976). Waltraud Anna Mitgutsch's *Die Züchtigung* (1985, *Three Daughters* 1987)[27] is a literary illustration of this idea. It focuses on three generations of mothers and highlights the painful recognition by Vera, the narrator, that she is involuntarily reproducing some of her mother's attitudes and even her means of disciplining in her relationship with her own daughter. The text shifts from third-person accounts of Vera's mother Marie's upbringing and first-person recollections by Vera of her own childhood. However, if Mitgutsch dwells initially on the harsh, loveless treatment of Marie, the ugly, unwanted farmer's daughter, who was treated little better than a slave by her father and his wife, and often beaten for the slightest reason until she could hardly move, then this is 'meant to explain, if not excuse, the unfathomable degree of sadism exercised by Marie in the upbringing of her daughter Vera' (Kecht 1989: 361). As with Schwaiger's novel, here the daughter's relationship with the parent is also highly ambivalent. Highly dependent on her mother as her only source of attention and love, a love which her mother channels into trying to make her daughter into something superior, often by beating any signs of failure or misbehaviour out of her with her carpet beater, Vera complies by becoming the model daughter, interested only in her studies and adopting the required disgust for her own body and contempt for men.

The psychosexual consequences of a confining mother-daughter relationship are underlined more pointedly in Elfriede Jelinek's *Die Klavierspielerin* (1983, *The Piano Teacher* 1988), a novel with which *Die Züchtigung* has been compared. Both novels involve powerful mother figures who are solely responsible for the upbringing of their daughters and who control them almost as if they were a physical extension of themselves. Where Jelinek concentrates on the masochistic and voyeuristic rebellion of the daughter against the (s)mothering to which she has been subjected, Mitgutsch, on the other hand, presents more background to the mother's own psychological make-up.[28] Although she beats her daughter and dominates her every action and thought, the behaviour of the mother in *Die Züchtigung* can also be seen as masochistic. Barbara Kosta has convincingly argued 'in punishing the daughter, the mother is punishing herself. Or, to put it another way, the mother in this mother-daughter constellation, punishes her own sex instead of the sex which has caused her discontent' (Kosta 1993: 244).

Mitgutsch's novel is a powerful and disturbing contribution to the feminist exploration of mother-daughter relations. Written in a tone of honest realism, the picture of hatred, love, jealousy, and physical abuse which emerges breaks abruptly with romantic notions of tender, motherly love and invites the reader to reflect on the potential of the maternal role as 'effective patriarchal surrogate and oppressor' (Kecht 1989: 358). To speak out loud about her mother in such terms, however, is to break a taboo and the narrator is fully aware of this:

> Do you know, I boomed into the gathering of relatives, that my
> mother beat me – until she drew blood? Oh, be quiet, your mother
> was a highly respectable woman who just wanted the best for you
> . . . you can't go saying things like that. Leave the dead in peace.
> And even if she did, you probably deserved it. . . I keep my mouth
> shut and stop trying to understand. (Mitgutsch 1985: 33)

Despite the legal-sounding caveat prefacing the book, critics have
seen the novel as autobiographical and have, indeed, sought 'similarities with living persons'. Mitgutsch tried to set the record
straight in an interview for *Cosmopolitan*. The interviewer reports
that, 'the book is not a book of self-discovery or personal reappraisal. It's not autobiographical either. . . It should be seen as a
study of violence, Mitgutsch says ...' (*Cosmopolitan* 1987: 236).
What is interesting is not whether or not the book is autobiographically inspired, but how the author intended her account to
be read. It is perhaps a hangover from the 1970s that novels by
women writers written in the 1980s are still measured by a voyeuristic literary press for their experiential authenticity, even if the
writer points her critic to the social or political factors she is analysing.[29] It remains to be seen whether the prose of the 1990s will
take a turn towards abstraction and move away from accounts of
personal and gender oppression.[30]

Women on Stage in the 1990s

In recent years Austria has produced a number of excellent plays
by women writers. The dramatic form lends itself less to subjective introspection and autobiographical account. It is partly due to
this, therefore, that the Austrian plays of the 1990s, to which I now
turn, are deliberately distanced from the writer's own lives, even
in the first-person monologue form chosen by Elisabeth Reichart.

The two writers I have chosen to conclude my discussion of
Austrian women's writing and to represent Austrian women's
'theatre of the 1990s' are Marlene Streeruwitz and Elisabeth Reichart. Despite her age, it was Marlene Streeruwitz (b. 1953) who, in
1992, was chosen by *Theater heute* as the best 'young dramatist
writing in German'.[31] Although critics often speak of Streeruwitz
in the same breath as Jelinek as one of the 'frequently cited and
often staged' dramatists (Wille 1993: 30), or comment that 'at present, she counts, along with Elfriede Jelinek, among the most successful Austrian women dramatists' (*Neues Volksblatt* 1993: 9),

German studies have yet to accord her any attention at all.[32] Like Elfriede Jelinek, whose dramatic work was fostered by the German stage long before it was accepted in her native Austria, Streeruwitz's plays have also been premiered in Germany – in Munich, Cologne and Berlin. The year 1994 saw both a production of her play *New York. New York.* at the Viennese Volkstheater and the premiere of her play *Tolmezzo* in the Schauspielhaus in Vienna.

If Streeruwitz writes exclusively for the stage, it can also be said that she writes *against* it. In interviews she has talked about her scepticism towards the theatre, which is primarily 'because of the unbroken trend towards sentimentalising the medium. There's a lot of dreadful stuff to be seen. It's rare that somebody approaches theatre as a forum for art' (Streeruwitz in Merschmeier 1993: 34). It is classical theatre, then, which takes the brunt of Streeruwitz's invective, in the main for its attempts at psychological realism and for being worlds apart from the realities of modern life. In this regard Shakespeare serves Streeruwitz as a good example, and in an appropriately irreverently titled interview with Stephan Dedalus, 'Shakespeare is a Real Bore', she wonders what on earth Shakespeare is doing on the contemporary stage when he is 'totally remote from the reality of our alienated world'. Pondering the role of Juliet, for example, she concludes: 'What has such a contrived female role still got in common with women today? ... Nothing!' (Streeruwitz in Dedalus 1993). Streeruwitz's choice of role here reflects the feminism which informs her work and also, in part at least, her aesthetic principles, too. Although her subjects are not what one might call expressly feminist, it is clear that a feminist consciousness is at work, for example, in the depiction of brutality against a prostitute by her pimp, in the play *New York. New York.* She describes the theatre she is reacting against as phallic in its preoccupation with the decisions and actions of an individual (usually male) central character. Moral dilemma and slow psychological development, then, have no place in Streeruwitz's altogether more fragmented plots and staccato style. Streeruwitz explains:

> Classical theatre ... is always about moments of decision. It always centres on the moment when the hero, or heroine as well today, decides. It always involves this phallic principle of assertion in patriarchy, the moment of decision ... Female contexts are different. They're about duration, about eternity, about fluidity, about the forever – forever preparing a meal to keep everyone fed, or forever making beds. This is what they're about, and men's lives, of course, also concern these things. Only, these are contexts which literature

... has denied because it's always been about political man and the moment of decision. (Streeruwitz in Fischer 1992: 34)

In Austria it is Vienna's Burgtheater which stands as the guardian of 'high' tradition, an institution which has been damningly criticised by Jelinek as having swept its own Nazi involvement and that of its actors under the political carpet.[33] Streeruwitz's hilarious suggestion of appointing Arnold Schwarzenegger as its next director and turning the theatre into a sauna, gym and cinema will not earn her the malicious criticism which Jelinek's rather more political criticism generated, but it is not just to be dismissed as a 'joke'. One senses that putting the Burgtheater to such use would be more acceptable for Streeruwitz than allowing it to continue with the sort of plays it currently offers![34]

The action of Streeruwitz's plays is crisp, fragmented and often without motivation, generally extending over twenty to thirty short scenes. The scenarios border on the absurd, while the locations are nothing other than totally everyday. *New York. New York.*, for example, is set not as one might expect in an exciting and expansive Manhattan, but in a gentlemen's toilet underneath the Viennese Stadtbahn station, Burggasse. The toilet attendant (*Klofrau*), Frau Horvath, is largely oblivious to the violence and sexual abuse which goes on under her nose and is preoccupied with keeping her toilets clean. Characters change identity and age, in one case metamorphosing from eighteen to sixty-year-olds. Groups of Japanese tourists are herded in to see this lavatorial leftover from the former Austrian Empire and to photograph the toilet where Kaiser Franz Joseph once urinated. Professor Chrobath – something of a ubiquitous character in Streeruwitz's work – finally succeeds in karate-chopping the toilet bowl, and thereby doing his bit for what he sees as the inexorable destruction of Western civilisation, however, not before he has had his eyes poked out by Frau Horvath's knitting needles.

Classical, popular, literary and filmic quotations and references abound in Streeruwitz's plays. Francis Ford Coppola's *The Godfather* provides *New York. New York.* with the dead horse of its final scene. Characters in the play, even the one designated as the deaf-mute, break into Shakespeare, Rilke, or Raymond Chandler.[35] In *Elysian Park* the nurses quote perfume adverts and *Tolmezzo* (1994) even has Spiderman and four Barbie dolls as some of its 'characters'. As one critic notes, the effect which is produced is that of chaotic simultaneity,[36] a fitting state for the postmodern consciousness, and one that is produced by Streeruwitz's own postmodern eclecticism. In *Tolmezzo*, Streeruwitz even, as it were, quotes herself, her opinions of the Burgtheater and of the Austrian culture industry are voiced by Krobath (here with a 'K'): 'The Burgtheater is the biggest rural folk theatre [*Bauerntheater*] in the world ... The German stage was once an instrument of the Enlightenment ... A place of genius. Today flabby sentimentality prevails' (1994: 54).

Despite the exotic, faraway titles of her plays, *New York. New York.* and *Tolmezzo* are both set in Vienna, the action of the latter taking place in and around a café which is described as resembling the famous literary café, the Café Central. Yet this does not make of Streeruwitz a provincial writer. As Sigfried Kienzle observes, Vienna is not so much a location as a state, it is an 'extremely precise localisation, an everywhere-and-nowhere location for the monstrous' (Kienzle 1992: 15). The reason Streeruwitz gives for choosing Vienna as the setting for *Tolmezzo*, which presents reminiscences of the First World War, is that it is 'more suitable as a location for describing the world than any other place in Germany: an Imperial capital which was put in a jamjar in 1917; on with the lid and that was that!' (Streeruwitz in Merschmaier 1993: 34). Vienna, then, has a quintessential quality: 'Vienna is everywhere' (Streeruwitz in Thieringer 1993: 12). Streeruwitz's theatre is an angry, cynical theatre, one which is highly critical of society, and which presents it in its worst light. As Jutta Baier remarks, it is 'Disgusting? Sometimes. But never more disgusting than reality, and a lot funnier' (Baier 1994). If Streeruwitz can be said to present a political picture on her stage, it is in her attempt to question and to make the audience think about her tableaux of 'everyday life' via formal experiment and above all via humour. For Streeruwitz, as for other Austrian women writers, such as Jelinek and Reichart, laughter is not the best cure, but the best provocation: 'How else can I set anything at all in motion these days, if not indirectly, via humour?' (Streeruwitz in Dedalus 1993).

Elisabeth Reichart's text *Sakkorausch* (1994) bears the description, 'a monologue', and is thus a thoroughly different kind of stage play to Streeruwitz's *New York. New York.*[37] The monologue form, however, is nothing new to the Austrian stage and Reichart is in good company here, with writers such as Elfriede Jelinek (*Wolken. Heim* 1990), Thomas Bernhard (*Der Weltverbesserer* 1988) and even Carl Merz and Helmut Qualtinger (*Der Herr Karl* 1982).

Reichart's earlier work takes as one of its central themes, the fascist legacy in post-war and contemporary Austria (see Schanda

1992). Her novels *Februarschatten* (1984) and *Komm über den See* (1988b) deal with Austria's failure to come to terms with its fascist past. *Februarschatten*, for example, builds on the author's own experience of asking around locally in her home town in Upper Austria for information regarding the persecution and execution of Russian officers who escaped from an Austrian concentration camp in February 1945. Given the involvement of local people in what apparently became a bloodthirsty chase, Reichart's questions often met with silence. In *Komm über den See* (1988b), Reichart thematises the resistance work of women in the Salzkammergut area of Austria, and presents an aspect of the National Socialist period which has been underplayed in literature, perhaps for political reasons. It is a side which is commemorated, too, in the documentary prose work *Der weibliche Name des Widerstands. Sieben Berichte* (1980) by Marie-Thérèse Kerschbaumer.

The title story of her collection of short stories, *La Valse* (1992), concerns a father-daughter relationship and the father's sexual abuse of his daughter. Schwaiger's protagonist's address to her dead father in *Lange Abwesenheit* is called to mind here, though Reichart's attempt to explore her dying father's past is, this time, not concerned with his National Socialist ideas and involvement. Jürgen Koppensteiner points out that the collection deals with some very Austrian themes, 'which are of concern in today's Austria: the influence of party politics in Austria's schools, teacher unemployment, nepotism, the oppression of women'. But such Austrian specificities belie a more general relevance and applicability which is also true of Reichart's play *Sakkorausch*. As in many of the works dealt with in this chapter, 'Vienna, or Austria, becomes a paradigm for ordinary, everyday fascism, a fascism you can encounter elsewhere too' (Koppensteiner 1992: 54). I have chosen to conclude my treatment of post-war Austrian women's writing with this recent play by Reichart because it illuminates in a very interesting way the theme of *Frauenunterdrückung* and characterises it as a form of everyday fascism, or in Reichart's terms, a kind of 'war'. These ideas have a long tradition in Austrian women's writing, whether in the work and ideas of Ingeborg Bachmann, for whom war was an eternal war between the sexes or in Elfriede Jelinek's 'materialist analysis of relationships in the form of a novel (*Lust*)' (Moser 1992).[38] In a sense, then, with *Sakkorausch* we have come full circle from Ilse Aichinger's *Die größere Hoffnung*, only in Reichart war serves mainly as a philosophical starting-point and only tangentially as a realist literary setting.

The guiding principle of Reichart's writing has been aptly described as a writing against the denial of history (Roscher 1987: 129). In *Sakkorausch* this principle is applied to the life of Helene von Druskowitz (1856–1918), the first Austrian woman to be awarded a doctorate – albeit at a Swiss university – since in 1872, when she received her higher degree, women were not even allowed to attend Austrian universities. Feminist historians and writers have done a great deal of important work since the 1960s reclaiming history for women. On the one hand this has taken the form of considering women's contributions, be they those of average and unnamed women or those of particular women whose achievements have long been ignored or categorised as unimportant by mainstream, patriarchal (literary) history. On the other hand, it has involved researching the effects of social, political, and philosophical developments on women's lives.[39] *Sakkorausch* is both a witty and linguistically inspired play and a clever and thoughtful example of how women can reclaim and adjust historiography.

At the age of thirty-five von Druskowitz was admitted to a mental asylum where she lived until her death twenty-seven years later. She was able to continue with her philosophical writings and kept in contact with her publishers, but her repeated pleas to be released were continually denied. Druskowitz also received little support from the likes of Marie von Ebner-Eschenbach with whom she corresponded. Reichart's text is peppered with quotations from Druskowitz's 'manifesto', *Der Mann als logische und sittliche Unmöglichkeit und als Fluch der Welt. Pessimistische Kardinalsätze* (1988).[40] This title was in its day possibly as hilarious and provocative as Valerie Solonas's organisation and ideas under the pithy acronym, SCUM (Society for Cutting Up Men) founded in 1968. According to Reichart, von Druskowitz was simply too radical for her day, and too much of a non-conformist. 'Her inheritance was soon used up, but she wanted neither to marry, nor did she want to work as a governess or a teacher, as Eschenbach and her circle of friends advised. Nobody helped her get out of the lunatic asylum, because even her friends thought she was mad' (Reichart in Kathrein 1994: 25). Members of this circle included Nietzsche and Conrad Ferdinand Meyer, of whom the character von Druskowitz comments: 'These clever men, who couldn't tolerate a clever woman in their midst' (Reichart 1994: 60).

Druskowitz's non-conformism or 'resistance', since she was indeed resisting prevailing norms, is expressed very bitingly in her attack on war, which, according to her, is a thoroughly masculine activity. War, to Reichart's Druskowitz, includes both the waging of war – the monologue is situated in the period of escalation towards the First World War – and the permanent state of living under patriarchy. The war which men wage on women, then, is the most atrocious crime which the male sex has committed. It is also one which never ends: 'All the other shameful deeds committed by the male species were of a temporary nature, from the perspective of history they were short-lived. Only the enslavement, rape and mass murder of women have accompanied his rule from the very beginning and we shall not see an end to these so long as men are in power!' One small positive outcome of physical war, Druskowitz notes to herself dryly and flippantly, is that women will be forced to live on their own for a while and will be made aware of their own capabilities (37). A sense of fun and an irreverent wit were doubtless a crucial source of support to the real Druskowitz, as indeed to the fictional character in Reichart's play who chuckles over a potential future treatise: 'Perhaps I'll write a piece one day comparing the thoughts of thick and thin philosophers: The Effects of Corpulence on the Contemplation of Ethical Problems' (9). Humour is the quality which allowed Druskowitz to live in the asylum *without* going mad; it is also a key factor in Reichart's personal philosophy: 'Living without humour is simply asking too much' (Reichart 1991: 136).

The playfulness of *Sakkorausch* is most apparent in Reichart's language games. She uses word association, rhyming words previously without association, and puts them together to form patterns. Evoking how, as a little girl, she was schooled to say 'thank you', the monologue breaks out into an apparent nonsense regression:

> Say thank you. Say please. Thanks, please, please, thanks, ta ta, please, peep peep, dope, nope, dadda, adda, tata, see ya tomorrow, parting is such sweet sorrow. (56)

Ridiculing the spoils of war, she plays with rhymes and near rhymes. [41] The play's title is playful, too, but unlike in *New York. New York.*, the reader does find clues in this text to help solve the puzzle of the title's meaning. 'Sakkorausch', 'Sakkrosankt', 'Herr D', and 'Foreign' were just some of the pseudonyms which the real Helene von Druskowitz used. A possible reason for this is offered by one of Druskowitz's characters in a play entitled *Unerwartet*, where she explains her use of false *noms de plume* to her niece as follows: 'Do you imagine that it is deemed permissible for someone suddenly to show himself from a side for which he is previously unknown?'

(quoted in 'Frauentafel', Reichart 1994: 70). Reichart's 'mad woman', then, is not suffering from some kind of multiple personality problem, a sort of extended schizophrenia, rather, she feels forced into adopting these names in order to avoid the trap of preconceptions attached to the notion of the single, unified, bourgeois subject.

Reichart's character is certainly not afraid to say 'I' and, if anything, knows herself to be superior, not inferior to men. She describes herself as 'I, the queen of world wisdom, who am superior in intellect to almost all men' (28). However, like many nineteenth-century women writers, she clearly found it easier to publish under an assumed male name. This statement of self-confidence is made in a section where Druskowitz laments the alcohol ban under which she is forced to live and write. She demands access to this substance which will produce in her the same intoxication which many famous male authors have exploited for their writing.

For her monologue Reichart borrows an extensive list of names compiled by 'a certain male-fixated Gottfried Benn' ranging from men who have taken drugs such as opium and hash to those who have drunk absinthe and alcohol (Benn 1968). The word 'Sakkoträger' (literally 'jacket wearers', but more idiomatically understandable to British women perhaps as 'the grey suits') denotes men generally, and more specifically the men who would be able to authorise her dismissal from the home. Druskowitz's neologism is there for the reader to decode. For me, the title symbolises the sense of phallic self-importance and readiness for war which the Austrian philosopher was criticising. It is also an ironic allusion to Druskowitz's own as it were 'masculine' pretensions, daring as she did to question her 'natural' role as wife and trespassing in the male world of letters. If Reichart's character presents her readers with ideas which are fiery and rousing, it is nevertheless quite clear that Druskowitz is also warning women against becoming 'pseudo men'.

Whereas in Aichinger's novel, *Die größere Hoffnung*, the pervading emotion is one of hope almost against all odds, Reichart's play seems at first glance to be set on a negative and pessimistic message. It is sobering to hear the character's warnings at the beginning of this century about the sham of female emancipation. Her evaluation takes on a prophetic air when she remarks of the male sex, that: 'he will set out a little bait for woman, and persuade her that these crumbs are half his power' (38). Reichart's use of historical material produces a timely reminder for today's reader in what is being heralded as a 'post-feminist' age, namely that the struggle for true equality between the sexes is not yet a reality. Moreover, the female reader is not allowed to wallow in self-satisfaction at her own innocence. Like the vocabulary book and its personified language in Aichinger's novel, women may become enthralled by a foreign power. It is in this sense that *Sakkorausch* may be read as a positive 'call to arms' and where it shows an affinity with the first Austrian novel in this chapter. Both texts are about integrity: Aichinger's character Ellen refuses to give in to the feeling of gloom and the destruction wrought by the war. It is more important to her not to capitulate to the ideas and warmongering of Nazism than it is to stay physically alive. Druskowitz's resistance is also one against the warriors, only her war is definitely a gender war. She does not want to capitulate to their ideas either, even if holding on to her own sanity means being labelled 'mad' by the outside world.

Notes

I would like to thank the University of Nottingham for a grant enabling me to undertake research in Vienna for my contributions to the present volume. Except for translations from published English editions listed in the bibliography, all translations from German texts cited in this chapter and in chapter 15 are by Allyson Fiddler.

1. Many critics of Austrian literature have shown how this state of mind is also reflected in Austrian culture. Greiner, for example, described Austria as experiencing world events as 'distant tremors', but Austria's entry into the European Union in 1995 may bring about decisive change. See Greiner 1979.
2. This is an assertion which is difficult to substantiate and one which is hotly denied in Austria. Nevertheless, examples such as Austrian politicians' reluctance to introduce the *Fristenlösung* abortion law in the late 1970s demonstrate their fear of upsetting the church. This point is mentioned in Konar's interesting *Diplomarbeit* 1988. The arguments about the role of conciliation and the strength of the Catholic Church made here are also confirmed in Benard and Schlaffer 1991.
3. See the very useful outline of the Austrian feminist movement and women's position in Austrian society in Vansant 1988 (chapters 1 and 2). This is Vansant's translation of *Gleichbehandlungsgebot*, see her explanation (27). Unless indicated, all other translations are my own.
4. Wisinger (1992: 197) may well be right when she argues that the media presence which this official, state-run bureau for women's affairs commands, itself stifles autonomous projects.
5. See Biffl 1994: 131.

6. While I was writing this chapter there was extensive media coverage of the *faux pas* committed by Chancellor Vranitzky's wife when she suggested that women with young children should not abandon them and go out to work. Her opinions acted as a kind of catalyst for heated debate and dealt a rather embarrassing blow to the Socialist Party. However, in all the press coverage, the issue of money was paramount, and the debate centred around the need or otherwise for women to earn a wage. The *right* of a woman to work and her needs for self-fulfilment were absent from the debate. Such a claim, it would seem, constitutes the real taboo.

7. Jelinek and Bachmann are perhaps the most important and certainly the best-known Austrian women writers. For these reasons separate chapters of the present volume have been devoted to each of them.

8. Aichinger (1952: 1) published a piece entitled 'Über das Erzählen in dieser Zeit' in which she denounced the *Kahlschlag* in any case as a 'Legende'.

9. Langer 1975 refers to a translation of *Die größere Hoffnung* as *Herod's Children*, which was unfortunately unavailable. See Aichinger 1963.

10. For a recent attempt to rectify this, see Lorenz 1993.

11. There are references to the Stadtbahn (now renamed as an underground line, 'U6'), the Stadtpark, to a canal and a fairground (probably Vienna's famous Prater funfair).

12. Schmid-Bortenschlager (1991) points out that Aichinger was using female protagonists at a time when Ingeborg Bachmann, for example, was still using male protagonists as a matter of course.

13. See Aichinger's, 'Meine Sprache und ich' (in Aichinger 1978), or Aichinger in Zimmermann 1990, where she again personifies language, and explains: 'Language, no, it's not really a friend. Sometimes I could really …'.

14. In addition to the common theme of childhood innocence, it may be of interest to note that Haushofer's lucky colour is also blue and that the hopeful image (a star), 'Stella', is here destroyed. See Venske 1991a.

15. Venske's chapter, 1991b, is an attempt to determine why these authors could never have been German. She makes an analogy here with Bachmann's opinion that writers such as Grillparzer, Hofmannsthal, Rilke and Musil could also never have been German.

16. 'The role of children's literature is rather controversial. Children's literature is a really tricky area. The ideal case for me is a book for parents and children' (Frischmuth in Ester 1982: 8).

17. In order to discourage vanity and individuality, there are not many mirrors in the convent. For a discussion of the importance of the mirror motif in Frischmuth's text and its meaning in psychoanalytic theory, see Gürtler 1983: 130, 178ff.

18. Daviau (1980: 177) traces the Austrian lineage from Wittgenstein and Kraus to experimental authors of the 1960s, such as Frischmuth and Handke.

19. Herminghouse (1987: xii) comments that changes in literary life 'are less feasible in the state-controlled publishing system of East Germany or in Switzerland and Austria, with their smaller populations and more traditional outlooks, which tend to resist feminist impulses'.

20. Verena Stefan was born and grew up in Switzerland. Arguably, therefore, we should see her as a Swiss woman writer.

21. Zeyringer cites the one lesbian story in Treudl 1988. The Wiener Frauenverlag has also published collections of lesbian texts. My thanks to Margaret Littler

for pointing out that as early as 1955, Marlen Haushofer had thematised lesbian love (see Haushofer 1955).

22. Brokop-Mauch (1989: 1225) describes Schwaiger rather aptly as 'the witty, unintentional feminist', arguing that her wit was a major selling factor.

23. The acronym stands for 'Vereinigte Österreichische Edelstahlwerke', the nationalised steel industry.

24. Though it may have been written, therefore, for 'the middle-class reading public', as Weigel suggests, Schwaiger's novel, paradoxically, seems the less bourgeois novel.

25. For a discussion of possible reasons for the timing of this wave of texts dealing with father-child relationships, see Schneider 1984. For an interpretation which does pick up on the feminine perspective in Schwaiger's text, see Eigler 1992.

26. For an account of some of the similarities between Schutting's and Schwaiger's novels, see Bagley 1990/1991.

27. The published translation of Mitgutsch's novel (1987) was unavailable, translations below are thus my own.

28. Kecht looks at the Kohuts' relationship in terms of this (s)mothering.

29. See chapter 15, 'Reading Elfriede Jelinek' in the present volume which documents Elfriede Jelinek's comments to this effect.

30. Lilian Faschinger's first-person narration in *Lustspiel* (1989) is a playful inner monologue which crosses the boundary of fiction and deals with the uneasy contradictions of erotic love (she has a married lover) and intellectual activity (writing is a kind of erotic act for her). The associative style and intellectual treatment of the issues is certainly much removed from plots such as Schwaiger's or Mitgutsch's which attempt to show linear developments and present reasons for gendered behaviour.

31. See Dedalus 1993.

32. This article can be found in the newspaper cuttings on Streeruwitz held at the Dokumentationsstelle für neuere österreichische Literatur in Vienna. I am grateful to Seán Allan for initially drawing my attention to Streeruwitz's work.

33. See Jelinek's play *Burgtheater* 1984a, and Fiddler 1993 for an analysis of the play in this context.

34. See Streeruwitz 1992.

35. See Schmitz-Burckhardt 1993.

36. See Kienzle 1992: 15.

37. *Sakkorausch* was premiered on 26 May 1994 as part of the annual festival, the *Wiener Festwochen*. Reichart is much better known as a prose writer.

38. Moser cites Czurda 1991 as a further example of this 'current trend in contemporary [Austrian] literature'.

39. See Gerstl's volume of essays (1985) by women writers about women writers. Reichart has also edited a volume of essays on Austrian women writers by women living or working in Austria (1993).

40. *Der Mann als logische und sittliche Unmöglichkeit und als Fluch der Welt. Pessimistische Kardinalsätze* was printed in 1905 according to Reichart (*Sakkorausch*, 75). For details of the recent edition, see von Druskowitz 1988. The above title is that of the sixth of her sections, and the volume entitled *Pessimistische Kardinalsätze: Ein Vademekum für die freiesten Geister* can be read in the Austrian National Library.

41. Reichart's linguistic experimentation puts her too in the Austrian tradition of language skepticism cited by Daviau earlier in this chapter (1980: 177).

Chapter Fourteen

 READING INGEBORG BACHMANN

Elizabeth Boa

During her lifetime, the Austrian writer Ingeborg Bachmann (1926–1973) was seen primarily as a poet in a modernist canon of the 1950s, when writers were responding to the foreign and exile literature which had been banned during the Third Reich.[1] Her position as primarily a novelist in a canon of women's writing came only posthumously. Even before the publication in 1953 of her first collection of poems, *Die gestundete Zeit*, Bachmann had been invited by the *Gruppe 47* to read from her work.[2] She was awarded the group's annual prize in 1953 and was catapulted to wider fame by the title story in the weekly news magazine *Der Spiegel* of 18 August 1954, an event which in itself launched Bachmann as a phenomenon, for never before had a news magazine made lyric poetry its lead story. *Der Spiegel* compared Bachmann's poetry to Goethe's *Roman Elegies*, other critics compared her with the modernist poets Rilke, Trakl and Hofmannsthal and with the two dominant figures in the post-war scene, Benn and Brecht. Following the publication in 1956 of a second volume of poetry, *Die Anrufung des großen Bären*, Bachmann's canonical status was established.[3] In retrospect the narrator of Bachmann's novel *Malina* (1971a, *Malina* 1989) and her male double, the eponymous Malina, echo the contrasting features of this new poetic star: sensuous lyricism yet intellectual abstraction, romantic pathos yet classical form, elegiac lament but also cerebral disharmony. The *frisson* offered by the work was heightened by the iconic appeal of the author, a young woman 'shy, very reserved, with very red lips and very charming', who yet was a *poeta docta* who had written a dissertation on Heidegger (cited in Hotz 1990: 39).

Opinion was divided, however, over *Das dreißigste Jahr* (1961, *The Thirtieth Year* 1987), a volume of short stories which enjoyed some acclaim but which some critics saw as *Kitsch*: was the *poeta docta* becoming not merely prosaic but purveying trivial women's writing? Then in 1971 *Malina* was published to competing choruses of vituperation: 'It is of course understandable that an unhappy woman might occasionally feel constrained to pass off her female minus as a literary plus, but what remains incomprehensible is that she should go as far as to dramatise her unhappiness in order to enjoy it to the full' (Korff, quoted in Tölpelmann 1987: 629), and of puzzled praise: 'Astonishing too is the distance dividing this fairy-tale, so brave in the face of death, from the political, from historical transformation or from the sociological … Poetic in gathering human possibilities, arrogant in fending off anything topical' (Kaiser, quoted in Hotz 1990: 144– 145). *Simultan* (1972), the collection of short stories published the following year, was greeted with relief for its comedy, though for many critics the seeming banality and light-weight tone did not become the high priestess of modernism. It was as if the Countess in *The Marriage of Figaro* had turned into the Countess in *Die Fledermaus* (Reich-Ranicki, quoted in Hotz 1990: 227–231). It now seems surprising that *Malina* and *Simultan* were perceived as unpolitical, given their publication date in the early 1970s just as so-called second-wave feminism was gathering pace. However, this was the first activist phase centring on the abortion issue. It was only after Bachmann's death, following the advent of more experimental women's writing and the rise of feminist criticism in the late 1970s that *Malina* acquired its foundational status and Bachmann turned from being a canonical modernist poet into a canonical woman novelist.

Following her death, and fuelled by the publication in 1978 of a collected edition, Bachmann criticism has been dominated, so Sara Lennox (1993) suggests, by feminist readings.[4] Lennox detects, however, two shifts: firstly from preoccupation with *Malina* to growing interest also in the other fragments of the planned *Todesarten* trilogy, and from a feminist highpoint in the mid-1980s to new interests in some later work. Lennox does not, however, propose post-feminist reading. What is required is to undo the split between the modernist poet and the feminist novelist, and rather than 'post-feminism', a shift from the singular to 'feminisms' does more justice to the current plurality of feminist theories. In the following a section on Bachmann's poems will relate modernism as a frame of reading to gender and will query their supposed ahistorical vision.[5] After a look at the short stories in a context of gender ideology stretching back to the early twentieth century, I shall discuss *Malina* as expressing less the dilemmas of all women under universal patriarchy than of an intellectual woman in twentieth-century Austria. I shall then look at *Der Fall Franza* (1979) another of the *Todesarten* texts, in the context of the supposed universal psycho-cultural structuring of subjectivity through a process of negation of an objectified Other.

Bachmann's Poetry: History or Myth?

In the early 1970s, at a time of political polarisation, *Malina* was attacked for its supposed ahistorical, elitist remoteness, whereas her poetry had been praised in the 1950s for much the same qualities: mythical power, autotelic self-containment, darkly hermetic lyricism. That earlier perception, which fed into the perversely apolitical readings of *Malina*, was in keeping with tendencies of the 1950s when a popularised existentialism served to distance an all too specific German past by collapsing history into a vision of an absurd universe. In academic criticism the *werkimmanent* approach elevated the literary text to the status of a verbal icon, its truth contained in a closed circle of self-referentiality, so setting pure poetry against the irremediably corrupted language of politics. In the mid-1950s, as the Cold War was intensifying, self-referentiality could seem to seal poetry off from suspect political ideology, whether of the National Socialist or Communist variety.[6]

At the opposite extreme from the verbal icon is the intertextual view of the text as having no hard and fast boundaries between the contexts of its writing and of its reading.[7] There are limits to textual meaning, of course, but just as the viewer's perception of contours of a landscape changes in different light, so changing the angle of vision will set different generic frames and highlight different elements and allusions in the dense literary text. Given Bachmann's recourse to natural imagery – often a classically infused, Mediterranean landscape – and the often hermetic symbolism, it is understandable that her poetry was read as 'the expression of a mythically timeless yet at the same time difficult and modern sensibility' (Fritsch, quoted in Hotz 1990: 386).[8] Bachmann's poetry does surely evoke apocalyptic and utopian visions couched in mythic terms; the title *Die Anrufung des großen Bären*, for example, evokes a lone human figure confronting the timeless constellation. But mythic and apocalyptic motifs are constantly embedded within images conveying temporal change, so that utopia appears as a direction of aspiration rather than an end-state and apocalypse as a threat not a necessity. Hans Höller (1987) makes this point in a reading of 'Ausfahrt', the opening poem in *Die gestundete Zeit*, with its image of the tree which has lost a branch but 'defiantly raises an arm' (I: 29). It is the wind which has broken off the branch, but the tree's unbalanced shape destabilises the conventional opposition between harmonious, organic nature and mutilating, historical violence: the 'natural' force of the wind becomes a metaphor for 'unnatural' historical change. The title 'Herbstmanöver' (I: 36) also destabilises two different discourses by grafting together the traditional lyric motif of autumn with contemporary reference to military manoeuvres.[9] The grafting produces (at least) five elements: military manoeuvres; autumn; autumn manoeuvres as a specific event; autumn manoeuvres as perennial human activity as inevitable as the seasons; and autumn/manoeuvres as a clashing discord between the natural and the historical, pointing perhaps beyond the seasonal cycle to an apocalyptic final winter. The middle verse may illuminate the point:

> In the newspapers I read a lot about the cold/ and its effects, about fools and dead men,/ about refugees, murderers and myriads/ of ice floes, but little of comfort to me./ Why should I? When the beggar comes at midday/ I shut the door, for it is peace time/ and one can spare oneself that sight, but not/ the joyless dying of the leaves in the rain. (I: 36)

Newspaper stories – political refugees following the Second World War; the *faits divers* of human evil which could as well appear in the newspaper or in the Bible (murder, turning the beggar from the door) – mix with natural phenomena – the ice-floes heralding the end of winter or an new ice-age. Such a mix – undoing simple oppositions between politics and morality or history and nature – opens up the last bitter image of the joyless dying of leaves, which unlike the human beggar cannot be ignored, to different possible readings, just as the mention of the beggar and his rejection in itself subverts the asocial, elegiac nature poetry by showing the inhumanity about which such poetry would be silent.

In effect the utopian and apocalyptic become perspectivistic, so that the lyric subject appears as a site of struggle between hope, despair and everyday awareness, an effect produced also by the frequent splitting between 'I' and an addressee 'you', who may be a partner in a discursive interchange or an aspect of the self. Thus reflection on ways of seeing, thinking and feeling proceeds at once as dialogue with another and as self-construction, so that the lyric subject appears not as static, but as a fluid process working through tensions and contradictions originating outside the self in the world of military manoeuvres and beggars. Self-referentiality thus need not seal off poetry from the social world but can open it up. As a (failed) fictional autobiography, *Malina*, too, conveys a process of writing the self and grafts together utopian, apocalyptic, and historical motifs. It begins with the kind of reflection on time which 'Herbstmanöver' conveys in miniature. The unnamed narrator, (hereafter *Ich*), who has great difficulty with the word 'today', first saw Malina her male *alter ego*, when he was standing at a bus stop reading a newspaper, like the newspaper in 'Herbstmanöver'. 'Today' in a newspaper means either a particular date or an epoch, 'nowadays'. Malina's 'today' is the 'Age of Technology', however, with the means of destruction which could bring an apocalyptic end of time. In *Ich*'s letters to her lover, by contrast, 'today' means the ever-present, urgent longing for union outside of time. Thus the empirical newspaper-today is torn apart in *Ich*'s imagination by the tug-of-war between the utopian dream of union with the other (Ivan) and the apocalyptic nightmare of being rent by the other (Malina or the monster Father).[10] In this psychic drama, the subject is feminine and the – half-internalised desired or feared – others masculine. And this subject, in whom *Ich* and Malina co-exist in uneasy truce, dreams and dreads and reads the newspapers.

Looking backwards through *Malina* highlights the gendering of figures in the poems. Thus in the poetological meditation 'Dunkles zu sagen' (I: 32) the subject is identified with the archetypal male poet, Orpheus, and the beloved other is Eurydice: 'The string of silence drawn taut across the wave of blood/ I grasped your sounding heart'.

Traditionally, the thought of the Muse (herself inactive and often asleep or even dead) prompts the emotion in the poet's heart which he then transmutes into poetry.[11] But here the emotion, which the poet *subsequently* forms into poetry, sounds *first* in the Muse's heart. Such a division of poetic labour suggests a regendering of Nietzsche's Dionysos/Apollo dualism as a feminine expressive core and a masculine formal impulse.[12] The poem laments the division – 'And I do not belong to you/ Now we both lament' – but reaches a paradoxical resolution in that Eurydice's closed eye is yet blue (like a sky?) within the lyric subject. The difference is that in *Malina* a Eurydice also claims the Orphic position of the writing subject. But the novel ends on a less reconcilatory note than the poem, for *Ich* – Eurydice-as-subject – is finally murdered and her Orpheus is the prime suspect. 'Dunkles zu sagen' deploys ancient figures of masculine activity, intellect and creativity set over against feminine suffering. In 'Die gestundete Zeit' an alienated masculine subject of history is divided into an ungendered speaker and a male 'you' addressee, who is called upon to observe a third figure, 'the Beloved in the Sand'. Sand blurs and absorbs the woman's human features and silences her voice. Such an image anticipates the desert setting in *Der Fall Franza* and the silencing of *Ich* in *Malina*. In the poem, an ungendered voice survives and peremptorily addresses a masculine 'you', who can be read as an element of the lyric subject in inner debate with itself. In the novel, Malina survives as a fragment of an otherwise dead subject and an ungendered voice utters the peremptory closing accusation of murder.

Reflections on Gender in *Das dreißigste Jahr* and *Simultan*

The above comparisons suggest that gender in Bachmann's work has always been problematic and always linked with historical issues, but they also indicate a more overt questioning of patriarchal categories in the prose writings, which I want now to place in a framework of debate about gender. Feminist theory distinguishes between biological sex and socially constructed gender, though some critics argue that biological discourse *follows* from the discourse of gender in the construction and meaning it gives to difference.[13] Current debate has roots in debates on gender which took place before the First World War, when some of the most influential voices were Austrian, notably Freud. Freud separates sex and gender: infants are born polymorphously sexual but acquire gender identity. However, this radical starting point leads to a conservative conclusion: adults should emerge from the dangerous passage through the Oedipal family drama with the characteristics of normal masculinity and femininity, for civilisation requires the sublimation of drives and the division of humanity into the two genders on whom different tasks fall. Thus man is the culture-maker and woman fulfils the maternal function.[14] Another feature of Freud's work is the structuring of the unconscious as a language, so that dreams or neurotic symptoms can be read as fragmentary texts. Neo-Freudians such as Jacques Lacan emphasise the child's entry into language as the threshold to gendered subjectivity, an idea that has been appropriated by some feminists who therefore see language as the prime terrain of struggle.

Almost as influential as Freud in the German-speaking world before 1914 was Otto Weininger whose *Geschlecht und Charakter* (1980) came out in 1903.[15] Whereas Freud was merely conservatively anti-feminist, Weininger was rabidly misogynistic. Weininger set a stark division between sexuality and 'character': the more human beings become emancipated from the instinctual heritage they share as an animal species to develop discrete, individual character, the more they approximate to the transcendent human potential. Weininger gendered the dualism as the masculine tendency towards individuality in contrast to the feminine entanglement in biology and set an ascetic masculinity against sensual femininity. Although all individuals, according to Weininger, have a mixture of masculine and feminine qualities, he simply asserted that men were more human than women. As 'the sex', women scarcely achieved subjecthood at all, enslaved as they were to impersonal sexual and maternal drives, for Weininger also sharply distinguished between the Mother and the Whore or sexual woman. At a time when bourgeois family ideology threatened to turn mothers into oppressive monsters of the imagination, stifling their sons and filling them with guilt, Weininger's popularity with male intellectuals was partly due to his promotion of the Whore who would not imprison men in domesticity. But there was also the *frisson* of a transgressive logic: if everybody had a mix of masculine and feminine features, then actual men and women could cross the line to display more of the tendencies of the opposite sex, so undoing the very opposition which the terms ostensibly established. Thus Weininger at once salved and fuelled gender anxiety in men by allowing for feminine traits which might yet threaten male identity, and he helped to construct the monstrous *Mann-Weib* (Man-Woman) as the threat posed by feminism.[16]

The woman as nothing but sex, but valued positively, also emerges from *Das Mutterrecht* by the Swiss anthropologist J.J. Bachofen, who envisioned a pre-patriarchal *and* pre-matriarchal world when women roamed the swampy marshlands between water and earth, nature and culture, and before fatherhood had been recognised.[17] Bachofen's hetaira has a close cousin in those nymphs such as Undine or Melusine who move through reedy landscapes in turn-of-the-century *Jugendstil* (art nouveau). Here water weeds and mermaid hair entwine to form sinuous decorative grotesques, mingling the human and the natural. In 'Die gestundete Zeit' the beloved's hair, as it is buried gradually in a sea of desert sand, lends her a deadly erotic enchantment. The hetaira may be mired in the man-made corruption of urban prostitution, like Wedekind's Lulu, or enchained in the banality of bourgeois marriage like Maeterlinck/Debussy's Mélisande.[18] Her opposites are patriarchal heads of households, but also the imprisoning wife/mother or the neurotic virgin. These types are less reflections of actual women than constructs born of the conflicting demands of masculinity which required that men sustain the patriarchal order which legitimates male dominance, yet that they transgress it in the new individualistic enterprise culture. However, given the greater socio-economic power of men at any one level of society and hence women's dependency, the imaginary figures affected women and were internalised. Thus among the educated intelligentsia, for every feminist such as Hedwig Dohm, who lucidly dissected the images, there was a Franziska zu Reventlow or a Lou Andreas-Salomé who played more ambiguous games. In trying to be writers without either posing a threat or succumbing to the men who controlled the institutions of culture, they played an exaggeratedly feminine role and so also avoided crossing the line to become the dreaded *Mann-Weib*.[19]

For heterosexual women, femininity *qua* sexual attractiveness to men offered relative power, yet it also perpetuated subjection, as Mary Wollstonecraft had argued when she called upon women to become, at least for a while, more masculine (1983:80).[20] Yet to 'be more masculine' or to play a lesbian role not out of desire but for political reasons, as advocated by some feminists in the 1970s, would be to don yet further masks. As Joan Rivière had argued in an essay of 1929: 'Womanliness therefore could be assumed and worn as a mask, both to hide the possession of masculinity and to avert reprisals expected if she was found to possess it' (1986:38). By 'masculinity' Rivière meant the professional skills and intellect which patriarchal ideology deemed to be male prerogatives, but which women who crossed the line mimicked or travestied, an analysis which turned femininity into a mask concealing a masquerade of masculinity behind which lay nothing at all. *Ich*'s death in *Malina* leaves perhaps such a vacuum, yet the end of the masquerades might open new possibilities for women beyond the either/or of *Ich*/Malina.[21]

Turning now to Bachmann's fiction, a common feature is oscillation between first and third person narration and between male and female narrators and focalisers.[22] Such a technique conveys not fixed identity, but subjectivity in flux. The opening story in *Das dreißigste Jahr*, 'Jugend in einer österreichischen Stadt' (II: 84–95), is narrated in the first person but is largely focused through a brother and sister composite in the years from just before to just after the Second World War, with some insets where retrospection gives way to the lyric present. That behind sibling androgyny there may be a girl focaliser, the earlier self of a woman narrator, is fleetingly suggested in the passage about the sex murderer as the children imagine the strangler's grasp. Of course a boy too might identify with the to-be-strangled female rather than the male strangler, but the moment points forwards to an end to androgyny with the arrival of a monstrous sexuality and sharply divided sex roles: 'They feel the strangler's grip, the mystery contained in the word sex that is more to be feared than the murderer' (1987:5). The motifs of childhood androgyny and sibling love, in keeping with the view that human beings are born sexed but acquire gender, mean that Bachmann avoids demonising males. In *Der Fall Franza*, Franza's brother, whom she protected as a child, becomes her protector in adulthood, a role the fraternal Malina also plays towards *Ich* until just before the end. But if men are not by nature violent, gender conditioning feeds into other power systems such as nationalism by producing a deep psychological structure of power and subjection: in 'Youth in an Austrian Town', the pointillistic juxtaposition of the sex murderer with Austria selling itself in 1938, allows the reader to draw such connections.[23]

Language is a key theme in several stories which thereby draw attention to their own medium as did the poetological lyrics, so continuing the modernist preoccupation with language which was especially strong in Austria. This was true not only in Freudian psychoanalysis, but also in the work of Wittgenstein or in Hofmannsthal's seminal 'Lord Chandos Letter' of 1902 which shows language not as a mirror but a barrier to truth.[24] More recently, Peter Handke's play *Kaspar* (1968) shows how the child-like hero can only achieve subjecthood through the acquisition of language, yet through that very process he is subjected to the oppressive social institutions and discourses which structure his identity. In Bachmann's 'Alles' (1959) a father laments his dead son:

> And I suddenly knew, it is all a question of language and not
> merely of this one language of ours that was created with others in
> Babel to confuse the world. For underneath it there smoulders
> another language that extends to gestures and looks, the unwind-
> ing of thoughts and the passage of feelings, and in it is all our mis-
> fortune. It was all a question of whether I could preserve the child
> from our language until he had established a new one and could
> introduce a new era. (II: 143)

The son, however, grows inexorably towards the masculinity
which the narrator inadvertently displays in his conduct as in his
language, for he and his wife transmit the old roles in the old language: no bridge leads to the new language and the wondrous
child dies prematurely. 'Everything' refers to one language underlying all natural languages, like the deep structures posited in
structuralist linguistics. Elsewhere Bachmann explores not language as such, but socio-historical discourses in the sense de-
ployed by poststructuralist theorists such as Michel Foucault, that
is, different linguistic fields associated with institutionalised
knowledge such as the law or medicine.[25] Thus 'Ein Wildermuth'
explores the incommensurability of 'truth' in different discourses.
The introduction and part one are highly reminiscent in manner of
the novella, 'Die Judenbuche' (1842) by Annette von Droste-Hülshoff (1797–1848), which also conveys the difficulty of knowing the
truth, or even of formulating what truth would be, given the
incommensurablity of legal, moral, psychological, religious and
sociological discourses. This theme has affinities with Nietzsche's
idea of perspectivism. From a patriarchal perspective the key sign
of truth is paternity, for the patriarchal order descends from
father to son and paternity forges links which stretch back to the
originary truth, the Word which in the beginning *is* the Father or
God. In such a discourse, woman introduces a terrible uncertainty, for she alone knows who the father is but has no interest in
a truth which sustains a system to which she is marginal. Nietzsche, an awful misogynist about actual women, frequently deploys 'woman' as a metaphor for elusive and illusive truth and
hence, so Jacques Derrida (1979) has argued, for undecidablity
between truth and lies because the opposites collapse into one
another as in the figure of 'woman'.

The title 'Ein Wildermuth' introduces patriarchal discourse also
complicated by class difference: who is 'a' Wildermuth; how does
he know that he has the right to the name; how will one Wildermuth, a prosperous judge, judge another Wildermuth, a poor

peasant and parricide. The judge's schoolteacher father was devoted to truth, but in both his mother and his wife Gerda he perceives a feminine indifference: 'Yes, my mother, whose Sunday joys had this appearance, was undoubtedly excluded from something – from the truth, of course' (II: 232).[26] The mother's hair, of a pre-Raphaelite red-blond colour and long like Mélisande's, is a signal of sexuality which threatens to exceed or to break out of the patriarchal order of truth. And: 'I don't know anyone who is close to me and cares so little about the truth as my wife' (II: 235). Gerda speaks a language of mourning for a stillborn child and of love for a husband, a language of flowers as the judge calls it, but which to him seems just lies: 'She has made us settle down in this language as she has made us settle down in the furniture which she brought from her home ...' (II: 245). From his perspective their lovemaking lacks truth, which the judge had once found in the silent lovemaking of another woman, but she was not a to-be-married woman. The truths of the mind (law and science), of the soul (grief and love), and of the body (sex) do not accord, for the patriarchal institution of marriage denies the truth of the flesh, so turning the language of love into a lie, and it divides the intellectual concerns of men from the emotional expressivity of women and from the wordless sensuality of the hetaira.

Paradoxically, in 'Ein Wildermuth', a woman author mimics the masculine perspective which reproduces the old images of femininity. And so 'Ein Wildermuth' might seem to repeat textually the dilemma conveyed in the story: by failing to represent feminine subjectivity in the double sense of showing woman characters from within and of writing the text as a woman, the author reproduces the sense of woman as a riddle. On the other hand, argument by ironic negation – woman is *not* this Mother, this Wife, this Whore as figured in this man's imagination – is perhaps preferable to direct representation – woman is *this* – which could merely set new oppressive norms.[27] Later in the collection, following three stories with a male perspective, 'Ein Schritt nach Gomorrha' comes as a shock: not just 'a step' towards lesbianism in the story, it is a textual shift to a woman's view. Yet perhaps the shift is not so great, for the focaliser Charlotte could seem similar to the *Mann-Weib* of antifeminist discourse, moved by the lust for social power and psychological mastery. Rather than offering a way out lesbianism may merely mimic the structure of dominance and subjection in compulsory heterosexuality.[28] On the other hand, following the trans/gression – literally the step across – the two women lie side-by-side: 'They were both dead and had killed something' (II: 213). This lesbian death/killing of the feminine is as full of ambiguities as *Ich*'s step behind the wall at the end of *Malina*.

The shift from masculine personas continues in 'Undine geht', the last story in *Das dreißigste Jahr* and in the *Simultan* collection. I cannot examine all of the stories here, but would like to raise two last issues. Sylvia Bovenschen (1979) argues that the feminine figures in male-authored texts either lack the positive features which men possess such as character (Weininger) or a sense of justice (Freud); or they represent that which men desire in order to achieve completion, for example selfless love or the hetaira's unalienated sensuality. Or, we might add, they oscillate undecidably between the negative and the positive to produce woman as riddle.[29] Women writers thus have to steer a path between such denigrating, idealising or mystifying images. In her thesis of the 'double focus', Sigrid Weigel argues that the images are so interwoven with women's sense of identity and so shape our desires, that to get rid of them would be more like plucking out an offending eye/I than simply removing patriarchal spectacles (1983c: 83–137).[30] Thus women writers must work through, and also distance the images, an idea close to Brecht's theory of the alienation effect which highlights class identity but also shows how it is produced through social relations which can be changed. Changing one's class position is easier to contemplate, however, than changing one's gender. Various dangers need to be avoided, for example reducing women to helpless victims without any responsibility for their own subjection, and also misogynistic or elitist contempt for typical 'feminine' behaviour. This is the meta-problem hanging over 'Probleme, Probleme' (II: 318–353). The old woman's closing words, 'Oh, men' are ironic, for what we (feminists and our 'New Man' friends) have seen is a woman's self-subjection and bad faith. But if 'Oh, men' is merely replaced by 'Oh, women' (which was more or less the response of Reich-Ranicki, not a 'New Man'), then 'Probleme, Probleme' would serve simply to confirm an ancient stereotype of female vanity and to blame women for their own subjection.[31] Neither 'Oh, men' nor 'Oh, women' is an adequate response: the layers of irony in this ending run deep, and turn the hitherto comic tone bitter, an effect even more evident in the close of 'Ihr glücklichen Augen'.

If 'Probleme, Probleme' attacks femininity as self-subjection, exemplifying Bovenschen's woman as negation, then 'Undine geht' raises converse problems by drawing on the figure of the hetaira or water nymph, an idealised and alienated image of the sexual woman against which male intellectuals measured their pathetic actual wives and found them wanting. Cora Kaplan has shown how critics evaluate fantasy in women's writing in diametrically opposed ways, either as a subversive breakthrough of the repressed or as reproducing the reduction of women to 'the sex' (1986b: 147–176). Does 'Undine geht' merely reproduce a motif demeaning to actual women in their practical lives, or does it appropriate and revalue the patriarchal image? I leave this question hanging tantalisingly in the air, which is where 'Undine geht' perhaps leaves the reader.

Woman As the Other and Other 'Others' in the *Todesarten* Novels

In a discussion of Bachmann's poem, 'Erklär mir, Liebe' (I: 109–110), D. G. Bond (1991) takes issue with Christa Wolf's reading of the salamander at the end as a still negative image of the alienated thinking self evoked earlier in the poem: 'Am I to hold company for the short, dreadful time only with thoughts and to know nothing alone of love and to do nothing loving'.[32] But Bond convincingly argues that the salamander is a utopian image of integration between the thinking self and the fire of passion: 'I see the salamander pass though every fire. No shudder moves him and he feels no pain'. The image also has tragic import, however, for although the salamander remains unhurt, human subjects come to grief on the divisions between mind and body, spirit and flesh, culture and nature. Thus the attack is not on one side or the other, but on the division. To gender the dilemma: the poem does not reject the masculine thinking subject in favour of a repressed femininity. It seeks rather to transcend such an opposition, which indeed turns reason into a ruthless instrumental rationality, demanding repression of the sensuous body and the feeling heart.

The dualisms in 'Erklär mir, Liebe' recall the idealist philosophical tradition which a range of more recent theories address – structuralism, Lacanian psychoanalysis, poststructuralism as well as feminism.[33] Such dualisms, it is variously argued, rest on a universal structure in the mind or in language, or on the 'binary opposition' of gender which, though supposedly culturally produced, seems in some theories to be as inescapable a destiny as anatomy. The oppositions are hierarchical in that the first term, the One and selfsame, takes priority over the second, the Other which is not self-same but always relative to the One.[34] A key passage is the dialectic of Lordship and Bondage in Hegel's *Phenomenology of Spirit* (also called 'master/slave') which introduces two figures of consciousness, 'one is the independent consciousness whose essential nature is to be for itself, the other is the dependent consciousness whose essential nature is to live or to be for another. The former is lord, the other is bondsman' (1977: 111). The lord is by essence *für sich*, that is self-aware, whereas the bondsman exists through his awareness of himself only as an object in another's consciousness. The opposition is but a stage in the movement towards universal humanity through self-consciousness and mutual recognition, but first comes a phase of struggle as each consciousness strives to overthrow the Other and set itself as the One by constraining the Other to recognise its mastery.[35] Paradoxically, however, it is not the master but the slave who is closer to humanity through his creative labour and his recognition of another who could by that very token respond in kind. For only a human subject, recognised as such, can in the eyes of the one seeking recognition provide such confirmation. Hence only through recognising the humanity of the slave could the master find confirmation of his own humanity, and in that step the master/slave dualism would be transcended.

This reconciliatory vision was first attacked by Marx on the grounds that the slave's alienated labour is no longer the creative expression of his human essence. Simone de Beauvoir undertook another critical appropriation in gendering the master as the male subject and the slave as the female Other (1989). Two elements in Beauvoir's argument stand in some tension. First is the claim that from time immemorial patriarchal culture has positioned woman as the Other and that this culture sustains and is sustained by the socio-economic inequality between the sexes. However, Beauvoir also posits an existential human freedom and on this view, the master/slave dialectic occurs *within* female subjectivity: rather than take up the burden of freedom in striving for transcendence, women remain in subjection; they play the inauthentic feminine role out of bad faith. However, Beauvoir's double position results in a sometimes astringent onslaught on femininity and a tendency to reinscribe the very dualistic categories of patriarchal ideology: transcendence gets set against women's entanglement in biology (shades of Weininger!).

Doubleness also runs through Bachmann's texts. In 'Erklär mir, Liebe', for example, the lyric subject may be male or female; the masculine *einer* (one) may be an internal aspect of a male or female self or the beloved of a female subject; *'Liebe'* may be an emotion within a male or female self or the beloved of a male subject.[36] In other words the poem intertwines gender identity within the self and relations between the sexes. And so it is with the novels. *Malina* (written 1967–1970) was planned as the first in a trilogy to be entitled *Todesarten*, although *Der Fall Franza* (written 1963–1966) was written first. (For reasons of space I omit from consideration *Requiem für Fanny Goldmann* [1971] which was to come, revised and expanded, between the other two.) Broadly speaking, *Malina* centres on splitting within the subject and *Der Fall Franza* (hereafter shortened to *Franza*) on relations between the sexes. Thus *Ich* is a woman who writes a first-person narration; Franza is a woman who is written about in a third-person narrative, though she occasionally assumes the first person, and her perspective briefly prevails, sandwiched between that of her brother Martin at the beginning and end. Malina, at once an actual male friend but increasingly also *Ich*'s uncanny double, plays a similar helper role as Martin who is, however, clearly separate from Franza, though their incestuous closeness recalls the motif of sibling *alter egos* (Ulrich and his twin sister Agathe in Musil's *The Man Without Qualities,* for example). *Malina* is more psychologically complex, *Franza* is more radical because overtly political, but both cross-reflect within the trilogy.

Malina can be read as the inner drama of woman as the Other. Like Hegel's slave who is aware of himself only as an object in another's consciousness, *Ich* is in thrall to her lover Ivan and plays the masquerade of cooking for him, worrying about her makeup, losing at chess. But through writing her self in auto/biography *Ich* strives towards transcendence, as Beauvoir advocates or Wolstonecraft when she advises women to be more masculine. Women are perfectly capable of 'masculine' logic or practicality, and Bachmann depicts with high comedy another *alter ego,* the competent Fräulein Jelinek. The problem comes with Malina's mephistophelian order that *Ich* must give up love (which positions her in her own imagination as the Other of Ivan) in order to be a writing subject. *Ich* finally refuses and disappears behind the wall. But even were a transformation of consciousness, such as Beauvoir and Malina envisage, possible, it would be insufficient, for woman is positioned as the Other through social power accruing to men which cannot just be abolished by an act of will.

'Der dritte Mann' opens a wider perspective in adding a third figure to the patriarchal trinity: Ivan associated with love; Malina associated with intellect; and the terrible Father.[37] How the ogre-like Father relates to *Ich*'s empirical father and how the imaginary melodramas relate to *Ich*'s actual family and her childhood during the war remain ambiguous: is the father the shadow of the Father; was the war an instantiation of a universal principle as the closing words of the chapter, 'It is unending war' (III: 236) might suggest? Or are childhood experiences during the war the historical causes of a damaged psyche? This latter reading need not reduce *Ich* to a female hysteric, which is how she is played in Werner Schröter's film.[38] Rather her nightmares can be read as visionary responses to real historical events; textually they constitute a question rather than an assertion. *Ich*'s statement 'It is unending war' comes not at the end of the novel, but rather the more limited 'It was murder' (II: 337).[39]

Malina survives as does a covert narrator who speaks the accusation. Thus much hangs not only on whodunnit, but on how we understand the main suspect, Malina, who can be seen as an aspect of an eternal trinity, yet also as a moment in the history of relations between the sexes in Europe, an effect of women's admission to education and the entry of middle-class women intellectuals into the public sphere. The murder of *Ich* in this view conveys the insufficiency of liberal emancipation to change deep-rooted (but not unchanging) gender conditioning. Seen in this light, *Malina* is the work of an author in much the same position as Beauvoir, a well-known writer respected by a male cultural establishment, but highly conscious of the limits to that respect and of the hard choices to be made in order to succeed in the institution of literature. 'Woman under patriarchy' is a double-edged speculation, for it signals a consciousness which might lead to political action, but it could also tend to perpetuate woman as the Other, as the eternal victim. *Ich*/Malina is perhaps better seen as a woman intellectual of the mid-twentieth century.

Ich/Malina is also very Austrian in inhabiting an old empire: in thrall to Hungarian Ivan, *Ich* belongs to the once hegemonic German nation. Among the intertextual reflections between *Malina* and *Franza* is the mirroring of continents between Europe and Africa, of old and new empires between Austria and colonial and neo-colonial domination, of victims between the Jews in Europe and the Arabs and between the colonised and women. In her fourth *Kassandra* lecture Christa Wolf singled out the parallel between patriarchy and imperialism: the first sets woman as the Other, and the second makes Others of the colonised. The novel opens by showing the extreme anguish Franza has suffered at being objectified by her husband Leo Jordan, a psychologist who has made a case study of her. Particularly gruesome are Jordan's observations of and on his wife's sexual behaviour, which he later leaves lying around for her to find. The allusion to Freud's Dora case or his essays on female sexuality is clear. Psychoanalysis came in the wake of other nineteenth-century medical, biological and anthropological discourses which produced a flood of theorising about 'woman' (*das Weib*); Bachofen or Weininger are examples. In tandem with scientific analysis is the huge literary output of men writing about women which can be seen as a metaphorical colonisation intended, like Jordan's notes, for the colonised to read, so that women see themselves mediated through the male gaze.[40] The anthropologists who wrote about women as if they were a sub-human species wrote similarly about supposedly primitive peoples who in ethnographic discourse are positioned, like the Hegelian Other, as the object of specialised knowledge by the white expert. As Robert Young puts it:

> Hegel articulates a philosophical structure of the appropriation of the other as a form of knowledge which uncannily simulates the project of nineteenth-century imperialism; the construction of knowledge which all operates through forms of expropriation and incorporation of the other mimics at a conceptual level the geographical and economic absorption of the non-European world by the West. (1990: 3)

The cover of Young's book, *White Mythologies*, showing a lone figure in a businessman's suit standing in the sand looking at a pyramid, could almost serve as an illustration for *Franza*. But that is perhaps the trouble. Edward Said (1978) has written of the pervasive tradition of 'orientalism' in English and French Arabist scholarship and in literature and painting: in choosing an exotic location, has not Bachmann herself perpetrated the ethnocentric use of others as a mirror for European concerns, just as male writers turn women into metaphor? Does not the monolithic term 'die Weißen' (the whites) imply as its opposite a faceless collective of non-white subaltern peoples, so half-undoing the critique of neo-colonialism by such an empty figuring of the colonised. To equate such different phenomena as the murder of six million Jews, colonial oppression in North Africa and neo-colonial economic exploitation with the subordination of women, which in turn mean such different things under different conditions – the sufferings of women slaves in sugar plantations are incommensurable with those of women intellectuals in the literary market – flattens out the historical specificity of particular evils, which *could* be combatted, to produce a monolith which *cannot*. *Franza* can in my view be defended against most of these charges precisely because the Other is left largely blank.

Franza sees herself as 'of inferior race' (III: 412) but is later clearly positioned as a white woman (III: 418); and she meets mainly Americans or Europeans such as the former concentration camp doctor; her death results from an encounter with a white man. True, the heat and the desert become metaphors, but that is not the same as making Egyptians into metaphors. There are 'orientalist' moments: the choice of the name Jordan sets up uncontrollable associations; a belly dancer is set against a generalised collective of Arab village women, but the comparison does at least half undo the main orientalist female stereotype of luxurious sensuality. Franza dies a victim, but the symbol of patriarchal power, the phallus, loses something of its aura. For hidden behind the pyramid against which Franza hits her head is not some archaic figure of sempereternal power but a flasher. 'Look on my works, ye mighty, and despair' were the words, but Keats' Ozymandias was just a heap of dust. Franza's death conveys a complex vision of the undeniable real injustice and suffering entailed in current gender relations, but also of absurdity. 'Look on my phallus, ye women, and despair': to remain in thrall to imaginary phallic power when the trouble comes from an intellectual flasher like Leo Jordan or the miserable man behind the pyramid would be indeed absurd.

More analysis would be needed to follow through the tensions in this perhaps ethnocentric and yet radically political text. That Bachmann's work continues to resonate through the shifting phases of feminist debates is a measure of its dense complexity. In addition, her work has engaged the imagination of other writers and artists. Uwe Johnson, a friend and fellow author who adopted a female persona as narrator of his tetralogy *Jahrestage*, the first volume of which came out almost simultaneously with *Malina* in 1970, wrote an essay in homage (1974). Bachmann and Wolf constitute twin peaks in the post-war range of women's writing. In tandem with the difficulty of saying 'I' which Wolf's Christa T. experienced, the shifting pronouns and gender identities in Bachmann's fictions feed into an intriguing field cutting across the borders between East and West in such works as the sex-change stories by

Kirsch, Morgner and Wolf in *Geschlechtertausch* (1980) or Monika Maron's novel *Flugasche* (1981), which changes from first to third person in mid-flight. Maron's *Die Überläuferin* (1986a) is also peopled by multiple *alter egos*, and in *Stille Zeile Sechs* (1991) in which 'the woman writes back', though the oscillation between first and third person is still there. In Austria Elfriede Jelinek adapted *Malina* for the screen version (though she subsequently distanced herself from the film), and her monster mother in *Die Klavierspielerin* (1983 *The Pianist* 1988) resonates fascinatingly with the monster Father in *Malina* (Jelinek/Bachmann 1991). Ingeborg Bachmann's writing thus still has a central place in the literary landscape.

Notes

Except for translations from published English editions listed in the bibliography, all translations from German texts cited are by Elizabeth Boa.

1. Bachmann also collaborated as librettist with Hans Werner Henze and wrote radio plays; her first, *Die Zikaden* broadcast in 1955, had music by Henze; the best known, *Der gute Gott von Manhatten* was first broadcast in 1958.
2. For more on *Gruppe 47* see chapter 4 and Leonhardt 1981. *The Respite* is the translation chosen by Hamburger 1977: 332.
3. See Hotz 1990 on the reception of Bachmann during her lifetime.
4. 'Erfolg mit Gedichten. Ingeborg Bachmann' in the *Abendzeitung* Munich, 13 June 1953, 5, cited in Hotz 1990: 39.
5. Hereafter page numbers, preceded by a volume number in Roman numerals, following quotations refer to Bachmann 1982. Lennox 1993 covers some ninety items.
6. On frames of reference see Rimmon-Kenan 1983: 122–124.
7. On connections between philosophical existentialism and aesthetic formalism see Kreuzer 1990.
8. On intertextuality see Worton and Still 1990: 1–44.
9. Also cited in Hotz 1990:77.
10. See Culler 1983: 134–56 on the grafting together of different discourses as a topic in deconstructive criticism. Here it merely serves to explain why Bachmann's texts have been read in different ways. Such mixing, sometimes termed heteroglossia or intertextuality, is a theme also in Bakhtin 1981: 257–422 and Kristeva 1980. Bakhtin, wrongly in my view, associates the phenomenon with the dialogic novel as against supposedly monologic lyric poetry, but as Bachmann's work shows, poetry may mix many voices.

11. For a fuller reading of the disunities of time, place and action in *Malina*, see Boa 1990.

12. In two canonical poetic cycles, with which Bachmann's poetry has been compared, Goethe's *Römische Elegien* and Rilke's *Sonette an Orpheus*, the Muse is asleep. See also Boa 1992.

13. This is precisely the move that Kristeva makes in her theory of the masculine syntactical symbolic order and the rhythmic feminine semiotic *chora*. Moi 1986: 93–98.

14. See Butler 1990.

15. A predominanty conservative psychoanalytic practice in the United States made Freud a prime target of radical feminists such as Kate Millett (1971) and Shulamith Firestone (1971). See Mitchell 1975 for a critical appropriation of Freudian theory.

16. It is available in facsimile reprint. The author committed suicide in 1904.

17. Weininger's cult of asceticism perhaps also came from abhorrence of heterosexuality, yet fear of homosexuality as threating masculine identity; of Jewish origin himself, he also saw Jews as a feminine race lacking in identity.

18. J.J. Bachofen's volume was originally published in 1861, and influenced Friedrich Engels in his critique of the family and was reissued in the 1890s.

19. On such figures see Boa 1987: 60–65, 186–189; Hermand 1968; and Roebling 1992.

20. On Dohm see Reed 1987; also Weedon 1994. On Salomé see Martin 1991.

21. On this double bind see Kaplan 1986: 31–56.

22. A more radical step would be to deconstruct not just cultural gender stereotypes but the categories of sexual difference, of women and men. See Butler 1990.

23. On the distinction between narration (who tells) and focalisation (who sees), and on narrative levels and voices see Rimmon-Kenan, 1983, chapters 6 and 7.

24. Bachmann later stated that the marching columns were Hitler's troops, which could suggest a rape of Austria by her German neighbour, a view tending to absolve Austria and to strengthen a dubious metaphorical gendering of politics. Yet, the inner loss of *Heimat* would, as Gerhard Bötz argues, be intensified were the columns to be understood as the *Austrian* fascists who marched through Klagenfurt on 11 March 1938. See Botz 1993.

25. On a putative influence of Wittgenstein see Seidel 1979.

26. On the value of poststructuralist ideas to feminism see Weedon 1996.

27. Seeking truth is like seeking baskets of mushrooms, the narrator remarks, perhaps in an allusion to Hofmannsthal's abstract words which crumble in the mouth like 'modrige Pilze'. Hofmannsthal 1959: 7–20 (12).

28. Critics influenced by French psychoanalytic and deconstructive theory value modernist experimental writing over realist representation on such grounds.

29. Some of the essays in Snitow, Stansell and Thompson 1984 offer a starting point to a debate which raged throughout the 1980s over competing theories of lesbianism.

30. See also Ellmann 1979 who wittily brings out how the stereotypes produce diametrically opposed characterisations: fickle and duplicitous women lack men's natural frankness, but have a plant-like harmonious nature compared with complex, alienated man.

31. Bachmann's *Malina* is *the* exemplary case towards which the essay is angled.

32. See footnote 7 above.

33. Wolf's commentary comes in the fourth of her Frankfurt lectures of 1982, published subsequently as essays accompanying her novel *Kassandra* 1983: 126–55.

Wolf honours Bachmann whose Frankfurt lectures (IV, 182–274) were delivered in the winter of 1959/60.

34. Critics in the deconstructive school deploy the term 'Western philosophy' for this tradition, a monolithic construct which itself deserves deconstruction and which can lead to undiscriminating hostility to logical argument, science, historical evidence etc.

35. For a now classic formulation of such a view see Cixous and Clément 1987: 63ff.

36. My use of the initial capital 'O', indicating the personification in Hegel, implies no reference Lacan's influential appropriation of Hegel's term.

37. I assume, without arguing the point here, that the poem expresses a heterosexual eroticism. The male figuring of sexual arousal is perhaps inevitable given the practices in the animal kingdom. But perhaps not, it may be time to look at the peahen. That the thinking self *and* the figures of active desire are all male is disturbing, though, and *Malina* here marks a feminist shift.

38. On the trinity see Bail 1984.

39. On the the film *Malina* see Heidelberger-Leonard 1992.

40. I argue elsewhere that the novel is more universalising than *Die Überläuferin* (1986) by Monika Maron who limits her critique to the GDR. Compare 'Hier ist Krieg' (*Die Überläuferin*, 149) with 'Es ist der ewige Krieg', Boa 1994.

41. There may be a hermetic reference here to Max Frisch who deeply wounded Bachmann by using their affair as material for a work of literature.

Chapter Fifteen

READING ELFRIEDE JELINEK

Allyson Fiddler

Introduction: Elfriede Jelinek and the Question of Feminine Aesthetics

It was only after the appearance of Elfriede Jelinek's third novel, *Die Liebhaberinnen* (1975, *Women as Lovers* 1994), that the author became labelled a writer of *Frauenliteratur*. This is a label which she has personally rejected. Before looking in this chapter at three of Jelinek's novels, *Die Liebhaberinnen, Die Klavierspielerin* (1983, *The Piano Teacher*, 1988), and *Lust* (1989, *Lust*, 1992), all of which do indeed have feminist themes, it is important to consider Jelinek's negative reaction to the concept of 'women's writing', or indeed to the idea of feminine aesthetics and to characterise the interaction between her politics and her writing.[1]

In an interview with Josef-Hermann Sauter, Jelinek reminds us that she has written other works which are not feminist, or which do not deal with expressly feminist issues: 'it would be wrong to call me an author of "women's writing" because out of three books, I've written one which is about the fate of two women, who, because of their upbringing, unfortunately still tend to let their lives be moulded by men, instead of taking things into their own hands. To call me a representative of "women's writing" as a result, is, I find, unacceptable' (Jelinek in Sauter 1981: 109).[2] Indeed the variety of themes which Jelinek's *oeuvre* spans – class relations, the discourse of *Heimat* and the related danger of latent fascism in contemporary (Austrian) society, the popular culture industry and its function as a stabilising social mechanism, to name but a few – testify to her claim, and have established her as a writer whose importance reaches beyond a description as 'feminist writer'. Although it is as a novelist that Jelinek is most widely known, she has a strong reputation, too, as a dramatist and has written in forms as diverse as poetry, the radio play, libretti, film scripts, essays and articles on aesthetic and political themes.[3]

Jelinek began writing in the early 1970s, but in terms of the thematic and stylistic preoccupations of her work, her development as a feminist writer is not representative of German-language women's writing in the 1970s as a whole. The largely autobiographical self-thematisation and experiential focus of early second-wave women's writing which is exemplified in works such as Verena Stefan's *Häutungen* (1975, *Shedding and Literally Dreaming*, 1994) and Brigitte Schwaiger's *Wie kommt das Salz ins Meer* (1977, *Why Is There Salt in the Sea?*, 1988), is wholly absent in Jelinek. *The Piano Teacher* is the one novel into which she incorporates autobiographical ideas, by reworking some of the experiences from her own childhood into the character Erika Kohut's traumatic relationship with her mother. If the 'consciousness-raising' literature of the 1970s worked to encourage many women to write by showing that indeed, 'the private is the political', or, more importantly, the private is a worthwhile subject for literature, it may, arguably, also have held back many other women writers. Jelinek explains:

> The market is actually quite greedy for this new self-experiential literature by women, as long as they view it as suffering which is experienced by an individual or which is portrayed in an individualistic way. They become reluctant the moment you try to reduce individual experience to a common social denominator. They call this 'generalising' and are quite resentful normally. It is still basically the case that if a woman just writes a very personal book about how she's been beaten by her husband, she'll still get more readers than someone who's attempted a piece of social analysis (Jelinek in Vansant 1985: 4)

The attempt to promote an analysis of society and its structures, to use individuals to represent a more common experience or problem, is central to Jelinek's work and reflects her socialist beliefs. As a socialist feminist, Jelinek's aim is always to challenge patriarchal oppression as a symptom or corollary of capitalism, and not to see women's oppression in a political vacuum. A member of the Austrian Communist party (KPÖ) until 1991, Jelinek had always described herself first and foremost as a Marxist, and stated that the defeat of capitalism was a requisite condition for sexual equality.[4] It is easy to see why she might reject the term 'women's writing', concealing, as it does, the vast political divide between, say, liberal feminist, or lesbian feminist writers, and social feminist writers.[5] Against the predominantly radical mood of 1970s feminism, works such as the novel, *Die Liebhaberinnen*, and the play, *Was geschah, nachdem Nora ihren Mann verlassen hatte oder Stützen der Gesellschaften* (orig. 1977, 1984 published in *Theaterstücke*), can be seen as Marxist correctives to the celebrations of sisterhood being conducted in women's writing elsewhere.

Jelinek is suspicious of terms such as *écriture feminine* or feminine aesthetics when they are used to denote a mode of writing to which women have access by virtue of their body. She states her resistance to the idea, saying: 'there are women writers who think that women in general have a tendency to speak with their bodies. They express the suffering which they endure in society with their bodies, with their emotions. That's a bit of a cliché in my opinion' (Jelinek in Sauter 1981: 109). Jelinek's description evokes theories of 'writing the body' put forward, for example, by French feminist theorist, Hélène Cixous. For her, feminine writing is a bisexual mode of writing, available to both sexes but naturally stronger in woman. Cixous urges women to 'write your self. Your body must be heard. Only then will the immense resources of the unconscious spring forth' (Cixous 1976: 880).

In the interview with Sauter cited above, Jelinek goes on to comment on her own writing, 'I'd say that, on the contrary, my aesthetic methods are very unfeminine. I've more often heard people speaking of my language and methods, those of irony and satire, as actually being very harsh, so I'm still quite amazed about this categorisation as a "woman's writer"' (Jelinek in Sauter 1981: 109–110). Her statement unwittingly affirms some kind of distinction between masculine and feminine aesthetics. An examination of just three of Jelinek's novels must serve here to cast some light on this issue.

Die Liebhaberinnen

The theme of Jelinek's first realist novel, *Die Liebhaberinnen*, is certainly a feminist one.[6] In a mock-didactic tone, reminiscent of the school-teacherly address to the reader so characteristic of her previous novel, *Michael. Ein Jugendbuch für die Infantilgesellschaft* (1973), the narrator of *Die Liebhaberinnen* uses the eponymous 'lovers' as her examples – good, and bad – to explain the rules of love and marriage to the reader. The novel describes the attempts of two girls, brigitte and paula,[7] to find themselves a husband. There is a certain progression of the narrative in that the two do finally get married, and one of them, paula, is forced to turn to prostitution in order to make ends meet and feed her child, as her husband, erich, spends his wages on drink. Paula is found out and is forced to take a job in the brassière factory on her divorce from erich. The circle is completed as paula ends up in the same factory from which brigitte at the opening of the novel was trying to escape, to a 'better' life as housewife and mother.

It is not the plot of the novel, or the characters themselves which are of interest in *Die Liebhaberinnen*, indeed as the narrator tells us, 'the story of how the two of them [brigitte and heinz] got to know each other is not out of the ordinary. the two of them themselves are not out of the ordinary. they are simply symptomatic of everything that is not out of the ordinary' (8). The techniques employed by Jelinek, those of parody and satire, hint at what *is* important in this text. By constructing a parody of romantic fiction, Jelinek's intention is to show that marriage is based, not on altruistic love and sexual equality, but on the exploitation and subjugation of women. To this end she avoids involving the reader in an emotional account of the girls' 'love story' and points instead at the structures behind their ideas on marriage. These include their family upbringing and how their parents discourage them from doing anything other than leading the same kind of life as themselves, the gendered and limited job opportunities available to them, and the media images of love and beauty which are inculcated in them.[8]

Although the good example in this moral tale, brigitte, has managed to secure herself a husband with a good job, and a home of their own, this is no 'happily-ever-after' ending. Brigitte is full of hate at having had to ingratiate her way into heinz's family and has only borne a child in order to make heinz marry her. The tone, then, as everywhere else in Jelinek, is overwhelmingly negative, a characteristic for which she has been much criticised. The humour, too, is black and is often based on 'the negation of existing traditions of thought and evaluation' (Lorenz 1987: 35). An example of how Jelinek frustrates our expectations and provides a humorous inversion can be seen in her description of paula's happiness at having found her man, erich: 'all that matters is that love has come at last, and that it hasn't come to an ugly, worn out, drunken, exhausted, vulgar, common woodcutter and her, but to a handsome, worn out, drunken, strong, vulgar, common woodcutter and her' (42). The switching of 'ugly' for 'handsome' and 'exhausted' for 'strong' in the second part of the sentence reinforces paula's blind disregard for anything other than good looks. Having expected a new string of positive attributes, the reader laughs on hearing that as long as erich is handsome, it does not matter to paula if he is a vulgar, good-for-nothing drunkard.

Dagmar Lorenz sees this use of humour as ultimately affirmative, since it does not fundamentally question hierarchical social structures or suggest alternatives to these: 'Women writers' use of such humour [based on the existing masculine discourse of humour] is very effective at mocking certain aspects of social reality, but it doesn't challenge the social hierarchy or any other kind of hierarchy ... Dominance is still the subject, and it is portrayed without the possibility of breaking out of the vicious circle of power and its abuse being conceivable' (Lorenz 1987: 35). Jelinek's writing leaves precious little space for positive alternatives, utopian moments or hopes,[9] but her aim is precisely to make sure that there can be no doubt in the reader's mind as to the existence of these patriarchal and capitalist hierarchies. Jelinek's contribution to the discourse of feminine aesthetics, then, and to feminine humour, is in constantly reminding her readers to remove the veil from their eyes and see things as they truly are. Admittedly, it could be argued that in the 1990s, women are well aware of the nature and structure of their oppression but are still greatly in need of suggestions and hopes for how this might be changed. That Jelinek's readership largely consists of men and women who are sympathetic to and aware of the socialist analysis she puts forward, rather than those whose eyes need opening, is a fact of which she is herself well aware.

In *Die Liebhaberinnen*, as in others of Jelinek's works, the finger is not only pointed at men. One of the most uncomfortable, and yet most important achievements of Jelinek's writing is precisely that she shows women's complicity with the patriarchal order. They are defined by and located in it and often help in perpetuating the patriarchal status quo. The family is the breeding ground for petty-bourgeois ideals such as individualism and competition. Paula's mother, for example, does not see why her daughter should escape her lot in life and train to be a seamstress. She should work at home for her brother and father just like paula's mother, and if she tries to do otherwise, she'll 'catch it' from the men, an act of retribution with which paula's mother clearly agrees:

> why and for what have i slaved all my life, if not for dada and gerald,
> and now when you could at last slave with me, you don't want to.
> you can put it out of your head! before dada and gerald put it out of
> your head for you. i'll tell dada and gerald right now. right now! (18)

The theme of sex and sexuality is a constant target for Jelinek's demystification. In contrast to the later text, *Lust, Die Liebhaberinnen* does not contain many passages dealing with the act itself. When heinz is on top of her and 'thrusts away' (55), brigitte is thinking about his colossal weight and about the possible consequences, consequences which brigitte *desires*. If she becomes pregnant, then heinz will be forced to marry her. Her thoughts are narrated to us: 'brigitte wants heinz to discharge and shoot the extract of the roast beef and the bread dumplings from today's dinner into her. by now this slimy muck must at last have been squirted into her and be safe inside, but no, it takes time to do a thing well' (53). Characterising sperm in terms of the food which has played its part in its production is a fitting thought to impute to brigitte who has probably contributed her labour towards making heinz's lunch! It is probably Jelinek's 'unsavoury' thematisation of sex and her negative picture of it which have earned her a certain disgust from male readers and reviewers. But the usurping of this very masculine of themes is itself a contribution towards expanding the dimensions of women's writing.

Lust

It was precisely such a motivation which led Jelinek to try to write a 'feminine pornography' with her novel, *Lust*, or at least this was the aim which she expressed in countless interviews before the appearance of the novel. At the same time, however, she prophesied the failure of such an enterprise, pointing out that it was impossible for women to take control of their own desire in this way, since to express desire in language meant to use a medium already controlled by men and one to which women had no access in their own right.

This argument can be seen in terms of the psychoanalytic theories of French theorists such as Jacques Lacan, who describes the infant's successful passage into adult life as an entry into the 'symbolic order'. In this patriarchal symbolic order, the order of laws, language, and social institutions, it is the phallus which guarantees meaning and symbolises control. If men can never fully become the symbolic 'father of creation', through their possession of a penis they can at least aspire to positions of authority within the system. Thus men, or 'man', in *Lust* is described wittily as: 'The Man. He is a largish room where talking is still possible' (8).[10]

Where Lacan's feminist followers Hélène Cixous, Luce Irigaray and Julia Kristeva have tried to counter the power of patriarchal language by creating a woman's language, an *écriture féminine*, Jelinek's texts translate onto the page a near fatalistic, if somewhat ironised exposition of these theories. Gerti, the house-wife protagonist of *Lust*, can only write her words in the air, to be carried off by the wind. Her husband will appropriate whatever it is she says. He does not merely produce 'characters' or 'signs', he can sign his name and seize authorship of her 'writing': 'The woman writes characters in the air with her hand. She does not have to earn her living, she is kept by her husband. When he returns home at the end of the day he has earned the right to set his signature to life' (54).

Control of sexuality and control of language are seen to be interdependent. In the above example 'setting one's signature' is one of the myriad ways of denoting sexual intercourse. When the managing director of the paper factory[11] returns home every evening he exerts his 'right' to have sexual intercourse with his wife, an object of gratification to which he must have frequent recourse, since in the scare surrounding the Aids virus his rapacious sexual appetite can no longer safely be satisfied by prostitutes. The 'plot' of *Lust* consists for the most part in fairly brutal, almost slapstick descriptions of the sex life of this married couple, but is interspersed with essay-style commentaries by the narrator on how Gerti's life is dictated by her husband and her son, and how the husband wields power over his employees. Gerti tries several methods of escapism or liberation from her sexual and social subjugation: she seeks escape through alcohol, though this cannot protect her from her husband's sexual attacks; she tries to seize the sexual initiative and have an affair with a student, but in the sexual economy of Jelinek's writing this is doomed to failure as he humiliates her and gang rapes her with his friends; and finally, she murders her son in order to prevent him from growing up to be a sexual tyrant like his father. In *Lust*, as in *Die Lieb-haberinnen*, the family is shown to be an important locus for the formation of the younger generation's attitudes and subsequent behaviour. The son tries to emulate his father, and is as brutal with his young friends as his father is with Gerti and with his employees. His confidence comes from seeing himself as 'a phrase expressed by his father' (54).

There is little which can be seen as subversive in terms of the novel's 'action', although the bleak and unexpected ending does offer a germ of rebellion and a kind of malicious hope, even if Gerti does not murder her husband, but merely his image, their son. The saturation of sexual abuse in the text functions on a narrative level to drive 'the woman' to despair, and ultimately to kill 'the son'.[12] This is mirrored on an interpretive level by the cumulative effect of Jelinek's portrayal of sex. The sheer number of acts of copulation, and the mechanical and metaphorical description of them combine to turn the reader 'off', not 'on'. In the following example, the sympathetic reader revels in the linguistic manipulation of the auto-mechanical metaphors and joins in with the black humour; the unsympathetic reader is perhaps disgusted and/or shocked at the brutality of the imagery and annoyed by both the narrator's patronising use of the first person plural and by the overtly political commentary:

> The Man takes hold of his wooden ding-a-ling and batters at the woman's astounded rear entry. She can hear the engine of his loins roaring closer from afar. She's beginning to banish all feeling from within her. But there's still room in the boot! And into the boot goes the heavy genital load, don't worry about the smell. The seats can't be kept clean anyway. Blindly the woman cashes in her security from the Man's spitting dispenser. He is milking her breasts. (*Lust*: 28)

Whatever the reader's reaction, there can be no doubt that in this barrage of sexual acts, the myth and mystique of male potency in conventional pornography is annulled as the permanently erect penis becomes a parody of itself. Once again, Jelinek's predilection for 'anti' genres becomes apparent. If, in *Die Liebhaberinnen*, she had created an anti-romance, with *Lust*, Jelinek produced not pornography, but anti-pornography.[13]

Lust can in many ways be seen to follow on from the much earlier novel, *Die Liebhaberinnen*. It is for this reason that I have discussed it here before the novel *Die Klavierspielerin*, which was published six years earlier. *Die Liebhaberinnen* deals with courtship and 'romance', and *Lust* presents the reader with a look at the 'reality' of marriage, that is, it picks up, thematically, where *Die Liebhaberinnen* leaves off. However, while belonging geographically to the same group of novels – *Oh Wildnis, oh Schutz vor ihr* (1985), *Lust* and *Die Liebhaberinnen* are all set in this forested, provincial Austrian location, which is the Styria of Jelinek's early childhood – *Lust* and *Die Lieb-haberinnen* do not belong together in terms of social milieu. Gerti's husband is the director of a paper-producing works which places them quite squarely in the upper-middle classes.

By concentrating on an upper middle-class woman in *Lust*, it could be said that Jelinek is concerned to show the non-class specific nature of all women's oppression and thus that the novel represents a departure from Marxism towards a radical feminist argument that women's oppression is a function not of capitalism but simply of male power. In fact, the choice of middle-class 'protagonists' for *Lust* adds another dimension to the Marxist perspective rather than detracting from it. As Marxists have argued, in the domestic economy of marriage, the wife becomes the proletarian to the bourgeois husband. The home is at least one place where men – oppressed by capitalism – can feel they are the boss and be in control, and to this end they need no special qualifications.[14] Or in Jelinek's terms, 'as we know, there is no man who is so poor, so exploited and worn out that he doesn't have somebody else who is still worse off – his wife' (Jelinek in Sauter 1981: 109). Indeed, Jelinek would seem to be illustrating Engels' thesis of bourgeois marriage equating to a kind of prostitution: the wife fulfils the role of courtesan with the only difference being that 'she does not let out her body on piecework as a wageworker, but sells it once and for all into slavery' (Engels in Jaggar 1983: 246). As Jelinek jokes in *Die Liebhaberinnen*, 'the women remain sales assistant or part-time sales assistant until their marriage, once they're married, that's the end of selling, then they are sold themselves' (12).

Die Klavierspielerin

In the 1970s Jelinek had been seen as a relative 'outsider', but the 1983 publication, *Die Klavierspielerin*, assured her growing reputation and brought her widespread acclaim and international acknowledgement. Due to the author's admission in interviews that the novel had incorporated autobiographically based ideas, it was also the text which seemed to endorse biographical readings of her work. Indeed, Jelinek's own life and upbringing, her political opinions, her manner of dressing, her make-up even, have all been subjects for discussion in the countless interviews with her and also in journalistic articles about her.[15] Jelinek cannot be said to have shied away from media contact and indeed talks about herself in quasi-psychoanalytic terms, fuelling those critics who try to sell her as a neurotic feminist who cannot be taken seriously because of her politics and personal inadequacies.[16] It is interesting to speculate whether Jelinek's sex has played a significant part in establishing her controversial status. To my mind, the fact that the harsh critique of Austria and the unpalatable heterosexuality of her novels have come from a vocal and forceful, Marxist *woman* has indeed contributed to some of the rather venomous reactions to her work.[17]

Die Klavierspielerin has caused debate among feminist readers due to its controversial depiction of the main character's sexuality and the oppressive mother-daughter relationship of Frau Kohut and her middle-aged daughter Erika. In keeping with her other novels, in *Die Klavierspielerin* Jelinek does not so much present a story as describe a situation. However, unlike both *Lust* and *Die Liebhaberinnen*, *Die Klavierspielerin* is much closer to a conventional narrative: Erika is less of a type than a fully-fledged character and is depicted with a degree of psychology and detail not present in many of Jelinek's other characters. Although it is tempting, therefore, to read *Die Klavierspielerin* as an individual, pathological 'case study' (Erika's sexual development can certainly be seen as a result of her traumatic and artificially prolonged 'infancy'), Jelinek repeatedly emphasises the representative nature of her figures by the use of generic terms such as 'the woman' 'the Man', 'Mother', 'the daughter', suggesting that there is something in the structure of these relationships which has much wider relevance. Karin Kathrein recognises in Jelinek's mother-daughter drama the hidden mechanisms of society, and argues against a reading of *Die Klavierspielerin* as a detached and individualised plot with no larger reverberations: 'as unusual as this story may seem, it does reflect the sinister mechanisms, the laws which secretly govern our lives' (Kathrein 1983). The novel confronts its female readers with some of the structures of dependency and guilt experienced and negotiated to more or less successful extent in all mother-daughter relationships. Who, for example, could fail to share Erika's guilt at having struck her mother: 'Mother swears that Erika's hand will drop off because she hit her mother and tore out her hair. Erika sobs louder and louder. She's sorry. After all, her mama works her fingers to the bone for her' (8).

The 'situation', then, against which Erika, the 'piano player' of the title tries to rebel, is her mother's treatment of her as a child and her refusal to allow her daughter to pursue relationships with men. Such a relationship might take Erika away from her and ultimately put an end to the mother's plans to save up her daughter's earnings so that they can buy their own house. The two women live alone, since the father is long dead, but their relationship is akin to that of husband and wife, with Erika as the bread-winning husband and the mother as caring wife. Indeed, the two share a bed.

The novel functions in a sense as an anti-artist's novel.[18] Erika's story is not one of the genius artist, but is the rather pitiful story of a would-be concert pianist, a woman who is pushed by her mother but does not have the necessary talent and must settle for her status as 'piano player'.[19] Jelinek thus points a satirical finger at the pursuit of musical excellence for material ends, as she shows the results of Frau Kohut's petty bourgeois aspirations and protective confinement of her daughter. Erika's sexuality has not developed 'normally', instead she has become a voyeur who visits peep shows and porn cinemas and watches couples copulating in the park. Prevented from forming physical relationships with men, Erika takes out her frustrations on her own body, mutilating it with a razor-blade and pinching it with clothes-pegs. Her self-mutilation is not a desperate attempt to feel something, however, to experience pain as a compensation for her lack of sexual pleasure. She sticks pins into her entire body but draws the line at poking them down behind her finger-nails, since this would really hurt! 'Erika doesn't dare prick herself under her fingernails; it's too painful' (249). Erika acts out of self-hatred, out of disgust at herself and out of her inability to enter into a loving relationship.

The second part of the novel focuses on Erika's attempted relationship with one of her pupils, Walter Klemmer. Klemmer has chosen Erika as a means of practising a thing or two before he moves on to a younger, prettier sexual partner, and, having at first scorned his advances, Erika enters into a relationship with him where the two vie for control. This is the crucial problem of the novel and links in with the issues of women's subjectivity and sexuality alluded to above with respect to *Lust*. Erika tries to take the initiative with Klemmer, writing him a letter with strict instructions as to what he may and may not do to her and containing a gruesome list of her sado-masochistic fantasies. Klemmer is disgusted, but more importantly, his masculinity is threatened as Erika tries to dictate to him how he should behave.

After a series of frustrated sexual encounters and having finally read Erika's letter, the tension culminates in Klemmer's brutal beating and rape of Erika. The fact that Klemmer has failed to recognise that Erika is not serious about her demands of him, in fact that 'instead of torturing her, she wants him to practice [*sic*] love with her according to Austrian standards' (231) is in a sense immaterial. It is not so much *what* Erika wishes to have done to her which angers Klemmer, but *that* she should presume to take command of his, Klemmer's, sexuality. Although Erika assures Klemmer that 'What I've written isn't carved in stone!' (230), Klemmer's musical ear is attuned to the sexual politics of what is happening between them, and her promises and assurances only vex him further. Klemmer can hear the command in her voice: 'Promises, emitted unclearly, drive the young man crazy: He hears the subliminal command as an intermediate tone' (243).

Conclusion

It is no coincidence that Erika should choose writing as her medium for trying to assert her sexuality in *Die Klavierspielerin*. This act of fixing words on paper stands metaphorically for women's attempts to express their desire, however contradictory, unpalatable, or 'un'-feminist this might be. But as the narrator ironically informs us, using Klemmer's comment to do so: 'There's nothing worse than a woman who wants to rewrite Creation' (263). These words might stand as a description of, and testimony to, Jelinek's own writing which remains fixed on the page for all to read. Jelinek's writing is all about uncovering oppressive structures in social interaction, about describing the world in different terms, indeed about 'rewriting'. Her writing is 'wicked', non-conformist, pessimistic and yet funny, it does not easily fit in with notions of how women should write, nor indeed with how feminists should write. It is in this sense that Jelinek's uncomfortable writing can be enlisted as a contribution to feminist aesthetics. Sigrid Weigel has advocated the adoption of a 'squinting gaze', or 'double focus' by women writers. She writes:

> What the liberated woman will look like cannot be imagined with any certainty or in any detail at the moment, let alone how she will be experienced. In order to live through this transitional space between the *no longer* and the *not yet* without going mad, it is necessary for woman to learn to look in two diverging directions simultaneously. She must learn to voice the contradictions, to see them, to comprehend them, to live in and with them, and also learn to gain strength from the rebellion against yesterday and from the anticipation of tomorrow. (Weigel 1985: 73)

The novels discussed here may be negative in outlook and present only small signs of rebellion in their subject-matter, but they undoubtedly work towards a better understanding of yesterday, a 'yesterday' which by Jelinek's analysis may not yet be over.

Notes

1. Quotations from the three novels discussed here are taken from the following English translations: *Women As Lovers* (1994), *The Piano Teacher* (1988) and *Lust* (1992). All other translations are my own.
2. As this book has noted on several occasions, the term *Frauenliteratur* is possibly less acceptable than the English terms 'women's writing', 'feminine aesthetics', or the French *écriture féminine*, since it carries strong connotations of a form of 'light fiction' (*Trivialliteratur*), specifically, as Sigrid Weigel points out, 'the nineteenth-century tradition of women's sentimental and often serialised popular novels'. See Weigel 1984: 53.
3. Other novels and plays not mentioned in the present chapter include: *wir sind lockvögel baby!* (1970), *Burgtheater* (1984b, original version 1982), *Clara S.* (1984a, original version 1981), *Wolken. Heim* (1990a), and *Totenauberg* (1991). Jelinek's poetry collections are: *Lisas Schatten* (1967) and *ende. gedichte 1966–1968* (1980). She also wrote the film script for *Malina* (1991), based on the novel by Ingeborg Bachmann.
4. On leaving the Austrian Communist party Jelinek admitted that her trust in the Communism of the GDR had been deluded. See her interview with Andrea Hodoschek (Hodoschek 1991).
5. The multiplicity of political standpoints in fact makes it more sensible to speak of feminist literatures.
6. Hans Christian Kosler calls this her first '*attempt* at a realist novel' (my emphasis) and criticises her for not achieving the sort of realism he demands. See Kosler 1981: 4. The problem of realism which beset early Jelinek criticism is discussed in Fiddler 1994: 26–34.
7. The lower case initials used for proper names in the original are reproduced here.
8. For an analysis of *Die Liebhaberinnen* as a parody of romantic fiction, see Fiddler 1994: 72–76.
9. Possible examples of positive figures are the vampires of *Krankheit oder Moderne Frauen* (1987), who threaten the patriarchal order, if only for a moment. A further example of a potentially positive moment is the hesitant ending to Jelinek's radio play, *Die Bienenkönige* (1982).
10. For a clear explanation of these psychoanalytic theories, see Weedon 1987: 54–55.
11. It is, of course, no coincidence that 'the Direktor' manufactures paper – the product onto which he can 'make his mark'. 'The Man uses and dirties the woman as if she were the paper he manufactures' (*Lust*: 57).
12. Jelinek works here as elsewhere with types. 'Die Frau' can of course mean both 'the woman' and 'the wife'.

13. For a reading of *Lust* as anti-pornography, see Fiddler 1991.
14. For Marxist feminist accounts of the family, see Delphy and Leonard 1992, especially chapter 3.
15. Consider, for example, titles such Agnes Hüfner's 'Warum ist das Schminken für Sie wichtig, Frau Jelinek?' (1986), or Hanna Molden's interview for 'Cosmo', 'Die kultivierte Neurose' (1985).
16. This process arguably reached its climax in an interview with André Müller. Müller's manipulation of Jelinek was skilful if impertinent, and he forced his interviewee to admit that, 'I carry the phrases out in front of me like placards behind which I can hide' (Jelinek in Müller 1990).
17. For one such venomous response, see Leitner 1986. For more information on Jelinek's reception, see Lamb-Faffelberger 1992, and Meyer 1994.
18. For a discussion of *Die Klavierspielerin* as an anti-*Künstlerroman*, see Wigmore 1990: 213-214.
19. The English title of 'The Piano *Teacher*' may have been chosen to evoke feminine connotations to match the feminine ending of the German original, but it does not do justice to this aspect: Jelinek deliberately refuses Erika the dignity of being called a piano 'teacher'.

Chapter Sixteen

WOMEN'S WRITING IN GERMAN-SPEAKING SWITZERLAND

Engaging with Tradition – Eveline Hasler and
Gertrud Leutenegger

Christine Flitner

Owing to Switzerland's neutrality during the Second World War,
1945 is a year which does not have the same significance in Swiss
literature or indeed Swiss history as in the literature of the German states and Austria. This fact does little, however, to explain
what sets German-Swiss literature apart from the literature of
other German-speaking regions, something which is a subject of
much debate.[1]

The existence of this debate testifies to the problematic search
for identity which Switzerland, a 'nation by intent', is undergoing
now-a-days. This is illustrated most markedly by the differences
between the various linguistic regions, highlighted particularly in
recent referenda over closer ties with Europe. Whereas the cantons
in French-speaking Switzerland welcomed greater links with
Europe and voted in favour of membership of the European
Union, people in German-speaking Switzerland voted against it.

Historical Context: Switzerland and Europe

The historical reasons for the country's detachment from its neighbours lie in Switzerland's vulnerable position in the Second World
War when, hemmed in by the fascist governments of Germany
and Italy, it kept to its policy of neutrality, and capitalising on the
population's desire to defend itself, united its people. The need to

fall back on its own resources culturally, economically, politically and militarily resulted among other things in a movement to defend the country's intellectual heritage and preserve its cultural independence from the axis powers, Germany and Italy. Swiss-German dialects, for example, were cultivated in order to accentuate the country's separateness from Germany. The cultural organisation 'Pro Helvetia' was founded in 1938 with the aim of spreading Swiss culture abroad and underlining Swiss independence. The organisation still promotes culture today. 'Landi 39', an exhibition of Swiss technology and culture, was staged to reinforce domestic awareness of Swiss products and values. A land-use scheme called the 'Wahlen-Plan' (also known as the 'cultivation battle') was devised to ensure that, with the aid of the entire population, enough food could be produced to make the country self sufficient.

The success of Swiss policy during the Second World War reinforced the people's confidence in the superiority of their government and political institutions. In retrospect, many Swiss men and women came to see their country's conduct only in terms of resistance to fascism. Critical voices, on the other hand, pointed to the extent to which Switzerland supported and profited from German fascism by its willingness to undertake money and gold transactions for the Nazis. There was particular criticism of the country's restrictive refugee policy which refused admission to numerous, mainly Jewish refugees and handed back illegal immigrants to the German authorities.[2]

The post-war years up to the 1970s saw a period of continuous economic growth in Switzerland which brought individual prosperity to large sectors of the population and gave Switzerland one of the highest living standards of anywhere in the world. This trend was accompanied by a loss of interest in politics on the part of the general public. Since 1959 the seven-member federal government has been constituted according to the so-called 'magic formula' which divides seats between the political parties regardless of election results. Thus there is no real opposition even in parliament, since all the major parties are part of the government. Since 1937 there have been peace agreements between employers and trade unions which prevent strikes and lock outs. These agreements were retained even after the fascist threat had disappeared. The resulting stability has led to a steady decline in turnout in elections and referenda, with 60 percent of the electorate voting in general elections and under 40 percent in referenda on individual issues.

In the 1930s the political and economic situation also persuaded bourgeois and socialist women's organisations to join together to form the Arbeitsgemeinschaft Frau und Demokratie (Organisation for Women and Democracy). The most important issues of the period between the wars were obtaining the vote for women and improving the position of working women. Many women hoped that they would be given the vote after the war in recognition of the part they played in defending the country. However, the reticence of middle-class women and their wish to avoid conflict meant that their demands were not taken seriously. The referendum in February 1959 (in which, of course, only men were allowed to vote) was a disaster, with 69 percent of votes cast against women's suffrage. Nevertheless, during the 1960s individual cantons introduced the right of women to vote at canton level. In 1968 the discussion on equal rights was given fresh impetus when Switzerland intended to sign the European Convention on Human Rights (which guarantees the equality of men and women) subject to an opt-out clause on this question.

At the same time the emergence of a New Left towards the end of the 1960s saw an increase in the numbers of people involving themselves in politics and questioning authority in Switzerland. In 1968 violent conflicts between young people and the police in Zurich and the scandal of the Bührle armaments factory, which had broken an embargo to export arms to Nigeria, shattered Switzerland's image of itself as a stable, democratic state. The formation of the POCH (Progressive Organisations of Switzerland) provided a platform for opposition voices to air left-wing and later ecological concerns. In 1969 a number of women organised a successful march to Berne to reinforce their demands, an action which also received support from a section of the traditional women's suffrage organisations. The government was finally forced to act and in 1971 introduced the vote for women at national level.

Uneasiness about the country's politics began to spread to writers in Switzerland. In 1970 an entire group of mainly young male and female writers broke away from the Association of Swiss Writers (Schweizerischer Schriftstellerverband, SSV) because of differences with the traditionalist stance of the executive. They founded an alternative writers' union *Gruppe Olten*, which expressed in its statutes the aim of creating a 'democratic socialist society'. Today both organisations are officially recognised as writers' unions and receive funding from the government.

The growing democratisation of large sections of the population was matched, however, on the other side by a reinforcing of reactionary forces which feared that traditional Swiss values were under threat. In September 1970 the radical right-wing organisation Nationale Aktion sponsored the Schwarzenbach Initiative to protest about the foreign workers brought into Switzerland since the beginning of the 1960s.[3] The turnout for the referendum was unusually high and the initiative was only narrowly defeated. Foreign workers were also the main victims of the economic crisis which gripped Switzerland – and other European countries – in the 1970s. By declining to renew large numbers of labour contracts and sending workers back to their countries of origin, Switzerland managed to maintain a sensationally low unemployment rate – under 1 percent – and reconfirm its image of stability.

Switzerland's official image of itself is based to a great extent on the belief that the country's democratic ideals, its neutrality and its army were the reasons why the country managed to escape involvement in the Second World War, and grow in stability and prosperity afterwards. All three factors therefore continue to occupy a prominent position in official Swiss thinking. Switzerland's political constitution, which is based on the concept of direct democracy, ensures that citizens have a direct vote on important issues affecting public life. The growth of grassroots democratic political forms in the 1970s, coupled with a growing wish among the people to become involved in political life, led to an enormous increase in the number of issues which became subjects of referenda. Today the Swiss electorate votes every four months on a whole series of questions at local, cantonal and national level, some of which require detailed, specialist knowledge. Issues on which the people might be called on to vote include loans for extending a gym hall, the naturalisation of immigrant children, charges for refuse disposal or the legalisation of abortion.

The frequency of referenda and their complexity has led, as in general elections, to a steady decline in turnout. The complexity of the issues also means that where they are in any doubt, voters tend to vote against change so that the results are generally conservative. Similar conservatism is evident in the wish of the German-Swiss population to retain political and economic neutrality. This represents an unspoken desire to ensure continuing prosperity and economic stability in Switzerland in the face of developments in the rest of Europe. Thus the population voted against joining the United Nations in 1986 and the European Union in

1992, going against the explicit recommendations of the government. Regardless of these decisions, the government, however, continues to pursue a policy of European integration and is pressing on with Switzerland's economic integration into Europe at the bilateral level.

Women in Switzerland

The country's separation from the outside world, coupled with the relatively high standard of living, has had the effect of slowing down the introduction of social legislation when compared with the rest of Western Europe – something which seems anachronistic to many outsiders. This has also affected the social status of women in Switzerland. Often quoted in the international press is the example of women in the rural canton of Appenzell-Innerrhoden, who were finally granted the vote by federal decree in 1990, against the declared will of their male counterparts. In fact, as stated above, universal suffrage was not introduced until 1971, some fifty years later than in most neighbouring countries. An official article guaranteeing equality has only existed since 1981 and some of the relevant amendments to legislation are still outstanding.

The effects of this late and halting development can be seen in the discrimination against women still written into legislation on issues ranging from maternity leave to retirement pensions. It is also revealed in family-related and social bills which almost without exception assume a traditional social division of labour with the man as bread-winner and the woman looking after the home and children. While the law officially gave husband and wife equal status in 1987, socially this is far from the case. Maternity leave lasts eight weeks and there is no long-term parental leave or provision to keep jobs open. There are hardly any state creches, after-school care, nurseries and the school system are organised on the assumption that mothers will be available all day. Child care has to be privately arranged and financed, and women (as is also the case in the rest of Europe) earn on average one third to a quarter less than men and are at a disadvantage in terms of pensions.

Nevertheless there are just as many working women in Switzerland as in other European countries. The 1990 national census reveals that nearly 60 percent of Swiss women go to work and women account for 40 percent of the workforce.[4] However, the proportion of women engaged in part-time work is very high (over 90 percent), career breaks to bring up children are longer, and the status of working women is generally more at risk, particularly in times of recession.

The firmly rooted trust of Swiss men and women in the effectiveness of democratic institutions has also manifested itself in the new women's movement: in 1977 POCH women founded a feminist organisation OFRA (Organisation for Women's Affairs) which over the years has attracted a major section of the women's movement and acted as their mouthpiece. As in other Western European countries, the focus of their work has been on socio-political issues such as the right to abortion, equal pay and improvements to social legislation.

How far from self-evident the right to equal treatment remains even today, was demonstrated by the 'women's strike', a day of action staged in 1991 to draw attention to the lower pay of women and other disadvantages. The wave of polemic and denunciation unleashed on this campaign for women's legal rights was out of all proportion to the peacefulness of the action and shows that many Swiss people pay little more than lip service to the concept of the legal and economic equality of women.

The traditional social division of labour is also reinforced by the importance of the army which, as a militia, calls up all men between the ages of twenty and forty for regular exercises, thus creating an excellent, highly efficient male network of informal contacts which extends into business and private lives. Few referenda in recent years have therefore attracted so much attention as the initiative in 1989 to abolish the army. The considerable success of the sponsors of the initiative, supported among others by the author Max Frisch, indicates that many Swiss men and women, particularly the young, are critical of this system and want to see it changed.

Literature

While 1945 is of limited significance in Swiss literature as a year marking a division between periods, two authors belonging clearly and unmistakably to the post-war generation have achieved international recognition: Max Frisch and Friedrich Dürrenmatt. They dominated German-speaking literature in Switzerland after 1945 and remain for many the only names known outside Switzerland. There are also, however, a number of 'second generation' writers including Adolf Muschg, Otto F. Walter, Hermann Burger, Urs

Jaeggi and Peter Bichsel who have found recognition beyond Swiss borders at least in the German-speaking world. Women's writing up until the 1970s has received little attention. Histories of literature tend to mention only two women writers, if any, from this period, the lyric poets Erika Burkhart and Silja Walter.

Writers in Switzerland are very much dependent on the German book market. Although Switzerland is regarded as a country of readers, and statistics show that the Swiss spend on average more time and money on books than the Germans for instance, or the British, Swiss publishing houses and Swiss writers are economically dependent on finding an audience in Germany.[5] There are therefore a whole series of writers who prefer to be published by German publishers. The Swiss literary scene is consequently strongly influenced by developments in Germany and trends and currents in the German book market are reflected in Switzerland. A good example of this situation is the case of Verena Stefan from Berne, whose first book *Häutungen* (1975, *Shedding,* 1978) became a cult work for the women's movement in Germany in the 1970s and, following this success, found its way back to Switzerland. Very few readers were aware that the writer, whose book had been published by the then newly established Verlag Frauenoffensive in Munich, was Swiss.

The increased awareness in women's interests and therefore women's writing led to an improvement in publishing conditions for women in Switzerland as elsewhere, and many women writers published works in the 1970s and 1980s, among them Laure Wyss, Erica Pedretti, Eveline Hasler, Ingeborg Kaiser, Maja Beutler, Margrit Schriber, Hanna Johansen, Rahel Hutmacher, Ilma Rakusa, Mariella Mehr, Verena Stefan and Gertrud Leutenegger.[6] Many of them were over forty when their first books were published, coming on the scene significantly later than their male colleagues, a fact ascribed at the time to the lifestyles of the women, who did not begin to write until after bringing up families. In reality, the large number of publications by women writers which have appeared since the beginning of the 1970s is more an expression of increased public awareness and improved publishing conditions, than an increase in literary output. This is confirmed by research which has since been carried out into women's writing in Switzerland. It disproves the claim that there were hardly any women writing prior to 1970. In fact a group of women researchers identified over 900 women publishing in the period between 1700 and 1945.[7]

The earliest known example of women's writing is the work of the fourteenth-century nun Elisabeth Stagel who wrote *Das Leben der hl. Schwestern zu Toess* and a biography of her teacher.[8] Thereafter, up to the eighteenth century only isolated texts by women are documented, but for the nineteenth and early twentieth century a large number of women writers have been found, some of whom have since been successfully republished.[9]

A more recent example of a female writer whose work was ahead of her time and therefore not properly recognised is the lawyer Iris von Roten, a campaigner for votes for women. In the 1950s she wrote *Frauen im Laufgitter*, a seminal work on the situation of women in modern society, 'the book that I would like to have read at twenty but could not find', as she wrote in the foreword. The book was mauled by the press at the time and dismissed even by the women's movement as too aggressive. It soon sank into oblivion, much to the bitterness of the author, who then turned her mind to other subjects and would have nothing more to do with women's rights. The work was reissued to great acclaim after the author's death at the beginning of the 1990s and remained on the bestseller lists for many weeks. Thirty years after its first publication, the book, still topical, finally found an audience.

It would be futile to try to extract specific characteristics or dominant themes from the wide range of contemporary literature by women writers in Switzerland. It is possible, for example, to find as many items of proof in support of, as against, the claim that women writers concentrate particularly on matters of the home.[10] Any attempt to do so should therefore be understood more as a possible method of classification than as a statement on dominant themes.

In fact it is very difficult to identify such currents in the modern works of German-Swiss women writers, so varied are the writers and their works. The spectrum of styles includes radically subjective narratives (e.g., the works of Erica Pedretti and Ilma Rakusa), dialect literature (Helene Beyeler), experimental prose (Margrit von Dach), experiential reportage (Rosalia Wenger, Mariella Mehr), immigrant literature (Irena Brezna), historical novels (Eveline Hasler), reports (Laure Wyss) and lyric poetry (Ingeborg Kaiser). What characterises many of these writers, however, is the importance of Switzerland as a setting for their work. Living conditions and experiences in very hidebound and patriarchal circumstances are often the reason for writing or in other cases form a background to the work.

The great significance of tradition and its effect on the way of life of women, and the tendency of society 'to stress continuity and overlook discrepancy' (Rasmussen 1989: 164) raises the question of how women writers in Switzerland see the literary and social traditions and how they deal with them. Two writers who very consciously confront the question of tradition in their works are Eveline Hasler and Gertrud Leutenegger. Both began writing and publishing in the 1970s and are today among Switzerland's better known women writers, whose progress is followed with interest by the press and public.

The traditions of Swiss society, their continued effect in the present, and their impact on the reality of women's lives play a central role in the works of both writers. They have, however, developed quite different forms in which to confront these issues. While Hasler uses historical sources to write novels about the lives of Swiss women from the past, Leutenegger draws on mythical material, reinterpreting it and linking it to subjective experiences.

'Searching for the cultivators of the stony soil' – Eveline Hasler

Eveline Hasler (b. 1933) studied psychology and history before working as a teacher and writing children's books for which she received a number of awards. Her first novel *Novemberinsel* was published in 1979. She first achieved fame, however, with her extremely successful historical novel *Anna Göldin. Letzte Hexe*, which was published in 1982. Her simple use of language, coupled with the great success of her books, has meant that she has tended to be disregarded or treated with condescension by some literary critics.

Anna Göldin. Letzte Hexe

The last witchcraft trial in Europe was held in 1782 in Eveline Hasler's home canton of Glarus. A servant woman, Anna Göldin, was accused of having bewitched a child of the household in which she worked, making it spit needles and pins. The accused confessed, was sentenced by the court and executed. Sources show that the trial provoked great controversy even at the time. The courts in Glarus were ridiculed and criticised by more enlightened cities in Switzerland and Germany. In her novel, Hasler attempts to explain how a witchcraft trial could come to take place in the heart of Europe during the heyday of the Enlightenment.

In order to write her novel the author studied the trial documents and further sources on living conditions in the steep Swiss
mountain valley. The novel is faithful to the historical facts, em-
bellishing them in order to flesh out the life of a servant woman in
the eighteenth century. The book takes up the story at the point
when the protagonist starts her last job which is to seal her fate.
The ongoing narrative of the 'bewitched' daughter of the household falling ill, the accusations against the servant woman, her
flight, subsequent capture and condemnation is interrupted by
various flashbacks which gradually reveal the story of Anna
Göldin's life.

The child of a poor peasant family, she is placed in service as a
maid. Made pregnant by a servant in the household who then
deserts her, she is accused of infanticide when the child dies at
birth. She becomes pregnant a second time by a young master, is
once again deserted and has to foster out the child before finding
another situation. Anna Göldin is on the bottom rung of the social
ladder. Her story is the story of any woman from a poor background in the Swiss mountains in the eighteenth century. As a
stranger she is regarded with mistrust in Glarus, lacking continuity and family ties, her life does not follow the prevailing pattern:

> She'd been in Glarus before, moved away, then come back again;
> she'd changed her job several times, a tricky path.
>   Here, there.
>   And at an age where others had long settled down. A woman
> shouldn't do that.
>   At least not one from her station in life.
>   You know what they say about picking up stones which are
> lying where they fell. She should have stayed in Sennwald, the rel-
> atives say. You should stay where you belong. If you don't stay, you
> don't belong anywhere.
>   You have only yourself to blame. (Hasler 1992a: 9)

By deviating from the narrow prescribed path, Anna Göldin cuts
herself off from a society which will not tolerate anything out of
the ordinary. As a maid and a single woman she has no rights and
is seen as a dangerous outsider. For the women of the village she
symbolises independence, self-determination and even sexual
freedom and thus represents a threat to the established order.
Because her stylish clothing is not the customary garb of servants,
she is suspected of challenging the divide between master/mis-
tress and servant:

Come to think of it, this person is dressed too haughtily for her station. Frau Tschudi examines Göldin's skirt. A skirt in fashionable
colours! Only Lieutenant Marti's wife wears a skirt like that; this
shimmering, almost brownish violet is supposed to be all the rage in
Paris. The ladies saw it for themselves at the last tea party: today you
have to look twice to see who's the mistress and who the maid. (14)

Thus the story of witch-hunting becomes a story of the persecution of the oppressed. Witch-hunting becomes a question of power
and powerlessness, of social hierarchies. The servant girl, Anna
Göldin, is too independent in the eyes of those around her and
therefore represents a threat to the established order which must
be upheld at the cost of her destruction.

Scattered throughout the narrative are extracts from the court
documents and contemporary reports. These extracts appear in a
different typeface and are therefore readily identifiable as original
sources. The writer also lists the sources she uses in an appendix
and makes a reference at the beginning of the text to her historical
research: 'On Anna's trail I looked in these books for those who
cultivated the stony soil' (7). Thus she draws attention to the historical content of her novel and at the same time describes her
work in terms of following a trail to reveal the history of women
hidden behind official history.

Ibicaba oder Das Paradies in den Köpfen

Historical sources were also the basis of Hasler's book *Ibicaba oder
Das Paradies in den Köpfen* (1992b). In the nineteenth century, poverty
forced numerous Swiss people to emigrate, some of them to Brazil
where they were promised riches and prosperity in the coffee plantations. Touting organisations recruited likely emigrants in Switzerland, arranged for the local authorities to advance their travel
costs and published reports from emigrants extolling the virtues of
life on the plantations. In reality, instead of the promised paradise,
those emigrants who survived the voyage encountered slave-like
working conditions and were ruthlessly exploited. A teacher from
the canton Graubünden, who led a group of emigrants in 1855,
managed after years of perseverance, to return to Switzerland and
report on the true conditions in the plantations. His report eventually led the Swiss authorities to intervene, albeit without much
forcefulness or success, on behalf of the Swiss people remaining
there. The report written by the teacher, Thomas Davatz, his hand-
written records, the emigrant newspapers and other sources form
the basis of Hasler's novel. It tells the story of a group of people led

by a teacher who emigrate to Ibicaba in the hope of finding a better life. After their arrival, however, all the extravagant promises gradually prove to be lies. In order to start their new life the emigrants are forced deeply into debt, and the barren land and leasehold conditions offer little possibility for them ever to extricate themselves. Only the tenacity of the teacher makes it possible for his family finally to return to Switzerland.

The writer brings the historical documents to life through her sympathetic description and psychological interpretation of the characters. Hasler contrasts the central, historical figure of the teacher who leads the group and acts as its representative in the outside world with a female character, an 'unmarried mother' attached to the teacher's family who hopes to find a better life abroad and possibly to live one day with the father of her son. Thus Hasler supplements the historical material with a female figure with whom her readers can identify. This character is able to conceive of an independent life as a woman, in opposition to society's narrow norms, even if this might be a purely utopian dream.

Die Wachsflügelfrau

Die Wachsflügelfrau, which appeared in 1991, once again has at its centre the fate of a Swiss woman. Emily Kempin-Spyri (1853–1901), a niece of Johanna Spyri, author of *Heidi*, was the first woman lawyer in Europe. With the support of her husband she took her school-leaving certificate after the birth of her third child, and studied jurisprudence at Zurich University, gaining her doctorate in 1887. But although Zurich was the first German-speaking university in Europe to admit women, (doing so from the 1860s onwards, when women came from all over Europe to study there), Emily Kempin was not permitted to practise her profession in Switzerland. Her attempts to work both as a lawyer and university lecturer were blocked by Zurich society. She then went to the United States with her family, where she founded the Women's Law School in New York. Out of consideration for her husband, who was unable to make a living in the United States, and in the (unfulfilled) hope of a chair, Emily Kempin returned to Zurich in 1892. In 1896 she separated from her husband and eventually moved to Berlin to practise law. Despite her brilliance and commitment, Emily Kempin-Spyri was thwarted by the narrow-mindedness of those around her, who refused to accept an independent female lawyer and placed numerous obstacles in her path. After suffering a nervous breakdown in Berlin, she entered a psychiatric clinic in Basel where she was detained against her will until she died of cancer in 1901. The few remaining personal records of Emily Kempin-Spyri include a letter from the qualified lawyer applying for a position as housekeeper in an attempt to escape the institution – a tragic document testifying to one woman's depressing fate. Like other letters it was held back by the clinic and never reached its recipient.

Hasler's novel attempts to reconstruct the life of this remarkable woman, about whom only a few personal documents survive. The fact that the Basel clinic allegedly has no records of its former patient, although the author gained access by other means to documents from her medical file, is evidence in Eveline Hasler's eyes of the suppression of an 'undesirable', which persists even to the present day:

> There is no trace here of Kempin; they have erased all resistance, the cancer did its work from the inside, a thin skin, decayed. The Director of the Basel institution has written: *Not even so much as a personal record*. Even today, one hundred years later, she is not allowed to exist, Emily Kempin-Spyri, the first woman lawyer. (Hasler 1991: 333)

As in the preceding novels, original sources blend with contemporary documents in the text which reconstructs the life of the lawyer in narrative and in fictitious dialogues. While the mixture of fiction and historical sources generates a convincing picture of the times, particularly where the fate of individuals reflects the history of the ordinary people of the eighteenth and nineteenth centuries, the method is less convincing in the *Die Wachsflügelfrau*. The writer adopts the standpoint of omniscient narrator, turning the central figure into a character in a novel, whose inner life is as accessible to the writer as her legal publications. Her portrayal blurs the boundaries between fact and fiction, making it unclear where the writer is recounting what is known and where she is inventing. Thus the novel creates a complete and unbroken picture which turns Kempin-Spyri into a storybook character and obscures rather than highlights the suppression of the real historical figure.

'This Vulnerable Bird called Love' – Gertrud Leutenegger

Gertrud Leutenegger's method of dealing with and handing down tradition is very different from Hasler's. Born in Schwyz in central Switzerland in 1948 and brought up there, Leutenegger studied directing at the Drama Academy in Zurich while writing her first novels. Unlike Hasler she does not write stories with a developing narrative; her works consist of impressions, thoughts and memories expressed in dense, symbol-laden language. Disparate experiences, facts and perceptions are woven together to form a dense, often almost impenetrable whole. It is therefore almost impossible to recount what happens in Leutenegger's works since the action generally forms only the barest of skeletons. 'My subject is that I have none' she writes in her first novel *Vorabend* which appeared in 1975.

Vorabend describes a walk that the narrator takes, along streets through which a protest march will pass the following day. The walk evokes memories: past friendships, a love affair, work in a psychiatric clinic. The narrator's own painful memories are interwoven with a sensitive description of the feelings of alienation experienced by others: the insane person in the psychiatric clinic, the Italian maid excluded by society. Open-ended chapters and paragraphs emphasise that the memories are not finite for the narrator but reach into the present. *Vorabend* touches on a number of themes that recur throughout Leutenegger's writing: the linking of subjective and social experiences, the patriarchal order, women's need for autonomy and longing for love, the petrification of human relations and the destruction of nature.

In her next novel *Ninive*, which appeared in 1977, a young couple, Fabrizio and the female first-person narrator, meet in their home village to see a giant whale which is on display. They pass the night in conversation in front of the whale. Once again the text comprises memories, dream images and reflections, as well as concrete references to recent Swiss history. With Nineveh and the whale, the writer is taking up a biblical motif which contains both an apocalyptic vision and the hope of salvation. The fall of Nineveh is prophesied in biblical history. The whale that swallowed Jonah and disgorged him on land, thereby saving Nineveh from destruction, is an allegory for an almost irrational hope for the future.

No such optimism is evident in *Gouverneur* (1981a), Leutenegger's third prose work in which, despite the female narrator's longing for love, the dominant theme is one of alienation and violence between the sexes. The narrator has a hill constructed in the middle of a capital city as a monument to her love for the governor. Her intention is to plant the hill with lavish hanging gardens, but her plan is threatened by the governor's mausoleum. The story highlights, in an almost simplified manner, the contrast between male concern for order and its associations with death, and female activity which is concerned with growth, blossoming and ripening. The governor, as symbol of the male principle, represses the chaotically prolific female element. As in *Ninive*, the author once again makes use of motifs from Babylonian-Assyrian culture. The hanging gardens of the fabled Assyrian Queen Semiramis are among the wonders of the ancient world, reputedly built by Nebuchanezzar II for the woman he loved. In Leutenegger's story, however, the female 'I' herself designs and plants the gardens as an expression of extravagant folly, a gesture that is threatened by the male power of the governor. The use of myths from Assyrian culture highlights the continuity of patriarchal domination in Western thinking.

The perplexing or impossible utopia of love; memory and past as part of the present; antagonism between man and woman, and the destruction of the living world are the central themes which also dominate Leutenegger's two following works. *Komm ins Schiff* (1983) takes the form of a dream monologue on love and loss addressed by the first-person female narrator to a silent male, seated opposite her on a boat after she has fled from a summer festival. In contrast *Kontinent* (1985) is more realistically narrated. A young woman spends time in a village in a wine-growing region to record the noises of the village for an anniversary record for the local factory. Very gradually she is drawn into the scenery of the village which has an almost surreal quality. Into the observations and thoughts of the female protagonist flow memories of a trip to China and a love affair there. Her experience of love brings the foreign country closer than her everyday surroundings, which are made all the more disconcerting by the indifference of the village people.[11]

Lebewohl, Gute Reise

Leutenegger's third work *Lebewohl, Gute Reise*, published in 1980 and described by the author as a dramatic poem, is dominated by the same central themes as her prose: the constraints and paralyses of love affairs, female autonomy and subjectivity, antagonism between the sexes, patriarchal striving for power and the destruction of nature.

The basis of the piece, which was performed for the first time in Wuppertal in 1984, is the 'Epic of Gilgamesh'. Leutenegger uses large sections of this complex story in her poem. In the original epic, Gilgamesh, mythical king of the Sumerians, is a harsh and intemperate ruler. It is the task of Enkidu, who lives at one with nature looking after his animals, to curb Gilgamesh's excesses. A temple whore entices Enkidu to renounce his former life and live as Gilgamesh's friend. In order to make his name as a hero, Gilgamesh decides with Enkidu to conquer the sacred cedar forest of the goddess Ishtar (or Inanna). The goddess falls in love with Gilgamesh and promises him happiness at her side, but Gilgamesh rejects her. The divine bull is sent to destroy him but Gilgamesh kills it. The turning point comes when Enkidu falls ill and dies. Losing interest in power and glory, Gilgamesh is overcome by grief for his friend and fear of death. Restlessly he wanders from place to place in search of everlasting life.

The theme of the Gilgamesh epic is the breaking up of matriarchal forms of society by male domination. In her poem Leutenegger not only makes use of this motif and the subject matter of the epic, but even quotes verbatim, changing, however, the importance of the characters and including modern elements – a cassette recorder, military installations – to introduce contemporary relevance.[12] The framework of the poem is formed by the monologues of a female first-person narrator who is lying in a coffin on a mountain, reflecting on past events.

Central to Leutenegger's interpretation of the epic is the prominence she gives to the whore, an importance not ascribed to her in the original. As in *Gouverneur*, which was written at the same time, man and woman stand in opposition to one another, representing different, incompatible principles. In contrast to Gilgamesh's principle of power, the whore represents the principle of love. Gilgamesh's striving for power inevitably destroys love:

> *Gilgamesh*: … Your love frightens me like something that has been irretrievably lost; I'm not fit for such things any more, I have experienced too much. (Leutenegger 1980a: 25)

He discards and abuses the whore, and even Enkidu is snatched from the whore's embrace. The Great Mother sees in his actions Gilgamesh's fear of death:

> *Great Mother*: You are scared of death …
> He who does not fear love is immortal …
> You would not have banished her to the steppes if you had not been awed by the power of her love. (25)

The bull, which is a symbol of fertility in many cultures, stands, like the sacred rite of marriage, for the past order and is therefore killed. After killing the bull, Gilgamesh declares the goddess of fertility to be 'not only the goddess of sexual love but the goddess of war! The violent act of war is like the fiery passion of the sex act, what difference is there?!' (64). Gilgamesh can only conceive of the relationship between man and woman in terms of a battle or war. The relationship between the sexes is pervaded by the war-like character of society; marriage as a sacred ritual to overcome the antagonism between the sexes has no place in his world.

Gilgamesh's rule is based on violence and destruction: he seizes power from the Great Mother, turns the temple whore into a common prostitute, wrecks the sacred rite of marriage and destroys the goddess Inanna. Humans and nature are abused and destroyed: the suburbs turn into slums, the mountains are covered in military installations, the mountain dwellers are driven out and the fruit rots on the trees. The fertile country falls into ruin, 'it lies there sick like a mother animal left to die in the heat once it has produced enough young' (35). Contempt for humans and the destruction of nature are linked together, the product of the boundless lust for power displayed by Gilgamesh, who can only find enjoyment and satisfaction in the total subjection of the earth. Gilgamesh himself sees this as the antithesis of human love:

> *Gilgamesh*: The times are past when love could have been rapture, nothing but oblivion and warming stillness over the world; now I need other madnesses! It is not the vulnerable bird called love I crave to fly, no! I want to blast my way through the centre of the earth on a beam of pure energy and shake up its protective crust to expose it in all its nakedness. I want to harness it again, this flaming and pulsating earth, even if it hurls me out into space! (23–24)

The text repeatedly makes connections between Gilgamesh's rule and fascism – even the title of the piece points to it. '*Lebewohl, Gute Reise*' was the title of a song performed by the Comedian Harmonists popular in Germany at the time when fascism was starting to gain ground. The sentimental song runs through the piece as a leitmotif, played on a cassette recorder carried by the Great Mother and is a reminder of the beginning of a murderous and violent period of rule. Thus a parallel is drawn between Gilgamesh's rule and German fascism. At the same time the song highlights the irony of the utopia of joyous love which can only be portrayed as kitsch. Further references underline the link with fascism. These include references to a selection and race ordinance introduced by Gilgamesh (31), allusions to extermination camps and self-accusation by the victims: 'I, oaf that I am, still believe that people are being gassed in the mountains' (107), Gilgamesh's dictatorial style of leadership and the comprehensive militarisation of society.

The patriarchal domination of the world, based on the exclusion of women and the establishment of hierarchies between the sexes, is equated with the rule of the fascists and fascism is interpreted as the ultimate consequence of patriarchy. The recurring motif of blood also emphasises the bloodthirsty nature of Gilgamesh's rule. The whore has specks of blood on her garment, bleeding doves testify to the death of the Goddess Inanna, and even the walls sweat blood.

Gilgamesh's destructive actions are offset by the figure of the whore who represents the principle of love and life and tries to salvage the old traditions. The character of the whore is an amalgam of various female characters from the original Gilgamesh epic: the temple whore, the Goddess Ishtar, the innkeeper Siduri and the wife of Utnapishtim (who in the original epic meets Gilgamesh during his search for eternal life). These are all fused by the author into one character whom Gilgamesh meets again and again in the various stations of his life. Thus, the whore comes to represent the essence of womanhood whom Gilgamesh repeatedly encounters, humiliates and rejects but whom he nevertheless needs and searches for. Despite Gilgamesh's cruelty and disdain, she retains her love for him in the hope of curbing the destructive energy of both Gilgamesh and Enkidu:

> *Whore*: … I can scarcely distinguish myself any longer in you and him, as if I had no boundaries anymore and had become only a moving, flowing red. Whore! you cry, but how can I pull myself together again when I have to direct all my energies into drawing all these dark, destructive forces of yours and his to myself and not become enslaved by them. (100)

Her awareness of Gilgamesh's crimes and cruelty does not alter her courtship of him which is concerned not with individual fulfilment but with restoring the original unity of male and female principles, 'for the creation of the world separated not only light from darkness but gender from gender' (22).

Nevertheless it is impossible for the whore to remain untouched by Gilgamesh's cruelty and escape the curse of power. Through her closeness to Gilgamesh she is inevitably drawn into the circle of power and destruction, for which she curses Gilgamesh:

Whore: ... Away, away! Let the blood blind you until death, let it persecute you until your burnt-out eternity, the dove's blood of a whore who set out to learn of love and was forced to hate; thus I curse you for making me greedy for power, the power to seize your history from you, the power to destroy your hollow victories, the power to destroy your murderous achievements! (102)

Leutenegger does not attempt to mythicise womanhood, in the world of destructivity the woman cannot remain innocent. The brief love between the whore and Enkidu, which represents a utopian contrast to the ruined man-woman relationship, cannot possibly last. Their happiness in each other's company is upset by the sudden invasion of power represented by Gilgamesh's emissaries. Love becomes destruction: '*Whore*: ... How can I carry around a dead love inside me, I am being destroyed by its poison' (73).

The all-destructive power of patriarchal domination is the central theme of this work. Leutenegger does not contrast it, however, with a utopian 'natural' femininity. The factor that distinguishes the matriarchal period before Gilgamesh seized power is the lack of hierarchies between men and women. The only true alternative to patriarchal rule is co-existence between the sexes based on the absence of controlling power.

The framework of the piece is provided by the monologues of the first-person narrator reminiscing in the coffin. These monologues sometimes recount past events and sometimes predict the future. Experience can be overcome by memory: at the end the narrator rises from her coffin and starts to take action. 'Gilgamesh lives!' the narrator cries out at the end of the poem, words which can be taken to mean that Gilgamesh ultimately achieves deliverance.

Conclusion

In their approach to different historical and literary traditions Swiss women writers belong in the wider context of German-speaking contemporary women's writing, whose foremost representatives have continued to tackle the past and its legacy in very different and innovative ways, searching for the evidence of female repression and the repressed. Eveline Hasler and Gertrud Leutenegger have found two quite different but successful forms for doing so.

Hasler takes characters and events from Swiss history and gives them a meaning which differs from the accepted interpretation or puts them in a new perspective. In doing so, she supplies fragments to form a mosaic of the (as yet unwritten) history of women in Switzerland which revises and sets straight the traditional record. She fills the empty space marked 'women's history' with 'what might have been'.

Leutenegger, on the other hand, takes up myths and traditions from a wide variety of cultures to reveal their patriarchal content in the context of the present, offering new ways of interpreting the myths or reworking the old ones. What she presents, however, is not a constructive, positive image of womanhood or even a revival of the matriarchal myth. The female in her work is presented much more as an oppressed, repressed but also subversive element. She depicts women who rebel against oppression and, in her more optimistic works, creates a utopian co-existence between the sexes free of controlling power, which is a the necessary precondition for the emancipation of women.

What both writers have in common despite all their differences is a shifting of the narrator's perspective. The stories are told from the angle of women who thereby document their claim to their own historically conditioned perspective of the world.

Translated by Elizabeth Doyle

Notes

I should like to thank Yolanda Cadalbert and Barbara Spalinger for their constructive criticism and helpful suggestions. Translations from German texts cited are by Elizabeth Doyle.

1. The following deals only with the literature of German-speaking Switzerland and does not cover the literature of French or Italian Switzerland. For a discussion of the special features of German-Swiss literature, see Acker and Burkhard 1987.
2. The practice adopted by the German authorities of stamping a large 'J' in the passports of Jews in order to make them easier to identify, was introduced in 1938 at the request of the Swiss authorities who wanted to prevent Jews immigrating secretly. See Häsler 1968.
3. The main targets of the initiative were Italian workers and refugees from the countries of Africa, Asia and Latin America. In 1970, however, statistics show that German nationals constituted the largest group of foreigners in Switzerland.
4. This data is taken from the Swiss Federal Statistical Office, BFS, Berne 1993.
5. See Stiftung Lesen 1990.
6. See Elsbeth Pulver's introduction in Pulver and Dallach 1985 and Pezold 1991: 262.

7. See Stump, Widmer and Wyss 1994.
8. See *Schweizer Lexikon* 91, 1992: 718.
9. The anthology *Viel Köpfe, viel Sinn*, 1994, offers a selection of texts from the eighteenth to the twentieth centuries. Texts from the nineteenth and twentieth century are included in Wörle 1991.
10. See, for instance, Burkhard 1981. The author makes reference to a 'topical and symbolic orientation toward all forms of houses and places as closely structured living spaces that define and confine existential possibilities' (611).
11. A more detailed presentation of Leutenegger's prose works is contained in Boa 1991, which interprets Leutenegger's work as a successful fusing of socialist and psychoanalytically oriented feminism: 'Leutenegger's work conveys the variety of women's experience at different times and places and sets psychological explorations of dreams, desires and fantasies in social contexts. In that sense it interestingly bridges the division between socialist feminism and feminism influenced by psychoanalytic theory' (219).
12. A detailed presentation and interpretation of Leutenegger's handling of the Gilgamesh epic can be found in Schuscheng 1987.

AFTERWORD
Chris Weedon

Post-war Women's Writing in German-Speaking Europe is in many ways a product of the feminist cultural politics of the last thirty years. Feminism has created both the space for taking gender seriously in the study of literature and the theoretical tools necessary for its critical investigation. Developments in publishing, scholarship and teaching have radically expanded access to women's writing and enabled a rediscovery and revaluation of women writers pre-1968.

As the different parts of this book demonstrate, post-war developments in women's writing have been country specific. In Austria, Switzerland, the Federal Republic and the former German Democratic Republic the different sexual-political and cultural contexts have shaped women's writing. Its themes range from attempts to address apparently universal issues to quite specific engagements with feminist issues such as the family, lesbianism or violence against women.

The coverage of post-war women's writing in German-speaking Europe in this book has been necessarily selective. Much scope remains for further studies of women writers. Yet, we are sure that we have made the case for a rethinking of canonical views of post-war literary history. If there is one thing that this volume shows, it is that the increase in interest in women's writing over the last three decades is well-deserved. Since the Second World War, women have written powerful texts, often under difficult conditions, which should not be ghettoised under a dismissive heading *Frauenliteratur*.

The very term *Frauenliteratur*, so long associated with triviality and reclaimed in an explicitly political way by feminist critics in the 1970s, needs rethinking in mainstream literary history and criticism. In societies in which gender is a fundamental category marking difference in hierarchical ways, 'women's writing' as a category is likely to signify a difference of view given by women's different placing within the patriarchal social and cultural orders. To claim that women and men are the same is to deny the structural relations that produce difference. What is important is not to essentialise women's difference.

This point holds, too, in the area of women's writing. 'Women's writing' in post-war German-speaking Europe clearly does not express or reflect some fundamental unchanging difference between women and men. Yet, as the range of studies in this volume suggest, both the issues women write about and the ways in which they write often do differ from their male contemporaries. These differences are best explained by recourse to the social and cultural relations of patriarchal societies. Shared concerns across different social and historical contexts, for example, the questioning of meaning and subjectivity in the work of Ingeborg Bachmann and Christa Wolf, can be understood in terms of women's restricted access to apparently unified subject positions and forms of subjectivity in patriarchal societies which privilege a male norm. Here it is feminist theory which helps explain similarities without reducing different writers to the sameness implied by biologically grounded theories of women's difference.

Despite their differences of approach, the various chapters in this book share the assumption that gender is a key structuring principle in all writing and that feminist theory, in its various forms, offers useful ways of understanding the role of gender in reading and writing. Not only does feminist theory throw explicit light on implicit conceptions of gender, it enables rereadings of texts which are sensitive to questions of power. Manifestations of 'feminine' aesthetics can be seen as historically produced engagements with male-defined institutions and traditions which undervalue or marginalise women. Women's writing can be understood as shaped by both complicity and resistance to patriarchal relations of power.

# Notes on Contributors

Elizabeth Boa is Professor of Modern German Literature at the University of Nottingham. She is author of *The Sexual Circus: Wedekind's Theatre of Subversion* (1987) and co-editor along with Janet Wharton of *Women and the Wende: Social Effects and Cultural Reflection of the German Unification Process* (1994). She has also published extensively on German fiction by contemporary women writers and has just completed a feminist study of Kafka.

Johanna Bossinade is Professor (*Privatdozentin*) of Modern German Literature at the Freie Universität Berlin. She has published a book on Ödön von Horvath (1988) and *Das Beispiel Antigone* (1990). She has written on a wide range of authors, periods, themes and theoretical questions in modern literary studies. She currently teaches at the University of Hamburg.

Allyson Fiddler lectures in German Studies at the University of Lancaster where she teaches cinema and women's writing. Her research interests are in contemporary Austrian literature. She has published articles on Elfriede Jelinek as well as a full length study of Jelinek's writing entitled *Rewriting Reality: an Introduction to Jelinek* (1994).

Christine Flitner studied German and currently works in publishing in Basel. Her doctoral thesis is on the critical reception of women's writing: *Frauen in der Literaturkritik. Gisela Elsner und Elfriede Jelinek im Feuilleton der Bundesrepublik Deutschland* (1995). She has edited an anthology of British women's writing, *Frauen in Großbritannien* (1992).

Eva Kaufmann is Emeritus Professor of Modern German Literature at the Humboldt University Berlin. She is a specialist in nineteenth- and twentieth-century literature with particular emphasis on the

GDR and comparative literature. Since the 1970s she has written numerous reviews and essays on women's writing, especially from the GDR. She has edited an anthology of women's writing from 1871 to the First World War, *Herr im Haus* (1989).

Margaret Littler is a lecturer in German at the University of Manchester. She is the author of *Alfred Andersch (1914–1980) and the Reception of French Thought in the Federal Republic of Germany* (1991). She has also published on Brigitte Kronauer, Anne Duden and Claire Goll.

Franziska Meyer is lecturer in German at the University of Wales, Cardiff. She has published on East and West German post-war literature (Volker Braun, Hans Mayer and the literary policy of the Cold War). Her research interests cover German women's literature since 1918. She has recently completed her doctoral thesis on the reception of romanticism in GDR literature of the 1970s and 1980s. This focuses in particular on the image of Caroline Schlegel-Schelling. She is currently working on a book on women's writing 1850–1990.

Isolde Neubert graduated from the University of Greifswald and teaches nineteenth- and twentieth-century English literature, feminist cultural studies and literary theory at the Humboldt University Berlin. She wrote her doctoral thesis on the novels of Colin McInnes and has published on working-class writing and feminist thought. She is currently working on feminist appropriations of the fantastic in science fiction, fantasy and fairy tales.

Cettina Rapisarda taught in the Department of Modern German Literature at the Freie Universität Berlin until 1994. She is currently working on research projects at the Freie Universität and at the University of Wales, Cardiff. Her research and publications focus on eighteenth-century travelogues, educated women of the eighteenth century, the city in literature and the work of Ingeborg Bachmann.

Chris Weedon is Reader in Critical and Cultural Theory at the University of Wales, Cardiff. She has published widely on feminist theory, critical theory and women's writing. Her books include *Feminist Practice and Poststructuralist Theory* (1987, second edition 1996) and *Cultural Politics: Class, Gender, Race and the Postmodern World* (1995) written together with Glenn Jordan. She is currently working on a book on German women's writing 1850–1990. Her volume *Feminism and the Politics of Difference* will be published in 1997.

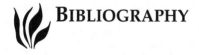

BIBLIOGRAPHY

Acker, Robert and Marianne Burkhard (eds) (1987) *Blick auf die Schweiz. Zur Frage der Eigenständigkeit der Schweizer Literatur seit 1970*. Amsterdam: Rodopi.

Adelson, Leslie (1988) 'Racism and Feminist Aesthetics: The Provocation of Anne Duden's "Opening of the Mouth"' in *Signs. Journal of Women in Culture and Society*, vol. 13, no. 2, 1988, 234–252.

Adorno, Theodor W. (1969) *Minima Moralia. Reflexionen aus dem beschädigten Leben*. Frankfurt a.M.: Suhrkamp (orig. 1951).

—— (1987) *Minima Moralia. Reflections from Damaged Life*, trans. E.F.N. Jephcott. London: Verso, (orig. 1974).

Aichinger, Ilse (1952) 'Über das Erzählen in dieser Zeit' in *Die Literatur*, vol. 1, no. 6, 1952, 1.

—— (1963) *Herod's Children*, trans. Cornelia Schaeffer. New York: Athenäum.

—— (1972) 'Story in Reverse', trans. Christopher Levenson in Richard Newnham (ed.) *German Short Stories. Deutsche Kurzgeschichten*. Harmondsworth: Penguin (orig. 1964).

—— (1978a) *Meine Sprache und ich. Erzählungen*. Frankfurt a.M.: Fischer.

—— (1978b) 'Spiegelgeschichte' in Aichinger 1978a (orig. 1952).

—— (1991) *Die größere Hoffnung*. Frankfurt a.M.: Fischer (orig. 1948).

Akzente. Zeitschrift für Dichtung (1954–1974) ed. Hans Bender. Munich: Hanser. Reprinted Frankfurt a.M. 1975: Zweitausendeins.

Alexander, Elisabeth (1978) *Die törichte Jungfrau*. Cologne: Braun.

—— (1982) *Sie hätte ihre Kinder töten sollen*. Düsseldorf: Erb.

—— (1992) *Bauchschuß*. Trier: éditions trèves.

Allerkamp, Andrea (1991) *Die innere Kolonialisierung. Bilder und Darstellungen des/der Anderen in deutschsprachigen, französischen und afrikanischen Literaturen des 20. Jahrhunderts (Studien zur Literatur- und Kulturgeschichte)*. Cologne, Weimar and Vienna: Böhlau.

Altbach, Edith Hoshino, Jeanette Clausen, Naomi Stephann and Dagmar Schultz (eds) (1984) *German Feminism. Readings in Politics and Literature*. Albany: State University of New York Press.

Althusser, Louis (with Étienne Balibar) (1970) *Reading Capital*. London: New Left Books.

Anz, Thomas (ed.) (1995) *Es geht nicht um Christa Wolf. Der Literaturstreit im vereinten Deutschland*. Frankfurt a.M.: Fischer.

Apel, Friedmar, Maria Kublitz-Kramer and Thomas Steinfeld (1993) *Kultur in der Stadt*. Paderborner Universitätsreden 36.

Bachér, Ingrid (1988) '… und die Frauen in der Gruppe 47? Bruchstücke zu einem Thema' in Schutte 1988, 91–92.

Bachmann, Ingeborg (1953) *Die gestundete Zeit*. Frankfurt a.M.: Frankfurter Verlagsanstalt.

—— (1956) *Die Anrufung des großen Bären*. Munich: Piper.

——— (1961/86) *Das dreißigste Jahr*. Munich: Piper/dtv.
——— (1964) 'Ein Ort für Zufälle. Rede zur Verleihung des Georg-Büchner-Preises' in Bachmann 1982, vol IV, 278–293.
——— (1971a) *Malina*. Frankfurt a.M.: Suhrkamp.
——— (1971b) *Requiem für Fanny Goldmann*. Munich and Zurich: Piper.
——— (1972) *Simultan*. Munich: Piper.
——— (1979) *Der Fall Franza*. Munich and Zurich: Piper.
——— (1980) *Frankfurter Vorlesungen*. Munich: Piper.
——— (1982) *Werke*, ed. Christine Koschel, Inge von Weidenbaum and Clemens Münster. Munich and Zurich: Piper.
——— (1987) *The Thirtieth Year*, trans. Michael Bullock. New York: Holmes & Meier.
——— (1989) *Malina*, trans. Philip Boehm. New York: Holmes & Meier.
Bachofen, J.J. (1975) *Das Mutterrecht*. Frankfurt a.M.: Suhrkamp (orig. 1861).
Bagley, Petra M. (1990/1991) 'The Death of a Father: the Start of a Story. Bereavement in Elisabeth Plessen, Brigitte Schwaiger and Jutta Schutting' in *New German Studies*, vol. 16, no. 1, 1990/1991, 21–38.
Baier, Jutta (1994) 'Die Kloake als Ort der Poesie' in *Frankfurter Rundschau*, 15 April 1994.
Bail, Gabriele (1984) *Weibliche Identität. Ingeborg Bachmanns Malina*. Göttingen: Heredot.
Bakhtin, M. M. (1981) *The Dialogic Imagination*. Austin, Texas: University of Texas.
Bammer, Angelika (1986) 'Testing the Limits: Christa Reinig's Radical Vision' in *Women in German Yearbook 2*, 1986. Lincoln: University of Nebraska Press, 107–127.
Barthes, Roland (1988) *Fragmente einer Sprache der Liebe*. Frankfurt a.M.: Suhrkamp.
Bartsch, Kurt and Gerhard Melzer (1993) *Ilse Aichinger*. Graz: Droschl.
Bartsch, Kurt and Günther Höfler (eds) (1991) *Elfriede Jelinek*. Graz: Droschl.
Beauvoir, Simone de (1983) *The Second Sex*. Penguin: Harmondsworth.
Bebel, August (1971) *Women Under Socialism*. New York: Schocken.
Becker, Renate (1992) *Inszenierungen des Weiblichen. Die literarische Darstellung weiblicher Subjektivität in der westdeutschen Frauenliteratur der siebziger und achtziger Jahre*. Frankfurt a.M., Berne, New York and Paris: Lang.
Behrens, Katja (1981) *Frauenbriefe der Romantik*. Frankfurt a.M.: Insel.
Beig, Maria (1982) *Rabenkrächzen*. Sigmaringen: Jan Thorbecke Verlag.
——— (1983a) *Rabenkrächzen*. Frankfurt a.M.: Suhrkamp.
——— (1983b) *Hochzeitlose, komm*. Sigmaringen: Jan Thorbecke Verlag.
——— (1983c); *Urgroßelternzeit*. Sigmaringen: Jan Thorbecke Verlag.
Belsey, Catherine and Jane Moore (1989) *The Feminist Reader: Essays in Gender and the Politics of Literary Criticism*. Basingstoke and London: Macmillan.
Benard, Cheryl and Edit Schlaffer (1991) 'Austria: Can Women's Capitalism have a Social Conscience?' in *Politics and Society in Germany, Austria and Switzerland*, vol. 3, no. 3, 1991, 34–39.
Benjamin, Jessica (1990) *Die Fesseln der Liebe. Psychoanalyse, Feminismus und das Problem der Macht*. Basel and Frankfurt a.M.: Stroemfeld/Roter Stern.
Benjamin, Walter (1973) *Illuminations*, trans. Harry Zohn. London: Fontana (orig. 1968).
——— (1980) *Illuminationen. Ausgewählte Schriften*. Frankfurt a.M.: Suhrkamp (orig. 1972–77).
Benn, Gottfried (1968) 'Genie und Gesundheit' in *Gesammelte Werke*, vol. 3, ed. Dieter Wellershoff, Wiesbaden: Limes, 1968, 646–651.
Berkéwicz, Ulla (1984/8) *Michel, sag ich*. Frankfurt a.M.: Suhrkamp.
——— (1992) *Engel sind schwarz und weiß*. Frankfurt a.M.: Suhrkamp.
Bernhard, Thomas (1988) *Der Weltverbesserer*. Frankfurt a.M.: Suhrkamp.
Biffl, Gudrun (1993) 'Die Arbeitswelt der Frauen in Österreich – Erwerbsarbeit und Hausarbeit' in Good et al. 1993, 120–145.
Bloch, Ernst (1962) *Erbschaft unserer Zeit*. Frankfurt a.M.: Suhrkamp.
——— (1991) *Heritage of our Times*, trans. Neville and Stephen Plaice. Cambridge: Polity Press.
Blumer, Arnold (1983) 'Kulturelle Fremde in der Frauenliteratur am Beispiel von Barbara Frischmuths *Die Klosterschule*' in Jurgensen 1983, 181–195.
Boa, Elizabeth (1987) *The Sexual Circus. Wedekind's Theatre of Subversion*. Oxford: Blackwell.

—— (1990) 'Women Writing about Women Writing and Ingeborg Bachmann's *Malina*' in Sheppard 1990, 128–144.

—— (1991) 'Gertrud Leutenegger: A Feminist Synthesis' in Butler and Pender 1991, 202–221.

—— (1992) 'The Murder of the Muse or the Wound and the Pen: Figures of Inspiration in Wedekind's Diaries and Kafka's Letters to Felice' in Rolf Kieser and Reinhold Grimm (eds), *Frank Wedekind Yearbook 1991*. Bern: Peter Lang, 1992, 81–100.

—— (1994) 'Schwierigkeiten mit der ersten Person: Ingeborg Bachmanns *Malina* und Monika Marons *Flugasche, Die Überläuferin* und *Stille Zeile Sechs*' in Robert Pichl and Alexander Stillmark (eds), *Kritische Wege der Landnahme. Ingeborg Bachmann im Blickfeld der neunziger Jahre*. Vienna: Hora, 125–146.

Bohn, Volker (1993) *Deutsche Literatur seit 1945*. Frankfurt a.M.: Suhrkamp.

Böll, Heinrich (1961) 'Bekenntnis zur Trümmerliteratur' in *Erzählungen, Hörspiele, Aufsätze*. Cologne and Berlin: Kiepenheuer & Witsch, 339–343, (orig. 1952).

—— (1977) 'My Pal with the long Hair' in *Children are Civilians Too*, trans. Leila Vennewitz. New York, St. Louis, San Francisco, Toronto, Mexico and Panama: McGraw-Hill Book Company, 7–12.

—— (1987) 'Kumpel mit dem langen Haar' in *Werke. Romane und Erzählungen I 1947–1952*, ed. Bernd Balzer. Bornheim-Merten and Cologne: Lamuv & Kiepenheuer & Witsch, 63–67 (orig. 1947).

Bond, D.G. (1991) 'Gedanken über die ganze Bildungsstufe der Männer: Fire Imagery in the Work of Ingeborg Bachmann' in *Forum for Modern Language Studies*, vol. xxvii, no. 3, 1991, 238–254.

Borchert, Wolfgang (1949) *Das ist unser Manifest*. Hamburg: Rowohlt.

Bossinade, Johanna (1993) 'Prolegomena zu einer geschlechtsdifferenzierten Literaturbetrachtung. Am Beispiel von Wedekinds "Lulu"-Dramen' in *Jahrbuch für Internationale Germanistik* vol. 1, 1993, 97–120.

Botz, Gerhard (1993) 'Historische Brüche und Kontinuitäten als Herausforderungen – Ingeborg Bachmann und post-katastrophische Geschichtsmentalitäten in Österreich' in Göttsche and Ohl 1993, 199–214.

Bovenschen, Silvia (1976) 'Über die Frage: Gibt es eine weibliche Ästhetik?' in *Ästhetik und Kommunikation* vol. 15, 1976, 60–75. Also in Dietze (ed.) 1989, 82–115.

—— (1979) *Die imaginierte Weiblichkeit. Exemplarische Untersuchungen zu kulturgeschichtlichen und literarischen Präsentationsformen des Weiblichen*. Frankfurt a.M.: Suhrkamp.

—— (1985) 'Is There a Feminine Aesthetic' in Ecker (ed.) 1985: 23–50.

Braidotti, Rosi (1994) *Nomadic Subjects. Embodiment and Sexual Difference in Contemporary Feminist Theory*. New York: Columbia University Press.

Brandt, Gisela, Johanna Kootz and Gisela Steppke (1973) *Zur Frauenfrage im Kapitalismus*. Frankfurt a.M.: Suhrkamp.

Braun, Michael (1994) 'Ulla Hahn' in *Kritisches Lexikon zur deutschsprachigen Gegenwartsliteratur* (1 April 1994).

Braun, Volker (1989) 'Transit Europa. Der Ausflug der Toten' in *Stücke II*. Berlin: Henschel.

Briegleb, Klaus (1992) '"Unsere Vergeßlichkeit". Neue Schreibweisen des Erinnerns' in Briegleb and Weigel (eds) 1992, 133–140.

Briegleb, Klaus and Sigrid Weigel (eds) (1992) *Gegenwartsliteratur seit 1968*. (Hansers Sozialgeschichte der deutschen Literatur vom 16. Jahrhundert bis zur Gegenwart, vol. 12). Munich and Vienna: Hanser.

Brinker-Gabler, Gisela (ed.) (1988a) *Deutsche Dichterinnen vom 16. Jahrhundert bis zur Gegenwart*. Frankfurt a.M.: Fischer (orig. 1978).

—— (1988b) *Deutsche Literatur von Frauen*, 2 vols, Munich: Beck.

Brinker-Gabler, Gisela, Karola Ludwig and Andrea Wöffen (eds) (1986) *Lexikon deutschsprachiger Schriftstellerinnen 1800–1945*. Munich: dtv.

Brokoph-Mauch, Gudrun (1989) 'Die Prosa österreichischer Schriftstellerinnen zwischen 1968 und 1983 (Frischmuth, Jelinek, Schwaiger)' in Zeman vol. 2, no. 1, 1989, 201–226.

Bronnen, Barbara (1980) *Die Tochter*. Munich and Zurich: Piper.

Brügmann, Margret (1986) *Amazonen der Literatur. Studien zur deutschsprachigen Frauenliteratur der 70er Jahre*. Amsterdam: Rodopi.

—— (1989) 'Das gläserne Ich: Überlegungen zum Verhältnis von Frauenliteratur und Postmoderne am Beispiel von Anne Dudens *Das Judasschaf*' in *Amsterdamer Beiträge zur neueren Germanistik*, vol. 29, 1989, 253–274.

Brüning, Elfriede (n.d.) *Lästige Zeugen*. Halle: Mitteldeutscher Verlag.

Burkhard, Marianne (1981) 'Gauging Existential Space. The Emergence of Women Writers in Switzerland' in *World Literature Today* 55, 1981, 607–612.

Burmeister, Brigitte (1987) *Anders oder Aufenthalt in der Fremde*. Berlin: Verlag der Nation. (West German edition 1988, Darmstadt & Neuwied: Luchterhand.)

—— (1994) *Unter dem Namen Norma*. Stuttgart: Klett-Cotta.

Butler, Judith (1990) *Gender Trouble: Feminism and the Subversion of Identity*. New York and London: Routledge.

—— (1993) *Bodies that Matter: On the Discursive Limits of 'Sex'*. New York and London: Routledge.

Butler, M. and M. Pender (eds) (1991) *Rejection and Emancipation. Writing in German-speaking Switzerland 1945–1991*. New York and Oxford: Berg.

Calvino, Italo (1979) *Invisible Cities*, trans. William Weaver. London: Picador.

Chodorow, Nancy (1978) *The Reproduction of Mothering: Psychoanalysis and the Sociology of Gender*. Berkeley: University of California Press.

Cixous, Hélène (1976) 'The Laugh of the Medusa', trans. Keith Cohen and Paula Cohen in *Signs* vol. 1, no. 4, 1976, 874–893.

Cixous, Hélène and Catherine Clément (1987) *The Newly Born Woman*. Manchester: Manchester University Press.

Classen, Brigitte and Gabriele Goettle (1979) '"Häutungen", eine Verwechslung von Anemone und Amazone' in Dietze 1979, 55–59. (Orig. 1976 in the magazine *Courage*, no. 1.)

Cocalis, Susan L. (ed.) (1986) *The Defiant Muse. German Feminist Poems form the Middle Ages to the Present*. New York: Feminist Press at City University of New York.

Conrad, Judith and Ursula Konnertz (eds) (1986) *Weiblichkeit in der Moderne. Ansätze feministischer Vernunftkritik*. Tübingen: Edition Diskord.

Cosmopolitan (1987) 'Nicht nur vom Erfolg verfolgt', no. 4 , 1987, 233, 236 and 237.

Coward, Rosalind (1984) *Female Desire*. London: Paladin.

Culler, Jonathan (1983) *On Deconstruction: Theory and Criticism after Structuralism*. London: Routledge and Kegan Paul.

Czurda, Elfriede (1991) *Die Giftmörderinnen*. Reinbek bei Hamburg: Rowohlt.

Dahn, Daniela (1987) *Prenzlauer Berg-Tour*. Halle: Mitteldeutscher Verlag. (West German edition 1989: *Kunst und Kohle. Die 'Szene' am Prenzlauer Berg*. Frankfurt a.M.: Luchterhand.)

Daly, Mary (1979) *Gyn/Ecology*. London: The Women's Press.

Damm, Sigrid (1980) *Caroline Schlegel-Schelling. 'Lieber Freund, ich komme weit her schon an diesem frühen Morgen'. Briefe*. Darmstadt: Luchterhand.

Dangel, Elsbeth (1990) 'Übergang und Ankunft. Positionen neuerer Frauenliteratur. Zu Anne Dudens "Übergang" und Verena Stefans "Wortgetreu ich träume"', in *Jahrbuch für Internationale Germanistik*, vol. 2, 1990, 80–94.

Daviau, Donald G. (1980) 'Neuere Entwicklungen in der modernen österreichischen Prosa: Die Werke von Barbara Frischmuth' in *Modern Austrian Literature*, vol. 13, no. 1, 1980, 177–216.

Dedalus, Stephan (1993) '"Shakespeare ist ein echter Langeweiler": Gespräch mit Marlene Streeruwitz – Ihr neues Stück Elysian Park wird heute in Berlin uraufgeführt' in *Die Welt*, 17 June 1993.

Delphy, Christine and Diana Leonard (1992) *Familiar Exploitation: A New Analysis of Marriage in Contemporary Western Societies*. Cambridge: Polity Press.

Demirkan, Renan (1991) *Schwarzer Tee mit drei Stück Zucker*. Cologne: Kiepenheuer & Witsch.

Demski, Eva (1987) *Hotel Hölle, guten Tag*. Vienna: Hanser.

—— (1992a) *Unterwegs*. Frankfurt a.M.: Fischer (orig. 1988).

—— (1992b) 'Abschied von der Larmoyanz. Frauen und Literatur' in Demski 1992, 202–213.

Derrida, Jacques (1968): 'Die Différance' in Engelmann 1988, 29–52.
——— (1973) *Speech and Phenomenon*. Evanston: Northwestern University Press.
——— (1976) *Of Grammatology*. Baltimore: The Johns Hopkins University Press.
——— (1979) *Spurs/Éperons: Nietzsche's Styles*. Chicago: University of Chicago Press.
Dieterle, Bernhard (1990) 'Hommage der Literatur an die Malerei. Zu Michel Butors *Embarquement de la Reine de Saba* and Anne Duden's *The Judas Goat*' in Lea Ritter-Santini (ed.) *Mit den Augen geschrieben. Von gedichteten und erzählten Bildern*, (*Hanser Dichtung und Sprache*, vol. 10). Munich and Vienna: Hanser, 260–283.
Dietze, Gabriele (ed.) (1979/89) *Die Überwindung der Sprachlosigkeit. Texte aus der neuen Frauenbewegung*. Darmstadt and Neuwied: Luchterhand.
Dinnerstein, Dorothy (1987) *The Rocking of the Cradle and the Ruling of the World*. London: The Women's Press.
Domin, Hilde (1974) 'Über die Schwierigkeiten, eine berufstätige Frau zu sein' in *Von der Natur nicht vorgesehen. Autobiographisches*. Munich: Piper, 1974, 42–46.
Dor, Milo (1988) 'Das andere Deutschland' in *Sprache im technischen Zeitalter. Teil II: Literatur im technischen Zeitalter*, 26, 1988, 55–59.
Drescher, Angela (ed.) (1990) *Christa Wolf. Ein Arbeitsbuch. Studien. Dokumente. Bibliographie*. Frankfurt a.M.: Luchterhand.
——— (1992) *Dokumentation zu Christa Wolf. Nachdenken über Christa T.* Hamburg and Zurich: Luchterhand.
Drewitz, Ingeborg (1978) *Gestern war Heute. Hundert Jahre Gegenwart*. Düsseldorf: Claassen.
Droste-Hülshoff, Annette von (1970) *Die Judenbuche*. Bad Homburg, Berlin and Zurich: Gehlen Verlag (orig. 1842).
Druskowitz, Helene von (1988) *Der Mann als logische und sittliche Unmöglichkeit und als Fluch der Welt. Pessimistische Kardinalsätze* in *Pessimistische Kardinalsätze* ed. Traute Hensch. Freiburg: Kore.
Duden, Anne (1982) *Übergang*. Berlin: Rotbuch.
——— (1985a) *Opening of the Mouth,* trans. Della Couling. London: Pluto Press.
——— (1985b) 'Day and Night' in Duden 1985a, 97–106.
——— (1985c) 'Wimpertier', in *Literaturmagazin 20*, 1985, 10–12. Reinbek bei Hamburg: Rowohlt. Also in *Wimpertier*, Cologne: Kiepenheuer & Witsch, 1995.
——— (1985d) 'The Art of Drowning' in Duden 1985a, 124–128.
——— (1985e) 'The Country Cottage' in Duden 1985a, 11–39.
——— (1986) 'Übergang: Zum Verhältnis von Angst und Postmoderne in der Literatur der achtziger Jahre', in *Orbis Litterarum*, 41, 1986, 279–288.
——— (1990a) 'Gegenstrebige Fügung', in *Literaturmagazin 25*, 1990, 80–87. Reinbek bei Hamburg: Rowohlt. Also in Duden 1995.
——— (1990b) 'Zeichen auf der Erde', Column 3.
——— (1993) *Steinschlag*. Cologne: Kiepenheuer & Witsch.
——— (1994) *Das Judasschaf*. Berlin: Rotbuch (orig. 1985).
——— (1995) *Der wunde Punkt im Alphabet. Essays*. Berlin: Rotbuch.
Duden, Anne and Sigrid Weigel (1989) 'Schrei und Körper – Zum Verhältnis von Bildern und Schrift. Ein Gespräch über *Das Judasschaf*' in Koebner 1989, 120–148.
Duden, Anne, Jeannie Ebner, Irmela von der Lühe et al. (1986) '*Oder war da manchmal noch etwas anderes?' Texte zu Marlen Haushofer*. Frankfurt a.M.: Verlag Neue Kritik.
Durzak, Manfred (ed.) (1980a) *Erzählte Zeit. 50 deutsche Kurzgeschichten der Gegenwart*. Stuttgart: Reclam.
——— (1980b) *Die deutsche Kurzgeschichte der Gegenwart. Autorenporträts. Werkstattgespräche. Interpretationen*. Stuttgart: Reclam.
——— (1981) *Deutsche Gegenwartsliteratur. Ausgangspositionen und aktuelle Entwicklungen*. Stuttgart: Reclam.
Eagleton, Mary (1991) *Feminist Literary Criticism*. London and New York: Longman.
Eck, Ines (1991) *Steppenwolfidyllen*. Berlin and Weimar: Aufbau.
Eckart, Gabriele (ed.) (1984) *So sehe ick die Sache. Protokolle aus der DDR*. Cologne: Kiepenheuer & Witsch.
Ecker, Gisela (ed.) (1985) *Feminist Aesthetics*, trans. Harriet Anderson. London: The Women's Press.

Edschmid, Ulrike (1990) *Diesseits des Schreibtischs. Lebensgeschichten von Frauen schreibender Männer*. Frankfurt a.M.: Fischer.
—— (1992) *Zwei Frauen, zwei Lebensgeschichten*. Darmstadt: Luchterhand.
Edvardson, Cordelia (1991a) *Gebranntes Kind sucht das Feuer*. Munich: dtv (orig. Swedish 1984).
—— (1991b) *Die Welt zusammenfügen*. Munich: dtv (orig. Swedish 1988).
Eigler, Friederike (1992) 'Trauerarbeit in Brigitte Schwaigers *Lange Abwesenheit* als konfliktreiche Suche nach einer weiblichen Identität' in *The Germanic Review* vol. 67, no. 1, 1992: 26–34.
Ellmann, Mary (1979) *Thinking about Women*. London: Virago.
Elsner, Eva-Maria and Lothar Elsner (1992) *Ausländer und Ausländerpolitik in der DDR*. In *hefte zur ddr-geschichte*. Berlin: Gesellschaftswissenschaftliches Forum e.V.
Elsner, Gisela (1965) *The Giant Dwarfs. A Contribution*, trans. Joel Carmichael. New York: Grove Press.
—— (1983) 'Autorinnen im literarischen Ghetto' in *Kürbiskern* 2, 1983, 136–144.
—— (1985) *Die Riesenzwerge. Ein Beitrag*. Reinbek bei Hamburg: Rowohlt (orig. 1964).
—— (1989) 'Interview mit Gisela Elsner am 12. August 1985', in Hoffmeister 1989, 103–119.
Endres, Ria (1982) *Milena antwortet. Ein Brief*. Reinbek bei Hamburg: Rowohlt.
—— (1989) 'Das Schöne am Theater ist sein Anachronismus' in Roeder 1989, 93–108.
—— (1992) *Werde, was du bist. Literarische Frauenporträts*. Frankfurt a.M.: Suhrkamp.
Engelmann, Peter (ed.) (1988) *Randgänge der Philosophie*. Vienna: Passagen.
—— (ed.) (1990) *Postmoderne und Dekonstruktion. Texte französischer Philosophen der Gegenwart*. Stuttgart: Reclam.
Engels, Frederick (1972) *The Origin of the Family, Private Property and the State*. London: Lawrence and Wishart.
Erb, Elke (1975) *Gutachten*. Berlin and Weimar: Aufbau.
—— (1978) *Der Faden der Geduld*. Berlin and Weimar: Aufbau.
—— (1983) *Vexierbild*. Berlin and Weimar: Aufbau.
—— (1987) *Kastanienallee*. Berlin and Weimar: Aufbau.
—— (1991) *Winkelzüge*. Berlin: Edition Galrev.
Esselborn, Karl (1986) 'Neuer Realismus' in Fischer 1986a, 460–468.
Faschinger, Lilian (1989) *Lustspiel*. Munich: List.
Fast, Irene (1984): *Gender Identity. A Differentiation Model (Advances in Psychoanalysis: Theory, Research and Practice 2)*. London: Hillsdale.
Fetscher, Justus, Eberhard Lämmert and Jürgen Schutte (eds) (1991) *Die Gruppe 47 in der Geschichte der Bundesrepublik*. Würzburg: Königshausen & Neumann.
Feyl, Renate (1977) *Bilder ohne Rahmen*. Rudolfstadt: Greifenverlag.
—— (1981) *Der lautlose Aufbruch. Frauen in der Wissenschaft*. Berlin: Verlag Neues Leben.
—— (1986) *Idylle mit Professor*. Berlin: Verlag Neues Leben.
—— (1991) *Ausharren im Paradies*. Cologne: Kiepenheuer & Witsch.
Fiddler, Allyson (1991) 'Problems with Porn: Situating Elfriede Jelinek's *Lust*' in *German Life and Letters* vol. 44, no. 5, 1991, 404–415.
—— (1993) 'Demythologizing the Austrian *Heimat*: Elfriede Jelinek As *Nestbeschmutzer*' in Ricarda Schmidt and Moray McGowan (eds) *From High Priests to Desecrators: Contemporary Austrian Women Writers*. Sheffield: Sheffield Academic Press, 1993, 25–44.
—— (1994) *Rewriting Reality: An Introduction to Elfriede Jelinek*. Oxford: Berg.
Firestone, Shulamith (1970) *The Dialectic of Sex. The Case for Feminist Revolution*. New York: William Morrow.
Fischbeck, Helmut (ed.) (1979) *Literatur und Literaturpolitik in der DDR. Eine Dokumentation*. Frankfurt a.M.: Verlag Moritz Diesterweg.
Fischer, Ludwig (ed.) (1986a) *Literatur in der Bundesrepublik Deutschland bis 1967. (Hansers Sozialgeschichte der deutschen Literatur vom 16. Jahrhundert bis zur Gegenwart*, vol. 10) Munich and Vienna: Hanser.
—— (1986b) 'Die Zeit von 1945 bis 1967 als Phase der Gesellschafts- und Literaturentwicklung' in Fischer 1986a, 29–96.

Fischer, Michael (1991) *Trivialmythen in Elfriede Jelineks Romanen 'Die Liebhaberinnen' und 'Die Klavierspielerin'*. St. Ingbert: Werner J. Röhrig.

Fischer, Ulrich (1992) 'Ein verheißungsvolles Debüt' in *Neue Zeit*, 9 August 1992, 34.

Fleisser, Marieluise (1968) 'Wie es heut' noch zugeht auf dem Land' in *Der Tagesspiegel* (West Berlin) 8 September 1968.

Flitner, Christine (1995) *Frauen in der Literaturkritik. Gisela Elsner und Elfriede Jelinek im Feuillton der Bundesrepublik Deutschland*. Pfaffenweiler: Centaurus..

Foucault, Michel (1979) *Discipline and Punish*. Harmondsworth: Penguin.

—— (1981) *The History of Sexuality, vol. I. An Introduction*. Harmondsworth: Penguin.

Franger, Gaby (1990) *Wir haben es uns anders vorgestellt. Türkische Frauen in der Bundesrepublik*. Frankfurt a.M.: Fischer.

Frank, Manfred (1988) 'Subjekt, Person, Individuum' in Manfred Frank, Gérard Raulet, Willem van Rijen (eds) *Die Frage nach dem Subjekt*. Frankfurt a.M.: Suhrkamp, 7–28.

Frederiksen, Elke (ed.) (1989a) *Women Writers of Germany, Austria, and Switzerland. An Annotated Bio-Bibliographical Guide*. New York, Westport (Connecticut) and London: Greenwood Press.

—— (1989b) 'Literarische (Gegen-)entwürfe von Frauen nach 1945' in Knapp and Labroisse 1989, 83–110.

Freud, Sigmund (1974) 'Some Psychic Consequences of the Anatomical Differences Between the Sexes' in *Women and Analysis. Dialogues on Psychoanalytic Views of Femininity*, ed. Jean Strouse. New York: Dell.

—— (1982a) 32nd lecture in *Studienausgabe* vol. I, *Vorlesungen zur Einführung in die Psychoanalyse*, 517–543. Frankfurt a.M.: Fischer.

—— (1982b) 'Die Zerlegung der psychischen Persönlichkeit' in *Studienausgabe*, vol. I, 495–516. Frankfurt a.M.: Fischer.

—— (1982c): 'Zur Einführung des Narzißmus' in *Studienausgabe* Vol. III: *Psychologie des Unbewußten*, 41–68. Frankfurt a.M.: Fischer (orig. 1914).

—— (1982d) 'Hemmung, Symptom und Angst' in *Studienausgabe* Vol. VI: *Hysterie und Angst*, 1982, 233–308. Frankfurt a.M.: Fischer (orig. 1926).

—— (1984): 'Beyond the Pleasure Principle' in *On Metapsychology*, The Penguin Freud Library, vol. II. Harmondsworth: Penguin.

Friedan, Betty (1963) *The Feminine Mystique*. New York: Norton.

Friedländer, Veronika (1982) *Späte Notizen*. Berlin: Verlag Neues Leben.

Fries, Marilyn Sibley (1993) 'Zur Rezeption deutschsprachiger Autorinnen in den USA' in *Weimarer Beiträge* vol. 39, no. 3, 1993, 410–446.

Frischmuth, Barbara (1984) *Die Klosterschule*. Reinbek bei Hamburg: Rowohlt (orig. 1968).

—— (1993) *The Convent School*, trans. Gerald Chapple and James B. Lawson. Riverside, California: Ariadne Press.

Frischmuth, Barbara and Hans Ester (1982) 'Gespräch mit Barbara Frischmuth' in *Deutsche Bücher* vol. 12, no. 1, 1982, 1–11. Amsterdam: Rodopi.

Fritsch, Gerhard (1957) 'Im Blickfeld liegt die Lyrik', *Wort und Wahrheit*, vol. 5, 1957, in Hotz 1990, 77.

Gallop, Jane (1985) *Reading Lacan*. Ithaca New York: Cornell University Press.

Gerhardt, Marlies (1980) 'Gisela Elsner' in Puknus 1980, 88–94.

Gerstl, Elfriede (ed.) (1985) *Eine frau ist eine frau ist eine frau … Autorinnen über Autorinnen*. Vienna: Promedia.

Geyer-Ryan, Helga (ed.) (1982) *Was geschah, nachdem Nora ihren Mann verlassen hatte? Acht Hörspiele von Elfriede Jelinek, Ursula Krechel, Friederike Mayröcker, Inge Müller, Erica Pedretti, Ruth Rehmann und Gabriele Wohmann*. Munich: dtv.

Gilbert, Sandra and Susan Gubar (1979) *The Mad Woman in the Attic*. New Haven: Yale University Press.

Gnüg, Hiltrud and Renate Möhrmann (eds) (1985/9) *Frauen Literatur Geschichte. Schreibende Frauen vom Mittelalter bis zur Gegenwart*. Frankfurt a.M.: Suhrkamp.

Good, David, Margarete Grandner and Mary Jo Maynes (eds) (1993) *Frauen in Österreich: Beiträge zu ihrer Situation im 19. und 20. Jahrhundert*. Vienna: Böhlau.

Gorky, Maxim et al. (1977) *Soviet Writers Congress 1934: The Debate on Socialist Realism and Modernism in the Soviet Union*. London: Lawrence and Wishart.

Görtz, Franz Josef et al. (eds) (1992) *Deutsche Literatur 1991. Jahresüberblick*. Stuttgart: Reclam.

Göttsche, Dirk and Hubert Ohl (eds) (1993) *Ingeborg Bachmann. Neun Beiträge zu ihrem Werk*. Würzburg: Königshausen und Neumann.

Grass, Günter (1962) *Die Blechtrommel*. Frankfurt a.M. and Hamburg: Fischer (orig. 1959).

―――― (1989) *The Tin Drum*, trans. Ralph Manheim. London: Picador (orig. 1961).

Greene, Gayle and Coppélia Kahn (eds) (1985) *Making a Difference: Feminist Literary Criticism*. London and New York: Methuen.

Greer, Germaine (1971) *The Female Eunuch*. London: Paladin.

Greiner, Ulrich (1979) 'Über das "Österreichische" in der österreichischen Literatur' in Ulrich Greiner, *Der Tod des Nachsommers. Aufsätze, Portraits, Kritisches zur österreichischen Gegenwartsliteratur*. Munich and Vienna: Hanser.

Greuner, Suzanne (1990) *Schmerzton Musik in der Schreibweise Ingeborg Bachmanns und Anne Dudens*. Berlin and Hamburg: Argument.

Griffin, Susan (1982) *Made From This Earth*. London: The Women's Press.

―――― (1984) *Woman and Nature: the Roaring Inside Her*. London: The Women's Press.

Gröschner, Annett and Tina Bara (1993) *Herzdame Knochensammler*. Berlin: Kontext.

Grosz, Elizabeth (1994) *Volatile Bodies. Toward a Corporeal Feminism*. Bloomington, Indianapolis: Indiana University Press.

Gruenter, Undine (1986) *Ein Bild der Unruhe*. Munich: Hanser.

Gürtler, Christa (1983) *Schreiben Frauen anders? Untersuchungen zu Ingeborg Bachmann und Barbara Frischmuth*. Stuttgart: Heinz.

Gürtler, Christa (ed.) (1990) *Gegen den schönen Schein. Texte zu Elfriede Jelinek*. Frankfurt a.M.: Verlag Neue Kritik.

Hahn, Ulla (1981) *Herz über Kopf*. Stuttgart: Deutsche Verlagsanstalt.

―――― (1983) *Spielende*. Stuttgart: Deutsche Verlagsanstalt.

―――― (1985) *Freudenfeuer*. Stuttgart: Deutsche Verlagsanstalt.

―――― (1988) *Unerhörte Nähe*. Stuttgart: Deutsche Verlagsanstalt.

Hamburger, Michael (ed.) (1977) *German Poetry 1910–1975: an Anthology in German and English*. Manchester: Manchester University Press.

Hannsmann, Margaret (1986) *Der helle Tag bricht an*. Hamburg: Knaus.

Härtling, Peter (1980) 'Ein Buch, das geduldig auf uns wartet' in *Süddeutsche Zeitung*, 22/23 November 1980.

Hasler, Eveline (1979/92) *Novemberinsel*. Munich: dtv.

―――― (1991) *Die Wachsflügelfrau. Geschichte der Emily Kempin-Spyri*. Zurich: Nagel und Kimche.

―――― (1992a) *Anna Göldin. Letzte Hexe*. Munich: dtv (orig. 1982).

―――― (1992b) *Ibicaba. Das Paradies in den Köpfen*. Munich: dtv (orig. 1985).

Häsler, Alfred Adolf (1989) *Das Boot ist voll – Die Schweiz und die Flüchtlinge 1933–1945*. Zurich: Diogenes.

Haushofer, Marlen (1955) *Ein Handvoll Leben*. Vienna and Hamburg: Paul Zsolnay Verlag.

―――― (1986) *Die Tapetentür*. Munich: Knaur (orig. 1957).

―――― (1993) *Wir töten Stella*. Munich: Knaur (orig. 1958).

Hegel, G. W .F. (1977) 'Independence and Dependence of Self-Consciousness: Lordship and Bondage' in *Phenomenology of Spirit*, trans. by A. V. Miller. Oxford: Oxford University Press, 111–119 (orig. 1807).

Heidelberger-Leonard, Irene (1992) 'War es Doppelmord? Anmerkungen zu Elfriede Jelineks Bachmann-Rezeption und ihrem Filmbuch "Malina"' in *Elfriede Jelinek. Text + Kritik*, vol. 117, 1992, 78–85.

Heinrich, Jutta (1977) *Das Geschlecht der Gedanken*. Munich: Frauenoffensive.

―――― (1984) *The Gender of Thoughts* (excerpt), trans. Jeanette Clausen, in Altbach et al. 1984, 276–283.

―――― (1986) '"Männlich schreiben – weiblich schreiben" oder "Gibt es eine Geschlechterspur in der Gegenwartsliteratur?"' in Conrad and Konnertz 1986, 215–223.

―――― (1991) *Alles ist Körper*. Frankfurt a.M.: Fischer.

Heller, Erdmute and Hassouna Mosbahi (1993) *Hinter den Schleiern des Islam. Erotik und Sexualität in der Arabischen Kultur*. Munich: Beck.

Hensel, Kerstin (1989) *Hallimasch*. Halle: Mitteldeutscher Verlag.

—— (1991a) *Auditorium Panoptikum*. Halle: Mitteldeutscher Verlag.

—— (1991b) *Gewitterfront*. Halle: Mitteldeutscher Verlag.

Hermand, Jost (1968) 'Undinenzauber: Zum Frauenbild des Jugendstils' in Renate von Heydebrand and Klaus Günther Just (eds) *Wissenschaft als Dialog. Studien zur Kunst und Literatur seit der Jahrhundertwende*. Stuttgart: Metzler, 1991, 9–29.

Herminghouse, Patricia (ed.) (1987) *Frauen im Mittelpunkt: Contemporary German Women Writers*. New York: Feminist Press at City University of New York.

Hetmann, Frederik (1990) *Schlafe meine Rose. Die Lebensgeschichte der Elisabeth Langgässer*. Weinheim and Basel: Beltz & Gelberg.

Heuser, Magdalene (1983) 'Literatur von Frauen/Frauen in der Literatur. Feministische Ansätze in der Literaturwissenschaft' in Pusch 1983, 117–148.

—— (1989) '"Die Gegenstände abstauben" und "Mit Blicken wie mit Pfeilen und Messern": Brigitte Kronauer im Kontext der Gegenwartsliteratur von Frauen lesen' in Knapp and Labroisse 1989, 343–375.

Höbel, Wolfgang (1994) 'Leichter, sanfter Schwindel' in *Der Spiegel. Bücher '94*, October 1994, 36–37.

Hodoschek, Andrea (1991) 'Endzeit in der Heimat' in *Kurier*, 16 March 1991.

Hoffmann, Freia (ed.) (1976) *Ledige Mütter, Protokolle, Analysen, Juristische Informationen, Sozialarbeit, Selbstorganisation*. Frankfurt a.M.: Stroemfeld/Roter Stern.

Hoffmeister, Donna L. (1989) *Vertrautes, Alltag, gemischte Gefühle. Gespräche mit Schriftstellern über Arbeit in der Literatur*. Bonn: Bouvier.

Hofmannsthal, Hugo von (1959) 'Ein Brief', in *Gesammelte Werke in Einzelausgaben. Prosa*, vol. 2, ed. Herbert Steiner. Frankfurt a.M.: Fischer.

Höller, Hans (1987) *Ingeborg Bachmann. Das Werk von den frühesten Gedichten bis zum 'Todesarten'-Zyklus*. Frankfurt a.M.: Athenäum.

Honigmann, Barbara (1986) *Roman von einem Kinde*. Darmstadt: Luchterhand.

Höntsch-Harendt, Ursula (1985) *Wir Flüchtlingskinder*. Halle: Mitteldeutscher Verlag. (West German edition 1986, Frankfurt a.M.: Röderberg.)

Horvat, Dragica et al. (1987) *Eine Kulturmetropole wird geteilt. Literarisches Leben in Berlin (West) 1945–49*. Berlin: Berliner Kulturrat.

Hotz, Constance (1990) *Die Bachmann. Das Image der Dichterin: Ingeborg Bachmann im journalistischen Diskurs*. Konstanz: Ekkehard Faude.

Hüfner, Agnes (1986) 'Warum ist das Schminken für Sie wichtig, Frau Jelinek?' in *Frankfurter Allgemeine Zeitung* (Magazin), 31 October 1986.

Irigaray, Luce (1985a) *Éthique de la différence sexuelle*. Paris: Minuit.

Irigaray, Luce (1985b) *This sex which is not one*, trans. Catherine Porter and Carolyn Burke. Ithaca, New York: Cornell University Press.

Jaggar, Alison M. (1983) *Feminist Politics and Human Nature*. Brighton: Harvester.

Jelinek, Elfriede (1970) *wir sind lockvögel baby!* Reinbek bei Hamburg: Rowohlt.

—— (1973) *Michael, Ein Jugendbuch für die Infantilgesellschaft*. Reinbek bei Hamburg: Rowohlt.

—— (1980) *ende. gedichte 1966–1968*. Munich: Schwiftinger Galerie-Verlag.

—— (1982) *Die Bienenkönige*, in Geyer-Ryan 1982, 7–48.

—— (1983) *Die Klavierspielerin*. Reinbek bei Hamburg: Rowohlt.

—— (1984a) *Clara S.*, in Ute Nyssen (ed.) *Theaterstücke*. Cologne: Prometh 1984 (orig. 1981).

—— (1984b) *Burgtheater*, in Ute Nyssen (ed.) *Theaterstücke*. Cologne: Prometh 1984 (orig. 1982).

—— (1985) *Die Liebhaberinnen*. Reinbek bei Hamburg: Rowohlt (orig. 1975).

—— (1987) *Krankheit oder Moderne Frauen* with an afterword by Regine Friedrich (ed.). Cologne: Prometh.

—— (1988/9) *The Piano Teacher*, trans. Joachim Neugroschel. New York: Weidenfeld & Nicolson/London: Serpent's Tail.

—— (1989) *Lust*. Reinbek bei Hamburg: Rowohlt.

—— (1990a) *Wolken. Heim*. Göttingen: Steidl.

—— (1990b) *Wonderful, Wonderful Times*, trans. Michael Hulse. London: Serpent's Tail.

—— (1991) *Totenauberg*. Reinbek bei Hamburg: Rowohlt.

—— (1992) *Lust*, trans. Michael Hulse. London: Serpent's Tail.

—— (1994) *women as lovers*, trans. Martin Chalmers. London: Serpent's Tail.

Jelinek, Elfriede and Ingeborg Bachmann (1991) *Malina. Ein Filmbuch*. Frankfurt a.M.: Suhrkamp.

Johns, Jorun B. and Katherine Arens (eds) (1994) *Elfriede Jelinek: Framed by Language*. Riverside, California: Ariadne Press.

Johnson, Uwe (1974) *Eine Reise nach Klagenfurt*. Frankfurt a.M.: Suhrkamp.

Jonas, Anna (1981) *Nichts mehr an seinem Platz*. Munich: List.

—— (1985a) *Das Frettchen*. Berlin: Rotbuch.

—— (1985b) 'Die Gattung' in *Neue Literatur*, 6, 1985, 39–44.

Joris, Elisabeth and Heidi Witzig (eds) (1986) *Frauengeschichte(n). Dokumente aus zwei Jahrhunderten zur Situation der Frauen in der Schweiz*. Zurich: Limmat.

Jurgensen, Manfred (1983/5) *Frauenliteratur, Autorinnen, Perspektiven, Konzepte*. Munich: dtv.

Kachold, Gabriele (1989) *zügel-los*. Berlin and Weimar: Aufbau.

Kaiser, Joachim (1971) 'Liebe und Tod einer Prinzessin. Ingeborg Bachmanns neuer Roman', *Süddeutsche Zeitung*, 25 March 1971, Beilage Buch und Zeit, 1 in Hotz 1990, 144–145.

Kaplan, Cora (1986a) *Sea Changes: Culture and Feminism*. London: Verso.

—— (1986b) 'Pandora's Box: Subjectivity, Class and Sexuality in Socialist Feminist Criticism' in Kaplan 1986a, 147–176.

Kappeler, Susanne (1986) *The Pornography of Representation*. Cambridge: Cambridge University Press.

Kaschnitz, Marie Luise (1979) *Orte*. Frankfurt a.M.: Suhrkamp (orig. 1973).

Kathrein, Karin (1983) 'Höllenfahrt der Wünsche' in *Die Presse*, 27 April 1983.

—— (1994) 'Der Mann ... als Fluch der Welt: Elisabeth Reicharts *Sakkorausch* zum Thema Patriarchat der Zeit/Schnitte bei den Festwochen' in *Kurier*, 25 May 1994.

Kecht, Maria-Regina (1989) 'In the Name of Obedience, Reason, and Fear: Mother-Daughter Relations in W.A. Mitgutsch and E. Jelinek' in *The German Quarterly* vol. 62, no. 3, 1989, 357–372.

Kerschbaumer, Marie-Thérèse (1980) *Der weibliche Name des Widerstands. Sieben Berichte*. Olten and Freiburg im Breisgau: Walter.

Kienzle, Siegfried (1992) 'Die Austro-Berserker. Werner Schwab, Harald Kislinger, Marlene Streeruwitz – drei neue Stückeschreiber aus Österreich brechen über die Theater herein. Schon die Titel dampfen und ächzen' in *Die deutsche Bühne* 9, 1992, 12–15.

Kirsch, Sarah (1967) *Landaufenthalt. Gedichte*. Berlin: Aufbau. (West German edition 1977, Ebenhausen: Langewiesche-Brandt, orig. 1969.)

—— (1973a) *Die ungeheuren bergehohen Wellen auf See*. Berlin: Eulenspiegel. Also in Wolff 1979, 193–197.

—— (1973b) *Zaubersprüche*. Berlin and Weimar: Aufbau.

—— (1973c) *Die Pantherfrau. Fünf unfrisierte Erzählungen aus dem Kassetten Recorder*. Berlin and Weimar: Aufbau. (West German edition 1985, Reinbek bei Hamburg: Rowohlt.)

—— (1975) *Blitz aus heiterm Himmel*. Berlin and Weimar: Aufbau. (West German edition 1980: *Geschlechtertausch. Drei Erzählungen* with Christa Wolf and Irmtraud Morgner. Darmstadt and Neuwied: Luchterhand.)

—— (1989) *The Panther Woman. Five Tales from the Cassette Recorder*, trans. Marion Faber. Lincoln: University of Nebraska Press.

Kirsch, Sarah and Rainer Kirsch (1965) *Gespräch mit dem Saurier*. Berlin: Verlag Neues Leben.

Kiwus, Karin (1981) *39 Gedichte*. Stuttgart: Reclam.

—— (1992) *Das chinesische Examen*. Frankfurt a.M.: Suhrkamp.

Kiwus, Karin and Ille Oelhaf (1994) *Tiere wie wild*. Frankfurt a.M. and Leipzig: Insel.

Klüssendorf, Angelika (1990) *Sehnsüchte*. Munich: Hanser.

Knapp, Gerhard P. and Mona (1981) *Gabriele Wohmann*. Königstein: Athenäum.

Knapp, Mona and Gerd Labroisse (eds) (1989) *Frauen-Fragen in der deutschsprachigen Literatur seit 1945*. Amsterdam: Rodopi.

Koebner, Thomas (ed.) (1989): *Laokoon und kein Ende: Der Wettstreit der Künste*. Munich: edition text + kritik.

Köhler, Barbara (1991) *Deutsches Roulette. Gedichte 1984–89*. Frankfurt a.M.: Suhrkamp.
Kolb, Ulrike, (1985) *Idas Idee*. Frankfurt: tende.
Kolinsky, Eva (ed.) (1991) *The Federal Republic of Germany. The End of an Era*. New York and Oxford: Berg.
Kollontai, Alexandra (1982) *Wege der Liebe* with an afterword by Hedda Zinner. Berlin: Buchverlag Der Morgen (orig. 1925).
Konar, Violäne (1988) 'Überblick über die Situation der Frau und die Frauenbewegung in Irland, Großbritannien und Österreich (ab 1970)', unpublished *Diplomarbeit*, University of Vienna.
König, Barbara (1988) 'Tagebuch', in *Sprache im technischen Zeitalter, Teil II: Literatur im technischen Zeitalter*, 26, 1988, 72–78.
Königsdorf, Helga (1979) *Meine ungehörigen Träume*. Berlin and Weimar: Aufbau.
—— (1982) *Der Lauf der Dinge*. Berlin and Weimar: Aufbau.
—— (1986) *Respektloser Umgang*. Berlin and Weimar: Aufbau.
—— (1988) *Lichtverhältnisse*. Berlin and Weimar: Aufbau.
—— (1990a) *1989 oder Ein Moment Schönheit*. Berlin and Weimar: Aufbau.
—— (1990b) *Ungelegener Befund*. Berlin and Weimar: Aufbau.
—— (1991a) *Adieu DDR. Protokolle eines Abschieds*. Reinbek bei Hamburg: Rowohlt.
—— (1991b) *Aus dem Dilemma eine Chance machen*. Hamburg and Zurich: Luchterhand.
—— (1992) *Gleich neben Afrika*. Berlin: Rowohlt.
—— (1993) *Im Schatten des Regenbogens*. Berlin: Rowohlt.
Koppensteiner, Jürgen (1992) 'Zwischen Anpassung und Widerstand: Bemerkungen zu zeitkritischen Prosawerken von Peter Henisch, Elisabeth Reichart und Gerald Szyszkowitz' in *Modern Austrian Literature* vol. 25, no. 1, 1992, 41–59.
Kosler, H.C. (1981) 'Elfriede Jelinek' in *Kritisches Lexikon zur deutschsprachigen Gegenwartsliteratur* (1 January 1989).
Kosta, Barbara (1993) 'Muttertrauma: Anerzogener Masochismus' in Kraft and Liebs 1993, 243–265.
Kraft, Helga and Elke Liebs (eds) (1993) *Mütter-Töchter-Frauen: Weiblichkeitsbilder in der Literatur*. Stuttgart and Weimar: Metzler.
Kraft, Ruth (1959/86) *Insel ohne Leuchtfeuer*. Berlin: Verlag der Nation.
Krauss, Angela (1984) *Das Vergnügen*. Berlin and Weimar: Aufbau (West German edition 1988, Frankfurt a.M.: Suhrkamp).
—— (1988) *Das Glashaus*. Berlin and Weimar: Aufbau.
Krechel, Ursula (1975) *Selbsterfahrung und Fremdbestimmung. Bericht aus der neuen Frauenbewegung*. Darmstadt and Neuwied: Luchterhand.
—— (1978) 'Freie Formen oder das unfreie Gedicht in der Mangel' in *Frauenoffensive Journal* 11, 1978, 6–10, also in Dietze 1989, 60–69.
—— (1979) 'Leben in Anführungszeichen. Das Authentische in der gegenwärtigen Literatur' in *Literaturmagazin 11*, 1979, 80–107.
Kreuzer, Helmut (1990) 'From Being-Itself to Post-Modernism – Four Decades of Literature and Literary Criticism in the Federal Republic of Germany' in Sheppard 1990, 9–33.
Kristeva, Julia (1977) 'Le sujet en procès' in *Polylogue*. Paris: Editions du Seuil, 1977.
—— (1980a) *Desire in Language. A Semiotic Approach to Literature and Art*. Oxford: Blackwell.
—— (1980b) 'Das Subjekt im Prozeß: die poetische Sprache' in Jean-Marie Benoiste (ed.) *Identität. Ein interdisziplinäres Seminar unter Leitung von Claude Lévi-Strauss*. Stuttgart: Klett-Cotta, 1980, 187–221.
—— (1984) *Revolution in Poetic Language*, trans. Margaret Waller. New York: Columbia University Press.
Kritisches Lexikon zur deutschsprachigen Gegenwartsliteratur, ed. Heinz Ludwig Arnold. Munich: edition text + kritik 1978
Kronauer, Brigitte (1983) *Rita Münster*. Munich: dtv.
—— (1986) *Berittener Bogenschütze*. Munich: dtv.
—— (1991) *Frau Mühlenbeck im Gehäus*. Stuttgart: Klett-Cotta (orig. 1980).
—— (1993) *Die Wiese*. Stuttgart: Reclam.
Kubli, Sabine and Doris Stump (1994) *Viel Köpfe, viel Sinn. Schweizer Schriftstellerinnen von 1800–1945. Eine Textsammlung*. Zurich: eFeF.

Kublitz-Kramer, Maria (1993) 'Die Freiheiten der Straße. Stadtläuferinnen in neueren Texten von Frauen' in Apel et al. 1993, 15–36.

Lacan, Jacques (1977) Écrits, trans. Alan Sheridan. London: Tavistock.

Lamb-Faffelberger, Margarete (1992) Valie Export und Elfriede Jelinek im Spiegel der Presse: Zur Rezeption der feministischen Avantgarde Österreichs. New York: Lang.

Lambrecht, Christine (1986) Männerbekanntschaften. Freimütige Protokolle. Halle: Mitteldeutscher Verlag.

Lange-Müller, Katja (1986) Wehleid – wie im Leben. Frankfurt a.M.: Fischer.

——— (1988) Kasper Mauser – die Feigheit vorm Freund. Cologne: Kiepenheuer & Witsch.

Langer, Lawrence L. (1975) 'Suffer the little children' in Lawrence L. Langer, The Holocaust and the Literary Imagination. New Haven and London: Yale University Press, 1975, 124–165.

Langgässer, Elisabeth (1947) 'Schriftsteller unter der Hitlerdiktatur' in Ost und West 1, 4, 1947. Reprinted Königstein: Athenäum, 1979, 36–58.

——— (1979) Das unauslöschliche Siegel, vol. 1 and 2 with an afterword by Ursula Krechel. Darmstadt and Neuwied: Luchterhand (orig. 1946).

——— (1980a) Ausgewählte Erzählungen, with an afterword by Horst Krüger. Frankfurt a.M., Berlin and Vienna: Ullstein.

——— (1980b) ... so viel berauschende Vergänglichkeit. Briefe. Frankfurt a.M., Berlin and Vienna: Ullstein.

——— (1984) 'In Hiding' in 3 German Stories by Elisabeth Langgässer, Anna Seghers, Johannes Bobrowski, trans. Michael Bullock. London: Oasis Books.

Laplanche, Jean and J. B. Pontalis (1972) Das Vokabular der Psychoanalyse, trans. Emma Moersch. Frankfurt a.M.: Suhrkamp (orig. 1967).

——— (1973) The Language of Psycho-Analysis, trans. Donald Nicholson-Smith. New York and London: Norton.

Leitner, Sebastian (1986) 'Das Gespeibsel der Elfriede Jelinek' in Kurier, 12 December 1986.

Lennox, Sara (1993) 'The Feminist Reception of Ingeborg Bachmann' in Jeannette Clausen and Sara Friedrichsmeyer (eds), Women in German Yearbook, vol. 8, 1993. Lincoln and London: University of Nebraska Press, 73–111.

Leonhardt, Rudolf Walter (1981), 'Aufstieg und Niedergang der Gruppe 47' in Durzak 1981, 61–76.

Lersch, Barbara (1988) 'Der Ort der Leerstelle. Weiblichkeit als Poetik der Negativität und der Differenz' in Brinker-Gabler 1988b, 487–502.

Lettau, Reinhart (ed.) (1967) Die Gruppe 47. Ein Handbuch. Berlin and Neuwied: Luchterhand.

Leutenegger, Gertrud (1980a) Lebewohl, Gute Reise. Ein dramatisches Poem. Frankfurt a.M.: Suhrkamp.

——— (1980b) Vorabend. Frankfurt a.M.: Suhrkamp.

——— (1981a) Gouverneur. Frankfurt a.M.: Suhrkamp.

——— (1981b) Ninive. Frankfurt a.M.: Suhrkamp.

——— (1983) Komm ins Schiff. Frankfurt a.M.: Suhrkamp.

——— (1985) Kontinent. Frankfurt a.M.: Suhrkamp.

Levi-Strauss, Claude (1969) The Elementary Structures of Kinship. Boston: Beacon Press.

Liersch, Werner (ed.) (1975) Was zählt ist die Wahrheit. Briefe von Schriftstellern der DDR. Halle: Mitteldeutscher Verlag.

Lindemann, Gisela (1988) Ilse Aichinger. Munich: Beck.

Literaturmagazin 11 (1979) Schreiben oder Literatur. Reinbek bei Hamburg: Rowohlt.

Lorenz, Dagmar C. G. (1979) 'Marlen Haushofer – eine Feministin aus Österreich' in Modern Austrian Literature vol. 12, 3/4, 1979, 171–191.

——— (1987) 'Humor bei zeitgenössischen Autorinnen' in The Germanic Review 62, 1987, 28–36.

——— (1993) 'Männlichkeits- und Weiblichkeitskonstruktionen bei Ilse Aichinger' in Bartsch and Melzer 1993, 15–35.

Lühe, Irmela von der (ed.) (1982a) Entwürfe von Frauen in der Literatur des 20. Jahrhunderts. Berlin: Argument.

——— (1982b) 'Ich ohne Gewähr' in von d. Lühe 1982a, 106–131.

——— (1988) 'Schriftstellerinnen in der Gruppe 47' in Schutte 1988, 94–102.

—— (1994) *Erika Mann. Eine Biographie*. Frankfurt a.M. and New York: Campus.

Lukács, Georg (1963) *The Meaning of Contemporary Realism*. London: Merlin.

Lukens, Nancy and Dorothy Rosenberg (eds and trans.) (1993) *Daughters of Eve. Contemporary Women Writers of the German Democratic Republic*. Lincoln and London: University of Nebraska Press.

Lyotard, Jean-François (1991) 'Emma', in Hans Ulrich Gumbrecht and K. Ludwig Pfeiffer (eds) *Paradoxien, Dissonanzen, Zusammenbrüche*. Frankfurt a.M.: Suhrkamp, 1991, 671–708.

Marcuse, Herbert (1969) *Eros and Civilization*. London: Sphere.

Maron, Monika (1981) *Flugasche*. Frankfurt a.M.: Fischer.

—— (1986a) *Die Überläuferin*. Frankfurt a.M.: Fischer.

—— (1986b) *Flight of Ashes*, trans. David Newton Marinelli. London: Readers International.

—— (1988) *The Defector*, trans. David Newton Marinelli. London: Readers International.

—— (1992) *Stille Zeile Sechs*. Frankfurt a.M.: Fischer.

Martin, Biddy (1991) *Woman and Modernity: The (Life)Styles of Lou Andreas-Salomé*. Ithaca and London: Cornell University Press.

Mechtel, Angelika (1977) 'Der weiße Rabe hat fliegen gelernt' in *Die Zeit*, 16 September 1977, 49.

—— (1983) *Gott und die Liedermacherin*. Munich: Paul List.

Menke, Tim (1986) 'Anne Dudens Erzählband *Übergang*: Zum Verhältnis von Angst und Postmoderne in der Literatur der achtziger Jahre' in *Orbis Litterarum*, 41, 1986, 279–288.

Menschik, Jutta (1971) *Gleichberechtigung oder Emanzipation? Die Frau im Erwerbsleben der Bundesrepublik*. Frankfurt a.M.: Fischer.

Merian, Svende (1980) *Der Tod des Märchenprinzen. Frauenroman*. Hamburg: Rowohlt.

Merschmeier, Michael (1993) 'Schrecklich schön. Marlene Streeruwitz über das Theater im allgemeinen und die Nicht-Uraufführung ihres Stückes *Elysian Park* im besonderen' in *Theater heute* 8, 1993, 34.

Meyer, Anja (1994) *Elfriede Jelinek in der Geschlechterpresse: Die Klavierspielerin und Lust im printmedialen Diskurs*. Hildesheim: Olms.

Meyer, Franziska (1987) '"Auch die Wahrheit bedarf der Propaganda": Der Kongreß für kulturelle Freiheit und die Folgen' in Horvat et al. 1987, 33–48.

Meyer-Gosau, Frauke (ed.) (1993) *Text und Kritik. Elfriede Jelinek*, 117. Munich: edition text + kritik.

Millett, Kate (1970) *Sexual Politics*. New York: Doubleday.

Minai, Naila (1981) *Women in Islam. Tradition and Transition in the Middle East*. New York: Seaview Books.

Minces, Juliette (1992) *Verschleiert – Frauen im Islam*. Reinbek bei Hamburg: Rowohlt (orig. *La Femme Voilee. L' Islam au feminin*. Paris: Calmann-Levy, 1990).

Mitchell, Juliet (1975) *Psychoanalysis and Feminism*. Harmondsworth: Penguin.

Mitgutsch, Waltraud Anna (1985) *Die Züchtigung*. Düsseldorf: Claassen.

—— (1987) *Three Daughters*, trans. Lisel Müller. New York: Harcourt Brace.

Mitscherlich, Margarete and Brigitte Burmeister (1991) *Wir haben ein Berührungstabu. Zwei deutsche Seelen – einander fremd geworden*. Hamburg: Klein.

Möbius, Paul J. (1900/1907) *Über den physiologischen Schwachsinn des Weibes*. Halle a.d.S.: Marhold.

Möhrmann, Renate (1979) 'Feministische Ansätze in der Germanistik seit 1945' in *Jahrbuch für internationale Germanistik* 11, 2, 1979, 63–84. Berne, Frankfurt a.M. and Las Vegas: Lang.

—— (1981) 'Feministische Trends in der deutschen Gegenwartsliteratur' in Durzak 1981, 336–358.

Moi, Toril (1985) *Sexual/Textual Politics*. London: Methuen.

—— (ed.) (1986) *The Kristeva Reader*. Oxford: Blackwell.

Molden, Hanna (1985) Interview for 'Cosmo': 'Die kultivierte Neurose' in *Cosmopolitan*, 5 May 1985.

Moníková, Libuše (1981/90) *Eine Schädigung*. Munich: dtv.

—— (1983/8) *Pavane für eine verstorbene Infantin.* Munich: dtv.

—— (1994) *Prager Fenster. Essays.* Munich: Hanser.

Moog, Christa (1986) *Die Fans von Union.* Düsseldorf: Claassen.

—— (1989) *Aus tausend grünen Spiegeln.* Düsseldorf: Claassen.

Moosdorf, Johanna (1988) *Die Freundinnen* with an afterword by Regula Venske. Frankfurt a.M.: Fischer (orig. 1977).

—— (1989) *Jahrhundertträume.* Frankfurt a.M.: Fischer.

Morgner, Irmtraud (1962) *Ein Haus am Rand der Stadt.* Berlin: Aufbau.

—— (1968) *Hochzeit in Konstantinopel.* Berlin and Weimar: Aufbau. (West German edition 1984, Darmstadt and Neuwied: Luchterhand, orig. 1969.)

—— (1974) *Leben und Abenteuer der Trobadora Beatriz nach Zeugnissen ihrer Spielfrau Laura. Roman in dreizehn Büchern und sieben Intermezzos.* Berlin: Aufbau. (West German edition 1984, Darmstadt and Neuwied: Luchterhand, orig. 1977.)

—— (1978) 'Life and Adventures of the Troubadora Beatriz As Chronicled by Her Minstrel Laura' (Twelfth Book), trans. Karen and Friedrich Achberger in *new german critique* 15, 1978, 121–146.

—— (1983) *Amanda. Ein Hexenroman.* Berlin and Weimar: Aufbau. (West German edition 1984, Darmstadt and Neuwied: Luchterhand.)

—— (1990) 'Interview mit Alice Schwarzer' in *Emma. Das Magazin von Frauen für Frauen* 2, 1990, 32.

—— (1992) *Rumba auf einen Herbst,* ed. Rudolf Bussmann. Hamburg and Zurich: Luchterhand.

Moser, Gerhard (1992) Review of *La Valse,* 'Es begann mit dem Krieg und der Kindheit' in *Der Standard,* 30 April 1992.

Moser, Sigrid (1991) *Bald nach Hause – skoro domoi. Das Leben der Eva-Maria Stege.* Berlin: Aufbau.

Mudry, Anna (ed.) (1991) *Gute Nacht, du Schöne. Autorinnen blicken zurück.* Frankfurt a.M.: Luchterhand.

Müller, André (1990) 'Ich lebe nicht. André Müller spricht mit der Schriftstellerin Elfriede Jelinek', in *Die Zeit,* 22 June 1990.

Müller, Christine (1985) *Männerprotokolle* with an afterword by Ursula Püschel. Berlin: Buchverlag Der Morgen.

Müller, Herta (1989) *Reisende auf einem Bein.* Berlin: Rotbuch.

Musil, Robert (1985) *The Man Without Qualities.* New York: Putnam Publishing Group.

Neues Volksblatt (1993) Article on Marlene Streeruwitz. 14 April 1993.

Nicholson, Linda J. (ed.) (1990) *Feminism/Postmodernism.* New York and London: Routledge.

Niehaus, Herbert (ed.) (1967) *Handbuch der Sekretärin. Ein modernes Sach- und Fachbuch.* Frankfurt a.M.: Verlag für Bürotechnik.

Nonnenmann, Peter (ed.) (1963) *Schriftsteller der Gegenwart. Deutsche Literatur. 53 Porträts.* Olten and Freiburg im Breisgau: Walter.

Novak, Helga M. (1979) *Die Eisheiligen.* Darmstadt and Neuwied: Luchterhand.

Nowoselsky-Müller, Sonia (ed.) (1989) *ein mund von welt: ginka steinwachs. TEXT/S/ORTE/N/.* Bremen: Zeichen + Spuren.

Othmer-Vetter, Regina (1988) '"Weibliches Schreiben": Streifzüge durch Noch-Nicht-Vergangenes' in *Feministische Studien* 1, 1988, 116–124.

Özakin, Aysel (1983) *Die Leidenschaft der Anderen.* Hamburg and Zurich: Luchterhand.

—— (1987) *Der fliegende Teppich. Auf der Spur meines Vaters.* Reinbek bei Hamburg: Rowohlt.

—— (1989a) *Die blaue Maske.* Hamburg and Zurich: Luchterhand.

—— (1989b) *Die Preisvergabe.* Hamburg and Zurich: Luchterhand 1989.

—— (1991a) *Die Vögel auf der Stirn.* Hamburg and Zurich: Luchterhand.

—— (1991b) *Glaube, Liebe, Aircondition. Eine türkische Kindheit.* Hamburg and Zurich: Luchterhand.

Özdamar, Emine Sevgi (1991) *Mutterzunge. Erzählungen.* Berlin: Rotbuch.

—— (1992) *Das Leben ist eine Karawanserei, hat zwei Türen, aus einer kam ich rein, aus der anderen ging ich raus.* Cologne: Kiepenheuer & Witsch.

Pauli, Ruth (1986) *Emanzipation in Österreich: Der lange Marsch in die Sackgasse.* Vienna: Böhlau.

Pausch, Birgit (1977) *Die Verweigerungen der Johanna Glauflügel*. Berlin: Rotbuch.
—— (1985) *Bildnis der Jakobina Völker*. Frankfurt a.M.: Ullstein (orig. 1980).
Peitsch, Helmut (1991) 'Built on Sand? Prose Writings in the Fifties and Sixties' in Kolinsky 1991, 297–322.
Petersen, Karin (1978) *Das fette Jahr*. Cologne: Kiepenheuer & Witsch.
Pezold, Klaus and Autorenkollektiv (eds) (1991) *Geschichte der deutschsprachigen Schweizer Literatur im 20. Jahrhundert*. Berlin: Volk und Wissen.
Pfister, Eva (1992) 'Ein Land wie eine Tür', in *Der Standard. Album* 25 September 1992, 1–2.
Pirskawetz, Lia (1984) *Der stille Grund*. Berlin: Verlag Neues Leben.
Plessen, Elisabeth (1976) *Mitteilung an den Adel*. Zurich: Benziger.
—— (1979) *Such Sad Tidings*, trans. Ruth Hein. New York: The Viking Press.
Plogstedt, Sibylle (1991) *Niemandstochter*. Munich: Piper.
Puknus, Heinz (ed.) (1980) *Neue Literatur der Frauen. Deutschsprachige Autorinnen der Gegenwart* with an introductory essay by Elisabeth Endres. Munich: Beck.
Pulver, Elsbeth and Sybille Dallach (eds) (1985) *Zwischenzeilen – Schriftstellerinnen der deutschen Schweiz*. Berne: Zytglogge.
Pusch, Luise F. (ed.) (1983) *Feminismus. Inspektion der Herrenkultur*. Frankfurt a.M.: Suhrkamp.
Qualtinger, Helmut and Carl Merz (1982) *Der Herr Karl*. Vienna: Preiser.
Rapisarda, Cettina (1987a) 'Anfang Zwischenreich Zukunft. Autorinnen im Berlin der Nachkriegszeit' in Horvat et al. 1987, 88–101.
—— (1987b) '"… und damit waren unsere Anfangsjahre richtig zerteppert." Interview mit Ingeborg Drewitz am 30 October 1986' in Horvat et al. 1987, 10–14.
—— (1991) 'Zu den literarischen Anfängen Ingeborg Bachmanns' in Fetscher et al. 1991, 188–202.
Rasmussen, Ann Marie (1989) 'Women and Literature in German-speaking Switzerland: Tendencies in the 1980s' in Knapp and Labroisse 1989, 159–182.
Rasp, Renate (1967) *Ein ungeratener Sohn*. Cologne: Kiepenheuer & Witsch.
—— (1968) 'Fünf Gedichte' in *Akzente* 15, 1968, 54–58.
—— (1970) *A Family Failure*, trans. Eva Figes. New York: Orion Press.
Reed, Philippa (1987) *Alles was ich schreibe steht im Dienst der Frauen. Zum essayistischen und fiktionalen Werk Hedwig Dohms (1833–1919)*. Frankfurt a.M.: Lang.
Rehmann, Ruth (1961) *Saturday to Monday*, trans. Catherine Hutter. New York: The Viking Press.
—— (1968) *Die Leute im Tal*. Frankfurt a.M.: Suhrkamp (paperback 1989, Munich: dtv).
—— (1979) *Der Mann auf der Kanzel. Fragen an einen Vater*. Munich: Hanser.
—— (1983) *Paare. Erzählungen*. Munich: dtv (orig. 1978).
—— (1985) *Abschied von der Meisterklasse*. Munich: Hanser.
—— (1987) *Die Schwaigerin*. Munich: Hanser.
—— (1988a) 'Schriftsteller arbeiten ziemlich einsam. Ein Gespräch mit Wilfried Ihrig und Wolfgang Rath' in *Sprache im technischen Zeitalter*, 26, 1988, 115–122.
—— (1988b) 'Was ist das für ein Verein?' in Schutte 1988, 48–51.
—— (1989) *Illusionen*. Munich: dtv (orig. 1959).
—— (1993) *Unterwegs in fremden Träumen. Begegnungen mit dem anderen Deutschland*. Munich and Vienna: Hanser.
—— (1994) *Travelling in Alien Dreams* (excerpts), trans. Christoph Lohmann, in *Dimension²*, 1, 1994, 470–495 (translation forthcoming: Lincoln: University of Nebraska Press).
—— (1995a) *Bootsfahrt mit Damen. Erzählungen*. Munich and Vienna: Hanser.
—— (1995b) *The Man on the Pulpit*. Lincoln: University of Nebraska Press.
—— (1995c) 'Kompliziertes einfach machen. Literatur, Politik und Moral. Gespräch mit Ruth Rehmann.' Werner Jung in *Juni. Magazin für Literatur und Politik*, 23, 83–94.
Reich-Ranicki, Marcel (1962) *Wer schreibt, provoziert. Kommentare und Pamphlete*. Munich: dtv.
—— (1967) *Literatur der kleinen Schritte. Deutsche Schriftsteller heute*. Munich: R. Piper and Co.

——— (1972) 'Eine einst bedeutende Lyrikerin auf sonderbaren Abwegen. Am liebsten beim Friseur. Ingeborg Bachmanns neuer Erzählungsband *Simultan*', *Die Zeit*, 27 September 1972, in Hotz 1990, 227–231.

Reichart, Elisabeth (1984) *Februarschatten*. Vienna: Verlag der österreichischen Staatsdruckerei.

——— (1988a) *February Shadows. A Novel of Austria under Fascism*, trans. with a commentary by Donna L. Hoffmeister. London: The Women's Press.

——— (1988b) *Komm über den See*. Salzburg: Otto Müller.

——— (1991) '"Die Grenzen meiner Welt sind die Grenzen meiner Sprache". Wiener Vorlesungen zur Literatur' in *Wespennest* 82, 1991, 114–142.

——— (1992) *La Valse*. Salzburg: Otto Müller.

——— (1993) (ed.) *Österreichische Dichterinnen*. Salzburg: Otto Müller.

——— (1994) *Sakkorausch. Ein Monolog*. Salzburg: Otto Müller.

Reimann, Brigitte (1961) *Ankunft im Alltag*. Berlin: Verlag Neues Leben. (West German edition 1986, Munich: dtv.)

——— (1965) *Das grüne Licht der Steppen*. Berlin: Verlag Neues Leben.

——— (1974) *Franziska Linkerhand*. Berlin: Verlag Neues Leben. (West German edition 1986, Munich: dtv.)

Reimann, Brigitte and Christa Wolf (1993) *Sei gegrüßt und lebe. Eine Freundschaft in Briefen*. Berlin and Weimar: Aufbau.

Reinig, Christa (1961) *Der Traum meiner Verkommenheit*. Berlin (West): Wolfgang Fietkau.

——— (1976a) 'Das weibliche Ich' in Hildegard Brenner (ed.) *alternative (Das Lächeln der Medusa. Frauenbewegung. Sprache. Psychoanalyse)* 108/109, 1976, 119–120. Berlin: alternative-Verlag.

——— (1976b) 'Eindrücke auf dem Treffen schreibender Frauen' in *Frauenoffensive-Journal*, 5, 1976. Munich: Frauenoffensive.

——— (1977) *Entmannung. Die Geschichte Ottos und seiner vier Frauen erzählt von Christa Reinig* (orig. 1976). Darmstadt and Neuwied: Luchterhand.

——— (1978) *Mein Herz ist eine gelbe Blume. Christa Reinig im Gespräch mit Ekkehart Rudolf*. Düsseldorf: Eremitenpresse.

——— (1979) *Müßiggang ist aller Liebe Anfang*. Düsseldorf: Eremitenpresse.

——— (1980) *Der Wolf und die Witwen*. Düsseldorf: Eremitenpresse.

——— (1984) *Die Frau im Brunnen*. Munich: Frauenoffensive.

——— (1985) *Gesammelte Gedichte 1960–1979*. Darmstadt and Neuwied: Luchterhand.

——— (1986a) *Erkennen was die Rettung ist. Christa Reinig im Gespräch mit Marie-Luise Gansberg und Mechthild Beerlage*. Munich: Frauenoffensive.

——— (1986b) *Gesammelte Erzählungen*. Darmstadt and Neuwied: Luchterhand.

——— (1989) 'Eine Ruine' in Helmut Peitsch and Rhys Williams (eds) *Berlin seit dem Kriegsende*. Manchester: Manchester University Press, 1989, 40–41 (orig. 1949).

——— (1991) *Idleness is the Root of All Love*, trans. Ilze Mueller. Corvallis: Oregon State University Press.

Reinshagen, Gerlind (1984) *Die flüchtige Braut*. Frankfurt a.M.: Suhrkamp.

——— (1985) *Die Clownin*. Frankfurt a.M.: Suhrkamp.

Reith, Hartmut (1987) 'Das Berliner Verlagsleben in der Nachkriegszeit' in Horvat et al. 1987, 117–127.

Reschke, Karin (1982) *Verfolgte des Glücks. Findebuch der Henriette Vogel*. Berlin: Rotbuch.

——— (1984) *Dieser Tage über Nacht*. Berlin: Rotbuch.

Resnick, Margery and Isabelle de Courtivron (eds) (1984) *Women Writers in Translation: An Annotated Bibliography, 1945–1982*. New York and London: Garland.

Rich, Adrienne (1976) *Of Woman Born*. New York: Norton.

——— (1981) *Compulsory Heterosexuality and Lesbian Experience*. London: Onlywomen Press.

Richter, Hans Werner (ed.) (1962) *Almanach der Gruppe 47. 1947–1962*. Reinbek bei Hamburg: Rowohlt.

——— (1986) *Im Etablissement der Schmetterlinge. Einundzwanzig Porträts aus der Gruppe 47*. Munich: Hanser.

Richter-Schröder, Karin (1986) *Frauenliteratur und weibliche Identität. Theoretische Ansätze zu einer weiblichen Ästhetik und zur Entwicklung der neuen deutschen Frauenliteratur*. Frankfurt a.M.: Anton Hain.

Rimmon-Kenan, Shlomith (1983) *Narrative Fiction: Contemporary Poetics*. London and New York: Methuen.

Rinser, Luise (1977) *Gefängnistagebuch*. Frankfurt a.M.: Fischer (orig. 1946).

—— (1980) 'Die rote Katze' in Durzak 1980a and Weyrauch 1989, 70–76 (orig. 1949).

—— (1981) *Den Wolf umarmen*. Frankfurt a.M.: Fischer.

—— (1987) *A Woman's Prison Journal*, trans. Michael Hulse. New York: Schocken Books.

Riviere, Joan (1986) 'Womanliness As Masquerade' in Victor Burgin, James Donald and Cora Kaplan (eds) *Formations of Fantasy*. London: Methuen, 1986, 35–44.

Roebling, Irmgard (ed.) (1992) *Sehnsucht und Sirene. Vierzehn Abhandlungen zu Wasserphantasien*. Pfaffenweiler: Centaurus.

Roeder, Anke (ed.) (1989) *Autorinnen: Herausforderungen an das Theater*. Frankfurt a.M.: Suhrkamp.

Roschner, Achim (1987) 'Elisabeth Reichart im Gespräch' in *Neue Deutsche Literatur*, 35, 9, 1987, 129–32.

Roten, Iris von (1991) *Frauen im Laufgitter. Offene Worte zur Stellung der Frau*. Zurich: eFeF (orig. 1958).

Roth, Friederike (1983) *Das Buch des Lebens. Ein Plagiat. Erste Folge*. Darmstadt and Neuwied: Luchterhand.

—— (1986) *Das Ganze ein Stück*. Frankfurt a.M.: Suhrkamp.

Rudolph, Kurt and Ernst Werner (eds) (1984) *Der Koran*. Leipzig: Reclam.

Rundbrief Frauen in der Literaturwissenschaft, ed. Sibylle Benninghoff-Lühl, Dagmar von Hoff, Inge Stephan, Heike Vedder, Kerstin Wilhelms. Universität Hamburg: Frauen in der Literaturwissenschaft.

Runge, Erika (1968) *Bottroper Protokolle*. Frankfurt a.M.: Suhrkamp.

—— (1970) *Frauen. Versuche zur Emanzipation*. 2nd revised and enlarged edition. Frankfurt a.M.: Suhrkamp.

—— (1976) 'Überlegungen beim Abschied von der Dokumentarliteratur' in *Kontext*, vol. 1. *Literatur und Wirklichkeit*, 1976, 97–120. Munich: Autoren-Edition.

Rütschi-Hermann, Elisabeth and Edna Huttenmaier Spitz (1978) *German Women Writers of the Twentieth Century*. Oxford: Pergamon Press.

Said, Edward (1978) *Orientalism*, Harmondsworth: Penguin.

Sander, Helke (1975) 'Rede des "Aktionsrats zur Befreiung der Frau"' in *Frauenjahrbuch* 1. Frankfurt a.M.: Frankfurter Frauen, 1975, 10–15.

—— (1984) 'Speech by the Action Council for Women's Liberation', trans. Edith. H. Altbach in Altbach et al. 1984, 307–310.

Saussure, Ferdinand de (1974) *A Course in General Linguistics*. London: Fontana.

Sauter, Josef-Hermann (1981) 'Interviews mit Barbara Frischmuth, Elfriede Jelinek, Michael Scharang' in *Weimarer Beiträge* 27, 6, 1981, 109–117.

Schanda, Susanne (1992) 'Mit messerscharfen Sätzen ins Fleisch der Wirklichkeit. Neue Bücher von österreichischen Autorinnen: *Hochzeit. Ein Fall* von Ingrid Puganigg und *La Valse* von Elisabeth Reichart' in *Der kleine Bund*, Kultur-Beilage, 8 August 1992, 1.

Scheer, Regina (1992) *Ahawah. Das vergessene Haus. Spurensuche in der Berliner Auguststraße*. Berlin: Aufbau.

Scheuffelen, Thomas (ed.) (1977) *Gabriele Wohmann. Materialienbuch*. Darmstadt and Neuwied: Luchterhand.

Schlich, Jutta (1994) *Phänomenologie der Wahrnehmung von Literatur: Am Beispiel von Elfriede Jelineks 'Lust' (1989)*. Tübingen: Max Niemeyer.

Schmid-Bortenschlager, Sigrid (1991) 'Der Ort der Sprache. Zu Ilse Aichinger' in Walter-Buchebner-Gesellschaft (ed.) 1991, 86–94.

Schmidt, Ricarda (1982/90) *Westdeutsche Frauenliteratur in den siebziger Jahren*. Frankfurt a.M.: Rita G. Fischer.

—— (1988) 'Erzählende Prosa der 70er und 80er Jahre' in Brinker-Gabler 1988b, 459–477.

Schmitz-Burckhardt, Barbara (1993) 'Die kalte Komik des Gemeinen' in *Frankfurter Rundschau*, 4 February 1993.

Schneider, Michael (1984) 'Fathers and Sons, Retrospectively: The Damaged Relationship Between Two Generations' in *new german critique* 31, 1984, 3–51.

Schnell, Ralf (1986) *Die Literatur der Bundesrepublik. Autoren, Geschichte, Literaturbetrieb*. Stuttgart: Metzler.

Scholl, Sabine (1990) *Unica Zürn: Fehler Fallen Kunst.* Meisenheim and Frankfurt a.M.: Anton Hain.

Schostack, Renate (1985) *Heiratsversuche oder die Einschiffung nach Cythera.* Munich: Piper.

Schroeder, Margot (1975) *Ich stehe meine Frau.* Published with the collaboration of the *Hamburger Werkstatt schreibender Arbeiter,* Frankfurt a.M.: Fischer.

———— (1976) *Der Schlachter empfiehlt noch immer Herz.* Munich: Frauenoffensive.

Schubert, Helga (1975) *Lauter Leben.* Berlin and Weimar: Aufbau.

———— (1982) *Das verbotene Zimmer.* Darmstadt and Neuwied: Luchterhand. (East German edition 1984: *Blickwinkel.* Berlin and Weimar: Aufbau.)

———— (1984) 'Innenhöfe' in *Blickwinkel.* Berlin and Weimar: Aufbau.

———— (1990) *Judasfrauen.* Berlin and Weimar: Aufbau.

Schubert, Helga and Rita Süssmuth (1992) *Bezahlen Frauen die Wiedervereinigung?* ed. Michael Halle. Munich and Zurich: Piper.

Schulte, Axel, Monika Müller, Jan Vink et al. (1985) *Ausländer in der Bundesrepublik. Integration, Marginalisierung, Identität.* Frankfurt a.M.: Materialis MP 29.

Schuscheng, Dorothe (1987) *Arbeit am Mythos Frau. Weiblichkeit und Autonomie in der literarischen Mythenrezeption Ingeborg Bachmanns, Christa Wolfs und Gertrud Leuteneggers.* Frankfurt a.M. and Berne: Lang.

Schutte, Jürgen (ed.) (1988) *Dichter und Richter. Die Gruppe 47 und die deutsche Nachkriegsliteratur.* Berlin: Akademie der Künste.

Schutting, Jutta (1980) *Der Vater.* Salzburg and Vienna: Residenz.

Schütz, Helga (1970) *Vorgeschichten oder Schöne Gegend Probstein.* Berlin and Weimar: Aufbau. (West German edition 1977, Munich: dtv, orig. 1972.)

———— (1972) *Das Erdbeben bei Sangerhausen und andere Geschichten.* Berlin and Weimar: Aufbau.

———— (1973) *Festbeleuchtung.* Berlin and Weimar: Aufbau. (West German edition 1982, Darmstadt and Neuwied: Luchterhand, orig. 1976.)

———— (1980) *Julia oder Erziehung zum Chorgesang.* Berlin and Weimar: Aufbau. (West German edition 1983: *Erziehung zum Chorgesang.* Munich: dtv, orig. 1981.)

———— (1992) *Heimat, süße Heimat.* Berlin and Weimar: Aufbau.

Schwaiger, Brigitte (1977) *Wie kommt das Salz ins Meer.* Vienna and Hamburg: Zsolnay.

———— (1980) *Lange Abwesenheit.* Vienna and Hamburg: Zsolnay.

———— (1988) *Why is there Salt in the Sea?* trans. Sieglinde Lug. Lincoln: University of Nebraska Press.

Schwarzer, Alice (1975) *Der 'kleine Unterschied' und seine große Folgen. Frauen über sich – Beginn einer Befreiung.* Frankfurt a.M.: Fischer.

———— (1983) (ed.) *So fing es an!: die neue Frauenbewegung.* Munich: dtv (orig. 1981).

Schweizer Lexikon 91 (1992), 6 volumes. Lucerne: Verlag Schweizer Lexikon.

Seghers, Anna (1944) *Transit,* trans. James A. Galston. Boston: Little Brown.

———— (1946) *Das siebte Kreuz .* Berlin and Weimar: Aufbau. (West edition 1962, Darmstadt and Neuwied: Luchterhand; 1965, Reinbek bei Hamburg: Rowohlt, orig. 1942 Mexico)

———— (1948) *Transit.* Konstanz: Weller.

———— (1951a) *Die Kinder.* Berlin: Aufbau.

———— (1951b) 'Die Tochter der Delegierten' in Seghers 1951a.

———— (1953a) 'Friedensgeschichten', in *Der Bienenstock* vol. 2, 1953. Berlin: Aufbau

———— (1953b) 'Der erste Schritt' in *Der Bienenstock* vol. 2, 1953. Berlin: Aufbau.

———— (1953c) 'Die Umsiedlerin', in *Der Bienenstock* vol. 2, 1953. Berlin: Aufbau.

———— (1959) *Die Entscheidung.* Berlin: Aufbau. (West German edition 1985, Darmstadt and Neuwied: Luchterhand.)

———— (1961) 'Das Licht auf dem Galgen' in *Karibische Geschichten.* Berlin and Weimar: Aufbau, 1977.

———— (1965) *Die Kraft der Schwachen. Neun Erzählungen.* Berlin and Weimar: Aufbau. (West German edition 1965, Darmstadt and Neuwied: Luchterhand.)

———— (1967) *Das wirkliche Blau.* Berlin and Weimar: Aufbau.

———— (1968) *Das Vertrauen.* Berlin and Weimar: Aufbau.

———— (1973a) *Benito's Blue and Nine Other Stories,* trans. Joan Becker. Berlin: Seven Seas.

———— (1973b) *Überfahrt.* Berlin and Weimar: Aufbau.

———— (1973c) *Sonderbare Begegnungen.* Berlin and Weimar: Aufbau.

────── (1973d) 'Sagen von Unirdischen', in Seghers 1973c.

────── (1980) *Drei Frauen aus Haiti*. Berlin and Weimar: Aufbau. (West German edition Darmstadt and Neuwied: Luchterhand.)

────── (1987) *The Seventh Cross*, trans. James A. Galston. New York: The Monthly Review Press (orig. 1942).

Seidel, Heide (1979) 'Ingeborg Bachmann und Ludwig Wittgenstein. Person und Werk Ludwig Wittgensteins in den Erzählungen *Das dreißigste Jahr* und *Ein Wildermuth*' in *Zeitschrift für deutsche Philologie*, Heft 2, 1979, 267–282.

Sellers, Susan (1994) *The Hélène Cixous Reader*. London: Routledge.

Serke, Jürgen (1979/82) *Frauen schreiben. Ein neues Kapitel deutschsprachiger Literatur*. Hamburg: Stern/Frankfurt a.M.: Fischer.

Seyffarth, Ursula (1946) 'Vom Wesen und Werden der Frauendichtung' in *Welt und Wort* 1. 1946, 193–197. Wörishofen: Drei-Säulen-Verlag.

Sheppard, Richard (ed.) (1990) *New Ways in Germanistik*. Oxford: Berg.

Showalter, Elaine (ed.) (1985/6) *The New Feminist Criticism*. New York: Pantheon/London: Virago.

Siblewski, Klaus (ed.) (1982) *Gabriele Wohmann. Auskunft für Leser*. Darmstadt and Neuwied: Luchterhand.

Snitow, Ann, Christine Stansell and Sharon Thompson (eds) (1984) *Desire: The Politics of Sexuality*. London: Virago.

Spanlang, Elisabeth (1992) *Elfriede Jelinek: Studien zum Frühwerk*. Vienna: Verband der wissenschaftlichen Gesellschaften Österreichs.

Stefan, Verena (1975) *Häutungen. Autobiographische Aufzeichnungen, Gedichte, Träume, Analysen*. Munich: Frauenoffensive.

────── (1978) *Shedding*, trans. Beth Weckmüller and Johanna Moore. New York: Daughters.

────── (1994a) 'Shedding', trans. Johanna Steigleder Moore and Beth E. Weckmueller in *Shedding & Literally Dreaming* with an afterword by Tobe Levin. New York: Feminist Press at City University of New York, 1994, 3–79.

────── (1994b) *Häutungen. Mit einem Vorwort zur Neuausgabe*. Frankfurt a.M.: Fischer.

Steinwachs, Ginka (1971/85) *Mythologie des Surrealismus oder die Rückverwandlung von Kultur in Natur*. Basel and Frankfurt a.M.: Stroemfeld/Roter Stern.

────── (1978) *marylinparis. montageroman*. Vienna: Rhombus.

────── (1979) *Berliner Trichter. Berliner Bilderbogen*. Vienna: Rhombus.

────── (1985) *Erzherzog Herzherzog oder: Das unglückliche Haus Österreich heiratet die Insel der Stille*. Munich: Raben Verlag.

────── (1989) 'Die entfesselte Titanin. Ich will ein Theater der Fülle' in Roeder 1989, 109–122.

────── (1992a) *G-L-Ü-C-K*. Frankfurt a.M.: Suhrkamp.

────── (1992b) *George Sand: eine Frau in Bewegung, die Frau von Stand* (orig 1980). Basel and Frankfurt a.M.: Stroemfeld/Roter Stern.

────── (1992c) 'George Sand', trans. Jamie Owen Daniel, Katrin Sieg and Sue-Ellen Case in Sue-Ellen Case (ed.) *The Divided Homeland. Contemporary German Women's Plays*. Ann Arbor: University of Michigan Press, 1992, 287–339.

Steinwachs, Ginka and Sonia Nowoselsky-Müller (1989) 'Alles plus eine Tomate'. Interview in Nowoselsky-Müller 1989, 32–42.

Steinwendtner, Brita (1993) 'Ein paar Fragen in Briefen – Gespräch mit Ilse Aichinger' in Bartsch and Melzer 1993, 7–13.

Stephan, Inge (1986) 'Von Bildern umstellt: Zu den Frauenfiguren bei Ruth Rehmann' in Stephan et al. 1986, 221–240.

Stephan, Inge and Sigrid Weigel (eds) (1983) *Die verborgene Frau: sechs Beiträge zu einer feministischen Literaturwissenschaft*. Berlin: Argument.

Stephan, Inge, Sigrid Weigel and Renate Berger (eds) (1984) *Feministische Literaturwissenschaft*. Berlin: Argument.

Stephan, Inge, Regula Venske and Sigrid Weigel (eds) (1986a) *Frauenliteratur ohne Tradition? Neun Autorinnenporträts*. Frankfurt a.M.: Fischer.

Stephan, Inge, Sigrid Weigel, Renate Berger, Monika Hengsbach, Maria Kublitz (eds) (1986b) *Frauen – Weiblichkeit – Schrift*. Berlin: Argument.

Stern, Carola (1994) *Der Text meines Lebens*. Reinbek bei Hamburg: Rowohlt.
Stiftung Lesen (1990) *Lesen im internationalen Vergleich*. Ein Forschungsgutachten der Stiftung Lesen für das Bundesministerium für Bildung und Wissenschaft. Teil 1. Mainz: Stiftung Lesen.
Stötzer-Kachold, Gabi (1992) *grenzen los fremd gehen*. Berlin: janus press.
Streeruwitz, Marlene (1992) '''Helb auer mischon!'': Schwarzenegger for Burgtheater' in *Frankfurter Rundschau*, 29 February 1992.
—— (1993). *New York. New York. Elysian Park. Zwei Stücke*. Frankfurt a.M.: Suhrkamp.
—— (1994) *Tolmezzo. Eine symphonische Dichtung*. Frankfurt a.M.: Suhrkamp.
Strittmatter, Eva (1975) *Ich mach ein Lied aus Stille*. Berlin and Weimar: Aufbau.
—— (1977) *Mondschnee liegt auf den Wiesen*. Berlin and Weimar: Aufbau.
Struck, Karin (1973) *Klassenliebe*. Frankfurt a.M.: Suhrkamp.
—— (1983) 'Ist nur eine tote erotische Autorin eine gute erotische Autorin?' in *Monatshefte* 75, 4, 1983, 353–357.
Struzyk, Brigitte (1984) *Leben auf der Kippe*. Berlin and Weimar: Aufbau.
—— (1988) *Caroline unterm Freiheitsbaum. Ansichtssachen*. Berlin and Weimar: Aufbau.
—— (1994) *In vollen Zügen – Rück-Sichten*. Berlin and Weimar: Aufbau.
Stump, Doris, Maya Widmer and Regula Wyss (eds) (1994) *Deutschsprachige Schriftstellerinnen in der Schweiz 1700–1945. Eine Bibliographie*. Zurich: Limmat.
Taschau, Hannelies (1967) *Die Taube auf dem Dach*. Hamburg: Christian Wegner.
—— (1980) *Landfriede* . Frankfurt a.M.: Fischer (orig. 1978).
Tetzner, Gerti (1974) *Karen W.* Halle: Mitteldeutscher Verlag. (West German edition 1989, Frankfurt a.M.: Luchterhand Literaturverlag, orig. 1979.)
Thieringer, Thomas (1993) 'Mensch – kaputt: Marlene Streeruwitz', *New York. New York*. in München' in *Süddeutsche Zeitung*, 1 February 1993, 12.
Töpelmann, Sigrid (ed.) (1987) *Ingeborg Bachmann. Ausgewählte Werke*. Berlin: Aufbau.
—— (1988) *Tradition entdecken – Tradition schaffen. Schweizer Frauenliteratur im 19. und 20. Jahrhundert*. (1988) Dokumentation der Tagung vom 31. Mai/1. Juni 1986 in der Paulus-Akademie Zurich. Zurich: Paulus-Akademie.
Treudl, Sylvia (1988) *Domino mit Domina*. Vienna: Wiener Frauenverlag.
Tunner, Erika (1988) 'Tradition und Aufbruch: Literatur in der Bundesrepublik in Österreich und der deutschsprachigen Schweiz seit 1945. Ein Überblick' in Brinker-Gabler 1988b, vol. 2, 401–416.
Vansant, Jacqueline (1988) *Against the Horizon: Feminism and Postwar Austrian Women Writers*. New York, Westport (Connecticut) and London: Greenwood Press.
Venske, Regula (1988) *Mannsbilder – Männerbilder. Konstruktion und Kritik des Männlichen in zeitgenössischer deutschsprachiger Literatur von Frauen*. Hildesheim and Zurich: Olms.
—— (1991a) *Das Verschwinden des Mannes in der weiblichen Schreibmaschine. Männerbilder in der Literatur von Frauen*. Hamburg and Zurich: Luchterhand.
—— (1991b) '''Schriftstellerin mit der Seele eines Möbelpackers'': Marlen Haushofer' in Walter-Buchebner-Gesellschaft 1991, 22–32.
—— (1992) 'Kritik der Männlichkeit' in Briegleb and Weigel (eds) 1992, 267–276.
Vinke, Hermann (ed.) (1993) *Akteneinsicht Christa Wolf. Zerrspiegel und Dialog*. Hamburg and Zurich: Luchterhand.
Walser, Martin (1968) 'Berichte aus der Klassengesellschaft' in Runge 1968, 7–10.
Walter-Buchebner-Gesellschaft (ed.) (1991) *Das Schreiben der Frauen in Österreich seit 1950*. Vienna: Böhlau.
Wander, Maxie (1977) *Guten Morgen, du Schöne*. Berlin: Buchverlag Der Morgen. (West German edition 1978: *Guten Morgen, du Schöne. Frauen in der DDR. Protokolle*. Darmstadt and Neuwied: Luchterhand.)
Wartmann, Brigitte (1979) 'Schreiben als Angriff auf das Patriarchat' in *Literaturmagazin 11*, 1979, 108–32.
Wartmann, Brigitte (1984) 'Writing As an Attack Against Patriarchy', trans. Jeanette Clausen in Altbach et al. 1984, 55–63.
Weber, Ingeborg (ed.) (1994) *Weiblichkeit und weibliches Schreiben*. Darmstadt: Wissenschaftliche Buchgesellschaft.
Weber, Richard (ed.) (1992) *Deutsches Drama der 80er Jahre*. Frankfurt a.M.: Suhrkamp.

Weedon, Chris (1987/1996) *Feminist Practice and Poststructuralist Theory*. Oxford: Blackwell. Second edition 1996.

—— (1994) 'The Struggle for Women's Emancipation in the Work of Hedwig Dohm' in *German Life and Letters*, XLVII, 1994, 182–192.

—— (ed.) (1988) *Die Frau in der DDR*. Oxford: Blackwell.

Weigel, Sigrid (1983a) 'Die geopferte Heldin und das Opfer als Heldin. Zum Entwurf weiblicher Helden in der Literatur von Männern und Frauen' in Stephan and Weigel 1983, 138–152.

—— (1983b) 'Das Schreiben des Mangels als Produktion von Utopie. Reflektionen' in *horen* 28, 3, 1983, 149–155.

—— (1983c) 'Der schielende Blick: Thesen zur Geschichte weiblicher Schreibpraxis' in Stephan and Weigel 1983, 83–137.

—— (1984a) '"Woman Begins Relating to Herself": Contemporary German Women's Literature (Part One)' trans. Luke Springman in *new german critique* 31, 1984, 53–94.

—— (1984b) 'Deutschsprachige Literatur von Frauen nach 1945' in *Frauen sehen ihre Zeit*. Literaturausstellung des Landesfrauenbeirates Rheinland Pfalz. Mainz: Landesfrauenbeirat Rheinland Pfalz, 1984, 62–75.

—— (1985) 'Double Focus', trans. Hamet Anderson in Ecker 1985, 59–80.

—— (1989) *Die Stimme der Medusa. Schreibweisen in der Gegenwartsliteratur von Frauen*. Reinbek bei Hamburg: Rowohlt (orig. 1987).

—— (1990) *Topographien der Geschlechter. Kulturgeschichtliche Studien zur Literatur*. Reinbek bei Hamburg: Rowohlt.

Weigel, Sigrid (1994) *Bilder des kulturellen Gedächtnisses. Beiträge zur Gegenwartsliteratur*. Dülmen-Hiddingsel: tende.

Weil, Grete (1980) *Meine Schwester Antigone*. Zurich and Cologne: Benziger Verlag.

Weininger, Otto (1980) *Geschlecht und Charakter. Eine prinzipielle Untersuchung*. Munich: Matthes & Seitz (orig. 1903).

Wellershoff, Dieter (1988) 'Ein sozialer Raum ohne Entfremdung? Rückblick auf die Gruppe 47' in *Sprache im technischen Zeitalter* 26, 1988, 122–128.

Werkkreis Literatur der Arbeitswelt (1973) *Liebe Kollegin. Texte zur Emanzipation der Frau in der Bundesrepublik*. Frankfurt a.M.: Fischer.

—— (1979) *Für Frauen. Ein Lesebuch*. Frankfurt a.M.: Fischer.

Werner, Ruth (1977) *Sonjas Rapport*. Berlin: Verlag Neues Leben.

—— (1989) *Sonya's Report*, trans. Renate Simpson. London: Chatto & Windus.

Weyrauch, Wolfgang (ed.) (1989) *Tausend Gramm. Ein deutsches Bekenntnis in dreißig Geschichten aus dem Jahr 1949*. Reinbek bei Hamburg: Rowohlt (orig. 1949).

Whitford, Margaret (1991) *Luce Irigaray. Philosophy in the Feminine*. London: Routledge.

Widmeier, Ellen (1992) *Eis im Schuh*. Dortmund: edition ebersbach.

Wiggershaus, Renate (1989) 'Neue Tendenzen in der Bundesrepublik Deutschland in Österreich und in der Schweiz' in Gnüg and Möhrmann 1989, 416–433.

Wigmore, Juliet (1990) 'Power, Politics and Pornography: Elfriede Jelinek's Satirical Exposés' in Williams et al. 1990, 209–220.

Wille, Franz (1993) 'Farewell, my lovely? An den Grenzen der Aufklärung' in *Theater heute* 9, 1993, 30–39.

Williams, Arthur, Stuart Parkes and Roland Smith (eds) (1990) *Literature on the Threshold: The German Novel in the 1980s*. New York, Oxford and Munich: Berg.

Willingham, Heike (1992) *vom fegen weiß ich wird man besen*. Berlin: janus press.

Winkels, Hubert (1988a) *Einschnitte. Zur Literatur der 80er Jahre*. Cologne: Kiepenheuer & Witsch.

—— (1988b) 'Mundtot. Die leibhaftige Prosa Anne Dudens' in Winkels 1988a, 42–58.

Winter, Riki (1980) 'Gertrud Leutenegger' in *Kritisches Lexikon zur deutschsprachigen Gegenwartsliteratur* (1 June 1980).

Wisinger, Marion (1992) *Land der Töchter: 150 Jahre Frauenleben in Österreich*. Vienna: Promedia.

Wittowski, Joachim (1991) *Lyrik in der Presse. Eine Untersuchung der Kritik an Wolf Biermann, Erich Fried und Ulla Hahn*. Würzburg: Königshausen & Neumann.

Wohmann, Gabriele (1966) 'Die Schwestern' in *Erzählungen*. Ebenhausen bei Munich: Langewiesche-Brandt.

—— (1974) 'The Sisters', trans. Edna Spitz and Elisabeth Rütschi-Hermann, in *Dimension* 7, 3, 1974, 450–459.

—— (1975) *Schönes Gehege*. Darmstadt and Neuwied: Luchterhand.

Wolf, Christa (1961) *Moskauer Novelle*. Halle: Mitteldeutscher Verlag.

—— (1963) *Der geteilte Himmel*. Halle: Mitteldeutscher Verlag. (West German edition, 1968, Darmstadt and Neuwied: Luchterhand.)

—— (1965/76) *Divided Heaven*, trans. Joan Becker. New York: Adler's Foreign Books/Berlin: Seven Seas.

—— (1968) *Nachdenken über Christa T.* Halle: Mitteldeutscher Verlag. (West German edition Darmstadt and Neuwied: Luchterhand, 1968.)

—— (1972) *Lesen und Schreiben. Aufsätze und Betrachtungen*. Berlin and Weimar: Aufbau. (West German edition, *Lesen und Schreiben: Aufsätze und Prosastücke*. Darmstadt and Neuwied: Luchterhand, 1972. Reprinted 1980/4 as *Neue Sammlung. Essays, Aufsätze, Reden*. Darmstadt and Neuwied: Luchterhand.)

—— (1973) *Unter den Linden*. Berlin and Weimar: Aufbau.

—— (1974/80) 'Selbstversuch' in *Geschlechtertausch. Drei Erzählungen* with Sarah Kirsch and Irmtraud Morgner. Darmstadt and Neuwied: Luchterhand.

—— (1976) *Kindheitsmuster*. Berlin and Weimar: Aufbau. (West German edition Darmstadt and Neuwied: Luchterhand, 1977.)

—— (1977) *The Reader and the Writer. Essays, Sketches, Memories*, trans. Joan Becker. Berlin: Seven Seas/New York: International Publishers.

—— (1978) 'Self-Experiment', trans. Jeanette Clausen in *new german critique: Special Feminist Issue* 13, 1978, 109–131.

—— (1979) *Kein Ort Nirgends*. Berlin and Weimar: Aufbau. (West German edition Darmstadt and Neuwied: Luchterhand, 1979.)

—— (1980) *Von Büchner sprechen. Darmstädter Rede* in Wolf 1986a II, 155–169.

—— (1980/3) *A Model Childhood*, trans. U. Molinaro and H. Rappolt. New York: Farrar, Straus & Giroux/London: Virago.

—— (1982) *The Quest for Christa T.*, trans. Christopher Middleton. London: Virago.

—— (1982/3) *No Place on Earth*, trans. H. Rappolt and U. Molinaro. New York: Farrar Straus & Giroux/London: Virago.

—— (1983) *Kassandra*. Berlin and Weimar: Aufbau. (West German edition Darmstadt and Neuwied: Luchterhand, 1983.)

—— (1984a) *Cassandra. A Novel and Four Essays*, trans. Jan van Heurck. London: Virago.

—— (1984b) *Krankheit und Liebesentzug*. In Wolf 1986a, vol. II, 271–292.

—— (1986a) *Die Dimension des Autors* vols. I and II. Berlin and Weimar: Aufbau.

—— (1986b) *Berliner Begegnung*, in Wolf 1986a, vol. I, 438–442.

—— (1990a) *Reden im Herbst*. Berlin and Weimar: Aufbau.

—— (1990b) *Was bleibt*. Berlin and Weimar: Aufbau.

—— (1993a) *What Remains and Other Stories*, trans. Rick Takvorian and Heike Schwarzbauer. New York: Farrar Straus & Giroux.

—— (1993b) *Akteneinsicht Christa Wolf. Zerrspiegel und Dialog*, ed. Hermann Vinke. Hamburg and Zurich: Luchterhand.

Woolf, Virginia (1929) *A Room of One's Own*. London: Hogarth Press.

Wolff, Lutz W. (ed.) (1979) *Frauen in der DDR. Zwanzig Erzählungen*. Munich: dtv.

Wollstonecraft, Mary (1983) *Vindication of the Rights of Women*. Harmondsworth: Penguin.

Wolter, Christine (1976) 'Ich habe wieder geheiratet' in Christine Wolter, *Wie ich meine Unschuld verlor*. Berlin and Weimar: Aufbau, 1976.

—— (1982) 'Meine italienische Reise' in Christine Wolter, *Italienfahrten*. Berlin and Weimar: Aufbau, 1982.

—— (1984) 'I Have Married Again', trans. Friedrich Achberger, in Altbach et al. 1984, 220–225.

—— (1990) *Das Stendhal-Syndrom*. Berlin and Weimar: Aufbau.

Worgitzky, Charlotte (1982) *Meine ungeborenen Kinder*. Berlin: Buchverlag Der Morgen.

Wörle, Andrea (ed.) (1991) *Frauen in der Schweiz. Erzählungen*. Munich: dtv.

Worton, Michael and Judith Still (eds) (1990) *Intertextuality: Theories and Practices*. Manchester: Manchester University Press.

Wright, Elizabeth (1984) *Psychoanalytic Criticism: Theory in Practice*. London: Methuen.

—— (1992) *Feminism and Psychoanalysis. A Critical Dictionary*. Oxford: Blackwell.

Wysocki, Gisela von (1980a) *Die Fröste der Freiheit: Aufbruchsphantasien*. Frankfurt a.M.: Syndikat.

—— (1980b) 'Weiblichkeit als Anagramm. Unica Zürn' in von Wysocki 1980a, 37–54.

—— (1988) 'Schauspieler, Tänzer, Sängerin' in *Theater heute* 6, 1988, 18–32.

Young, Robert (1990) *White Mythologies: Writing History and the West*. London: Routledge.

Zeman, Herbert (ed.) (1989) *Die österreichische Literatur. Ihr Profil von der Jahrhundertwende bis zur Gegenwart*, 2 vols. Graz: Akademische Druck- und Verlagsanstalt.

Zeplin, Rosemarie (1984) *Alpträume aus der Provinz*. Berlin and Weimar: Aufbau.

—— (1990a) *Ein holdes Liebkerlchen*. Unpublished radio play.

—— (1990b) *Maulwurf oder fatales Beispiel weiblicher Gradlinigkeit*. Berlin and Weimar: Aufbau.

Zetkin, Clara (1987) *Zur Geschichte der proletarischen Frauenbewegung Deutschlands*. Frankfurt a.M.: Verlag Marxistische Blätter.

Zeyringer, Klaus (1993) 'Österreichische Literatur von und über Frauen in den achtziger Jahren' in Good et al. 1993, 247–272.

INDEX